PUBLICATIONS ON ASIA
OF THE SCHOOL OF
INTERNATIONAL STUDIES
UNIVERSITY OF WASHINGTON

Number 36

POLICY AND TRADE ISSUES

AMERICAN

OF THE JAPANESE ECONOMY

AND JAPANESE PERSPECTIVES

Edited by

KOZO YAMAMURA

UNIVERSITY OF WASHINGTON PRESS

SEATTLE AND LONDON

This book is sponsored by
The Japanese Studies Program
School of International Studies
University of Washington

Library of Congress Cataloging in Publication Data

Main entry under title:

Policy and trade issues of the Japanese economy.

    (Publications on Asia of the School of International Studies, University of Washington ; no. 36)
    Based on a binational symposium held in Hawaii, Mar. 1981, under auspices of the Committee for Japanese Economic Studies of the Association for Asian Studies.
    Includes index.
    1. Japan--Economic policy--1945-   Congresses.
2. Japan--Economic conditions, --1945-   Congresses.
3. Japan--Commerce--United States--Congresses.
4. United States--Commerce--Japan--Congresses.
I. Yamamura, Kōzō. II. Association for Asian Studies. Committee for Japanese Economic Studies. III. Series.
HC462.9.P54 1982   338.952   82-15918
ISBN 0-295-95900-2

Foreword

The Japan-United States Friendship Commission has been trying to encourage joint ventures between American and Japanese scholars on issues of current or prospective importance to the relationships between our two countries. It is hard to imagine a more successful example of the fruits of this policy than this volume. Certainly, few matters are of greater importance to the international sector of the American economy than the Japanese relationship. Similarly, no single binational economic relationship has simultaneously generated more advantages or more problems for the United States. These are so complex in nature and so deeply imbedded in the culture and politics as well as the economies of both countries as to defy resolution by government or business alone. Under these circumstances the Friendship Commission believes that a constructive and enlightening contribution can be made by the scholars of both countries. We hope that the essays that follow will demonstrate the merits of this belief.

ROBERT E. WARD, CHAIRMAN
Japan-United States Friendship Commission

CONTENTS

Introduction

Today, no data are needed to convince Americans of the importance of Japan as a trading partner and many more Americans are better informed about the Japanese economy and the issues involved in the bilateral economic relationship than there were a decade ago. However, what we know of the Japanese economy and these trade issues is still inadequate. Because of the complexity of the issues and the rapid changes in the Japanese economy, even American executives, policy makers, academic specialists, and others who can claim substantial knowledge about trade issues and the working of the Japanese economy, must make constant efforts to increase and update that knowledge. Such efforts are necessary if we are to minimize the economic and political friction that at times mars the otherwise harmonious relationship we now maintain with Japan. Such efforts are also important if we wish to assess and evaluate the wisdom of our economic policies against those adopted by Japan —a nation that continues to increase productivity, minimize unemployment, avoid rapid inflation, and achieve economic growth more successfully than other industrial economies are able to accomplish today.

To help us better understand the Japanese economy and bilateral trade issues, this volume presents essays by ten Japanese and American economists (and one co-author who is a political scientist specializing in Japanese politics). All the authors were asked to meet these three requirements: to increase our knowledge of the Japanese economy to aid in reducing friction in economic relations; to make the essay readable to as many of those interested as possible; and to ensure technical accuracy along with new analytic insight. Meeting the second requirement was difficult for authors dealing with highly technical subjects, but we believe that the essays can be read by noneconomists. Technical discussions are limited to an identified section or an appended technical note. Thus, we are confident many readers will find the essays rewarding even though a basic familiarity with the subjects may sometimes be required.

Part 1, "Japanese Policies and the Behavior of Firms and Individuals," is limited to examinations of Japanese economic policies and the changing behavior of Japanese firms and individuals, with analyses of their significance in bilateral economic relations.

Murakami's wide-ranging opening essay provides an overview of the changes that are now occurring in economic policy, in the structure of the industries, and in the behavior of firms and individuals. His essay is rich in analytic insight, acute observations, and reflections on the Japanese economy and Japanese society. He sets the stage for other essays to follow, and those who read his essay carefully will find why Murakami, an economic theorist, has come to be highly regarded as a social scientist capable of offering thought-provoking analyses of the economic, political, and social issues of contemporary Japan.

Imai's broad analyses of the changes in industrial policy and in the structure and behavior of firms demonstrates how government control declined over time and how the economy gradually grew more competitive in response to changing needs and circumstances. He describes the changes in the roles of subcontractors, in the rapidly evolving distribution system, in the goals and characteristics of "grouping of firms" (keiretsu), and in other important industrial characteristics. His analysis that some of the strengths of the Japanese economy can become weaknesses is especially illuminating coming from Japan's leading scholar of industrial policy.

Yamamura's essay is a critical discussion of the reasons why the once successful administrative guidance and what he regards as "pro-cartel" policy ceased to be effective and even became detrimental to the Japanese economy and to a harmonious bilateral trade relationship. His analysis, developed by making extensive use of the discussions of the guidance and antimonopoly policy among Japanese officials and scholars themselves, suggests the inherent difficulties involved in changing the cooperative relationship once developed between government and industry. He cautions against uncritical acceptance of suggestions that the United States, in its efforts to revitalize its economy, emulate the Japanese and adopt policies that are intended to relax antitrust statutes and to increase cooperation between government and industry.

Noguchi is concerned with the changes that have occurred in the use of the fiscal resources of the government, from aiding industrial recovery and growth to financing rapidly increasing social welfare expenditures. Especially interesting is his analysis of the role played by the huge amount of savings in the Postal Savings (which has no counterpart in the United States). He warns of the dangers of a big government and continued large deficit spending and suggests that the Japanese government is well advised to allocate a larger proportion of its fiscal resources to improve the lives of the urban population and less to promote industrial growth, thereby minimizing trade conflict with the United States.

Noting that Japan's often envied high savings rate is "no longer the virtue it used to be," Sato analyzes the problems it has created. He examines with care savings-investment patterns and their possible trend and effects on the Japanese economy and on Japan's economic relationship with the United States. Though he is fully aware of the difficulties involved, he sees a rapid increase in direct investment by Japanese firms in the United States as an important means to reduce economic tension between the two nations.

Shinkai's paper examines how and why the Japanese economy was able to cope successfully with the effects of the first oil crisis of 1973 and the second oil crisis that resulted from the Iranian Revolution of 1979. He shows how the Japanese policies, managerial reactions, and moderate wage demands enabled Japan to overcome the effects of the crises: to "belie the notion that there is a trade-off between price stability and vigorous growth." Shinkai's study highlights the importance of increasing productivity and of moderate wage demands if an economy is to overcome stagflation. Can the American economy also grow without rapid inflation? In his analysis of the reasons for the resiliency of the Japanese economy, Shinkai's message is clear.

The first essay presented in Part 2, "The Political Economy of United States-Japan Trade in Steel" studies the political and economic issues raised by the Japanese export of steel to the United States and the "trigger price mechanism" that was adopted to minimize trade conflicts. Co-authored by Patrick and Sato, this is a lucid examination of the structures of the American and Japanese steel industries, their relative productive efficiency, the differing perceptions of trade friction between American and Japanese policy makers and industry leaders, and other important issues raised by the increasing export of Japanese steel to the United Staes. This essay should be extremely useful for anyone wishing to understand causes of, and difficulties involved in seeking solutions to, a major bilateral trade conflict. And more important, many of the issues raised and many of the analyses offered are applicable in analyzing similar bilateral trade issues that are being faced (or may be faced in the near future) by other American industries.

Saxonhouse's study asks a very important question, Does the relatively small amount of manufactured products imported by Japan indicate that Japan is somehow extra-legally restricting imports? Or does it show that Japan is no more restrictive than other nations and the amount it imports can be explained in terms of differences, vis-à-vis other industrial nations, in quantity and quality of labor and capital and natural resources and distance from its trading partners? His careful econometrics study, adapting the international trade theory and data gathered from a wide range of sources, leads him to the conclusion that Japan in the 1970s was no more restrictive in importing manufacturing products than other industrial nations. His finding is extremely significant for policy makers as well as for others interested in the Japanese trade policy. Undoubtedly his analysis, assumptions, and conclusion will be questioned, but this is as it should be, as this is the first rigorous analysis of contradictory views on this crucial question.

Hamada, one of Japan's leading specialists of monetary theory and international economics, analyzes a highly technical issue: how bilateral exchange rates are determined when the United States and Japan pursue their differing monetary and other macroeconomic policies. After reviewing the major developments since 1971, he summarizes his and other Japanese scholars' efforts to "model" the recent behavior of the bilateral exchange rates, and examines how Japanese and American monetary policies and interventions influence the rates. Specialists will find his balanced discussion of various theoretical approaches illuminating and nonspecialists will have little difficulty in understanding why he argues for bilateral cooperation to achieve better management of the yen-dollar exchange rates.

Dealing with the same subject examined by Hamada, the central aim of Makin's essay is clear. It is to demonstrate the usefulness to policy makers of analyzing yen-dollar exchange rates by adopting hypotheses that the rates are determined by stock-equilibrium conditions in the asset markets and that market participants make rational expectations of all future values of pertinent variables. Presenting the most technical part of his discussion in an appendix and writing with care, Makin accomplishes his purpose. In addition, his essay contains knowledgeable discussion of current and expected policies of the Reagan and Suzuki administrations, an analysis of 1973-79 data, and his policy recommendations.

The essays grew out of a binational symposium on the bilateral economic relationship that was held in Hawaii in March 1981. The purpose of the symposium was to discuss a wide range of trade issues, to increase participants' understanding of the rapidly changing Japanese economy, and to create a forum in which Japanese and American economists (and invited political scientists) could exchange views and research results. The intent of the Committee for Japanese Economic Studies of the Association for Asian Studies, under whose auspices the symposium was held, is to hold such symposia in the future as well as to contribute to the effort toward minimizing trade friction and increasing knowledge about the Japanese economy. Currently, the members of the committee are Gary Saxonhouse, Hugh Patrick, Henry Rosovsky, Kazuo Sato, and Kozo Yamamura. Yamamura, who was charged with the organization of the Hawaii symposium, edited this volume on behalf of the committee, since "this was his turn" to assume such responsibilities, which are rotated among committee members.

Other activities of the committee include organizing symposia and seminars for government officials, business leaders, and academic specialists; holding seminars for graduate students interested in the Japanese economy; inviting Japanese economists to lecture-seminar tours in the United States; assisting young American specialists of the Japanese economy in finding an appropriate Japanese or American government agency or a university where they can most profitably continue their research; and carrying out other similar activities that can contribute to increasing our knowledge of the Japanese economy and thereby contribute to maintaining as harmonious as possible an economic relationship with Japan.

The committee wishes to express its appreciation to the Japan-United

States Friendship Commission for the financial assistance it provided to hold the Hawaii symposium. (The commission, we also gratefully acknowledge, is an important contributor to most of the activities of the committee.) The committee also wishes to express its appreciation to Professor Sho'ichi Royama of Osaka University for attending the symposium and actively participating in its programs, and to Professor Daniel Okimoto, a political scientist of Stanford University, who also was an active discussant at the symposium.

The committee and especially the editor of this volume also wish to thank Martha L. Lane for most ably assisting in all aspects of the often difficult administrative and secretarial work that was involved in organizing a binational symposium and in publishing a volume containing many essays written by nonnative speakers of English. In the words of one committee member, "It is unfair for anyone so charming to be so capable." And, finally we wish to express our appreciation to the University of Washington Press, the Publications Committee of the School of International Studies of the University of Washington, and to the Publications Program of the School of International Studies for expediting the publication of this volume.

JAPANESE POLICIES

AND THE BEHAVIOR OF FIRMS AND INDIVIDUALS

Toward a Socioinstitutional Explanation

of Japan's Economic Performance

YASUSUKE MURAKAMI

EVEN AN ECONOMIST would agree that the economy is only one aspect of society as a whole. The polity is another essential ingredient of society, although the economy in capitalist societies may often be relatively independent of the polity. Behind these manifest aspects of society, there also lies a more latent domain that might roughly be called the culture. The economy, the polity, and the culture are interacting and often interpenetrating, and we must remain cognizant of this fact as we begin to study an economy in an over-all context.

Among these three societal ingredients, the economy would be viewed by an orthodox economist as a relatively independent system, subject to its own quasi-deterministic laws. In the economist's perception, the economic system is subject to the laws of market mechanism, and the polity is guided by the rules of parliamentary democracy. The autonomy of the market mechanism is maintained by a fixed legal framework that guarantees, among other things, the right to private property. Political decisions reached in the parliament can intervene in the market system only if they concern a remedy for market failure, the promotion of infant industries, the supply of public goods, or the redistribution of income. This classic perception of a capitalist

This article is a radically revised version of the paper the author presented at the binational symposium of economists on U.S.-Japan Economic Relations in March 1981 in Honolulu, Hawaii. The article owes much to all participants at the symposium, particularly the discussants of the paper: Professors Yukio Noguchi and Kazuo Sato. I am also immensely indebted to Professor Kozo Yamamura, my colleague at the University of Washington. Also, my gratitude to Elizabeth Hanson, Diane Caviezel, and Martha Lane for their efforts to improve and edit my English expressions.

industrial society may well be a good first approximation of reality when we try to grasp the general features common to all capitalist economies. The many social changes of the last hundred years notwithstanding, the market mechanism and parliamentary democracy remain the two pillars of any non-socialist industrial society, including the so-called mixed economies.

However, once we start to compare the performances of different capitalist economies or of the same economy in different periods, we need to examine more carefully the interaction between the economy, the polity, and the culture. For example, if we attempt to compare the Japanese economy with other advanced industrial economies, we will have to pay closer attention to the rigidity of each legal framework, range, and mode of government intervention, strength and persistence of underlying values, and so forth.

If we focus our attention only on the purely economic aspects of the Japanese economy, we will overlook what I believe are the Japanese economy's important features, those that distinguish it from other industrial nations' economies. In the second section, I will attempt to formulate a socioinstitutional model of the Japanese economy during the period of rapid economic growth by briefly reviewing major related arguments, past and present. Then I will examine more closely some recent socioinstitutional or even cultural changes that are likely to crucially affect the future of the Japanese economy. Finally, the arguments will be summarized to give a possible picture of the Japanese economy in the near future and to point out its inherent problems. As space is limited, I can only touch on two important problems essentially related to the present topic, the problem of Japanese politics and the problem of the "Japanese employment system."

THE JAPANESE ECONOMIC SYSTEM BEFORE THE OIL CRISIS

THE BILEVEL SYSTEM

This section attempts to spell out characteristic features of the Japanese economy including its politico-institutional background during the period of rapid economic growth from the mid-fifties to the early seventies. The 1953 amendment of the Antimonopoly Act was probably the most apparent indication of a series of growth-oriented institutional restructuring that ushered in an era of economic growth, which ended with the beginning of the 1973 oil crisis.

There has been a wide spectrum of ideas about what the essential features of the Japanese economy were in this period. On one extreme, the "Japan Inc." theory emphasizes a strong cohesion within the Japanese society between the government and every major private business. The naïveté of this theory has often been criticized by Japanese and foreign Japan specialists; I will add only that it seems impossible to reject totally the concept that the connection between government and business in Japan was somehow closer than in most other capitalistic type industrial countries. On the other extreme, the "excessive competition" (katō kyōsō) theory stresses that Japanese firms were suffering from cutthroat competition, not only in the export market but also in many domestic scenes such as the "investment race," "deposit collection competition," and so on. Although business spokesmen and a particular branch of the government (the Ministry of International Trade and Industry—MITI) subscribed to this view, most academic economists were highly critical of it, basing their arguments on the standard reasoning of price theory. Yet, at least as far as the rapid growth period is concerned, the evidence seems to be against a generalization that strong restrictive practices dominated the markets in Japan, causing inefficiency.

These theories represent, in extreme forms, two perceptions about the Japanese economy, one stressing government regulation and the other marketlike competition. Nevertheless, each seems to be a half-truth, merely describing one aspect of the total picture. There is a clear need for a hypothesis that can consistently explain how two seemingly contradictory elements, regulation and competition, could be combined into one viable system. As one attempt, this paper offers the hypothesis that the central part of the postwar Japanese economic system consisted of two levels. At the "upper" level, an array of administrative regulations and guidance provided a quasi-legal framework (on top of the existing legal framework) that was relatively free from discretionary or arbitrary changes. This framework, in effect, compartmentalized the Japanese economy into relatively separate subsystems. Then, at the "lower" level, each subsystem was generally subject to marketlike competition. This competition could be local, not as global as an economist would like to find in an idealized market economy, but it could still be quite competitive.

When asked what the systemic essence of the Japanese economy was, the answer cannot be given in one word, neither "regulation" nor "competition." The central part of the system was a bilevel combination of competition and regulation, a constellation of localized competitive systems, each being under a specific quasi-legal system of regulations. This bilevel "regulation and competition" system carried out what a "competition only" system, within a universal legal framework, did in an idealized market economy.

The explanation we are now presenting is highly abstract and schematic. As a more concrete and detailed explanation, the following main points are to be considered as part of the total picture of an economic system Japanese style: (a) the long-run orientation of Japanese firms; (b) the competitive product markets; (c) the regulated allocation of investment, including the regulated financial system with low interest rates and the investment guidance and intervention by government. We should note as a common key factor underlying these characteristics the remarkable convergence of Japanese opinion about the goals of their society as well as its expected future course, which might be called the consensus about the "catch-up-type" growth.

The Long-run Orientation of Japanese Firms

It is widely held that Japanese firms in leading modern industries took a long-run rather than a short-run view. As many opinion surveys indicated, short-run profit was apparently not the primary goal but probably only one of the constraints to be satisfied. On the surface at least, firms were more conscious of long-run goals or surrogates such as market share, the firm's growth rate, and so forth. Hence, we may accept as a prima facie fact that Japanese firms were somehow long-run oriented. A more basic question to ask is how they were long-run oriented and why. An often suggested answer is the theory that this orientation is closely linked to the so-called permanent employment practice and ultimately due to the "collectivist" tradition inherent in Japanese culture. However, as the following argument will show, the experiences during the rapid growth period do not necessarily substantiate, nor do they totally falsify, this cultural explanation.

To pinpoint essential features of the behavior of Japanese firms, we may first examine two alternative behavioral hypotheses, market share maximization and profit maximization. As illustrated in chapter 4, the two types of behavior shown by a firm under these two different assumptions are not qualitatively distinguishable,[1] provided that the firm faces an increasing average cost situation. Particularly, the two types of supply curves derived from these assumptions will both guarantee stable market equilibrium, if coupled with a well-behaved downward sloping demand curve. Therefore, if average cost is increasing, a market share-maximizing firm will show no particularly unusual behavior compared to a profit-maximizing firm.

If average cost is assumed to be decreasing, two types of firms, profit maximizer and market share maximizer, will again behave in almost the same way, not only qualitatively but also even quantitatively; they will both maximize their output on an average cost curve or its slight modification (see chap. 4). In fact, market instability may be caused by the two type of indistinguishable supply behavior. That is, once a price falls below the equilibrium level, it will increase supply more than demand so that the price will become even lower, and the excess supply will continue to worsen. This is what many people had in mind by saying that competition was "excessive." Thus, in a decreasing cost situation, both a market share maximizer and a profit maximizer will have a rather unusual outcome that might be called "excessive competition."

Most cultural explanations argue that a typical Japanese firm is not an economic, profit-maximizing association but a communitylike organization that always strives to arrive and expand. Hence market share maximization

1. It is true that there is a quantitative difference, because a market-share-maximizing firm produces more output and creates a greater consumer surplus, as well as a small producer surplus, than a profit-maximizing firm. Yet even this distinction might be of little significance if the profit maximizer operates on a long-run cost curve while the market share maximizer is on a short-run cost curve. See chapter 4.

is often identified as an economic expression of this "group oriented" culture. However, the above argument implies that such maximization will not give rise to any visibly different behavior from firms under profit maximization. An issue of excessive competition suggests that whether average cost is increasing or decreasing might make a difference, but not whether a firm is maximizing profit or market share. The case of decreasing average cost should draw our particular attention.

In most economics textbooks, the case of decreasing average cost is treated as exceptional, mainly for the sake of theoretical expediency. There is a lack of empirical evidence to show that such cases are rare. With respect to short-run average cost, that is, an average cost under a given amount of fixed capital (factories, machines, and related facilities), this preclusion of the decreasing case may still be permissible because an optimal scale of production is fixed and so is likely to soon be reached and surpassed. However, with respect to a long-run average cost, that is, an average cost when an amount of fixed capital is adjustable, the decreasing case is by no means exceptional as is seen in such process industries as steel, nonferrous metals, cement, petrochemicals, and so on, or in some manufacturing industries such as automobiles, electric appliances, and so forth. Having these observations in mind, I will now offer the hypothesis that Japanese firms in leading postwar industries were operating generally on decreasing long-run cost curves, at least during the period of rapid economic growth. Japanese firms at that time were long-run oriented primarily in this sense rather than in the sense that their objective was longevity or expansion per se.

Long-run cost is a tricky concept and this trickiness is central to our hypothesis. In discussing a firm's short-run cost, there are fewer conceptual ambiguities. The state of fixed capital (factories, machines, and related facilities) is given, embodying presumably optimal technology. Within this technological framework, a decision on an output level leads to a particular choice of a combination of variable inputs such as materials, energies, labor, and so on. In a long-run situation, however, a technological framework has yet to be embodied, that is, a new factory may be built, new machines introduced, or a new job system created. The process of using (embodying) a new state of fixed capital ought to include a variety of innovations or at least developments, technological as well as organizational. As a firm's decisions become more and more long-run oriented, the difference between a change within a given technology and a change in technology itself will be less and less discernible.[2] Symbolically, a short-run cost curve may be shown as a line, while a long-run cost curve can be represented only as a band, and the width of the band depends on the amount of uncertainty involved.

Generally speaking, the amount of uncertainty involved will be influ-

2. Actually, no econometrician can discern two changes without a rather artificial assumption of "homotheticity."

enced by the following factors: (1) whether a firm is a pioneer or a late-comer in attempting to embody the new technological horizon in question; (2) how well a firm can bear the cost of risk or transfer it to other economic actors in the society via long-term financing in some way or another; (3) how well a firm can adapt workers' abilities and willingness to changing techno-logical situations. In a perspective broader than each individual firm, another crucial factor enters: (4) how demand can expand in response to an increased supply capacity. As John M. Keynes emphasized, a firm's long-run decision (usually called an investment), unlike its short-run decision, is irreversible and involves expectations for financing, labor-management relations, demand response, and so on. This decision thus virtually depends on a society's ability to bear investment risk, to mediate labor issues, and to create necessary demand. Hence, even for each individual firm, the long-run cost curve depends on the politico-institutional capability of society as a whole. Even if they belong to the same industry, firms in different countries are likely to have different long-run cost curves.

During the period of rapid economic growth, these four factors reduced the uncertainty for Japanese firms in leading industries. With respect to the first factor, Japanese industries were late-comers, particularly with the new technology that originated in wartime research and development. Viewed retrospectively or ex post facto, the long-run average cost curves in postwar leading industries throughout the world were declining because of successive technological progress. However, a pioneering economy had to face an ex ante curve and there was no guarantee the curve would be declining. On the other hand, late-comers such as the Japanese economy could make full use of an ex post facto average cost curve that incorporated new postwar technology already tested by pioneers.

With respect to the second factor, the postwar Japanese economy was so institutionalized that it could develop a financial system of risk-sharing among firms, households, and government—a topic that will be addressed in a later section. Concerning the third factor, one of the prominent features of the so-called Japanese employment system is intrafirm job mobility as well as extensive use of on-the-job training, and these features enabled the Japanese firms to adjust their job systems to constantly changing technology.[3] This contrasts, for example, with the craft union style practice that tended to strongly resist any type of job change. The problems of the Japanese employment system as a whole will be discussed briefly later. Regarding the fourth factor, note that once growth expectation permeates the business sector, investment-led growth, as in the case of postwar Japan, is self-fulfilling, so to speak, unlike in export- or consumption-led growth. For most of the demands of such an economy are interindustrial demands for investment goods and intermediate products. Moreover, consumer demand for all mass-consumption products, such as televisions, automobiles, and air con-

3. All students of the Japanese economy are indebted to Kazuo Koike (1977) for pointing out the importance of these features.

ditioners, was in its early explosive stage of diffusion in pre-oil crisis Japan. The expanding world market under the International Monetary Fund–General Agreement on Tariffs and Trade (IMF–GATT) regime also provided Japanese industries a demand that was secondary in the growth period as a whole but crucial at the time of relative recession. Primarily, this fourth problem was a part rather than an outcome of how the consensus about catch-up growth was formed at the beginning of rapid economic growth.

I am now hypothesizing that the Japanese firms in major industries were at a vantage point to exploit the decreasing long-run average cost situation, particularly because the long-run risk they faced was quite reduced, compared to most other industrial economies. However, as corollaries of this postulate, it is to be noted that Japanese firms had to deal with two difficulties. First, their behavior, in current activities as well as investments, created a kind of market instability that might be called "excessive competition," including the so-called "fixed investment race" in such industries as steel, petrochemicals, oil refining, and so forth, in the sixties. This seems to have led to government intervention in private investment at that time. Second, the Japanese firms' optimal scale of production tended to be larger than that actually used, compared to other economies as further discussed in chapter 4. Then, when a recession hit the economy, Japanese firms had a greater increase in average cost than less ambitious or more cautious firms in other countries. This seems to have led to the notorious Japanese export drive and the legalization of recession cartels.

We have thus assumed that a Japanese firm in a leading industry will be long-run oriented in the strong sense that the firm not only makes a decision over a long span of time, but also operates on a decreasing long-run average cost curve. An aforementioned cultural explanation, which implies a long-run orientation of only the first weaker sense, seems unnecessary for the growth period, though it is not inconsistent with, and sometimes even reinforces, our argument. The hypothesis presented here seems to consistently explain the behavior of Japanese firms, not only their vitality and long-run orientation but also instabilities inherent in this orientation, such as excessive competition and export drives.

THE COMPETITIVE PRODUCT MARKETS

For the competitiveness seen in product markets, I will postulate that major product markets in Japan during the rapid growth period were competitive, at least in the boom phase. Most of the years in this period were, in fact, boom years, with only intermittent relative recessions (not in terms of absolute level but in terms of growth rate). By competitiveness, I mean here that neither were product prices regulated by the government, nor were restrictive price practices, such as cartels, effective in comparison with other industrial economies. However, there are three important provisos to this statement.

The first is commonplace: there were exceptions. As in most countries, the Japanese government regulated prices of agricultural products—rice, wheat, beans, beef, and so on—often by controlling imports of these products. In tertiary industries, not only public utilities but transportation, communication, and miscellaneous service industries, prices were often effectively regulated by the central or local government as well as respective trade associations under administrative guidance. The financial markets were a particularly interesting case, which will be seen later. However, a list of these exceptions was, by and large, comparable to those of other industrial economies. If we focus on the secondary industries that led the postwar Japanese economic growth, the product markets were competitive in prices, though still subject to the following two provisos.

The second, more important, proviso is related to entry into industry. In leading modern industries in postwar Japan, entry of a new firm was often very difficult, if not impossible. Particularly in the case of large-scale process industries relying on import technology, such as petrochemicals, oil refining, steel, and so forth, the goverment (mainly MITI) could effectively regulate new entries by controlling licenses to import technology (even licenses to import materials at the early stage of the growth period) as well as by exerting influence on loan financing, which aspirants in those industries often needed in large amounts. It is true that entry was relatively free in industries where a new firm could start on a fairly small scale with limited reliance on imported technology. We can find examples of late entry even in such major industries as automobiles and electric appliances; Honda and Sony were prominent examples of successful later entrants. Generally, however, entry into a leading industry in postwar Japan was distinctly more difficult than in most other industrial economies. Until quite recently foreign firms were virtually prohibited from having their own factories inside Japan. In typical European industrial nations, many successful new entrants in modern industries are from different countries. This Japanese policy restricting the flow of capital precluded a major portion of potential entries. However, note also that even with no free entry there can still be price competition. Although such competition cannot be called perfect competition, it may still be what some economists call pure competition.

The third, most crucial proviso is related to the problem of whether the economy was in a boom or recession. As already noted, long-run oriented Japanese firms will get into serious trouble with rising costs when they face an unexpectedly slow growth of demand due to a recession. On the other hand, when demand is increasing as expected, the ensuing competition will be excessive competition, or, as I have characterized it, an unstable competition. Costs rise in a recession and fall in a boom, creating an inherent instability contrary to short-run oriented firm behavior. The Japanese government presented a twofold solution to this vexing problem. In the boom phase, the government or MITI tried to impose a restraint on the "investment race." In the recession phase, government-sponsored recession cartels were called for. In the 1953 amendment of the Antimonopoly Act, they were legalized, and many scholars since then have criticized this as a retrogression of antimonopoly policy. However, it is to be admitted by way of economic reasoning that the long-run orientation of Japanese firms would have been very difficult to maintain, unless recession cartels or other similar recession measures had been introduced. A long-run oriented industry without a recession cartel may not be a viable system. It is also likely to run into trouble in a boom, unless someone intervenes to restrain an investment race. I am not trying to be conclusive here, and the issue is probably part of a bigger question: can the market mechanism really take care of resource allocation in a dynamically growing economy?

In the present context, it is important to distinguish a boom phase from a recession phase. To be sure, recession cartels and other illegal practices were almost rampant in recession phases. In boom phases, every firm made maximum effort to expand its output and so its market share, giving rise to a fierce price competition as well as a potentially hectic investment race. Many observers of the Japanese economy have been puzzled by a mixed impression of competitiveness and cartel practices, but the truth is probably an alternating of competition and restrictive practice corresponding to alternating boom and recession periods. And after all, most years of the rapid economic growth were boom years, meaning that leading Japanese industries were usually competitive, in the sense defined here.

THE REGULATED FINANCIAL SYSTEM

The characteristics of Japan's postwar financial system are an issue for qualified specialists. However, as the role played by the financial system in postwar Japanese economic growth was so important, I will attempt a brief summary of the related arguments. One apparent feature of the Japanese financial system during the rapid growth period is evident to all. A huge amount of money was constantly flowing from the household sector to major leading industries mainly through bank loans, without averting the risks that might have accompanied growth oriented management in those industries. Japanese specialists called this characteristic "indirect finance" or "overborrowing." It made an especially striking contrast with the Anglo-American financial practice where most funds for industry are collected through the bond market or stock (equity share) market, facing substantial competition from households, government, and the outside world. The problem is, how could this Japanese characteristic come into being? The answer here is that it was mainly due to the (quasi-institutional) regulation by government.

In fact, a view emphasizing the role of regulation in Japanese financial system has long been accepted. Recently, however, a group of young economists has started to challenge this conventional view, contending that the system might be better understood as something closer to a competitive market. Specifically, the effective interest rate was not artificially low compared to the level that could equate demand and supply. Thus, the postwar Japanese financial system should be viewed not as a result of regulation but as a natural development subject to certain historical preconditions. Current controversy between the conventional regulation school and the new market school (both in the positive sense, not in the normative sense) is by no means settled. Being a reaction to many previous views of "Japan Inc.," this new argument is indeed contributing to correct some overemphasis on the role of regulation, as well as pointing out the lack of sufficient evidence supporting the conventional view. However, the evidence presented by the market school also seems to fall far short of establishing the opposite view—that the Japanese financial system was one big market mechanism.

I will now present an explanation of how the financial system in post-war Japan was regulated to create strong growth incentives for major leading industries. An essential role of the regulation was to compartmentalize the whole system into several subsystems, including (1) the interbank market, (2) the central bank credit, (3) the bank lending market, (4) the bond market, (5) the stock market, (6) the deposit market, and (7) the outside world. Regulations provided a quasi-institutional setting specific to each of them. I agree with the market school to the extent that each of those subsystems behaved, if taken separately, much like a competitive market. This explanation is thus another specific version of the bilevel system hypothesis.

On both sides of the controversy, there is broad agreement that the interbank market was most typically competitive, and also that the call rate (short-term interbank interest rate) was usually higher than all other kinds of interest rates for similar or even considerably longer terms, including the official discount rate, the time deposit interest rate (say, one year fixed term), the (nominal) bank lending rate, and the issuing terms for bonds. As the call rate is a very short-term interest rate, this interest rate ranking was unusual and was conventionally regarded as an indication that some form of regulation to effect artificially low interest rates existed in other markets vis-à-vis the competitive interbank market. That rates other than the call rate were so inflexible was also viewed as another indication of regulation.[4]

This argument, as the new market school emphasized, is insufficient to really verify the existence of regulation. Two issues have been raised and are now being debated. The first is whether or not the effective bank lending rate was high enough to equate demand and supply of bank loans, where the effective interest rate is the nominal interest rate adjusted by taking into account the compensatory deposit (such as *buzumi* or *ryōdate*) or the collateral (which is an accepted practice in Japan). However, the empirical evidence presented so far is obviously inconclusive either way.[5] The second

---

4. The best analytical account of the conventional view is probably Suzuki 1980, chap. 3.

5. Literature on this controversy includes an increasing number of articles and books. To mention a few recent works: Kaizuka and Onodera 1974 (the article belongs to the conventional "regulation school" and includes a survey of previous arguments on credit rationing); Teranishi 1974 (a criticism of the Kaizuka-Onodera article); Rimbara and Santamero 1976 (an attempt to prove the existence of credit rationing); Horiuchi

issue is whether or not credit rationing, called window guidance, really existed with Bank of Japan (BOJ) credit. With this issue also, there does not seem to be sufficient proof either way.[6]

Indeed, as the market school has suggested throughout the controversy, each submarket was, in a way, competitive. For example, even if the administrative guidance in the bank lending market was effective in artificially lowering the lending rate so that excess demand occurred and caused credit rationing, the banks' bargaining power in the loan market might not have been dominant. This was because the large number of banks competed for the more promising and credit-worthy borrowers. Thus, credit rationing itself was competitive so that, despite warnings of some Marxist economists in the late sixties, informal conglomerates around each big city bank *(yūshi keiretsuka)* have not occurred to date (Kōsai and Ogino 1980, p. 167).

Admittedly, the new market school has contributed to bringing to light many competitive elements in the Japanese financial system. However, the controversy until now has perhaps focused too much on two or three submarkets that are more amenable to economic analysis, namely, the bank lending market, central bank loans, and sometimes the interbank market. To have an over-all perspective, equal consideration should be given to other important submarkets, such as the securities (bond and stock) market and the deposit market. It is in these markets that there is ample, if indirect, evidence for the effectiveness of regulation in the postwar Japanese financial system.

As everyone admits, the bond market in postwar Japan was—and still is—strictly regulated by administrative guidance. The issuing terms were kept low enough to be on par with the controlled nominal bank lending rate. In spite of such poor (nominal) yield, new issues were usually purchased by banks because most of the issuing organizations were their clients and so were implicitly ready to accept the compensatory deposit practice. In other words, the banks regarded these bond purchases as simply another form of lending. To these banks and only to them, the effective issuing terms were on par with the effective lending rate. As a consequence, banks were unwilling to buy or sell bonds in unconditional open markets and the secondary bond market was extremely underdeveloped in postwar Japan. Only a small portion of new issues were assigned (by administrative guidance) to the general public via securities companies (brokerage houses), and the issuing

---

1980 (tends toward the market school); Iwata and Hamada 1980 (the regulation school); Kuroda 1979a (a criticism on part of the Iwata-Hamada book); Shimizu 1980 (emphasizes the role of mortgage practices together with the compensating deposit practice); Kamae 1980 (states that the evidence so far shown is inconclusive); Kuroda 1981 (includes bold speculative statements from the market school viewpoint); Sakakibara, Feldman, and Harada 1981 (a bold over-all argument from the market school viewpoint).

6. Works related to the recent controversy over the effectiveness of "window guidance" include: Horiuchi 1977; Kuroda 1979b, 1981; Furukawa 1980; Sakakibara, Feldman, and Harada 1981.

terms were seemingly competitive with the deposit interest rate. However, as there was no open secondary market, bond purchase was less attractive to the general public than it seemed or than it was in other countries. To ordinary households, the effective bond yield was, in this sense, lower than the nominal yield.

Further details cannot be included here, but what is the reason for all these artificial regulations? The only possible explanation is to block the direct fund flow via the bond market from the households to the industrial firms as final borrowers. This demands another question: what is the reason for this blockade? A plausible answer is to protect the artificially low interest rate that prevailed in the bank lending market as well as in the deposit market. If equilibrium interest rates had prevailed, as the market school asserts, in all markets and arbitrated among these markets, the whole regulation matter would have been much ado about nothing.

The deposit market in postwar Japan was also strictly regulated. Though strict supervision and regulation of the deposit market are common in many countries (for depositor protection), the Japanese deposit market was still unusual because the regulated interest rate was so inflexible and low. For example, during most of the growth period, the deposit interest rate for a one-year fixed term was almost pegged at 5.5 percent, a level much lower than the call rate. The deposit interest rate as an average over various terms was at an internationally comparable level of around 4 percent (Suzuki 1980, p. 58). Now suppose that the over-all effective interest rate of bank loans (not only bank lending but also bond holding) was, as the market school suggests, really an equilibrium rate. It is probably reasonable to suppose that such an equilibrium rate should be considerably higher than its counterpart in West Germany (because of the growth rate differential). Given that the overdraft rate for bank lending in West Germany in the same period was around 8.5 percent on average (ibid., p. 39), the Japanese equilibrium lending rate might have been at 9 percent or even much higher. If this had been the case, Japanese banks should have been exceptionally profitable compared to the banks of other countries.

This evidence may be circumstantial. However, if all relevant facts (only a part of which we have mentioned) are considered in a comprehensive way, it may be a sound judgment that the interest rate was regulated at an artificially low level in the following sense. The effective interest rates[7] in most financial markets would have been significantly higher, and never lower, if a network of financial regulations had been removed. This comparison with the hypothetical case leads us to another question: who incurred the greatest opportunity loss? In other words, what group in the Japanese economy would have gained the most if there had been no regu-

---

7. In this context, the word *effective* should be understood in a very broad sense. For example, if a strong goodwill relation exists between a bank and a borrower, it may virtually reduce an effective interest rate. But this holds only if the excess demand for funds exists. If excess supply exists, this might be the other way around.

lation? The answer is evidently the households. Industries would have suffered a loss due to greater financing costs, and the banks would have had neither a loss nor a gain because they could pass the higher deposit rate to a higher lending rate. In this sense, the Japanese households were the single most important mainstay of the low interest rate policy.

Then there is a mystery of sorts on our hands: why would Japanese households bear such potential loss? Many financial opportunities were closed to them. The bond market in postwar Japan was much more unfavorable to them than in other countries. Particularly, there was no open secondary bond market. The banks were very unwilling to lend to consumers. Until recently, ordinary Japanese could not acquire any foreign financial assets. In spite of this "unfair" treatment, Japanese households continued to increase their assets in the form of deposits. First, they were consistently eager to save. Second, they continued to hold their accumulated savings in the form of deposit, being insensitive to changes in real interest rates. Notice that this interest inelasticity was a secret of the low interest rate policy. For even if the interest rate is lower than the equilibrium level, the original supply of loanable funds from the households does not decrease.[8]

Why were the Japanese households insensitive to interest rate changes? Part of the reason was probably economic. It is generally accepted that an average person is likely to hold less risky assets, such as deposits, when he is poor, as were the Japanese in the earlier stage of economic growth. However, why did the Japanese continue to choose deposits throughout the whole growth period as they did? One less plausible assumption is that the Japanese are, by their culture, extreme risk-averters. A more plausible explanation is that there were no available financial assets closely substitutable for deposits. As mentioned earlier, bonds were poor substitutes. Stocks also seem to have been no close substitute. The Japanese firms during the growth period did not rely on stock financing, so their policy for dividends as well as for new issue were quite conservative. Therefore, the reason to buy Japanese stocks was potential long-term capital gain, but not short-term yield. Stocks must have been riskier assets in postwar Japan than in many other countries. It is to be noted that this was, in fact, due to the institutional framework of the Japanese financial system that was clearly biased in favor of lending to industries.

Again, why would average Japanese households accept an institutional arrangement that was so unfavorable and unfair to them? Any psychological or cultural explanation by itself cannot be a complete answer. A psychological trait or cultural legacy can be a determinant of a major social trend only if it is embodied in some institutional framework or social philosophy.

8. Some suggest that the subequilibrium interest rate assumption is inconsistent with the effectiveness of interest rate policy. Suppose that in the excess demand situation the supply rather than the demand determines the actual transaction. Then an increase in the interest rate will loosen rather than tighten the actual market situation. However, if the supply is interest-inelastic, this inconsistency cannot occur.

As we mentioned before, during the rapid economic growth period, there was a remarkable national consensus about "catch-up" economic growth. Almost all Japanese knew, though to differing extents, that the politico-economic institution was organized to promote growth. It would bring prosperity to big industrial corporations, at least as an immediate outcome, leaving the average Japanese lagging behind. Many Japanese were not satisfied. In the last analysis, however, a majority came to comply with the growth-oriented social framework, evidenced in the continuing majority by the conservative party that engineered this growth orientation. This compliance had been maintained and reinforced because the growth target was actually being achieved and the life of the average Japanese was being continuously improved. Perhaps an average person is not always making a meticulous, rational choice. Even if he does, the choice is usually overshadowed by his compliance with a broader institutional arrangement, such as the postwar Japanese social framework, including the financial system as a notable example.

INVESTMENT GUIDANCE AND INTERMEDIATION BY GOVERNMENT

In analyzing the Japanese economy, a typology of regulation-free economy versus regulated economy may be too simplistic. An idea basic to this typology is a contrast between the market economy and the command economy. In a market economy, everyone has full freedom of action subject only to a certain fixed, mandatory, and universal framework of law (the legal framework in its strict sense). On the other hand, in a command economy, everyone's action is always potentially subject to discretionary, mandatory, and specific direction by government. As suggested here, these two idealized systems indicate not one-dimensional, but multidimensional contrasts, such as fixed rule versus discretion, mandatory versus indicative, and universal versus specific. Therefore, an economy that is not an idealized market economy can have a variety of types, depending on how these multiple contrasts are combined.

As was discussed before, an essential feature of the postwar Japanese economy was a network of regulations distinct from the legal framework in its strict sense. In this network, which I called the quasi-institutional framework, each regulation was specific to a particular issue or, more concretely, a particular industry, and its execution was carried out by a particular administrative agency. The typical execution of these regulations may be best explained from a legal aspect. Administrative regulations in postwar Japan were legally based on numerous broadly phrased, presumably temporary, regulatory statutes that gave administrative agencies little power of enforcement (the only sanction given in these statutes was invariably the ability to impose a nominal fine). This meant that the regulations could not be mandatory but only indicative, so they were properly called administrative guidance. Thus, reliance on consensus for voluntary compliance was essential for effective regulation, and stable consensus necessitated some "fairness" among firms in an industry, giving rise to a fixed rule of some kind or other. Each regulation was an indication, not enforceable, from government of a fixed-rule agreement to a specific industry, thereby creating a quasi-institutional setting for each industry. Within that setting, each firm was given sufficient freedom so that compartmentalized competition occurred.

Such administrative guidance was notable in two main groups of industries in postwar Japan, financial industries and leading manufacturing industries. As discussed, the financial industries were a good example of a system of compartmentalized competition. A two-way flow of money was somehow checked among the deposit market, the bond market, the stock market, the bank lending market, and the outside world. All these markets were "compartments" and competition prevailed in each. It is interesting to note that essential to all these markets was administrative guidance such as BOJ's guideline on deposit interest rates, consultation with the Ministry of Finance (MOF) about bond issue schedules, voluntary ceilings on the lending rate, and so forth.

Another good example was the restraint on the potential fixed investment race in those major industries operating on decreasing long-run cost curves. MITI repeatedly tried to introduce a series of administrative guidelines called voluntary investment coordination (tōshi jishu kisei) into such typical large-scale industries as cement, fertilizer, petrochemicals, oil refining, steel, and automobiles. There was an interesting episode in this early phase of the growth period. To MITI bureaucrats at least, the results of investment guidance were unsatisfactory. This pushed MITI to attempt to legalize various government-led restrictive practices, particularly investment cartels, as was shown in the proposed amendment of the Antimonopoly Act in 1958 and a proposed Temporary Act for Specific Industries Promotion (Tokutei sangyō shinkō rinji hō) in 1963. In spite of the comfortable conservative majority in the Diet, neither proposal was enacted, probably because the industrial interests became concerned about "excessive bureaucratic control" (kanryō tōsei no yukisugi). This rare episode of a setback to the bureaucracy vis-à-vis business interests may be telling us that the Japanese method of regulation was closer to self-restraint by firms in each industry, and an administrative agency can function much more effectively as an arbiter or rule maker than as an enforcer of governmental design.

Thus, MITI's dissatisfaction may be interpreted as frustration with staying in an arbiterlike role, but not as a sign of ineffectiveness of regulation per se. In fact, investment guidance in the earlier part of the growth period seems to have been effective to the extent that size distribution of major firms in each strategic industry was getting more even (for example, in the degree of concentration in the top ten firms), by and large (Yamamura 1967, p. 102). Typical in investment guidance practice was a fixed rule that allocation of capacity increase be proportional to market shares. Nondiscretionary neutral rules seem to have been standard ways of regulation.

At least on the administrative level (not on a political level as in the case of the shipbuilding scandal or the Lockheed scandal), government intervention in the postwar Japanese economy was thus almost surprisingly free of such problems as nepotism and bribery-prone lobbying. Discretionary intervention may often be, in the long run, detrimental to competitiveness, while intervention by fixed rule is likely to encourage competition within that rule. Although investment allocation practice in major postwar Japanese industries was hardly a standard price mechanism, it could maintain a competitiveness and impartiality that many people, notably neoclassical economists, tend to attribute only to the market mechanism.

However, it should be admitted that government intervention was not always free from discretion. The major exception was government lending to particular projects or firms via the Japan Development Bank and the Japan Export and Import Bank. The size of this government lending was not large compared to the total amount of private fixed investment. Yet it played a central role in forming loan syndicates for particularly large projects, by demonstrating government's strong support and enhancing the credibility of borrowers. In this role, the government was a mediator in promoting the growth of major leading industries.

In summary, I will consider the question: was there really no prevalence of effective, if implicit, discretionary intervention? To be sure, branches of government like to give recommendations, advice, and opinions, and they also had numerous sources of leverage, such as financing, tax concessions, government contracts, research and development grants, licensing of mostly minor matters, and so on. An immediate impression is that there must have been a vast hidden network of highly discretionary intervention. Indeed, a particular move by a branch of government at a particular time might have been discretionary, not neutral, and even arbitrary. Also, it was obvious that government's basic policy was by no means impartial but was strongly biased to certain leading industries. However, all this differs from saying that the Japanese way of regulation was, in the long run, arbitrary, and not neutral to firms within each industry. The problem posed here is difficult to answer in an empirically substantiated way. However, a predominance of bureaucratic discretion can be a meaningful hypothesis only if the Japanese private sector is assumed to be extremely docile. To explain the mixed impression of competition and regulation that everyone seems to have of the postwar Japanese economy, our assumption of compartmentalized competition is probably a most plausible hypothesis.

SOME SOCIOECONOMIC CHANGES FROM PRE- TO POST-OIL-CRISIS

VALUE TREND: FROM INSTRUMENTALISM TO "CONSUMMATORISM"

At the outset of rapid economic growth, around 1955, the Japanese society was an amalgamation of various heterogeneous sectors and interests. Side by side with modernized industries, nearly half the labor force was still working in agriculture. Even within manufacturing industries, large-scale firms coexisted with small-scale, almost familylike firms, creating the "dual structure" *(nijū kōzō)*. Wage differentials seemed to show no immediate sign of narrowing in industries or firms of differing sizes. Thus, when the rapid economic growth started or when it seemed to get enough momentum, many analysts were concerned about an increasing heterogeneity and stratification within Japanese society as a result of accelerated growth; some of them even tried to point out that the dual structure would be an essential condition for successful rapid growth in Japan. There is not space here to review and criticize this "sociological pessimism," nor to illustrate that conservative politics since the late seventies were found to be, against many predictions, quite skillful in dealing with the danger of societal division as some had predicted. Attention in this section should be drawn only to what actually affected Japanese society toward the end of the rapid economic growth period, the early seventies. As I have said elsewhere (Murakami 1982) Japanese society is now becoming a certain new type of mass society, or what I call new middle mass society.

In this society, due to high mass consumption, high mass education, and visual mass media (television, in particular), people's life styles are being homogenized and the level of education and knowledge is being equalized. Stratification in such dimensions as occupation, income, wealth, educational background, life style, and political influence is becoming mutually inconsistent. Class barriers are blurred so that the ideology of class conflict is losing its influence. White-collar workers, blue-collar workers, self-employed people, and farmers are intermixed. In particular, the income differentials among these groups are narrowing rather than widening. Social welfare benefits are expanding to every segment of society. The concept of new middle mass society as outlined is particularly pertinent to Japanese society for several reasons we cannot delve into here, but the concept might even be applicable, in the long run, to other advanced industrial societies.

An important feature of the emerging new middle mass society is a change in values. All opinion survey data have indicated that, in the past thirty years, major changes have been occurring in the mind of the average Japanese, mainly in the way of thinking between generations. In the sixties, Japanese as well as non-Japanese observers tended to view these changes as a sign of Westernization of the Japanese and their society. The Japanese were becoming more like Westerners and more individualistic, and their society was converging with patterns of Western society as it achieved a comparable living standard. Today this interpretation seems insufficiently accurate. The Japanese are, to be sure, diverging from traditional values, but they are not necessarily getting more Westernized, as least not in the classic sense. Then how should these changes be described?

We might say that traditional or prewar Japanese values had two facets. On one hand, the Japanese valued diligence, frugality, efficiency in work, perfection of skill, and so forth. They were oriented toward work, the future, efficiency, and achievement. In other words, these were the same as values of modern Western society. On the other hande the Japanese, in comparison with Westerners, valued harmony within a society or group, as do people in many cultures based on Eastern religions such as Confucianism, Buddhism, or Hinduism. This first facet might be called "instrumental," and the second "group oriented." In talking about the Westernization of Japanese values, many people once considered the possibility that the second facet would be taken over by individualistic values, with the first facet probably remaining unchanged.

The interpretation to be offered here is nearly the opposite. Since the Japanese standard of living has approached the level of affluence, the instrumental values have been gradually weakening, with limited changes in group-oriented values. According to a recent Nippon Hōsō Kyōkai (NHK [Japan Broadcasting Corporation]) opinion survey, future orientation is changing to present orientation, work orientation to leisure (more exactly, nonwork) orientation, efficiency orientation to gratification orientation, and so on (NHK 1980; 1975). People's preference for action as a means to some end—that is, instrumental action—has been declining, while their interest in action for its own sake—"consummatory" action—has been increasing. As a number of studies have pointed out (Goldthorpe, et al. 1969; Inglehart 1977), this trend toward consummatory values seems to be spreading among affluent industrial societies. On a world-wide scale, new middle mass values are taking over traditional middle class values. In this limited sense, Japanese attitudes are converging with contemporary Western attitudes.

Group orientation in Japan is indeed changing in style. Respect for authority is generally weakening, as is the idea of male superiority (NHK 1980). Full-time commitment to an organization such as a firm is also gradually fading. However, these signs do not imply that the Japanese are beginning to have more belief in the self as an ultimate entity. Millennia-old cultural traditions will not die out, and probably with good reason. Judging from opinion survey data, the average Japanese, even in the younger generations, seems to keep holding to the idea that a group or organization can be something more than a mere collection of individuals or a mere instrument to self-actualization. Yet, as mentioned, this group orientation will change its style or its way of expression. The so-called Japanese employment system might have been a good expression for the period symbolized by economic growth as well as instrumental values. If the coming period is to be influenced by the trend toward consummatory values, a new type of group or organization may have to take the place of the Japanese employment system. However, we can now scarcely tell what specific form it will take.

The following sections will examine mainly how the trend toward consummatory values will persist and affect economic behavior, as well as shed some light on the future of what we call the new middle mass society. The future of Japanese group orientation, or more specifically, of the Japanese employment system, will not be dealt with as a main topic of this paper.

EMPLOYMENT AND INCOME

During the period of rapid economic growth, Japanese society surprised most other countries with its dynamism, but its over-all stability was also internationally remarkable. However, many people inside and outside Japan have suspected, and some still do, that Japanese society cannot remain stable when actually faced with decelerated growth. They argue that Japan's ability to restructure industry, stabilize labor-management relations, and create relative harmony among interest groups depends on ample redistributive choices created by rapid economic growth.

The question obviously requires us to examine various factors that might affect society's over-all stability. We may start with asking how the Japanese felt after the end of rapid economic growth and, more specifically, whether any specific section of the society remains particularly dissatisfied and may become a potential source of social instability. As is widely recognized, the conservative government in the latter part of the growth period virtually subsidized agriculture and the self-employed by price support and tax practices. According to popular concepts at least, employed workers in urban areas were the most neglected, suffering, in particular, poor housing conditions. The years after the first oil crisis in 1973-74 were hard ones for the average Japanese, particularly for the wage earners. The average growth rate of the real GNP from 1974 to 1978 fell to less than 4 percent, but most of this was accounted for by the growth in exports. The yearly increase in real wages during the same period was, on the average, less than 2 percent, and in 1975 it became negative. NHK opinion surveys that were conducted twice under the same format in 1973 and 1978 provide us with information on how the attitudes of the Japanese changed when faced with this sudden deceleration of economic growth.

One of the least expected findings is probably the response to the question, "On the whole, how satisfied are you with your present life?" The results are shown in table 1.1 below. More amazing is that this increase of

TABLE 1.1

SURVEY ON SATISFACTION WITH PRESENT LIFE, 1973 AND 1978

Answer	1973	1978
Satisfied	20.7%	24.0%
Satisfied rather than dissatisfied		
(Dochirakatto ieba manzoku shiteiru)	56.8	61.1
Dissatisfied rather than satisfied	18.2	12.3
Dissatisfied	3.2	1.9

satisfaction can be found in almost every sector of society, regardless of geographic area, educational background, sex, age, occupation, or political affiliation. Surprisingly, those indicating greater increases in satisfaction were the city dwellers, younger people (under 35), the wage earners, particularly white-collar workers, and students.[9] All of these persons, in obviously over-lapping categories, are usually viewed as least favored under the conservative government.

We should be very cautious in interpreting any questionnaire survey, particularly those concerning such subjective topics as satisfaction. In this NHK survey, however, the answers to other similar but more specific questions showed the same trend, implying that what I have just summarized is by no means a spurious observation.[10] In some way or other, the average Japanese became more "satisfied" after the economy decelerated and the rise in the living standard was nearly halted. Although various interpretations of this psychological fact are possible, the most straightforward one would be that, having achieved an almost affluent level of living, the Japanese now prefer a more stable life style with slower economic growth, and not the dynamic but restless life style that existed with the high-geared economic development before the first oil crisis. This psychology seems to cover all sections of society including urban dwellers, the young, and wage earners more evenly than the previous popular concept assumed (probably because the conservative government spent large amounts of money on social security and the urban infrastructure in the early seventies). Even though it was triggered by the oil crisis, deceleration of growth is the choice of the average Japanese and of every section of the Japanese populace.

Another important change can be found in the Japanese attitude toward work vis-à-vis leisure. A change was already obvious in the latter part of the growth period. According to previous smaller-scale NHK opinion surveys in 1967 and 1974 (NHK 1975, pp. 76-77) those who found their meaning in life *(ikigai)* primarily in work decreased from 54 percent in 1967 to 46 percent in 1974, those who found it in activities other than work increased from 10 percent to 15 percent, and those who found it in both work and nonwork *(dochira nimo ikigai)* also increased, from 32 to 35 percent. Particularly among people aged twenty to twenty-four, those who chose work were outnumbered by those who chose nonwork by a large difference of 20 percent against 39 percent in 1974, while in 1967, 39 percent were still work oriented and 19 percent were nonwork oriented. Before the oil crisis, Japanese "workaholism" had already started to decline, particularly in the younger generation.

In a sense, this trend away from work seemed to level off after the oil

---

9. NHK 1980, pp. 306-9. Those who are "satisfied" or "satisfied rather than dissatisfied" fell in ratio in only 2 of 75 subcategories. In the case of males of ages 50-54, the percentage fell from 76.5 to 76.4, only 0.1 percent. This group faced the most imminent danger of unemployment. The other exception is those who did not anwer regarding their educational background, but they are only 0.6 percent of the sample as a whole and so a negligible number.

10. The same survey asks four similar questions in more specific contexts before asking the question regarding satisfaction. The responses to these four questions show almost the same results. Ibid., pp. 290-305.

crisis. Table 1.2 lists responses collected in the large-scale NHK opinion surveys of 1973 and 1978 (NHK 1980, pp. 430-37). Weak leisure orientation, as shown in answer 2, declined, but work orientation as shown in answers 4 and 5 gives no definite sign of increase. The Japanese evidently go for an eclectic choice, shown by the increase in answer 3 from 20.9 percent in 1973 to 24.9 percent in 1978. Is this apparent leveling-off phenomenon temporary or lasting?

TABLE 1.2

SURVEY ON IMPORTANCE OF WORK AND LEISURE, 1973 AND 1978

	1973	1978
The meaning of life is in leisure, not in work	4.0%	4.1%
Work should not take too much time and leisure should be enjoyed as much as possible	28.1	25.3
Equal emphasis should be put on work and leisure	20.9	24.9
Leisure may be enjoyed sometimes but more emphasis should be put on work	35.7	34.9
Every effort should be made to work, pursuing the meaning of life in work	8.2	8.5

An answer can be given if the survey outcome is broken down into two age groups, those respondents under forty-five and those over forty-five. For the older group, work orientation as in answers 4 and 5 significantly increased, while leisure orientation as in answers 1 and 2 showed a significant decrease. On the other hand, for the group of younger people, work orientation showed a sizable decrease that was matched by an increase in answer 3, the eclectic choice. The percentage figures in table 1.2 are, in fact, a net result of these two different changes. As older people are unlikely to change their basic attitudes toward work versus leisure, the abrupt change in their responses might be regarded as a reaction to the economic uncertainty that mounted during the oil crisis. Anxiety about unemployment was evident for the first time in twenty years, and income motivation was rekindled. These apprehensions must have been stronger with older people who were aware of nearing retirement and families to be supported. As the older people's response was short term because of economic impact, the long-term trend is likely to mirror the younger people's response, that is, a shift from work to something other than just work (ibid., pp. 35-36).

As I mentioned earlier, a shift away from work orientation may be viewed as one aspect of the bigger change from instrumentalism to consummatorism. In spite of the oil crisis, there was no sign of change in other aspects less directly related to short-term economic problems, such as a shift from future orientation to present orientation, efficiency orientation to gratification orientation, and so on (ibid., pp. 8-12, 584-85). It may follow that these changes are still pushing people as a gradual latent trend.

Value transition from work to other kinds of activities is one symptom of this tendency.

Let me emphasize here that value change, being a latent factor, may not materialize in any immediate manner. Putting this in the present context, the trend away from work does not imply that the labor supply will become visibly smaller in the near future. It does imply a loss of intrinsic meaning in work as we find today. In other words, people's attitudes toward work will be polarized. On one hand, they will choose to work only as a means to some "higher" end, namely, as an "instrumental action." On the other hand, they will seek work that gives nondelayed gratification, or work for its own sake—"intrinsically satisfying work" in Goldthorpe's words or what I have called consummatory action.[11] More exactly, I should hypothesize that the contemporary affluent worker is faced with three alternatives—instrumental work, consummatory (intrinsically satisfying) work, and nonwork—instead of the classical assumption of the choice of work versus nonwork.

Given the present job system in industrial society and the usually poor pay for consummatory work, the average consumer-worker is still likely to decide on instrumental work rather than another choice. Two assumptions may explain this phenomenon. First, we may assume that nonwork activity, or leisure in its narrow sense, needs more and more material input from income. Second, the classical assumption that a consumer's relative preference of nonwork to work is greater in the higher real income range may be regarded as spurious. (More exactly, the substitution effect between work and nonwork becomes smaller and/or the income effect of nonwork becomes greater relative to work, as real income rises.) Instead, it can be assumed that the relative preference for consummatory work over instrumental work becomes greater as income increases, while the preference for nonwork over instrumental work does not increase much. Then, if wages paid for consummatory work are lower than those for instrumental work, the labor supply of instrumental work will remain strong for either of the above two reasons. A general remark to be made here is that people in an industrial society still adhere to the idea of work or, as Hannah Arendt puts it, the "generalization of the fabrication experience" (Arendt 1958, p. 305) while the system of industrialism demands only a limited variety of instrumental work. Therefore, in spite of a latent trend away from instrumental work, the supply of labor is unlikely to diminish in the near future. The "dilemma of the affluent worker" that puzzled Goldthorpe et al. may be explained in this way (Goldthorpe et al. 1969, p. 54). The choice of the younger Japanese for "both work and leisure," as found in the NHK survey, might be another expression of the dilemma-posing situation.

Thus, the value change from instrumental work to other activities will reveal itself only in more subtle but deep-rooted changes in workers' behavior patterns, including complaints about types of jobs, unwillingness to

11. The same topic was tackled by Goldthorpe et al., 1980. Argyris's interesting suggestion (1972) regarding this problem is somewhat similar to our argument here.

work overtime, demands for shorter working hours, absenteeism, declining integrity in maintenance work, inclination to change jobs for less significant reasons and so on—in short, an apparent creeping erosion of the work ethic. As has been widely discussed, the problem of the declining work ethic is now creating a serious challenge to labor management in affluent industrial countries.

It seems to be a popular belief that the Japanese employment system is exceptionally immune from this kind of trouble. There is no denying that the Japanese system fared better in this regard until the end of the seventies, but this does not guarantee its success in the eighties. The single most important factor of this success story is probably the work-oriented older generation of Japanese, say, people of forty or over. In the work versus leisure question in the 1978 NHK survey, work-oriented answers 4 and 5 were a majority in every male age group of thirty-five and over, while those answers were only a minority in every male age group under thirty-five. For a person of forty in 1980, being fifteen at the beginning of the rapid economic growth period may have been the turning point as to whether or not he remembers the austere life just after the war.

The problem is how the Japanese employment system in the coming decade can adapt to the arrival of the generation that knows only affluence, essentially the same problem of all industrial societies. The difference is in the timing of the coming of affluence, which has probably happened five to ten years later in Japan than in most Western advanced countries. Indeed, the Japanese response to this problem will probably be different from that in other societies, but its analysis is beyond the scope of this paper. Here I emphasize only that the value changes discussed here will first affect a microproblem of the employment system rather than a problem of macrobalance of the economy.

WOMEN AND THE AGED

In concluding the argument about labor supply, let me mention the issues of employment of women and older people. As in many other industrial countries, the status of women is improving in Japan. Women are asserting themselves and men, particularly those of the younger generation, are ready to accept change. In a question regarding marriage versus work in the NHK survey, those who support the idea that "women should continue to have careers after they have children" increased from 20.3 percent in 1973 to 27.1 percent in 1978 not only among women but also among men. The increase in support is almost the same, although the level still differs between male and female respondents.[12] The question is whether this attitudinal change will affect the supply of female labor or not.

12. NHK 1980, pp. 358-64. The increase among men was from 16.4 to 22.6 percent. Among women, it was from 23.5 to 30.8 percent. Correspondingly, the answer of "no career after marriage" decreased from 35.2 to 30.1 percent. The answer of "no career after having children" remained almost the same, going from 42.0 to 40.5 percent. Also, for the general improvement in women's status, see questions 10, 11, 12, and 28.

A strategic variable in this context is the labor force participation rate for female labor. Until the early seventies, the rate for Japanese women was very high at about 50 percent, one of the highest figures among industrial countries. Part of this high rate was, to be sure, due to the large percentage of women in Japan's agricultural labor force. However, according to Ichino's estimation for 1950-65, even for secondary and tertiary industries the labor force participation rate for women was probably higher in Japan than in typical industrial countries such as the United States or France (Ichino 1980). The popular idea that Japanese women are primarily engaged in household work has long been a misconception.

Figures for the seventies reveal interesting changes in international comparisons. The labor force participation rate for women dramatically rose in the United States and the United Kingdom, while it stayed at almost the same level in West Germany. The Japanese figure fell by 5 percent from 1970 to 1975 and then made an upward turn.[13] These different responses probably reflect each country's sociological framework. No solid explanation has been given for this international contrast, but one possible hypothesis is that each country has some sociological limit to women's participation in the labor force that depends on the society's perception of marriage and that is correlated, symbolically speaking, with the divorce rate, as may be exemplified by the recent change in the United States (see, e.g., Santas 1975). The Japanese attitude toward marriage is also changing but stays within a certain limit, as is shown by the divorce rate, which is even lower than in Catholic countries. We may then conjecture that the labor force participation rate for women in employee households may gradually increase. However, this increase will be mild enough to be offset by other factors, including a relative decrease in the younger members of the labor force and a reduction in labor force participation among women in nonemployee households. Therefore the problem in the eighties will be the structure of the female labor force rather than its mere size, including such factors as the supply shift from part-time work (mainly in tertiary industries) to regular work in large-scale firms or the problem of advancement to managerial status in large organizations. As both these examples suggest, women's liberation presents another challenge to the Japanese employment system.

The problem of elderly people has recently been one of the most frequently discussed topics in Japan. I will make only a few remarks here on this topic without delving into detailed arguments. The basic fact itself is well known. The Japanese population is aging with a speed incomparable to that of any other country. The percentage of people aged sixty-five and over was about 9 percent in 1980, still lower than in most other industrial countries. By 1990, however, it will be 11 percent, catching up with the other countries, and it will then continue to rise more rapidly until it reaches the un-

13. *White Paper on Labor, 1978*, p. 17, of data reference. The figures are different from OECD statistics, but the trends are the same.

usual level of 19 percent in 2020. It should be noted, however, that as far as the eighties are concerned, the aging population will be not so much an imminent economic burden as a factor contributing to sociopolitical pressure for institutional changes in employment practices or the social security system with a view to 1990 and beyond.

Speaking quite generally, the relative decrease of a population of productive age is, ceteris paribus, beneficial not only to the younger working population but also to those older people who are willing to work. Under the present Japanese employment system, however, it may have an adverse effect on older workers, since the system is well known for its permanent employment. However, this practice does not offer lifetime work but secure employment to retirement, which had been age fifty-five until recently. This retirement age is now outdated. In the mid-fifties, when the Japanese employment system started to emerge, the life expectancy of the Japanese male was around sixty-five, but it has now jumped to almost seventy-five. Longer life expectancy means longer working ability. If the retirement age remains fixed, an increasingly large part of the working population will be squeezed out of firms having a lifetime employment system—that is, virtually all of the large-scale firms. This implies a re-emergence of a dual structure in which one sector has greater job security and a younger work force, and the other has poor job security and an older work forces. Social tensions will probably increase. Considering this adverse effect (as well as that on the social security system), labor organizations, the government, and even business (as in Nikkeiren's *Yearly Review in 1973*) now seem to agree on delaying the retirement age to sixty, and some progress has been seen toward this end.

In the last several years, the national average retirement age among firms with a fixed retirement age system has been gradually nearing age sixty. We may predict that Japanese large-scale firms will finally comply with this societal demand partly because of pressures from outside but also partly for the sake of workers' morale within each firm. This change will force those firms to reshuffle other employment practices, however, particularly the seniority wage system.

In summarizing the above arguments, the Japanese households or worker-consumers of the seventies have experienced a change in their way of living and in their values from instrumentalism to consummatorism. Despite the recession due to the oil crisis, they are now feeling satisfied rather than dissatisfied with this change. By and large, the changes have been gradual and implicit rather than drastic and explicit. No drastic quantitative change in the labor supply is foreseen for the eighties, yet due to the undercurrent of changing values, the quality of labor will change, and the Japanese employers will have to remodel what has been called the Japanese employment system. The management of private firms rather than the governmental policy will be the main agent in solving the problems of the creeping value shift toward consummatorization, or toward work that is intrinsically satisfying.

DISTRIBUTION OF INCOME AND WEALTH

Equality of income and wealth is one of the essential conditions for the new middle mass society. This subsection will examine time trends as well as international comparisons with respect to the distribution of income and wealth in Japanese society. My argument will confirm the common understanding among specialists that Japan is a relatively egalitarian society compared to other advanced industrial societies.

According to OECD's *Economic Outlook* (1976), Japan achieved one of the lowest Gini coefficients for income distribution (0.316) along with Sweden (0.302). France with 0.414, West Germany with 0.383, and the United States with 0.381 seem less egalitarian than Japan. An international comparison of income distribution is a delicate subject to handle since Gini coefficients vary even within one country, depending on the survey data used. However, even if this kind of variability is taken into account, the difference between the Japanese coefficient and those of France, West Germany, and the United States may be viewed as significantly large.

Theoretically, the Gini coefficient—essentially a measure of variance—is only an incomplete index of inequality. Under a Gini coefficient of the same magnitude, one distribution might skew downward while another would skew upward. R. Atkinson's inequality index explicitly considers such differences. His parameter ε shows the degree of attention to be paid to the lower income stratum; $\varepsilon = 0$ means that no attention is to be paid to any difference in skewness, and, as ε increases, that greater attention be given to the lower stratum's distance in income from average. Y. Kosai and Y. Ogino (1980) attempted to compute Atkinson's index for Japan and some other countries (see table 1.3). Their results indicate that income distribution in

TABLE 1.3

ATKINSON INDEX OF INEQUALITY

ε	Japan	Sweden	West Germany	U.S.	OECD Average
0.5	0.08	0.08	0.12	0.12	0.10
1.5	0.22	0.24	0.30	0.36	0.29
3.0	0.38	0.46	0.46	0.62	0.50

Japan is skewed downward so that the income level of the lower stratum is relatively close to the average income. From a viewpoint centered on the lower stratum, Japan is more egalitarian than other countries, including Sweden. In the United States, the gap between the average income and the income of the lower stratum is relatively large. The lower stratum and the middle stratum are relatively indistinguishable in Japan, while in the United States the distinction between the middle stratum and the upper stratum is relatively weak.

Seen in a time series comparison, income distribution among Japanese households as a whole has shown a substantial increase in equality from the late fifties to the late seventies. This change has been particularly prominent among employee households (except single-member households). The Gini coefficient for these households declined almost steadily in the sixties. In the seventies, the coefficient showed ups and downs; it increased in years of recession or inflation, such as 1971, 1973, 1975, and 1976, but it declined in 1977 and 1978. The seventies as a whole may be said to have shown no definite trend in income equality for employee households. Agricultural households have shown a similar but less prominent pattern of change up to the end of the sixties, and then a gradual increase in inequality that might be due to increasing subsidies for large-scale farmers (Takayama 1980, p.31). In other types of households, such as the nonagricultural self-employed, the nonworking, and the single member (the first two categories do not include single-member households), the time series data showed a similar pattern to agricultural households, though the data were by far unreliable (ibid., pp. 33-35).

For Japanese households as a whole, it can be said that the income inequality significantly decreased during the rapid economic growth, mainly because the distribution of regular income showed a remarkable tendency toward equality. A trend in the seventies was more difficult to judge, but some turnaround toward inequality might have occurred. If so, its cause may be attributed not to the main earner's regular income, but to the main earner's temporary income, nonmain earner's income, unearned income, and so forth. The change in the seventies, if any, was due to a different factor than the dominant factor in the sixties.

Another important topic is distribution of wealth. Economic common sense says that distribution of wealth has to be more unequal than income distribution since if the average savings ratio of a household rises as its income rises and, at the same time, each household stays in the same income bracket, then it logically follows that wealth is less equally distributed than income. Table 1.4 is based on the *Chochiku dōkō chōsa (Saving trend survey)*, a survey on both income and financial assets of nonagricultural households. Table 1.4 may be used to make a comparison between wealth distribution and income distribution. Seen in this table, the Gini coefficients for financial asset distribution in Japan in the seventies were not significantly higher than those for income distribution, and moreover they showed a more pronounced tendency to decrease. In the previous twenty years, the Gini coefficient of income was slowly declining while that of financial assets was showing a rapid decrease. It is therefore predictable that financial assets finally became more equally distributed around 1977 or 1978, according to the table. Why has financial asset distribution become egalitarian more rapidly than income distribution?

The following hypothesis might partly explain this apparent paradox. That is, each Japanese household tends to move over a wide range of income brackets throughout its life cycle. A substantial part of income difference

TABLE 1.4

CHANGES IN GINI COEFFICIENTS

Year	Yearly income		Financial assets		Net financial assets	
	(1)	(2)	(3)	(4)	(5)	(6)
1959				0.4839		0.4830
1960				0.4690		0.4764
1961				0.4628		0.4296
1962		0.2972		0.4651		0.4727
1963		0.2968		0.4496		0.4536
1964		0.2872		0.3882		0.4094
1965		0.2988		0.3561		0.3972
1966		0.2916		0.3864		0.4084
1967		0.2864		0.3380		0.3483
1968		0.2712		0.3253		0.3312
1969		0.2652		0.3053		0.3010
1970	0.2669	0.2664	0.3033	0.3248	0.3075	0.3297
1971	0.2748	0.2756	0.3066	0.3275	0.3159	0.3399
1972	0.2705		0.3038		0.2978	
1973	0.2736		0.3012		0.2948	
1974	0.2711		0.2863		0.2687	
1975	0.2742		0.2878		0.2789	
1976	0.2771		0.2955		0.2916	
1977	0.2760		0.2872		0.2743	
1978	0.2655		0.2618		0.2256	

SOURCE: Cols. 1, 3, and 5 are from Economic Planning Agency 1979. Col. 2 is from Mizoguchi 1976, p. 231; Cols. 4 and 6 are from idem 1974, p. 363. All of these estimations are based on *Chuchiku dōkō chōsa* [Survey on changes in saving] by the Economic Planning Agency, and they cover the urban multimember households. See Mizoguchi 1974, 1976; Takayama 1980, for comparison with the figures based on other data sources.

NOTE: Gini coefficients of asset distribution are computed by using the data classified by income, not by the size of the financial assets, so that the Gini coefficients of income and those of financial assets are not immediately comparable. The true Gini coefficient of financial asset distribution seems to be higher than the figures presented here. See Mizoguchi 1974, p. 363, and Takayama 1980, p. 45. There may be two explanations to the question of why the Gini coefficient of financial assets has been decreasing more rapidly than the Gini cofficient of income: the saving ratios of the low income strata have been rising (see Takayama, p. 45), and accumulated income has been equalizing more rapidly than yearly income.

can be explained by age difference, so that lifetime income is much more equally distributed than the income flow in each year. This hypothesis fits nicely with the seniority wage system of Japanese employment.

We may now summarize that: (1) lifetime income in Japan is more equally distributed than income flow (yearly income); (2) lifetime income distribution in Japan has shown a more evident trend toward greater inequality than income flow distribution; (3) income in Japan is more equally distributed than in other industrial countries both in terms of lifetime income and the Atkinson index.

This assertion still must be tested with solid empirical data, but I might point out some indirect evidence. As many empirical studies have shown, age or length of service in a firm is a major factor in determining the wages of a Japanese worker because of the seniority wage system. Thus if the age variable is controlled by using, for example, lifetime income, inequality in income distribution will be much reduced. Another inequality factor is educational background, but this factor seems to be weakening if seen from the viewpoint of lifetime income (see table 1.5).

TABLE 1.5

COMPARISON OF LIFETIME INCOMES
OF MALES BY EDUCATIONAL BACKGROUND

	Manufacturers with 1000+ employees		All firms		
	1966	1974	1965	1975	1977
College graduate	100	100	100	100	100
High school graduate	80.3	94.2	70.2	77.2	75.6
Junior high graduate	85.1	92.3	57.7	66.9	74.5

SOURCE: Economic Planning Agency 1979; Ministry of Labor 1976

According to Mizoguchi's estimation for the years from 1963 to 1975, all important inequality factors concerning employee income except the age of the employee weakened in the sixties. In the early seventies, however, some factors such as differences in job, firm scale, and industry explained the reversal of the equality trend. Mizoguchi's estimation covered only the years up to 1975 (Toshiyuki et al. 1978). Future research should, therefore, include an investigation of what factors have contributed to an apparent return of the equality trend in 1977 and 1978. This prediction for the eighties depends on the results of such research. For the time being, let me suggest here that the Japanese economy has been and will be egalitarian in a stronger sense than what most of us have in mind.

TRENDS IN SAVINGS AND CONSUMPTION

In Japan, the average savings ratio (the income and the consumption used in this ratio do not include imputed rent) of households has been exceptionally high compared to that of other countries. In the early seventies, the ratio was more than 20 percent and, to everyone's surprise, rose to 25 percent in the stagflationary year of 1974. Since then, it has leveled off at a little more than 22 percent. Many people have attempted to explain this "unusual" Japanese savings behavior. Hisao Kanamori once presented the following possibilities: (1) a large number of households run their own family business; (2) population distribution is biased toward the younger generation; (3) income distribution in Japan is unequal; (4) living costs in Japan are low;

(5) liquid assets are too small; (6) rapid growth makes consumption lag behind; (7) Japan has a system of bonus payments; (8) the social security system is underdeveloped; (9) the consumer finance system is underdeveloped; (10) saving is a social custom. In addition to Kanamori's list, we may add two other possible theories: (11) savings are for housing; (12) savings are for the needs of grown-up children. Kanamori (1961) has rejected explanations 1 through 5 and 7 and has accepted the remaining four. For other examples, Ryutaro Komiya (1975) has supported numbers 6 and 7, as did Takafusa Nakamura (1980). Let us make our own brief review of the possible explanations.

Hypotheses 1 and 2 regarding family business and age structure were refuted by Kanamori through examination of the savings ratio of employed people versus self-employed and of elderly people versus younger people. Hypotheses 3, 4, and 5 regarding income distribution, liquid assets, and living costs may be rejected because it has been shown that income distribution, judged by international standards, is equal; that liquid assets are, as will be pointed out later, becoming comparable to those in wealthy countries; and that living costs in Japan are not unequivocally low.

Many economists in Japan preferred hypotheses 6 and 7 regarding rapid growth and the bonus system. These two hypotheses seem to explain well the increase in the savings ratio in the early phase of rapid economic growth. In that phase, the income increase was still so unexpected that consumption increase was influenced by past inertia and lagged behind. Bonus payments would have been a major form of such unexpected income increases. If the logic underlying these ideas is followed, however, I would predict a reduction in the savings ratio after rapid growth has continued for a sufficiently long time and the bonus system has become a part of regular wage practice. What actually happened in the later phase of rapid economic growth did not conform to this prediction. Moreover, after the oil crisis, the savings ratio soared and stayed at a high level in spite of the fact that the growth rate fell and bonus payments shrank.[14]

Compared to hypotheses 1 through 7, 8 to 12 may be viewed as less economic and more sociological or institutional. These socioinstitutional hypotheses seem harder to reject. Each of them needs more careful examination. Hypothesis 8, the social security hypothesis, appears to be rejectable, because the Japanese social security system is now, by and large, comparable to that of other countries. Particularly since 1976, when the indexation of old age pensions to current nominal wage was fully institutionalized, the Japanese system has greatly improved in its function of maintaining the living standard of elderly people.[15] Given that the savings ratio since 1976 has

14. Korea is at least one international counterexample to the rapid growth hypothesis, since it has a high growth rate and a very low savings rate.

15. A comparison of different countries' social security systems is always difficult. According to the *White Paper on National Livelihood 1976*, p. 161, old-age pensions for the standard retiree in West Germany and Japan are about the same (84,000 yen per

not shown any appreciable decrease, hypothesis 8 seems to be inconsistent. It is too early to deny the possibility that it takes many years for an institutional change to create a major turnaround in people's behavior, however. Sweden's experience supports this possibility.

Hypothesis 9, that the system of consumer finance is underdeveloped, seems acceptable, but needs an additional condition. If a consumer buys something by taking out a loan, he has to increase his savings after the purchase to repay it. Consumers as a whole are an aggregation of those who buy and those who repay. Thus, the theoretical problem is whether presaving purchase with borrowing or simple postsaving purchase will result in a greater savings ratio for consumers as a whole. Generally speaking, better financial opportunities will encourage each household to buy things sooner so that the household's time profile of consumption will have an earlier rise and an earlier peak. Thus, insofar as the number of households keeps increasing or decreasing, the aggregate ratio of consumption will be correspondingly higher or lower because of better financial opportunities.

A successive introduction of new products would have a similar effect. In postwar Japanese society, the number of households was increasing and new products were constantly being introduced, so that this hypothesis would account for a difference in the savings ratio between Japan (until the mid-seventies, when there was an expansion of consumer loans) and other countries with better consumer finance systems. In the eighties, however, the number of younger households will be decreasing in relative terms, and new major products seem to be appearing less often. Therefore an expansion of the system of consumer loans at this stage of maturity may not particularly lower the Japanese savings ratio (for similar conclusions, see Kosai and Ogino 1980, p. 191).

Hypothesis 11, regarding house-ownership demand, is partly related to the consumer finance problem, but it includes more than that. Many Japanese houses were destroyed by the war so that the postwar demand for housing in general was very high, although the same was true in Germany as well. Generally speaking, housing can be supplied through either public housing, or rented private housing, or resident-owned private housing. If a country tends to rely on public housing, a strong housing demand will increase government expenditure but not private savings. This was the case with countries ruled by labor (or labor coalition) governments such as Sweden, the Netherlands, and West Germany, but obviously not with Japan. If people have no particular preference for an owned house over a rented one, a strong housing demand will encourage investment in rental houses and as a consequence, some other types of private investments will be crowded

---

month in Japan and 86,000 yen per month in Germany). Most Japanese can receive a pension starting at age sixty and some even at fifty-five, while the German system and those of most other countries begin paying pensions at sixty-five. The Japanese system has many flaws of its own, but there is not space to delve into them here. See the *Chūkan hōkoku* 1979.

out, not necessarily resulting in an increase in private savings. However, if people have a strong preference for resident-owned housing, then the stronger housing demand must be matched by greater household savings. Judging from many opinion survey data, the Japanese have a strong preference for owned housing for reasons that are probably related to their cultural background (e.g., Economic Planning Agency 1977).

Actual economic data are consistent with the hypothesis of strong household-ownership demand. The ratio of private housing investment to GNP in Japan in the seventies was around 7 percent, which is significantly higher than any other industrial country. The ratio of houses owned by residents is very high in Japan. An international comparison of figures compiled around 1970 shows that Japan, with 58.2 percent, had one of the highest ratios along with such land-rich countries as Canada (60.0 percent), the United States (62.9 percent), and Australia (67.3 percent) (Sōrifu Tōkei Kyoku 1976, p. 212). The figures in all West European countries were lower than Japan, particularly those of the Netherlands (25.7 percent), Switzerland (28.5 percent), West Germany (33.5 percent), and Sweden (35.2 percent). (It should be noted that this ratio by no means reflects a degree of industrial development; most developing countries had higher figures than Japan. And in Japan, the ratio has declined from 62.4 percent in 1963 to 60.3 percent in 1968 and 59.2 percent in 1973.)[16]

The very high ratio of private housing investment together with the relatively high ratio of houses owned by residents in Japan would clearly suggest a high level of owned housing investment, which implies, as we pointed out, a higher level of private savings. In fact, according to Tetsuo Ihara, the savings ratio of those households that have definite plans for owning their houses is almost 10 percent higher than that of other households. It is also true that the savings ratio of those households that have to repay housing loans is higher than that of other households (Ihara 1979; Economic Planning Agency 1979, p. 194). Thus, we might argue that the strong demand for owned houses among Japanese can explain in part the high level of the savings ratio. Given this strong demand, hypothesis 9, regarding the underdeveloped consumer finance system, becomes relevant again in this context because until 1975, the government, banks, and other financial institutions had been unwilling to lend money for private housing.

However, we may offer a conjecture that things may be changing quickly. For the first time in the postwar period, the demand for new housing seems to be losing its momentum. Even in 1977 and 1978, the construction of new houses showed only a small increase in spite of still favorable financial conditions. This may be explained, at least in part, by the 7.2 percent vacancy rate of houses in 1979, a figure quite high from an international perspective. The

16. *White Paper on National Livelihood 1977*, p. 53. The decline was due to the decrease in the number of self-employed and the nonworking (probably the elderly). The ratio for employed people has been increasing.

deceleration of population increase and the halt of population movement into megalopolitan areas in the seventies contributed to this phenomenon. It is still true that among employed people in urban areas, the demand for owned housing is strong, but such a demand among the population as a whole seems to have begun to slacken. If this is so, the Japanese eagerness to save will gradually lose one of its major incentives. However, the short-run conclusion will not be much different, because the expansion of housing loans since 1975 will increase rather than decrease savings meant for repayment, as discussed in relation to consumer finance in general.

Hypothesis 12, regarding savings for grown-up children, has never been carefully examined. However, most Japanese parents seem to save for their children's college education, marriage ceremony and honeymoon, and new homes as well as to accumulate property that the children will one day inherit. This custom is rare in Western societies and so is worthy of mention. This type of saving is essentially the same as the postsaving purchase discussed earlier. Therefore on the one hand, it will result in an increase in the savings ratio if the size of the younger generation keeps increasing. On the other hand, however, if children themselves bear some of these expenses by borrowing money (parents are usually too old to be borrowers of the types of loans needed to meet their children's needs), they will probably be satisfied with more modest plans for education, marriage, and so forth. The net effect is uncertain so this hypothesis may be omitted as a major explanation of the high savings ratio.

Hypotheses 8 to 12 are more or less related to social customs and cultural background. Why did the Japanese in the sixties remain relatively indifferent to such problems as underdevelopment of social security or consumer finance? Why have Japanese continued to prefer owned houses to rented houses or public housing? Why are they willing to save for their children even after they are grown? In the end, the answers to these questions will be related to cultural factors. However, the problems raised above should be examined primarily as various aspects of Japan's postwar sociopolitical framework. Only through the choice of an institutional framework will a cultural factor materialize. What should be avoided is a naïve and almost tautological answer—for example, that the Japanese savings ratio is high because Japanese culture values frugality.

In the fifties, the earlier phase of the postwar reconstruction process, the ruling conservative government made the important institutional choice that probably was not a result of carefully planned design but that somehow achieved a de facto consistency. The choice was for a heavily growth-oriented economic institution that gave priority to industrial development over the immediate improvement of people's livelihood. Notable examples were, as discussed earlier, the growth-oriented financial structure, the industry-biased infrastructure, and so on. This choice may not necessarily have been harmful to people's welfare in the long run; it is quite likely that the opposite is the case. However, the institutional choice itself implied short-term discouraging effects on consumption because there was little policy emphasis on social security, public housing, and consumer finance. The high savings ratio of Japanese households is a consequence of this over-all institutional choice that includes, in effect, all the factors included in hypotheses 8 through 11.

What is going to happen to the savings rate of the Japanese or, more broadly, to their behavior patterns as consumer-workers? As a crucial factor in this context, it should be noted that the conservative government made another big change in its policy stance in the seventies that again may have been a result of ad hoc unplanned efforts of appeasement. The government was prepared to accept that the average Japanese was becoming less growth oriented. The government adopted one of the strictest counterpollution policies in the world, and the social security and consumer finance systems were improved. Public investment in the seventies shifted its emphasis visibly from the industrial infrastructure to such items as housing loans, sewer construction, and so forth.

Will these changes result in an explosion of much delayed consumption? The foregoing arguments tend to suggest that at least in the near future, there will be no explosive factors in the increase of private consumption. The improvement of the social security system has shown little sign of encouraging consumption; the relative decrease of the size of the younger generation, the end of megalopolitan sprawl, and the saturation of consumer durables (can IC create another wave of new consumer durables?) will all contribute to the deceleration of the growth of private consumption, even if consumer loans are amply supplied.

Many people are puzzled by the signs of increased satisfaction among the Japanese after the oil crisis, yet many opinion surveys such as those done by NHK testify to this phenomenon, as does an increasing conservative voting strength. But this may not be so puzzling after all. My previous arguments might indicate that the life of the average Japanese had been steadily improving through the seventies so as to almost reach maturity, although few Japanese are explicitly aware of this, probably because of the recent economic vicissitudes after the oil crisis. Equality of wealth and income as a trend has been increasing, which is beneficial to the middle and lower strata of Japanese society. Wealth is now increasing with accelerated speed.

One scarcely noticed fact is that the average Japanese household now has more financial assets than households in any other country except perhaps the United States. According to the *White Paper on National Livelihood 1977* (Economic Planning Agency 1977) personal financial assets per capita in 1975 (converted into yen by the exchange rate of 300 yen per dollar) were 3.57 million yen for the United States, 1.70 for West Germany, 1.15 for the United Kingdom, and 1.62 for Japan.[17] Due to the high savings ratio,

17. See ibid., p. 70. The exchange rate has gone from about 300 yen in 1975 to 200 yen per dollar in 1978. The figure for personal financial assets in 1979 comes from the Bank of Japan 1980.

the Japanese figure in 1979 soared to nearly 2.70 million yen, while my tentative estimate of the United States figure in the same year was around 3.10 million yen, converted by the exchange rate of 200 yen to the dollar. An exact comparison is not our concern. The point is the simple mathematical truth that a country with a high savings ratio as well as a high growth rate of real (adjusted by effective exchange rate) income will rapidly catch up with and finally pass other countries in terms of accumulated assets. When the gap in income compared with other countries is still large, the catch-up process is difficult to notice. However, once the gap closes, the process becomes suddenly visible with exponential acceleration. This is now happening in Japan vis-à-vis other industrial countries.

Many people have long entertained the idea that Japan may be well off in flow (income) but still poor in stock (wealth). However, my calculus of savings suggests that Japan will catch up and perhaps surpass other countries more quickly in terms of stock than in terms of flow.

The growth-oriented institutional structure that dominated postwar Japan seems to be changing, losing one after another of its prominent characteristics. On the other hand, the average Japanese consumer seems, as I have been arguing, to be entering a phase of saturation rather than of unsatisfied aspiration. (It may be noted that the lower stratum-centered income distribution in Japan is likely to create smaller demonstration effects on consumption than upper stratum-centered distribution such as that in the United States). It is difficult to predict exactly whether the new effects of these changes will lower or raise the Japanese savings rate. However, many signs indicate that the savings ratio is unlikely to fall in the next several years. Therefore the problem is how to deal with the high savings ratio and rapidly increasing assets. The list of issues includes a reappraisal of government expenditure in this new context, a search for investment based on new technologies, possible explosion of overseas investment, and most important, a restructuring of the financial system, and so forth. The problems in the eighties may have quite a different complexion.

PROBLEMS FOR THE FUTURE

THE BASIC INTERNAL CONDITION—THE END OF CATCH-UP CONSENSUS

As outlined earlier, the essential systemic characteristic of the postwar Japanese politico-economic structure was its bilevel system of regulation and competition. Thus, depending on what is emphasized, the Japanese system appeared regulative at times, and competitive at others. The vital point of this system is that the bilevel structure was never fully legalized, consisting of statutes of a presumably temporary nature, administrative guidance, voluntary agreements under such guidance, administrative consultations, and so forth. The system was indeed flexible, yet it would have suffered from loss of orientation and dynamism unless the basic consensus about the primary goal as well as major strategies worked to maintain consistency among all subsystems or to orchestrate them. In postwar Japan, the agreed goal was to catch up with advanced countries and the agreed strategy was to emulate the technology and industrial structure of advanced economies. Such consensus was the most important internal condition for the successful rapid economic growth.

This consensus provided an over-all design for almost all (not only economic but also diplomatic) policies including administrative regulations, thereby coordinating the otherwise sectionalism-prone ministries within government. It also provided an impartial rule for execution of each regulation to prevent potentially discretion-prone bureaucrats from favoritism or corruption. Private businesses would not have complied with administrative guidance or advice as willingly as they actually did if they had not felt themselves sharing this consensus. Even the average Japanese seemed to share the consensus, reinforcing the incentive toward hard work, a higher savings rate, and so forth, and this consensus somehow compensated for discontent with the primarily probusiness policy by government.

It is a serious misunderstanding often found not only in non-Japanese but also in the Japanese themselves that Japan is always capable of producing a consensus. Indeed, the typical Japanese organization such as a firm or a ministry tends to prefer consensual decisions, but the country as a whole is evidently too large to always be able to reach some consensus. In fact, the politics in modernizing Japan have been mostly (in terms of time) dominated by the so-called pluralistic hegemony, that is, conflict, compromise, and stalemate among major power groups. The period of postwar economic growth is, in this sense, exceptional perhaps only along with the period from the Sino-Japanese War to the Russo-Japanese War and five years of World War II. It may be noted in passing that on the eve of the Second World War, the then-ruling pluralistic hegemony was divided about external policies. As almost everyone may agree, the catch-up growth consensus is now disappearing, simply because it has almost achieved its goal. Can Japan build up a new and equally strong consensus for the future?

It is not likely. Some might argue that the Japanese economy overcame the oil crisis almost as if there were a solid nationwide consensus (the management accepted low profits to avoid layoffs or discharge of workers and labor restrained a wage increase). Indeed, a solution of the energy resource problem can be a primary national goal to Japan or almost any country. However, this goal, or for that matter, any other goal cannot be so strong a basis for new consensus as the catch-up goal for two reasons. First, the catch-up growth could be defined convincingly in terms of economic policies or even subpolicies by referring to the actual successful precedents of more advanced countries. This can hardly be the case with the energy resource problem. To save energy input in each industry is a unanimously agreed policy, and the Japanese economy during the oil crises pursued it to the fullest possible extent. Yet this policy has an obvious limit, and beyond that limit the policy choice is divided concerning, for example, whether a nuclear power policy should be adopted or not, how much foreign policy should be affected by energy issues, and so on. Second, the policy decisions under the growth consensus were virtually free from any major choice about foreign policy, because Japan's growth-only stance was protected and, in fact, made possible by Pax Americana including the IMF— GATT regime. Considering the historical lesson that prewar Japanese politics so often become divided when faced with external issues, this second condition will be of crucial importance. In the coming decade when international circumstances will become really fluid, it may thus be unlikely that any consensus will be built and maintained with an effectiveness equal to the catch-up consensus that the Japanese used to have.

Without an effective consensus, the loosely structured bilevel system of the Japanese political economy might behave in a totally different way. Given an extant system of industrywide consultation and guidance, each industry's interests will be more effectively organized than any other interests of broader range, and represented by a ministry or a particular branch of it. However, there will no longer be a simple criterion, such as contribution to economic growth, to judge which industry should be promoted or discouraged. Thus we may be facing the possibility that various sectionalist interests often represented by branches of government will form another "pluralist hegemony" but only reach a lukewarm compromise or even an inactive stalemate. This may be overstating one particular possibility, but in so doing I am attempting to emphasize how essential the consensus about catch-up growth was as a basic internal condition for the success of an economy Japanese-style.

THE BASIC EXTERNAL CONDITION–THE SLOWER GROWTH POTENTIAL

Like other industrial economies, the Japanese economy is facing different external environments than it did ten years ago. The differences may be summarized as follows. First, there is no more readily available technology for Japanese industries to borrow. The first wave of technological progress after World War II is fading away, and the second wave, if there is one, will be based on so-called mechatronic engineering and biological engineering. In this possible second wave, the Japanese industries will no longer have the advantage of being a late-comer. Second, the international economic system will be far less stable than in the fifties and sixties, the ideal of free trade will falter, and protectionism will be invoked more readily and frequently. As the Japanese share of total world trade is close to 10 percent, it will be increasingly difficult for Japanese exports to grow faster than world trade. Particularly, the downpouring of exports will no longer be a means to ease a recession. And third, energy resources, particularly petroleum, will be increasingly costly. As the Japanese economy is heavily reliant on imported oil, this problem will indeed be serious. From the viewpoint of competitiveness among industrial economies, however, the impact of an oil price hike will be a mixed blessing for the Japanese economy. Due to this impact, the Japanese economy will indeed fluctuate more than other economies in terms of output and prices; it will also have greater incentive to conserve oil and, more generally, to rationalize the whole industrial structure, as was indicated by the performance of the Japanese economy during the past two oil crises. This third issue may not be so fatal to the Japanese economy as it first appeared.

All these new basic external economic conditions of the coming decade will slow down the economic growth and force the Japanese economy to radically change its structure in ways explained below.

LONG-RUN ORIENTATION OF JAPANESE FIRMS: A REAPPRAISAL

Having reviewed the basic internal and external conditions, we may now summarize possible changes in each of those characteristic features of the pre-oil crisis Japanese economy formulated earlier. A Japanese firm's long-run orientation was not so much a characteristic inherent in Japanese culture as a product of a certain mixture of three economic environments, that is, the borrowable technology, the risk-reducing financial system, and the Japanese employment system, particularly intrafirm job mobility. As of today, the first advantage has disappeared and the second is, as I will discuss later, disappearing. These two changes seem cogent enough to conclude that Japanese firms can no longer operate on the decreasing long-run average cost curve. Leading industries before the oil crisis, such as steel, automobiles, electric appliances, petrochemicals, and so forth, are now facing the increasing long-run average cost situation just like others who are not late-comers.

This change will imply that in those (hitherto) leading industries the market mechanism is likely to be more stable or, in other words, less prey to excessive competition. During the growth period, administrative guidance to curb the investment race or to introduce a recession cartel was justifiable in the sense theorized earlier. From now on, however, continuation of such a policy stance is likely to cause a downturn toward inefficiency and stagnation in those formerly vigorous industries. In a similar vein the "downpouring" of Japanese exports will become not only increasingly difficult (due to international friction) but also less urgently needed by major Japanese industries. Economically speaking, there will hereafter be no powerful reason why Japanese firms should be particularly different from their Western counterparts.

While this paper cannot analyze the Japanese employment system, a good guess is that sociologically Japanese firms will remain considerably different and retain most features of the Japanese employment system, because inertia as well as group orientation is changing but not disappearing. Recently many Japanese seem to be seeking a panacea in this system. I agree with them to the extent that intrafirm job mobility as one of the system's features greatly contributed to the dynamism of Japanese firms. However, this feature is, in essence, a capability of adjustment but not of creating anything new so that it cannot be by itself a miracle medicine for continued vigor.

In my opinion, the group-oriented Japanese management and the individual-oriented Western (or rather Anglo-American) management are now on quite equal footing, facing the following challenges in the coming decades: (1) how to deal with short-term impact (such as the oil crisis) without causing a long-term adverse after-effect (such as a wage-price spiral or productivity decline); (2) how to create consummatory (intrinsically satisfying) work, or jobs for women or the aged; (3) how to innovate in a truly creative way; (4) how to make adjustments or even take leadership in interindustrial restructuring.

Concerning the capability for two types of firms to meet the challenges, there seems to be a preconception. An average view might be that a Japanese firm is better for (1) and part of (2), because it showed a better performance during the oil crisis stagflation and it also succeeded in keeping the work ethic alive. On the other hand, a Western firm might excel in (3) and (4), because a creative individual is better rewarded and interfirm mobility of workers is higher. However, it seems that this popularized view is only a preconception. An opposite conclusion about each of the four issues can be worked out, depending on what is premised, though this paper has to leave this interesting intellectual experiment open. My interim answer is that neither the success during the rapid growth period nor the praised performance during the oil crises guarantee better future performance of Japanese firms.

THE JAPANESE FINANCIAL SYSTEM: A REAPPRAISAL

In the early seventies, there emerged many signs of change in the Japanese financial system, including explosive expansion of the market of bonds with repurchase agreement (gensaki market), an internationalization of financial markets, a frequent revision of deposit interest rate, and so forth. After the oil crisis, further important changes appeared, such as a huge amount of national bond issue, a much-delayed development of consumer loans (mainly housing loans), an introduction of negotiable certificates of deposit, and so forth. These changes were mainly due to two factors. First, the government (MOF and BOJ) had to concede and respond to increasing complaints about the unfairness of regulations from various interested parties such as securities companies, corporate investors (mainly trust banks and insurance companies), households, and most notably the outside world.

This was an indication that the government could no longer hold in check the voices of various related interests by a dictum of catch-up growth. Actually, a constitutional suit was filed during the post-oil crisis inflation against the government because of the unfair depreciation of household savings due to the regulation of interest rates. Second, the excess supply of loanable funds seems to have occurred for the first time in the postwar period, because the sudden deceleration of growth triggered by the oil crisis created a sharp reduction in private investment and so in demand for loan-able funds, while household savings and so the supply of funds remained strong. Indirect evidence of excess supply is that the city banks became, for the first time after the war, seriously interested in lending to consumers. The situation has now changed from a dominance of excess demand to that of excess supply.

The poswar Japanese financial system symbolized by the artificially low interest rate policy is going to die a natural death. Two conditions are fatal to its survival. First, household savings in Japan will remain strong and asset-holding behavior will be more sensitive to the interest rate. Therefore, if the Japanese system still tries to peg the deposit interest rate at an artifi-cially low level, then a huge amount of assets will shift from the deposit to other forms as foretold by an explosive increase in postal savings compared to an increase in bank deposits. As we pointed out earlier, as the average Japanese household's financial assets are now comparable to those in the United States, there is no reason why only the Japanese household should stick to assets in the form of deposits. Second, the internationalization of the financial system will liberalize, particularly, the bond market. Yields on foreign yen-dominated issues are now liberalized, and only one-third of each issue is assigned to the banks. The rest is, via securities companies, placed with the smaller-scale financial institutions and households. Under this new development, it will soon be too difficult to continue to retain control of the yen-dominated bond issued by Japanese. Third, the large amount of na-tional bonds issued after the oil crisis to finance increased deficit spend-ing will work in favor of liberalization of the interest rate. Since all central government deposits are concentrated at the BOJ, the banks cannot resort to a compensatory deposit practice against the purchase of national bonds at artificially low nominal yields. As recent developments indicate, national bonds will have to be issued at the market rate. Therefore, the secondary market for outstanding national bonds will develop and be open to the general public. Too many changes are now occurring and need not be de-tailed here. All these signs obviously indicate that the growth-oriented Japa-nese financial system is gradually coming to an end.

ADMINISTRATIVE REGULATION: A REAPPRAISAL

The crux of the administrative regulation in postwar Japan was, as I dis-cussed earlier, the building of a consensus for voluntary compliance in each industry. There were two mainstays for this key practice. First, the nation-wide consensus about the catch-up growth worked as an ultimate rationale for industrywide agreements. This once paramount consensus is, however, now fading among the Japanese. Second, the voluntary compliance was buttressed by a miscellany of rewards and penalties, most of which have been justified as incentives for economic growth. Quite a few of them are now being repealed and their legitimacy is visibly in decline. The original mainstays of the consensus building are deteriorating. On the other hand, however, the accumulated experience of industrywide guidance and consultation over a quarter century seems to have created a kind of symbiosis between each industry (represented by the industry association) and the particular branch of government in charge. Thus, it may not be unreasonable to suspect that such a close relationship will primarily come to serve each industry's parochial interest as well as each administrative branch's sectional consideration. We cannot rely solely on Japanese bureaucrats' elitist morals and intelligence to avoid this hangover of growth-oriented regulation.

In fact, there are a number of catalysts to give rise to such industrywide protectionist practices. For one example, international trade conflicts are nurturing government-led cartels such as the trigger price system in the steel industry, the voluntary trade restriction in the automobile industry, and so on. For another example, expanding large-scale overseas projects are necessitating government loans to foreign countries as well as to Japanese firms in the projects, and administrative guidance (as exemplified by Iran Petro-Chemical, many industrial plants in China, and various mining investments all over the world). These recent developments are some of the most important politico-economic events in post-oil crisis Japan, and they might imply that the interests specific to each industry or ministry are getting too deeply involved in international politics and are increasingly difficult to coordinate with the national interests.

As suggested earlier, an inherent problem in the bilevel structure of the Japanese political economy is the potential unfairness between industries compared to the substantive fairness within each industry. As long as the Japanese economy was rapidly growing and all industries were more or less prosperous, interindustrial differences did not matter much. However, in the coming post-Pax Americana period when the economy will grow slowly and the second wave of technological innovation will not yet have come, conflicts in interindustrial interests are likely to be intense, beyond the control of implicit administrative guidance, which has now lost most of the persuasiveness it had based on the catch-up target as well as strategy. Many labor-intensive industries, let alone conventional agriculture, will have to be rationalized and probably abandoned, and even the hitherto leading industries, such as steel, will face competition from the newly developing countries. In these days of flexible exchange rates, the increasing productivity of export industries will imply a greater burden on the industries directly dependent on imported resources. All this will intensify the need for constant interindustrial restructuring, and will therefore require above all a fair rule between industries. In particular, the rule should be acceptable to foreign companies that will appear more and more often on the Japanese scene. The Japanese industrial policy up to now is likely to be less workable and less beneficial to the national interest, except possibly in such potentially innovative industries as the development of new energy sources, large-scale integrated circuits and their application, new communication systems, biological engineering, and so forth, in which the benefits of decreasing long-run average cost might remain.

The bilevel, loosely institutionalized politico-economic system in postwar Japan has proven effective in achieving the national consensual target of catch-up growth. As this article has been arguing, however, most of the prerequisites for this system are now fading. Because of the achieved material affluence, the consensus for catch-up growth no longer exists and average Japanese are getting less instrumental and more consummatory. Their desire to increase consumption will diminish and they will be increasingly motivated to hold more assets. In the years to come, macroeconomic policies in terms of aggregate demand or the labor supply will be as difficult in Japan as in other industrial countries. Yet a more serious challenge will come from the more structural or more institutional problems. At the start of rapid economic growth, many people were concerned that industrial growth would cause internal conflicts and societal division roughly in terms of class struggle. Their apprehensions were apparently unfounded. However, new types of structural friction now seem to be emerging—for example, the younger people versus the older people, female versus male, the hitherto leading industries versus the new innovative industries, the export-oriented industries versus the industries dependent on imported resources, and so forth. The old network of government regulation as well as the philosophy behind it seem to be, in many respects, ill-fitted to solve this new set of structural issues.

Above all, the Japanese economy will have to be internationalized in many senses of the word. The flow of commodities, capital, and even people will be liberalized in and out of Japan. The Tokyo market is likely to be one of the major financial centers of the world. Overseas investment will increase and automatically affect Japan's foreign policies. The commitment as well as the responsibility for international politics will inevitably increase. The past introverted, almost ethnocentric, economic policies should be abandoned, and a new set of policy stances as well as an institutional setting linked with them should be reformulated and implemented. These challenges might be regarded apprehensively by the established industries and branches of government. However, all this means is simply that the Japanese economy is on equal footing with other industrial countries of comparable magnitude. Even in this context, the Japanese characteristics might be incorporated in a beneficial way, for example, in the form of a new Japanese employment system. However, such an attempt should never be a perpetuation of the specific socioinstitutional framework that was effective only in the particular historical experience of the rapid economic growth period.

REFERENCES

Arendt, Hannah. 1958. *The Human Condition.* Chicago, University of Chicago Press.
Argyris, Chris. 1972. *The Applicability of Organization Sociology.* New York, Cambridge University Press.
Bank of Japan. 1980. *Shikin junkan kanjō* [Fund circulation account]. Tokyo.
Economic Planning Agency. See Keizai Kikakuchō.
Furukawa Akira. 1980. "Jisshō bunseki—'madoguchi shidō' no yūkōsei to ginkōjunbi no juyōkansū" [An empirical analysis—effectiveness of "window guidance" and demand

function for bank reserve] . *Tōyōkeizai rinji-zōkan shirizu*, no. 54 (October).

Goldthorpe, J. H. et al. 1969. *The Affluent Worker: Industrial Attitudes and Behavior*. New York, Cambridge University Press.

Horiuchi Akiyoshi. 1977. " 'Madoguchi shidō' no yūkōsei" [Effectiveness of "window guidance"] . *Keizai kenkyū* (July).

———. 1980. *Nihon no kinyū seisaku* [Financial policy in Japan] . Tokyo, Tōyō keizai shimpōsha.

Ichino Shozo. 1980. "The Structure of the Labor Force and Patterns of Mobility: 1950-65." In *The Labor Market in Japan—Selected Readings*, ed. Shunsaku Nishikawa; translated by Ross Mouer. Tokyo, University of Tokyo Press.

Ihara Tetsuo. 1979. *Kojin chochiku no kettei riron* [A theory of the determination of personal savings] . Tokyo, Tōyō keizai shimpōsha.

Inglehart, R. 1977. *The Silent Revolution*. Princeton, Princeton University Press.

Iwata Kazumasa, and Hamada Koichi. 1980. *Kinyū seisaku to ginkō kōdō* [Financial policy and bank behavior] . Tokyo, Tōyō keizai shimpōsha.

Kaizuka Keimei, and Onodera Hiroo. 1974. "Shinyō wariate ni tsuite" [On credit rationing] . *Keizai kenkyū*, vol. 25, no. 1 (January).

Kamae Hiroshi. 1980. "Nihon no kashidashi shijō no fukinkō no keisoku—kaizenshita dēta o mochiite" [An empirical study of the disequilibrium of the bank loan market in Japan—by improved data] . *Keizai kenkyū*, vol. 31, no. 1 (January).

Kanamori Hisao. 1961. "Chochikuritsu wa naze takai ka" [Why is the savings ratio high?] . In *Keizai geppō*, issued by the Economic Planning Agency (November).

Keizai Kikakuchō [Economic Planning Agency] . 1977. *Kokumin seikatsu hakusho* [White Paper on national livelihood] . Tokyo, Ministry of Finance.

———. 1979a. *Kokumin no seikatsu to ishiki no dōkō* [Changes in national livelihood and consciousness] . Tokyo, Government Printing Office.

———. 1979b. *Keizai hakusho* [White Paper on the economy] . Tokyo, Ministry of Finance.

Komiya Ryutaro. 1975. *Gendai Nihon keizai kenkyū* [A study of the contemporary Japanese economy] . Tokyo, University of Tokyo Press.

Kosai Yasushi, and Ogino Yoshitaro. 1980. *Nihon keizai tenbō* [Japanese economy in perspective] . Tokyo, Nihon hyōronsha.

Kuroda Iwao. 1979a. "Wagakuni ni okeru kashidashi-kinri no kettei ni tsuite" [On the determination of the loan rate in Japan] . *Kinyū kenkyū shiryō*, no. 2, pp. 25-51.

———. 1979b. " 'Madoguchi shidō' o meguru bunseki no saikentō" [A re-examination of the analyses of "window guidance"] . *Kikan gendai keizai* (Winter).

———. 1981. "Wagakuni kinyū seisaku no mekanizumu saikō" [The mechanism of Japanese financial policy reconsidered] . *Keizai kenkyū*, vol. 32, no. 1 (January).

Ministry of Labor. See Rōdōshō.

Mizoguchi Toshiyuki. 1974. "Sengo Nihon no shotoku bunpu to shisan bunpu" [Income and asset distributions in postwar Japan] . *Keizai kenkyū* 25, no. 9 (October):363.

———. 1976. "Wagakuni no zenshotai no shotoku bunpu suikei" [An estimate of income distribution of total households in Japan] . *Keizai kenkyū* 27, no. 3 (July):231.

—— et al. 1978. "Sengo Nihon no shotoku bunpu II" [Distribution of household income 1953-75] . *Keizai kenkyū*, vol. 29, no. 1 (January).

Murakami Yasusuke. 1982. "The Age of New Middle Mass Politics." *Journal of Japanese Studies* 8, no. 1:29-72.

Nakamura Takafusa. 1980. *Nihon keizai—sono seichō to kōzō* [The Japanese economy—its growth and structure] . 2nd ed., Tokyo, Tokyo University Press.

National Livelihood White Paper 1977. See Keizai Kikakuchō 1977.

Nenkin Kihonmondai Kondankai [Committee concerning the basic problems of old age] . 1979. *Chūkan hōkoku* [Interim report] . Tokyo.

NHK Yoron Chōsajo [The Opinion Survey Institute of the Japanese Broadcasting Corporation] , ed. 1980. *Daini Nihonjin no ishiki—NHK yoron chōsa* [The Japanese consciousness 2—NHK opinion survey] . Tokyo, Shiseidō.

———. 1975. *Zusetsu sengo yoronshi* [An illustrative history of postwar public opinion]. Tokyo, Nihon hōsō shuppan kyōkai.

Rimbara Yukio, and Santamero, A. M. 1976. "A Study of Credit Rationing in Japan." *International Economic Review*, vol. 17, no. 3 (October).

Rōdōshō [Ministry of Labor]. 1978. *Rōdō hakusho* [White Paper on labor]. Tokyo.

Rōdōshō Kambō Tōkeijōhōbu Jōhōkaisekika [Ministry of Labor, Department of Information and Analysis]. "Daigaku sotsugyōsha no koyō to chingin" [Employment and wages of college graduates]. *Rōdōtōkei chōsa geppō*, vol. 28, no. 1.

Sakakibara Eisuke, Feldman, Robert, and Harada Yuzo. 1981. "Japanese Financial System in Comparative Perspective." Unpublished working paper, Center for International Affairs, Harvard University.

Santas, F. 1975. "The Economics of Marital Status." In *Sex Discrimination and the Division of Labor*, ed. C. Lloyd. New York, Columbia University Press.

Shimizu Yoshinori. 1980. "Ginkō kashidashi shijō ni okeru kashidaore risuku" [Default risk in the bank loan market]. *Tōyōkeizai rinji-zōkan shirizu*, no. 54 (October).

Sōrifu Tōkei Kyoku [Prime Minister's Office, Bureau of Statistics]. 1976. *Kokusai tōkei yōran* [Handbook of international statistics]. Tokyo.

Suzuki Yoshio. 1980. *Money and Banking in Contemporary Japan*. New Haven, Yale University Press.

Takayama Noriyuki, 1980. *Fubyōdō no keizai bunseki* [Economic analysis of inequality]. Tokyo, Tōyō keizai shimpōsha.

Teranishi Shigeo. 1974. "Sengo kashidashi shijō no seikaku ni tsuite" [On the character of the postwar loan market]. *Keizai kenkyū*, vol. 25, no. 3 (July).

White Paper on Labor. See Rōdōshō 1978.

Yamamura Kozo. 1967. *Economic Policy in Postwar Japan*. Berkeley and Los Angeles, University of California Press.

Japan's Changing Industrial Structure
and United States–Japan Industrial Relations

THE STRUCTURAL CHANGE of Japanese industry can be portrayed in the following three chronological divisions. Phase 1 (1955 to 1964) was the period of initial rapid growth after postwar reconstruction. This phase was a period of widespread innovation when large-scale plants in raw material processing industries such as steel, chemicals, and electricity generation were introduced. Phase 2 (1965 to 1973) was a period of composite structural change. During the first part, machinery industries (broadly defined to include transportation, electrical, and all other types of machinery and equipment) began to form the core of Japan's industrial structure. The second part of phase 2 saw the change induced by efforts of the business world to solve environmental problems by relying on technological progress achieved by machinery industries. As will be elaborated later, Japanese industrial society in this period was at a crossroads in some respects. Phase 3 (1974 to the present) has been a difficult but successful period for Japan in the sense that rapid progress is being made toward becoming a superindustrial society through efforts to overcome the difficulties associated with the oil crisis.

In analyzing the structural changes of each phase, I shall pay special attention to three key concepts: technology, competition, and organization. Table 2.1 summarizes the basic characteristics of each phase with respect to these three variables.

PHASE 1: INNOVATION

Exactly when Japan's postwar economy began its period of high growth may be a subject for debate, but the political events of 1955 must have special significance. The year was marked by the formation of a power elite repre-

---

The author is professor of economic and management science, Institute of Business Research, Hitotsubashi University. This paper was presented at the Committee on Japanese Economic Studies conference on U.S.-Japan economic relations, March 23-27, 1981.

47

TABLE 2.1

CHANGING CHARACTERISTICS OF THE JAPANESE ECONOMY

	Technology	Competition	Organization
Phase 1 1955 ∿ 1964	Raw materials processing oriented	Competition vs Control	Internal organization
Phase 2 1965 ∿ 1973	Assembly oriented	Competition vs Monopoly	Hierarchy vs Market
Phase 3 1974 ∿	Electronic oriented	Competitive	Interfirm organization

senting a partnership between the Liberal Democratic party (LDP), government officials, and business. As a result, the government's economic objective of rapidly catching up with advanced countries combined with the business world's profit-motivated desire for rapid growth was converted into the political slogan of the ten-year "income-doubling plan." This slogan helped to produce a national consensus in favor of pressing along the road of high economic growth. The subsequent process of rapid growth that persisted until 1964 I shall call phase 1 of the structural change.

During phase 1, the Industrial Structure Investigation Committee (Sangyō Kōzō Chōsakai), an advisory body to the Ministry of International Trade and Industry (MITI), played a major role in organizing Japan's main industries. This committee was composed of subcommittees connected with specific industries, and committee members from representative firms in each industry compiled their respective industrial investment plans by harmonizing big business interests and bureaucratic views. In addition, industrial leaders sat on the general committee that fused business and government interests at the political level.

This system involving the LDP, government, and business was made all the more effective by a trend toward political centralism, produced by the increasing dependence of regional budgets on central finance. Although one of the objectives of postwar economic democratization was a parallel strengthening of regional political independence, the actual course of events produced a movement toward centralization of political power. Thus, as industries moved into new regions of development they came to depend on national funds for industrial land, water, transportation facilities, residential land, and educational and welfare facilities.

Underlying this policy was the basic concept that a strong industrial foundation speeds up the development of private enterprise and expedites the growth and development of the national economy, thus eventually benefiting the entire society. As part of its industrial policy, MITI often emphasized improving international competitive power. It is not easy to define competitive power, but at that time it was generally accepted that this meant organizing an efficient production system. As an objective it resembled the earlier American objective of space exploration, which also involved setting up a government-organized production system. However, in the case of Japan, there was no overt recognition that the push toward international competitiveness was a national plan as such; by using the method of "administrative guidance,"[1] it purportedly respected the independence of business.

The government justified administrative guidance ostensibly as a measure for preventing what it called excessive competition. From a physical organization aspect of an effective system of production, competition invariably appears to involve unnecessary duplication. Administrative guidance tends by nature toward assigning quotas, either overtly or covertly, and firms were engaged in hot competition for these quotas.

THE SUPPLY-FIRST SYSTEM

Since industrial policy involved introducing administrative guidance into the market mechanism, this complicated control system produced a peculiarly Japanese phenomenon: a system favoring the fast-growing producer. From the point of view of industrial organization, fixed-investment adjustment played the leading role in this process. Under the auspices of the Industrial Structure Investigation Committee, joint study groups were set up in each industry for firms to discuss and agree on investment plans. These were essentially authorized investment cartels in the form of coordination panels.

Plant investment coordination inevitably involved some form of allocation and placed those firms that increased their production capacity most rapidly in a favorable position. This prompted firms to compete for capacity expansion, and thus the very investment control that was aimed at preventing duplication of investment encouraged unexpected capacity expansion.

In this fashion, during the early stages of the high-growth era, normal plant investment based on an expectation of growth in demand came to be displaced by investment for its own sake, and this acquired a momentum of its own. The activities of firms, rather than reflecting the needs of the consumer, became distorted and reflected considerations of market share. Competition among enterprises ceased to be a matter of exploiting individual advantages to produce better products. Instead, during phase 1, undue emphasis was given to competition in securing more investment quotas. It is also undeniable that the driving force supporting the competition for investment involved entrepreneurs' nationalistic aspirations for catching up technologically with the advanced industrial nations, as well as their personal ambition for success.

1. Administrative guidance in this context means recommended restriction of production, whereby MITI makes recommendations to each of the firms in an industry concerning their pricing policies or the restriction of production. MITI has no explicit legal authority to enforce its recommendations. However, the firms in question usually have accepted the recommendations because of their underlying desire to reach some form of agreement.

Such unique features of competition based upon these external and internal motives are undoubtedly elements of what is generally referred to as excessive competition among Japanese firms. In the early 1960s, some Japanese economists hypothesized that "investment inviting further investment" explained the high growth of the Japanese economy. From the viewpoint of industrial organization, this corresponds to a mechanism that allows investment to expand by its own momentum through competition for a share of the market.

A system emphasizing the producer and the supply side—I shall call it a supply-first system—was unique to Japanese industrial organization in a number of industries such as steel, petrochemicals, and cement, which do not allow much product differentiation. Accelerated investment in these industries certainly contributed to rationalizing and modernizing Japanese firms, strengthening competitive power in overseas markets, and pushing economic development forward, This is, ipso facto, the process of technological innovations accompanying scale economies. The adoption of up-to-date, large scale, and large capacity equipment helped to lower production costs. Industrial organization attained the highest level of technological efficiency in this respect in many of Japan's industries.

THE CONSUMER GOODS MARKETS

At the same time, even in the consumer goods markets, where product differentiation is easy and scale economies not so large, the supply-first system also appeared, albeit through a different kind of mechanism. This was a system of captive distribution that came to be called the manufacturer controlled distribution system.

After the war, manufacturers replaced the prewar dealer-controlled distribution system with one that was under their own control, and during the period of high growth they expanded such "tied distribution" systems. In the economic climate of postwar Japan, especially during phase 1, it was commonly accepted that manufacturers should control the distribution channels of their own products. Antimonopoly policy ignored unfair practices in distribution such as restrictive or exclusive dealings. For instance, in the legal proceedings relating to the Matsushita resale case, the Matsushita Electric Industrial Company vigorously defended the legitimacy of its resale practices. Only recently has the company decided to acquiesce to the judgment.

Once control of distribution is established by an oligopolistic firm, a system of producer sovereignty exists in the field of distribution as well. The question of how to deal with the problem of nonprice competition under oligopoly is not limited to Japan alone but is a universal problem of capitalism today. However, Japan's distribution system during phase 1 was controlled by manufacturers more strongly than in any other country and produced a system of producer sovereignty to a degree that was unique to Japan.

STRUCTURAL CHANGES

Within the framework of the system described above, Japanese enterprises expanded rapidly and in the process introduced many innovations, broadened markets, extended the division of labor, and in general pursued a positive competitive policy. This process corresponds precisely to the Schumpeterian process of "creative destruction," a revolutionary process that cannot easily be summed up in a few statistical tables. Nevertheless, let me present here some statistical evidence that illustrates the dynamic changes in the Japanese economy. Table 2.2 presents an international comparison of the

TABLE 2.2

COEFFICIENTS OF CHANGE IN INDUSTRIAL STRUCTURE

	1954 ∿ 61	1960 ∿ 70	1971 ∿ 77
Japan	18.4	19.3	11.1
U.S.A.	5.6	10.9	1.2
U.K.	9.1	12.0	10.1
West Germany	7.0	10.6	10.6
France	5.4	12.9	7.5
Italy	14.3	11.4	7.8

SOURCES: 1954 ∿ 61, Economic Planning Agency 1964, p. 54. 1960 ∿ 70 based on material from United Nations 1973.
NOTE: Coefficient of change in industrial structure is obtained as follows. In both the base year and the end year the industrial composition of the gross national product is calculated and points given for differences between the two years. The coefficient of change is the sum total of such points.

variation coefficients of industrial structure as an indicator of the adaptability of the Japanese economy. Japan's variation coefficient during phase 1 was extremely high compared to other advanced countries, thus indicating that the industrial structure of the Japanese economy had undergone remarkable changes by giving full play to its adaptability.

Figure 2.1 reveals a decline of employment in agriculture, forestry, and fisheries from 48.3 percent of total employment in 1950 to 19.3 percent in 1970, despite substantial government protection. On the other hand, the key industries of chemicals, iron and steel, and machinery doubled their employment from 6.7 percent in 1950 to 13.8 percent in 1970. Such a rapid change is noteworthy in the history of modern economic growth—it took forty years for Britain to reduce primary employment from 22.8 to 12.3 percent. Although the social and political forces mentioned earlier tended to distort market forces in the Japanese economic structure, innovative forces were strong enough to cope with these obstacles and to achieve remarkable structural changes through an evolutionary growth process.

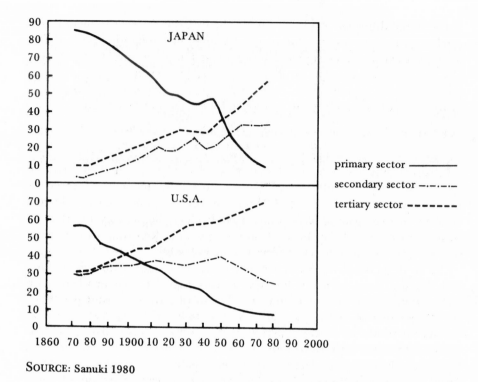

SOURCE: Sanuki 1980

Fig. 2.1. Structural changes in employment by sectors

PHASE 2: THE INDUSTRIAL TRANSFORMATION AT A CROSSROAD

Japanese corporations have grown by a dialectic wherein all energy is first expended in one direction and then redeployed in the opposite direction, transcending the original focus of endeavor. The tide of technological innovation after World War II was concentrated in manufacturing, especially in heavy and chemical industries, and created large-scale technology. Going along with this tide was, in a way, moving with the requirements of the times. In phase 1, it had probably been a good economic strategy to push investment to meet the potential demand from a population of 100 million. This strategy, however, did not give sufficient consideration to the social costs associated with Japan's deteriorating environment and ignored the tendency of plant investments to concentrate in a few industrial and residential areas because of Japan's geographical features. This created many environmental problems related to industrial pollution and also stimulated the formation of numerous consumer and citizen movements against producers' sovereignty.

The structural change during phase 2, from 1965 to 1973, was a composite induced by two kinds of effort. The first was the development of the machinery industry as the core of the Japanese manufacturing system. This industry used materials supplied by raw material processing industries that had been established in Japan during phase 1. The second was the effort of business circles to solve environmental problems by relying on technological instruments of pollution control supplied by the machinery industry.

THE SOURCE OF JAPANESE CORPORATE STRENGTH

Japanese corporations handled these two tasks by giving full play to their own adaptability, which may be seen as a basic source of their strength. There are many attempts to explain the strength of Japanese corporations but, in my view, the phenomenon can be readily comprehended by using the concept of experience curves, which have been emphasized by the Harvard Business School and the Boston Consulting Group. Resorting to some concept specific to Japan does not appear to be necessary.

A strategy based on the experience curve makes use of the observation that average costs in many business sectors diminish exponentially with cumulative volume of production. In other words, average cost depends not on the volume of production at any given time but on the cumulative volume of production over a period of time. This means that rapid investment at the initial stage is the indicated strategy. Since average cost decreases exponentially with cumulated output, the rapidly expanding firms, that is, firms that increase output steadily over a considerable period of time, realize the fastest decrease in average cost. The experience curve assumes that corporations learn from experience, meaning that the longer the production process continues, the more technical expertise, organizational efficiency, and other skills improve; product quality is enhanced and costs are reduced in the process. Experiential learning of this kind is particularly applicable to the Japanese, as can be clearly observed, for example, in agricultural cultivation where skills have been constantly refined.

The experience curve also coincides with the life cycle of demand for many products: gentle growth in the initial stage, rapid growth in the middle stage, and declining growth in the last stage. If there is aggressive investment at the initial stage when market demand for a product first occurs, corporate strategy gains a marked advantage in both cost and demand. Success on the market with one product, moreover, enables profits to be plowed back into initial-stage investment for the products expected to take off next. By repeating this strategy for successive products, a corporation realizes sustained growth.

The investment strategy of Japanese companies during phase 2 followed this model precisely. Even when profit rates were low during the initial stage of demand for a product, most corporations actively invested and thereby brought costs down through the experience-curve principle. By skillfully shifting their focus from the domestic market to overseas markets, from black-and-white television sets to color television sets, from motorcycles to automobiles, Japanese companies realized sustained corporate growth and outdid their foreign competitors.

Two preconditions for this corporate strength were the system of capital supply and the composition of Japan's labor force. An undeniable advantage for Japanese corporations is Japan's capital supply system, backed by a high savings ratio. By lowering capital costs and thereby the so-called cut-off ratio (determining whether or not it is profitable for a corporation to go ahead with a new investment), the capital supply system enables corporations to proceed boldly with a growth strategy.

In comparing the labor forces of Japan and the United States, I need not document anew that the skilled middle stratum of the labor force is proportionally larger in Japan. Important in this respect is the on-the-job training that the Japanese middle stratum receives within corporations. Accelerated learning made the high quality of Japanese goods possible.[2]

The experience curve is not limited to the production process; it reappears in research and development, sales, and other divisions as well, lowering general management costs. Japanese corporations' after-sale services and finely tuned sales management demonstrate the improvements that experience made possible. The Japanese tend to acquire the necessary experience and skills once fixed goals have been set and rules for their attainment prescribed. Self-improvement becomes its own object and the guiding purpose of an individual's life.

THE MACHINERY INDUSTRY AS THE CORE

Based on this strategy, Japanese firms succeeded during phase 2 in developing the machinery industry into the core of industrial structure. The skills of the Japanese labor force also contributed to this development. Production technology, especially the assembling process of machinery industries, was especially suitable for both the strategy and the skills.

Japanese firms learned the advantage of aggressive investment at the initial evolutionary stage of industrial development, and this investment strategy was pushed without hesitation in the machinery industries. MITI and financial institutions backed the strategy with government finance and nontariff barriers. Supporting the growth of machinery industries also conformed with the government policy that tried to promote the full utilization of the productive capacity of the raw materials processing industries. Thus, both government policy and corporate strategic concerns naturally led to the widespread adoption of the experience curve principle. The dynamic growth in the machinery industries—automobile and electrical machinery were representative—is shown in figure 2.2.

2. More concretely, as Hajime Karatsu has written, when learning is speeded up, the rate of inferior products decreases rapidly, and the cost is lowered faster and faster. If inferior products can be eliminated, the machine started in the morning can be run until closing time, increasing total production. As the rate of inferior products is reduced, the cost becomes lower and lower (H. Karatsu, "Quality Control: The Japanese Approach," *Speaking of Japan*, vol. 1, no. 1 [1981], Keizai Kōhō Center).

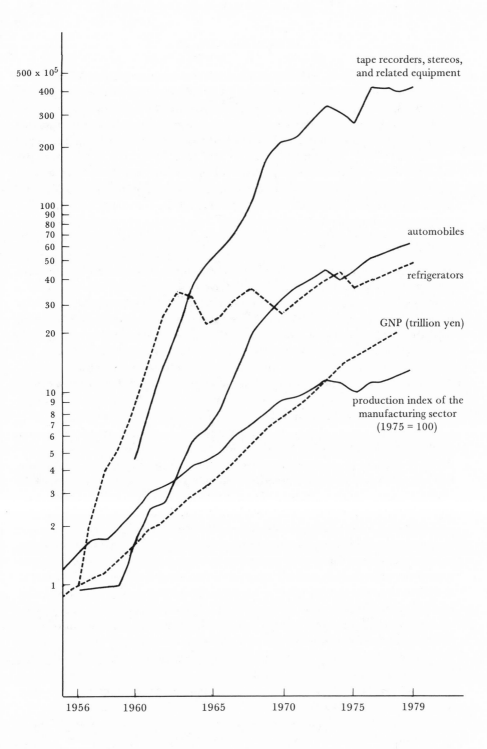

Fig. 2.2. Production trend in machinery sectors

Due to the substantial industrial development during phase 2, the quality of Japanese machinery and related technological capabilities progressed substantially, and these advances made it possible for Japanese industries to overcome pollution problems by technological measures. The ratio of investment for pollution control to total fixed investment increased from 2.3 percent in 1969 to 7.6 percent in 1973, and Japanese firms were perhaps the most successful in the world in reducing industrial pollution. This success may not represent a fundamental solution to the problem of industrial pollution but may be viewed as a technical patchwork approach at which the Japanese are quite skillful.

AT A POINT OF DECISION

The previous section characterized industrial change during phase 2 and highlighted the dimensions of change indicative of the good performance of the Japanese economy. Turning to other dimensions of industrial organization during phase 2, one can also make the observation that in several respects, Japan's economy was at a crossroads at that time.

First was the question of the degree of competition that would characterize Japan's future industrial structure. The issue was whether the industrial system would tend toward markets dominated by monopolies or competitive firms, or more precisely, whether the system would be dominated by monopolistic oligopoly or competitive oligopoly.

I do not believe that postwar Japanese industry as a whole shows any significant trend toward monopolization or concentration (see Imai 1980a, pp. 97-101). However, with 1970 as a turning point, a subtle change began occurring, and the average concentration ratio in manufacturing sectors began turning slightly upward. If one recalls that growth rates of industries then were generally declining, and advertising and other sales promotion activities were increasing in interfirm competition, the phenomenon of increasing concentration is not surprising. In addition, there was a strong concern that the declining growth rate would lead to interfirm cooperation and coordination, particularly in the raw material processing industries that had developed during phase 1. Also feared was the control of distribution channels, especially in the consumer goods markets. At a time when such factors were reinforcing one another, it was quite possible that monopolistic elements would become more prominent in the market structure.

A second sense in which Japanese industry was at a crossroads during phase 2 was related to the changing functions and performance of groups of firms, a feature of industrial organization peculiar to Japan. As is well known, the traditional groups of firms, such as the Mitsui or Mitsubishi group, exist in the Japanese market economy as special groups or clubs, with some similarities to custom unions. However, these groups do not have any formal internal structures or authority for explicit coordination of business, even though information exchange and occasional weak coordination can be effected through the presidents' clubs. This type of organization functions well only if informal coordination through information exchange is possible under the favorable conditions of growing demand or if conflicts are resolved by informal authority arising from information exchange.

During the rapid growth period of phase 1, it was possible for these informal organizations to coordinate growth plans of member firms because the vast majority of potential conflicts were resolved by demand growth itself. However, as the uncertainty surrounding the Japanese economy increased, authority and leadership based on an information advantage gradually began to decline, and the performance of traditional conglomerate groups gradually deteriorated (see table 2.3). At the same time, small inde-

TABLE 2.3

PROFIT PERFORMANCES OF GROUPS OF FIRMS IN JAPAN

	Profit Rates (%) on Total Assets	
	Average of traditional 6 groups	Average of independent groups
1960	4.2	8.0
1961	2.7	6.5
1962	3.4	7.5
1963	4.7	7.5
1964	2.7	4.3
1965	0.9	4.4

SOURCE: *Nippon Keizai Shimbun* 1977

NOTE: The independent groups are Hitachi, Toshiba, Matsushita, Nippon Steel, Toyota, and Nissan.

pendent groups were being formed in various sectors of the economy. Some examples are the Hitachi, Matsushita, and Toshiba groups in the electrical machinery industries; the Toyota, Nissan, and Honda groups in the motor vehicle industries; and the Nippon Steel group in the steel industry. These consist of a parent company and its diversified affiliated companies, all of which are strongly tied through stockholding and interlocking directorates. In these groups, the parent firm has authority and takes strong leadership in making group strategies. Such groups have frequently performed well in meeting their objectives. Thus, phase 2 led to a reshuffling of Japanese firm groupings, saw a decline in the importance of the traditional groups, and a notable rise and successful performance of a number of newly formed independent groups.

The third sense in which Japanese industry was at a crossroads relates to the labor policy of corporations. During the period of rapid economic growth, many corporations had accumulated large and relatively young labor forces. As growth slowed, the expenses associated with maintaining the slack labor forces during times of slump grew accordingly. Naturally, this provided a strong incentive for firms to use cartels and collusion to raise their selling prices and thus allow for wage increases. Japanese industry was faced with the choice of beginning to adopt a "management with slack" policy or a "management reducing slack" approach. The former approach undoubtedly represents one step down the road to stagflation.

A fourth crossroads for the Japanese economy concerned demographic trends. During phase 2 there was a movement toward regional decentralization that was expected to mitigate the problem of high business and population concentration in the Tokyo area. As the various social costs of congestion in the Tokyo area went beyond acceptable limits, people began to return to the regions of their birth, reversing a long-term trend to the contrary. This movement is known as the population "U-turn." Administrative centralization nevertheless remained unchanged.

In short, phase 2 can be understood as a period of conflict between centripetal forces toward monopoly-stagflation and centrifugal forces toward competition-efficiency. It was also a time that saw the rise of a variety of consumer or citizen movements as well as heated discussions for or against environmental and antitrust measures.

PHASE 3: TOWARD A SUPERINDUSTRIAL SOCIETY

The turning point from phase 2 to phase 3 was the oil crisis of 1973, which created severe difficulties for the Japanese economy since it coincided with the need to lower the nation's growth rate due to continuing inflationary pressures. However, in overcoming these difficulties, Japanese industries and corporations increased their efficiency, indicating that the choices made at the crossroads mentioned above were toward competition and efficiency rather than monopoly and stagflation.

In a sense, the oil crisis in Japan might be viewed as another one of the "divine winds," the chance storms that have, at least in Japanese folklore, appeared miraculously to save the nation from external threats. Since the nation is poorly endowed with natural resources, the oil crisis compelled Japanese corporations to save energy and increase productivity because of an almost life or death situation. This stands in sharp contrast to the experience of the United States, where the effects of the oil shock were mitigated by ample domestic resources. It appears that the United States is on the road to stagflation because of the scarcity of innovative efforts among manufacturers to overcome oil price increases.

The Japanese economy handled the decisions it faced in phase 2 in the following ways. First, Japanese raw material processing industries, characterized by little product differentiation and strong incentives for collusive behavior, were thrown into a competitive struggle for survival as they tried to overcome sharp increases in input prices and decreasing demand. Even if they could have taken a "live and let live" policy in the domestic market, it was impossible for them to do so in the international market, since they faced the danger of losing their international competitiveness. Japanese corporations had to absorb marginal (not average) increases in the price of oil by technological rationalization if they were to keep their competitive advantage. Thus, these firms made surprising efforts to adapt to a new environment and engaged in intense competition among themselves. The result is that they have succeeded in substantially increasing their productivity.

At the same time, through the working of the price mechanism that reflected oil price increases, demand has shifted from energy intensive sectors to nonintensive ones. That is, the industries of the mechatronics type (machinery plus electronics), such as numerically controlled machine tools or electrical machinery containing programmed integrated circuits, grew rapidly. In these industries the particular Japanese corporate strengths that are based on the experience curve and are supported by high-level labor skills can be brought into full play.

Second, and closely related to the above, already established firms that had created new-products departments and those that had set up joint ventures with other firms entered fields that were experiencing new growth. In this way, traditional conglomerate groups lost their economic justification and reshuffled to adapt to changes in the business environment. Member firms of each group are now pursuing their own objectives, choosing between internal and interfirm organization based on economic cost comparisons with alternate situations. In fact, tie-up contracts with firms in other groups and with outside firms have been increasing as shown in table 2.4

TABLE 2.4

TIE-UP CONTRACTS WITHIN AND
BETWEEN GROUPS AND WITH OTHERS
(Unit: Average number of cases per company)

	Within Group	With Firms in Other Groups	With Other Outside Firms
Mitsui group	7.2	11.8	52.7
Mitsubishi group	9.1	7.1	36.9
Sumitomo group	9.4	17.3	64.7
Fuyo group	2.7	6.3	27.7
Sanwa group	1.9	6.2	29.0
Daiichi group	2.0	7.5	24.3

SOURCE: Fair Trade Commision 1976

Third, after the oil crisis Japanese manufacturers actively pursued a management policy of employment reduction and efficient use of energy and other materials. This led to high productivity in manufacturing sectors and a rapid recovery from the oil shock. How was Japan able to achieve this rapid recovery without suffering from any transitional unemployment? For the special attention this issue deserves, it will be useful to begin with a detailed investigation of the Japanese vertical market structure. An understanding of that market structure makes it possible to offer a full explanation of the adaptability of the Japanese industrial system. This discussion should also serve to highlight the main features of recent structural changes in the Japanese economy.

CHANGES IN THE JAPANESE VERTICAL MARKET STRUCTURE

The basic characteristics of the Japanese vertical structure, compared with that of the United States, can be summarized as follows:

(1) In the Japanese nondifferentiated goods sector, most firms in intermediate goods industries such as steel or chemicals have not integrated backward into raw materials because Japan lacks natural resources. In the postwar period, when free trade of primary products prevailed, this factor actually favored Japanese economic growth. Industries could make the most of free contracts in a buyer's market for primary products, utilizing the trading skills of gigantic general trading companies. This stands in sharp contrast to American manufacturing sectors, where backward integration into raw materials is common, and firms, especially major oil companies, have made investment commitments in natural resource sectors. The Japanese advantage in this respect has completely disappeared, as can be seen in the apparent vulnerability of the Japanese economy after the oil crisis.

(2) In differentiated consumer goods industries such as automobiles, electrical appliances, and fashion goods, large firms possess the most modern technology at the center of their manufacturing processes. They attain a form of backward integration through the partial control of various small and medium subcontractors, and also in a forward direction through the establishment of special channels of distribution consisting of many small retailers. This is a basic characteristic of the Japanese vertical structure that can be contrasted with that of the United States, characterized by large-scale production and sales.

(3) In nondifferentiated consumer goods industries, such as mass-produced processed foods, clothes, or convenience goods, both large and small firms, including family enterprises, coexist in the production stage, and large and small retailers both perform their respective roles in the distribution stage. They are not vertically integrated, but various interfirm organizations connect a large manufacturing firm to small retailers, or a small manufacturer to a large retailer. This coexistence of large and small retailers is another characteristic of the Japanese vertical structure. A remarkable number of very small retailers have survived, as can be seen in Japanese shopping streets with their small- and medium-sized shops.

In short, compared to the vertical structure that connects large-scale production to large-scale sales in the United States, in Japan small manufacturers in backward stages (components and parts) and small retailers in forward stages are both connected through various forms of interfirm organization to large manufacturing firms at the core. In the United States, a large part of the vertical distribution of goods and services is controlled by the "visible hands" of managers, as is clearly analyzed in Alfred Chandler's book (1978). In Japan, however, market competition varies in each segment of the vertical market structure. This competition constitutes an essential element of Japanese economic adaptability, as will be analyzed below.

RELATIONSHIP OF SUBCONTRACTORS AND LARGE FIRMS

As noted above, there are hierarchical systems of subcontractors that supply many kinds of parts, components, and related goods under continuous contracts to large manufacturers in the automobile, electrical appliance, and related industries. These are hierarchical systems, with subcontractors further divided into secondary and tertiary subcontractors, as shown in the representative cases of automobiles and electrical appliances in figures 2.3 and 2.4.

As is well known, "make or buy" is a key strategic decision in the industrial organization of those sectors, and it is notable that the Japanese "buy ratios" are extremely high; in the case of automobiles, it is 75 percent and in electrical appliances, 72 percent. The large Japanese manufacturers in these industries concentrate on assembly, buying most of the parts and components they use from subcontractors. Although this buying is formally carried out through market contracts, it is not a pure market transaction and works as if it were an aspect of the firm's internal organization because of various forms of coordination between the manufacturer and subcontractors. In this sense, interfirm organizations play a key role in those sectors.

These subcontractors, however, are not completely controlled by large manufacturers. In the prewar and early postwar periods, they were subordinated to a parent firm and existed primarily because of cheap labor; however, many of these subcontractors later developed into quasi-independent firms that supplied their own products to other firms as well. Although interorganizational linkages between subcontractors and parent firms have continued to be tight, in more recent years subcontractors themselves have actively developed technological skill and management know-how, particularly during the phase 2 period.

In the United States, a hypothesis suggested by George Stigler (1968) explains the life-cycle pattern of vertical integration in the following way: In the first stage there are not enough markets for differentiated input, and firms have to integrate vertically. In the stage of demand growth, production of each input on a minimum efficient scale is allowed, and integrated sections are divested to separate firms, which may then sell their products to many more firms. The result is that they enjoy scale economies and quality development. In the last stage, when firms require very specialized input, production is again vertically integrated.

According to the Stigler hypothesis, the trend in Japan corresponds to the second stage. If his whole hypothesis were to hold for Japan, we would expect the last stage to be coming soon, with production again vertically integrated because Japanese manufacturing firms now require very specialized input. However, the trend in Japanese vertical relations appears to be quite

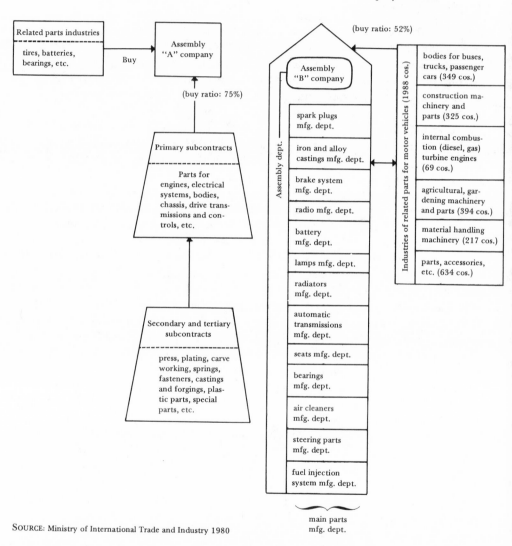

"A" company in Japan

"B" company in U.S.A.

Related parts industries

tires, batteries, bearings, etc.

Buy

Assembly "A" company

(buy ratio: 75%)

Primary subcontracts

Parts for engines, electrical systems, bodies, chassis, drive transmissions and controls, etc.

Secondary and tertiary subcontracts

press, plating, carve working, springs, fasteners, castings and forgings, plastic parts, special parts, etc.

(buy ratio: 52%)

Assembly "B" company

Assembly dept.

spark plugs mfg. dept.

iron and alloy castings mfg. dept.

brake system mfg. dept.

radio mfg. dept.

battery mfg. dept.

lamps mfg. dept.

radiators mfg. dept.

automatic transmissions mfg. dept.

seats mfg. dept.

bearings mfg. dept.

air cleaners mfg. dept.

steering parts mfg. dept.

fuel injection system mfg. dept.

main parts mfg. dept.

Industries of related parts for motor vehicles (1988 cos.)

bodies for buses, trucks, passenger cars (349 cos.)

construction machinery and parts (325 cos.)

internal combustion (diesel, gas) turbine engines (69 cos.)

agricultural, gardening machinery and parts (394 cos.)

material handling machinery (217 cos.)

parts, accessories, etc. (634 cos.)

SOURCE: Ministry of International Trade and Industry 1980

Fig. 2.3. Production structure of automobiles

"C" company in Japan

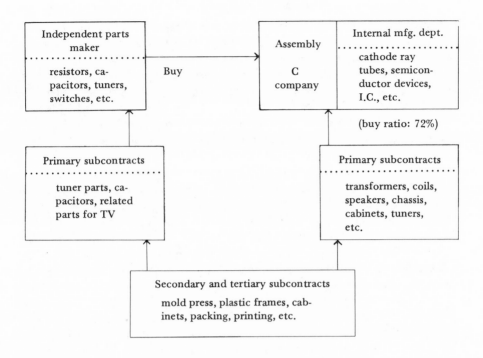

Independent parts maker		Assembly	Internal mfg. dept.

... (figure) ...

| Independent parts maker | ⟶ Buy | Assembly C company | Internal mfg. dept. |
| resistors, capacitors, tuners, switches, etc. | | | cathode ray tubes, semiconductor devices, I.C., etc. |

(buy ratio: 72%)

| Primary subcontracts | Primary subcontracts |
| tuner parts, capacitors, related parts for TV | transformers, coils, speakers, chassis, cabinets, tuners, etc. |

| Secondary and tertiary subcontracts |
| mold press, plastic frames, cabinets, packing, printing, etc. |

"D" company in U.S.A.

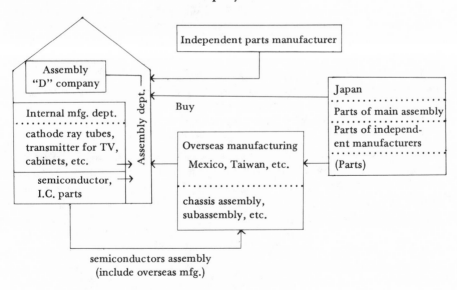

Independent parts manufacturer

Assembly "D" company

Assembly dept.

Buy

Internal mfg. dept.		Japan
cathode ray tubes, transmitter for TV, cabinets, etc.		Parts of main assembly
		Parts of independent manufacturers
semiconductor, I.C. parts		(Parts)

Overseas manufacturing
Mexico, Taiwan, etc.

chassis assembly, subassembly, etc.

semiconductors assembly
(include overseas mfg.)

SOURCE: Ministry of International Trade and Industry 1980

Fig. 2.4. Production structure of color televisions

different from this hypothesis. It is true that Japanese firms are now using highly specialized parts and components to make their final products adaptable to the diversified needs of Japanese consumers. However, small subcontractors have been able to supply even these highly specialized products by changing their specifications according to each customer's special order. This capability of making a small sharp turn is a special skill of small Japanese firms. Not only do they accept special orders from parent firms, they also have expanded their markets to include many customers whose orders require their technical skills.

This may help to explain why the Japanese manufacturing sector as a whole is capable of making quick adaptations to the changing, diversified needs of consumers. If Japan's industrial organization relied simply on large-scale production and concentrated on standardized products, this would undoubtedly be impossible. In this way small firms have been especially important in Japan's industrial organization and have been favored by the high growth rate of the Japanese economy. From an organizational point of view, they have taken advantage of interfirm organization.

Related to this, brief mention should be made of geographic groupings of very small firms in large Japanese cities, especially around Tokyo's inner city area. In Tokyo's Ota-ku area, crossed by the highway from Haneda airport to downtown Tokyo, are regional clusters of rather small firms that produce highly diverse kinds of machinery and parts. In Tokyo's "downtown" (shitamachi) area as well there is a concentration of small manufacturers that produce miscellaneous goods such as bags, shoes, and toys. These clusters of small firms often make up groups with very special characteristics that provide a source of technical skill in Japan's industrial organization. The owners of these small firms are themselves professional experts in machinery, and the level of technological skill is very high, so they are able to make a variety of goods to special order or produce experimental instruments in small lots, often handling special jobs from large firms' research laboratories or from large newspaper companies.

These specialized skills allow these firms to handle almost any type of order when they coordinate as a group. They establish interfirm organizations through which special jobs are subdivided into several subjobs or occasionally are forwarded to another specialist in a group if necessary. These regional interfirm organizations have excellent problem-solving skill, which contributes to making the Japanese industrial organization highly adaptable to changing environments.

THE JAPANESE DISTRIBUTION SYSTEM AND INTERFIRM ORGANIZATIONS

Within the Japanese distribution system, a number of small retailers coexist with large retailers and compete on a "live and let live" basis. This coexistence is a special characteristic of the Japanese vertical structure and will be discussed further in this section.

We should first note the statistical characteristics of the Japanese distribution system itself (for a general explanation of the Japanese marketing system, see Yoshino 1971). Table 2.5, which deals with the size distribution of Japanese retailers, shows that 61.9 percent of them have one to two employees, and that 23.7 percent have three to four employees—together this amounts to 85 percent of the total. Retailers employing twenty to forty persons, on the other hand, comprise only 1.1 percent, although they represent 11.4 percent of the total Japanese retail sales. This extreme predominance of small retailers, and therefore labor intensiveness as a whole, is a basic characteristic of the Japanese distribution system and is reflected in the international comparison of table 2.6, which shows that far more persons are employed in the Japanese distribution system than in the American and German.

TABLE 2.6

AN INTERNATIONAL COMPARISON OF
EMPLOYMENT IN THE DISTRIBUTION SECTORS
(Unit: Person per thousand of population)

	Japan 1977	U.S.A. 1976	West Germany 1977
Wholesale	30	20	8
Retail	56	46	30

SOURCE: Ministry of Labor 1980

TABLE 2.5

SIZE DISTRIBUTION OF JAPANESE RETAILERS, 1976

Number of Employees	Number of Establishments		Number of Employees	
	In 100s	%	In 1000s	%
1 ∿ 2	1000	61.9	1587	28.4
3 ∿ 4	382	23.7	1285	23.0
5 ∿ 9	166	10.3	1021	18.3
10 ∿ 19	43	2.7	570	10.2
20 ∿ 49	18	1.1	514	9.2
50 ∿	5	0.3	604	10.8
Total	1548	100.0	5580	100.0

SOURCE: Ministry of Labor 1980

Furthermore, this gap is widening at the present time. As can be seen in table 2.7, the number of employees in both the wholesale and retail sectors

TABLE 2.7

GROWTH OF EMPLOYMENT IN THE JAPANESE DISTRIBUTION SECTORS
(Unit: Million persons)

	1960	1964	1968	1972	1976
Wholesale	1.93	2.52	2.70	3.01	3.51
Retail	3.49	3.81	4.65	5.14	5.58

SOURCE: Ministry of Trade and Industry 1979

has been increasing in Japan. A decade ago, some modern economists predicted a revolution within Japanese distribution toward mass marketing, with a concomitant radical reduction in employment in the wholesale and retail sectors. The very reverse has been the case, however. Considering this, should we say that there is excessive employment in the Japanese distribution system, and therefore that it is quite inefficient from an economic point of view? I will argue against this conclusion.

As stated above, the main part of the Japanese distribution system is seen in the interfirm ties between manufacturers and retailers, and also in the organization of firms and the market. Interfirm organizations can evolve in the following three ways: (a) through the manufacturer's control of retailers by means of brand advertising; that is, retailers are controlled as if they were part of the internal organization of the manufacturer; (b) toward increased use of the market mechanism; that is, retailers develop into independent firms that sell many goods of various brands, gradually divorcing themselves from the control of a specific manufacturer; (c) toward making innovations without changing retailers' ties to manufacturing firms; that is, retailers attract consumers through an improved assortment of goods and variety of better quality services, and manufacturers also improve the quality of their goods and make modifications according to information they get from retailers.

If the Japanese distribution system had developed by taking course (a) or (b), employment in the distribution sector would have gradually declined. A mixture of (a) and (b) is characteristic of the American distribution system, where the development of an efficient system reduced employment. The Japanese system, however, has taken the third course (c), resulting in a labor-intensive distribution system that offers high quality services and is quickly adaptable to the diverse needs of consumers and changing environments.

Of course the Japanese distribution system has not been intentionally formed by the "visible hands" of government or big business, but has taken shape naturally through the market mechanisms resulting from Japan's particular economic and social circumstances. The conditions and forces that induced Japanese firms and distributors to take course (c) can be summarized as follows.

First, in Japan's industrial organization there has always been a tendency toward overproduction due to the adoption of large-scale production methods along with the best available technology and to the simultaneous competitive expansion of firms' capacities. This has been carried over from phase 1. Because of the vigorous competition induced by these factors, brand power in marketing has gradually declined in Japan. Each company in a particular market has been forced to develop differentiated goods and high quality services to meet consumers' changing needs.

If manufacturers want to control distribution channels as if distributors were part of their internal organization, a certain amount of economic power is required. The basis of authority in this case is brand power. If brand power declines, manufacturers cannot choose course (a), and they must attempt to develop their distribution channels in other ways.

On the other hand, there has been a long tradition of predominance of big manufacturers over retailers in Japan. Usually these manufacturers are big businesses, and they have capital funds, managerial resources, and an ample supply of manpower in contrast to small retailers. Most of the retailers have grown up under the umbrella of manufacturers, and they know well the merits of being affiliated with, or of being under, a manufacturer's leadership. Therefore they have chosen to keep close ties with large manufacturers rather than be completely independent, even if this were possible. Primarily because of this, course (b) has not been taken.

Additionally, if brand power in marketing declines, the power of retail marketing increases, and retail manpower becomes a key factor in expanding the size of the market. This has induced both manufacturers and retailers to make the most of the labor force that has existed as a kind of excess employment in the distribution sector. Generally, retailers have been able to increase their sales by increasing their manpower in direct and after services, information provision, and consulting services to consumers. Japanese consumers have differing preferences and are very demanding with regard to goods and services; to adapt to these demands, retailers require an increasingly large labor force in marketing. Manufacturers in turn are obliged to rely on the marketing power of retailers to deepen their markets, and they develop newly differentiated products on the basis of information they get from retailers.

In a modern consumer society, and especially in Japan, consumers' demands fluctuate according to the fashions of the day. To make the system sensitive to these demands, there must be a flexible supply system in the production sector, and at the same time, a quickly adaptable distribution system that can perform concentrated sales efforts in a short period. Japan's industrial organization has a flexible supply system that consists of large manufacturers that have a tendency toward overproduction and small firms that have the aforementioned capacity for quick turns; at the same time, there is an adaptable maketing system characterized by excess employment. These two systems combine to meet the changing needs of the Japanese middle class, which has a relatively high income and is responsive to current fashions.

THE DISTRIBUTION SYSTEM AND THE JAPANESE LIFE STYLE

The above argument applies mainly to differentiated consumer goods industries. However, even in the nondifferentiated convenience goods sector, where a large retailer might be expected to be predominant, small retailers have survived and play active roles in the Japanese "shopping street." Despite the competitive pressure of such large retailers as supermarkets, department stores, or the new types of retailing (the so-called box stores, for example), small retailers have been able to survive.

First, most small retailers are native to their cities or towns and their land and shops are inherited, enabling them to estimate their fixed costs as being very low if they neglect or underestimate imputed rents. Similarly, their labor forces include family members, who will work even without money wages in times of adversity. In contrast, large retailers, who have to build new stores by paying the characteristically high Japanese land prices and must also employ a regular wage-labor force, have not obtained enough competitive power to force small retailers out of the market even though they might be able to operate efficiently at low input costs. Second, manufacturers have maintained a policy of protecting the small retailers they supply. Sometimes, in fact, their supply prices are lower than market wholesale prices because under the continuous pressure of overproduction they want to retain various distribution channels for delivering their goods. And third, small retailers themselves have instituted special services, such as long business hours or special delivery to customers, which large retailers cannot provide.

Generally speaking, the small retailers fit in well with Japanese life. Japanese women usually go shopping every day, not only to buy fresh fish and vegetables, but also to enjoy walking around the shopping streets, sometimes chatting with the owner of a clothing store about current fashions or having coffee with a neighborhood friend met by chance. In this sense, the Japanese shopping streets provide one of the so-called public spheres that are naturally and casually established in the city. As is strongly advocated by such urban economists as Jane Jacobs (1969), these public spheres are indispensable in that they make the city more livable and provide an environment conducive to commercial and cultural activity. In this way, small retailers in Japan are performing quite an important role, supplying the differentiated services required by the Japanese.

TOWARD A "SUPERINDUSTRIAL" SOCIETY

The economic environment in recent years has continued to make the most of the adaptability of the Japanese industrial system. While fluctuations in the external environment have been extreme, the industrial responses in every country have been limited to marginal adjustments. The basic layout of any industrial structure is not easily altered, and the structure of demand as well makes for continuous but minor shifts. The recent challenge to industry has been for continual fine tuning within a largely predetermined industrial format. Having succeeded with growth strategy, Japanese corporations have turned quite naturally to a fine tuning strategy, exhibiting their resourcefulness in technological innovation, product diversification, and quality development.

The vitality and adaptability of the Japanese corporations have been clearly exhibited in the fast evolution of electronics (especially integrated circuits and microcomputers) and mechatronics. Integrate-circuit production is typical of a field in which the experience curve applies. Moreover, the microscopic operations involved in adding more and more features to already tiny objects seem to suit the skill and adaptability of many Japanese workers.

Since the techniques of programming machinery with microcomputers are applicable in almost every field requiring machinery, mechatronics is drawing attention as a new frontier of technological innovation. The labor pool that Japan can draw on to master electronic tehnology is deep indeed. Among consumers, especially the young, interest in electronic gadgets is strong and the desire to acquire the latest products intense. The multiplier effect of this convergence of supply and demand potential will no doubt propel Japanese corporations to the top of the competition that is now underway. Hence, the Japanese economy can be expected to begin a new growth phase in the 1980s, sustained to a large extent by mechatronics. Japan is now making steady progress toward becoming a superindustrial society, in which technological innovations combining information, communication, and machinery enable the fusion of manufacturing and information industries.

Strength, however, can turn into weakness. If Japanese firms are excessively single-minded in pursuing growth by the strategy outlined above, they may, in a sense, be digging their own graves. The danger in pursuing strength alone is that they may deprive themselves of the adaptability needed for the future. Another important issue concerns the way in which such innovations will be applied to economic and social life. There is the danger that ill-considered use of the new technology could result in a stifling and inhumane society.

A final word is called for here on some of the well-known demerits of Japan's system of industrial organization. First of all, Japanese consumers must pay higher consumer prices as the other side of the good service system of distribution. Similarly, they must pay the price of having a flexible supply and distribution system that involves a great number of small firms, in the sense of having to tolerate some disorder in big cities. Japan is now confronted with the issue of how to cope with these problems without damaging the genuine advantages of this system.

Taking the above discussion into consideration, I will turn to a discussion of policy issues in the final section, which includes a proposal for improving United States-Japan economic relations.

POLICY DISCUSSION: UNITED STATES-JAPAN INDUSTRIAL RELATIONS

How about the future? In my opinion, Japanese industrial organization is not showing any signs of becoming less flexible. On the contrary, its efficiency is improving through the adoption of "composite technologies" that unite information, electronics, machinery, and communications technology. Because these technologies are oriented toward small-scale production and are not particularly capital intensive, Japanese small firms are eager to adopt them and are thus contributing to the strengthening of Japanese export competitiveness.

Of course, there is a possibility that the high productivity of Japan's management system might be a transitory phenomenon, especially since there is a gradual change in the work ethic of the Japanese people. Nevertheless, the efficiency of Japanese management can be expected to continue at least through the eighties. I stress the competitive aspects of the Japanese management system rather than people's attitude toward work.

Therefore, we should predict that Japanese export competitiveness based on the flexible industrial organization and management system will further increase in the future. Does this necessarily mean that friction in United States-Japan economic relations as well will further increase from now on? I believe such frictions can be avoided.

To start, I would like to stress that despite the expected strengthening of Japan's export competitiveness, Japanese industries can avoid the problem of "torrential" export growth that is highly concentrated in specific goods and regions. This type of export growth has been the legacy of the simultaneous firm-by-firm expansion in private fixed investment accompanied by export-promoting policies of the government. We can predict that Japan's exports, now dominated by automobiles and steel, will shift to a more balanced mix of goods including many kinds of machinery and electronic goods as well as custom-ordered engineering products (one prediction of this type is shown in table 2.8).

The promotion of a more balanced pattern of exports is one way to avoid trade conflicts between Japan and the United States, and will require the modification of Japanese policies. First, the Japanese government should avoid relying on export-led recovery policies even though such policies are politically expedient at the domestic level. Second, in place of export-led recovery policies, the government should redirect its policies toward new objectives.

Among such objectives, the most important ones must be the development of alternative sources of energy, urban redevelopment, and the creation of new life styles. The energy crisis and the need to develop new forms of energy are well known, but it must be pointed out that this problem is also intimately related to the questions of infrastructure, urban environment, and patterns of living. For the quality of life to be further improved in Japan (as well as the United States), we must embark on a full-fledged effort to create comfortable cities and urban networks as well as inquire anew what true affluence consists of under conditions of energy constraint.

TABLE 2.8

A PREDICTION OF JAPAN'S MAJOR EXPORTS
(1970 prices, FOB, billion $)

	1980		1985		1990	
	real	%	real	%	real	%
Iron and steel products	10.9	13.0	15.1	11.7	20.5	11.3
Machinery and equipment	51.4	61.1	85.8	66.4	130.5	71.7
Motor vehicles	12.8	15.2	19.5	15.1	25.8	14.2
Vessels	3.0	0.4	5.3	0.4	5.9	0.3
Plants and engineering	16.5	19.6	29.1	22.5	48.1	26.4
Electronic goods	10.7	12.7	18.8	14.6	30.0	16.7
Others	21.8	25.9	28.3	21.9	31.1	17.1
Total	84.1	100.0	129.2	100.0	182.1	100.0
Share of exports to U.S.A.	23.8%		20.1%		18.8%	

SOURCE: Japanese Economic Research Center 1980

Many Japanese companies have already recognized this need and are dealing with it through diversification and marginal adjustment. But now they must move beyond fine tuning to medium-range adjustments, gambling on riskier investments, since an effective response is not possible utilizing only the acquisition of skills, innovations, and the industriousness of employees. Different abilities are required, which might be described as a combination of creativity and an adventuresome spirit.

In this respect, I would like to call attention to a facet of Japanese culture separate from the diligence of its people. The Japanese social system, as many writers have noted, is capable of directly absorbing and assimilating heterogeneous elements in "an undifferentiated form."[3] Japanese culture imparts a special meaning and value to what we shall call "blanks" or "blank spaces." This feature constitutes a strength in Japanese systems, and it seems to me that it should be brought under conscious scrutiny and made to work on behalf of corporate strategy.[4] Of course, the American market-oriented

3. Since limitation of space does not permit me to develop this topic in detail, let me simply present a useful metaphor conceived by Okada Susumu in *Nihonjin no imēji kōzō* [The composition of imagery used by the Japanese], (Chūō kōronsha, 1972): "In the brush strokes [of Japanese painting], the abstractness of the lines themselves and the concreteness of the shapes they delineate begin with the unfolding of these opposing elements and are completed by the blank spaces the brush has not touched." This reference succinctly suggests one way in which Japanese systems typically differ from European systems, which stress the opposition between the abstract and the concrete or between analysis and synthesis.

4. The idea of "blank spaces" is especially influential in unconsciously guiding the Japanese mode of behavior. The concept of a "pregnant pause" or short interval *(ma)* between beats or delivered lines in traditional Japanese music and Nō drama has a related meaning. In such a world, logic is not applied exhaustively; some things that might be said are left unspoken; arguments are left incomplete. The Japanese approach to systems has

approach has its advantages, but the Japanese approach has another kind of potential: the relevant combination of both approaches would provide the best method for solving the problems that now confront us.

Let me cite one possibility. The failure of urban development in the United States, for example, can be traced to the priority placed on separation of heterogeneous elements and deployment of facilities by function or, in other words, the insufficient recognition of the concept of mixture and intermingling as a necessary ingredient of urban planning.[5] The city is by nature a complex entity, and a basic error is made when it is thought of as a simple system. I would not claim that Japanese systems are already equipped with the means to overcome this problem, but I do believe that systems that can absorb heterogeneous elements in an undifferentiated form are more conducive to the problem's resolution.

I would like now to touch briefly upon some specific policies that embody the general principles outlined above, although a thorough examination of the proposals must be left for further research.

Urban Renewal

Urban renewal appears to be a common goal for both Japan and the United States. To create livable cities, the problem of how those engaged in efforts to achieve urban renewal should perceive and deal with the city's complexity must be solved. Most planners consider the concepts of such architects as Le Corbusier to be the ideal, and from those concepts they try to formulate a well-ordered three-dimensional design. However, this approach overlooks the essence of the city and the contemporary challenges it faces. As Lewis Mumford has written, urban planning must seek order between elements that lack a total design. A growing city that is also comfortable to live in requires not a separation of functions and simplification of layout but diversified communities, mobile arteries, and multipurpose centers.

The firms responsible for urban renewal in the United States are said to be far ahead of their Japanese counterparts, but they seem to have tackled only the easy problems. The American approach, it might even be said, makes the city an unattractive place to live. In contrast, Japanese firms are trying to deal with a far more complex and undifferentiated urban system, and the flexibility and loose structure of the Japanese system of business

---

been affected by this sensibility. When new systems have been imported from China and the West, invariably the assimilation has been less than complete. Even capitalism has not been assimilated in its entirety, and various "blanks" remain. By bold interpretation of the meaning of these blanks, hidden keys can be found enabling sudden leaps forward to the next generation of systems.

5. According to Jane Jacobs (1969, p. 101), a well-known urban economist, enterprises serving city consumers flourish when the following four conditions are simultaneously met: (1) different primary uses, such as residences and working places, are mingled together; (2) blocks are small and short; (3) buildings of differing ages, types, sizes, and conditions of upkeep are intimately mingled; and (4) population density is high.

contracts may also prove to be advantageous in managing its complexities. Moreover, Japanese architectural concepts concerning the use of small spaces with "blanks" and "gray areas" (for example, the *engawa* of the traditional Japanese house, which at times is part of the garden and at times is part of a room) may make a special contribution to the solution of urban problems.

Urban renewal and many other social endeavors should foster creativity in Japanese businesses. Unlike abilities realized through narrowly applied diligence today, these new approaches will provide the corporate strength needed for the world of medium-range adjustment and high-risk investments. If the new systems can be communicated in concise terminology and introduced abroad, they may be used to solve problems in U.S. urban renewal projects. If the outstanding goods and electronics of Japan are also made available for such projects, Japan-U.S. collaboration will be greatly facilitated.

DEVELOPMENT OF ENERGY RESOURCES

Japan's access to the world's shrinking supply of energy is the major source of the economy's vulnerability, and the reduction of this vulnerability and of the uncertainty it engenders in the Japanese business community is absolutely essential if Japan is to successfully manage the multiple transitions it faces. However, new energy development presents many alternatives, all of which contain elements of uncertainty regarding their practical applications, lead times, and costs. Under these circumstances, it would be dangerous as well as inefficient to single out one exclusive course of action. Because of this, the parallel development strategy that is well established in research and development management is directly applicable here. Even though this strategy is a financial burden, it must be used as a mechanism for guaranteeing Japan's access to some sort of energy supply during critical shortages. To that end, we must plan to use coal and to invest in foregn coal mining, transportation equipment, and coal utilization technology, endeavors that will necessarily engage Japan in joint ventures with other economies. In this area there are many tasks that will probably be accomplished with the help of American technology.

In the development of alternative energy sources, American companies have taken the lead in investment, and Japanese companies have little chance of pioneering original or unexplored fields. But if this is the case, it is all the more important that Japan gamble its investment in its areas of strength—filling in the blanks, so to speak, and complementing the endeavors of the American companies.

In the history of Japanese technological development, many breakthroughs have been the result of hiring talented people without giving them specific development objectives. Japan's Shinkansen (bullet train), for instance, was produced by outstanding aeronautical engineers who were hired at the end of World War II on the assumption that aeronautics would one day be applicable to railroad technology. Japanese corporations today have reached a position where gambles of this sort can be made.

These policy designs are not offered as a comprehensive plan encompassing all sectors of the economy, yet they can be regarded as the cornerstone for a whole policy system for leading Japan through the current transition period.

The important point suggested above is that the Japanese should undertake work in areas in which the skills as well as the products and services developed will be those that Americans are eager to acquire. In other words, in the long run we should aim at the areas that American systems have difficulty with and that frustrate American ingenuity. In this manner Japanese initiatives will not entail direct competition with U.S. industry, and any successes achieved will be useful in helping rejuvenate the American economy. Persistent diligence applied toward capturing markets now dominated by U.S. firms should not be the sole objective of Japanese firms. At the same time, in such important areas as communication and energy development, Japan should diversify with the help of related American technology.[6] A strategy that challenges the United States and Japan to face common goals together, instead of one requiring repeated acrimonious compromises, will enable both countries to more forward through industrial cooperation. Only in this way can Japan escape the nightmare of becoming the manufacturing center of the world, at the cost of its relations with its trading partners.

6. See Report of the Telecommunications Inquiry Committee (chaired by Dr. Shigeto Tsuru) January 1978.

REFERENCES

Caves, R., and Uekusa, M. 1976. *Industrial Organization in Japan.* Washington, D.C., Brookings Institution.

Chandler, A., Jr. 1978. *Visible Hands: The Managerial Revolution in American Business.* Cambridge, Harvard University Press.

Economic Planning Agency. See Keizai Kikakuchō.

Fair Trade Commission. See Kōsei Torihiki Iinkai.

Imai, K. 1980a. "Japan's Industrial Organization." In *Industry and Business in Japan,* ed. K. Sato. White Plains, N.Y., M. E. Sharpe.

——. 1980b. "Convergence or Collision: Alternative Scenarios for U.S.-Japanese Relations." In *U.S.-Japanese Economic Relations—Cooperation, Competition, and Confrontation,* ed. D. Tasca. Elmsford, N.Y., Pergamon Press.

——. 1980c. "Hard Work Is Not Enough." *Japan Echo,* vol. 7, no. 2.

——, and Goto, A. 1975. *Kigyō no tayōka ni kansuru jisshō bunseki* [Studies on diversification of Japanese manufacturing firms]. Mimeographed. Tokyo, Nippon keizai dētā kaihatsu sentā.

Jacobs, J. 1969. *The Economy of Cities.* Baltimore, Md., Penguin Books.

Keizai Kikakuchō [Economic Planning Agency]. 1964. *Keizai hakusho* [White Paper on the economy]. Tokyo, MOF Printing.

Keizai Kenkyū Sentā [Japanese Economic Research Center]. 1980.

Kōsei Torihiki Iinkai [Fair Trade Commission]. 1976. "Kigyō gōdō ni kansuru tokubetsu chōsa" [Special survey on business tie-up]. Tokyo, Government Printing Office.

Ministry of International Trade and Industry (MITI). 1979. *Commercial Statistics.* Tokyo, MITI.

———. 1980. *Chūshō kigyō hakusho* [White Paper on small and medium-sized firms]. Tokyo, Japan Economic Research Center.

Ministry of Labor. See Rōdōshō.

Nippon Keizai Shimbun. 1977. "Shin kigyō shūdan" [New groups of firms]. The Nippon Keizai Shimbunsha.

Remelt, R. P. 1974. *Strategy, Structure, and Economic Performance.* Cambridge, Harvard University Press.

Rōdōshō. 1980. *Labor Statistics.* Tokyo, Government Printing Office.

Sanuki, T. 1980. *Nippon keizai no kōzō bunseki* [A structural analysis of the Japanese economy]. Tokyo, Tōyō keizai shimpōsha.

Stigler, George. 1968. *The Organization of Industry.* Irwin, Inc.

United Nations. 1973. Economic and Social Council. *Yearbook of National Accounts Statistics.*

Williamson, O.E. 1975. *Markets and Hierarchies: Analysis and Antitrust Implications.* New York, Free Press.

Yoshino, Y. 1971. *Japanese Marketing System.* Cambridge, MIT Press.

Success that Soured:

Administrative Guidance and Cartels in Japan

KOZO YAMAMURA

DURING THE PAST FEW YEARS, the Japanese economy and managerial practices have been praised, envied, and touted with increasing frequency as an example that Americans must emulate. And, today, many experts continue to extol Japan's "highly rational and sophisticated economic policy" (Givens and Rapp 1979, p. 104), its close and effective government-business leaders, motivated and hard-working employees, and above all, its economic performance and the institutions that enabled it to capture more than one-fifth of the competitive American automobile market. The harsh criticisms of earlier years, once made against "Japan Inc." and a wide range of "unfair" trade tactics, have now been muted or have at least lost their former sting. More Americans today are asking "What can we learn from the Japanese?" or "If they can, why can't we?" A Harvard professor has even written a book entitled *Japan as Number One* (Vogel 1979).

There are, I believe, two major reasons for this visible shift in the American perception of the Japanese economy and business. One undoubtedly is the frustration most Americans have come to feel in the continued poor performance of their own economy. Of late, most Americans have been convinced of the basic futility of resorting to more of the same economic policies and to a series of ad hoc protectionist measures that seem only to favor the inefficient. And in frustration they have elected a new president because and in spite of his declared intention to adopt untried supply-side economics, accompanied by drastic budget cutting. In this atmosphere, who but the Japanese—the most able competitors whose economy is outperforming the Americans' on many fronts—should be selected as worthy of emulation?

The other obvious reason that rarely receives its due attention is that the Japanese model, as presented by these "experts," is extremely attractive to most American business executives, bankers, and some political leaders. The model contains taxes that are lower than what they now pay, enviable depreciation allowances, lax antitrust enforcement, and an obliging government always eager to adopt numerous other proindustry and progrowth policies. Better still, cooperative, if not docile, labor unions and employees willing to work unstintingly also seem to be integral parts of the model.

There is little wonder why many American businessmen now look upon the model longingly and are willing to sponsor and participate in conferences and seminars on "what can we learn from the Japanese." Consultants, business writers, and even some business school professors are quick to realize what the businessmen like to read and hear, and are now seemingly even more anxious to extol the virtues of Japanese policies, practices, and institutions. Mass media and after-dinner speakers are only half a step behind the "experts" and are almost always ready to promise a healthier bottom line if only the Japanese model were adopted.

However, if one carefully examines this recent outpouring of printed and spoken words praising the Japanese economy, one quickly discovers that much of it is replete with overgeneralizations, selected half-truths, hefty doses of misinformation, pseudoanalyses sprinkled with Japanese phrases, and generous servings of clichés. Some "experts" even seem to be trying to compensate for the sins of their predecessors who had busily condemned, on equally questionable ground, the "collusion" between the Japanese government and business, and all manner of "unfair" trade tactics adopted by Japanese exporters. To be sure, there are others who caution against such an abrupt shift in American perceptions; their caution, however, fails to attract the attention of many in search of not-so-painful (or better still, profitable) cures for our economic ills.

I believe that all this is quite dangerous. Little of the recent "emulate Japan" binge can really contribute to increasing our understanding of how and why the Japanese economy grew rapidly and continues to perform well relative to our own. Without such an understanding, any attempt to emulate the Japanese model will be impossible or unsuccessful. And, it could only reward us with unanticipated or unwelcome consequences, or with a result beneficial only to a small segment of American society. Furthermore, a superficial or one-sided view of the Japanese economy could not but be detrimental in achieving a true economic and political partnership across the Pacific.

Thus, the central goal of this essay is to contribute to a better understanding of the Japanese economy through an examination of postwar Japan's "guidance" policy—the policy of guiding industries to achieve rapid growth by coordinating their investment activity, permitting cartels, and adopting other progrowth policies. It is important to note that this guidance has recently attracted a significant amount of attention from those who urge us to emulate the Japanese model; it also exemplifies what was once called "Japan Inc." but today is called the "effective government-business cooperation."[1]

1. Government-business cooperation can have many dimensions and take many

My analysis here will be presented in two parts, one focusing on the period of rapid growth beginning in the mid-fifties and ending in the early seventies, and the other on the period of decelerated economic growth since then and especially since the oil crisis of 1973. Because of space limitations, I have had to exclude much of the relevant evidence, as well as any discussion topics closely related to the central issues of this paper.[2] Interested readers and specialists are referred to the list of references and the notes, which present sources containing essential evidence and further discussion of some issues, and to chapter 4, which follows this essay.

THE RAPID GROWTH PERIOD

In understanding Japanese economic performance, policies, and business practices of this period, we must first realize that rapid growth was achieved under a rather unusual set of economic and political conditions. Most important among the economic conditions were: availability of readily borrowable advanced Western technology; critical shortage of capital; sufficient supply of labor; open and expanding international market; and cheap raw materials (including petroleum). Most salient among the political conditions were Japan's total reliance on the U.S. nuclear umbrella and the stability of domestic politics dominated by the conservative Liberal Democratic party (LDP). The former enabled Japan to focus its national energies on economic recovery and growth, and the latter meant that Japan could adopt sustained and coherent progrowth policies.[3]

Given these conditions and reflecting the strong national consensus on the desirability of achieving rapid economic growth (the principal reason for the continuing electoral success of the LDP and thus political stability), Japan quickly created an effectively functioning political-economic machinery for rapid growth. That many parts of it closely resembled the prewar machinery was no accident. The leaders of the LDP and the senior officials of the central bureaucracy, most of whom survived the occupation, were the very same people who had once formulated and administered the economic policies to guide and control the economy during the 1930s and the war years.[4]

---

forms, as it does in Japan. Here I am examining two of its dimensions, the guidance and the procartel policy.

2. Even such directly related topics as changes in market structure, the industrial groups (keiretsu), protection from foreign competition (the liberalization issues), and others could not be discussed in this essay. On these topics, readers will find Sato 1980, Caves and Uekusa 1976, and Henderson 1973, most useful.

3. Some Japanese scholars went to far as to say that "There were no politics in the sense of the competitive advocacy of the fundamental goal of society," because rapid economic growth became a "war to be won, the first total war in Japanese history for which all of the nation's resources were mobilized voluntarily." See Sato, Kumon, and Murakami 1977, p. 82, and Sakakibara and Noguchi 1977, p. 110.

4. On the prewar legacies, see Chalmers Johnson's forthcoming book from Stanford University Press on the prewar Ministry of Commerce and Industry and the postwar MITI (Ministry of International Trade and Industry).

The machinery created to increase productive capacity and foster the adoption of new technology to produce more and become more competitive in the international market has two main components. These consist of a set of policies (monetary, fiscal, tax, and others) adopted to maximize the flow of low-cost capital to growing and innovative large firms, and of guiding industries to rapidly adopt more efficient larger scale technology (see Ackley and Ishi 1976; Wallich and Wallich 1976; Pechman and Kaizuka 1976). Our task here is to describe and analyze the guidance policy.

Its basic rationale was straightforward. If the largest firms were to grow rapidly by adopting new technology that was usually larger in scale than what it replaced, the firms had to produce more, often significantly more than before, to make optimum use of the new technology. The problem was that such an increase in productive capacity often tended to exceed the domestic demand and increases in exports often did not occur swiftly enough. And there always were occasional slumps that made the expected growth rate of demand falter. To overcome such a temporary gap in supply and demand, the firms, if they were to be motivated to grow, needed "freedom" to fix prices and/or limit output until domestic and international demand could increase. If the rapidly growing firms were allowed to engage in temporary "cooperative actions" to fix prices or limit output, no potentially ruinous price-cutting competition would occur, threatening bankruptcies, and no loss in profits would result, reducing the internal reserve needed for the next round of expansion enabling the firms to adopt even more advanced technology. Because new technology was larger in scale, firms had to be allowed to grow, even if it meant that the market structure could become highly oligopolistic. Anxious to encourage rapid growth and increases in productivity, the LDP and MITI needed no prompting to accommodate the wishes of industry, and the latter was always willing even to take the initiative in creating price-fixing (and/or output-limiting) cartels and a more oligopolistic market structure.[5]

Parenthetically, we should note that LDP and MITI officers had self-serving motivations in addition to the goal of achieving rapid growth. The LDP was understandably anxious to accommodate the wishes of the industry since the latter provided virtually all of the LDP's political fund (for campaigns and the political coffers of the party's faction leaders). Even beyond the long tradition of guiding the economy in cooperation with industry leaders and a great deal of bureaucratic pride in actively coordinating the nation's economy, some high-ranking MITI officers had an incentive to be most helpful to the largest firms that often invited them to fill high managerial posts after their retirement (also see Vogel 1975; Fukui 1970, 1972; Stockwin 1975; Thayer 1973; Campbell 1976; Johnson 1975; Pempel 1974, 1977a).

---

5. Observations contained in this paragraph will be re-examined later in this section. Also see Yamamura 1967 and chapter 4.

The result was a systematic undoing of the American-inspired Anti-monopoly Act, both in letter and spirit, and the adoption of extralegal policies and practices that permitted or encouraged de facto collusive conduct among firms. Let me summarize the policies followed during the period of rapid growth (for amplification, see Yamamura 1967). Though there had been earlier signs of a procartel policy, such as the MITI-initiated administrative guidance, issued immediately following the end of the Korean War, to limit output and/or fix prices in textiles, cement, steel, fertilizer, and other industries, its first major manifestation was the substantive revision to weaken the Antimonopoly Act in 1953.

One of the principal changes permitted formation of cartels to aid the firms in a "recession" and to enable them to "rationalize" their productive capacity. Request to form cartels were to be initiated by a group of firms and approved by the minister in charge (chiefly the minister of MITI). The definition of what constituted a "recession" was broad and flexible. "Rationalization" cartels could be authorized if the firms in an industry were to make investments to increase their productivity and catch up with the Western level of productivity. As we shall see, these cartels, which remain legal today, were readily permitted.

These amendments gave, in many instances, ex post facto legal recognition to the ongoing cartels. But they did much more. After 1953, "recession" cartels were liberally permitted and "rationalization" cartels were readily approved. Despite fluctuations determined by the magnitude of each "recession," the number of such cartels rose, as a trend, to reach a peak in 1966 when sixteen "recession" cartels and fourteen "rationalization" cartels were in effect (Fair Trade Commission 1951-69). Prosecution of illegal cartels also dropped sharply. Prosecution was initiated by the FTC (Fair Trade Commission of Japan) against sixty cartels in 1950, but this number dropped sharply to eighteen in 1951. The number of cases prosecuted continued to decline steadily to only one case in 1960. During the sixties, the FTC prosecuted about twenty cartels per year but most involved small firms that were not in innovative and rapidly growing industries (ibid.). The Export and Import Trading Act was also passed in 1953, formally permitting cartels to fix prices and limit imports. The basic policy, once formally proclaimed, was pursued in earnest.

More legal cartels, in addition to "recession" and "rationalization" cartels, were also authorized by more than a score of industry-specific laws enacted during the fifties and sixties to "promote," "stabilize," or "adjust the demand and supply" in the industries selected to achieve rapid increases in productive capacity and international competitive power. The Marine Products Export Industry Act and the Ammonium Sulphate Industry Rationalization and Ammonium Export Adjustment Temporary Measures Act of 1954 were the first of these laws to be enacted. Those that followed during the next two decades enabled shipbuilding, cement, iron, steel, chemical, machinery, electronics, textile, and other industries to form cartels and benefit from subsidies, low-interest loans, and other inducements to achieve the policy goals (for listing and intent of laws and data on cartels; see Yamamura 1975, pp. 67-100; Uekusa 1977, pp. 112-31).

The total number of legal cartels steadily rose from 162 in 1955 to around 1,000 in the late sixties and early seventies. Data concerning the laws authorizing cartels and the number of cartels permitted under each law as of March 1971 are presented in table 3.1. Here, I should stress, as Niino did, that "many cartels among small and medium firms that were not able

TABLE 3.1

LAWS AUTHORIZING CARTELS AND NUMBER OF
CARTELS AUTHORIZED UNDER EACH, MARCH 1971

Law	Number of cartels
Rationalization cartels, authorized under Antimonopoly Act	13
Emergency act for the promotion of the machine-tool industry	17
Emergency act for the promotion of the electronics industry	2
Emergency act for price stabilization in the fertilizer industry	4
Law concerning tax collection and trade organization in the sake and related industries	7
Law concerning the promotion of exports by the marine products industries	8
Trade association act for the adjustment of marine products	7
Law concerning the optimization of activities in the service industries relating to sanitation	123
Trade association act pertaining to domestic sea transportation	21
Export-import trading act	195
Law concerning the organization of trade associations of small-medium enterprises	439

SOURCE: Fair Trade Commission 1971, p. 96

to adopt new technology to achieve rapid growth" had to be permitted "in order to help them acquire some competitive ability against oligopolistic firms." That is, in many instances, "an active pro-cartel policy became necessary to protect the weak" from the large firms in cartelized industries that were producing the same or substitute products, or outcompeting smaller firms in obtaining labor and raw material (Niino 1981).

These were only the legally permitted cartels and certainly not all of the cartels. Extralegal collusive activities were also being practiced under the ministries' administrative guidance, including price fixing, output reduction, and engaging in other concerted activities relating to investment, market share, adoption of technology, methods and quantities of raw material purchasing (including importing), and so on. In some instances, the guidance to form cartels and engage in other collusive activities was given explicitly, but in others it was less explicit, though often as effective. Because of the importance of such guidance in understanding the nature of the procartel policy and the cooperative government-business relationship seen in Japan, let me add here, in lieu of the thorough discussion that is called for, the following observations and quotations.

No one denies that Japanese ministries issue a large amount of guidance in various forms to achieve their policy goals and perform their administrative functions. Virtually all of the guidance issued is based on the generally stated articles establishing each ministry (with ends such as "to administer its jurisdiction for the purposes of strengthening the national economy and welfare") and not on legislation empowering ministries to issue specific guidance. A Japanese scholar observed that:

The administrative guidance usually takes the form of "notification" *(tsutatsu)* which contains "recommendations" *(kankoku)*. The guidance, issued by the Ministries of Finance, International Trade and Industry, Construction, Agriculture and Forestry, and other governmental agencies, conveys the "advisory remarks" *(shiji jogen)*, "requests" *(yōsei)*, "notices" *(tsuchi)*, and "opinions" *(iken)* of these agencies to the private industries and businessmen. Such administrative guidance is usually effective in accomplishing the goals of the governmental agencies. . . . The number of "notifications" issued by the ministries is immense. For anyone wishing to analyze the effects of these notifications, it may take several years just to examine the notifications. [Ueno 1975, p. 17]

Most important, the guidance is, in many cases, issued following intensive discussion, negotiation, or an exchange of views between ministry officials and industry representatives. Such contact between ministries and industry can take place in very informal conversations or in more formal meetings. The following quotation gives a vivid account of one of the more formal contacts of special significance to this essay:

The Iron-Steel Building in Nihonbashi, Tokyo. Around noon every Monday, elderly gentlemen arrive in black cars. . . . They go to Room 704, on the entrance of which is a sign reading, "The Regular Monday Club Meeting." The members consist of the senior executives of eight major steel producers. They sit at a rectangular table around the section chief of the Ministry of International Trade and Industry, who is seated at the head of the table.

Ogawa, who heads the Iron and Steel Section of the Basic Industries Bureau of MITI, presides over the meeting. On his left is Vice President Ohashi of New Japan Steel and on his right is Senior Director Yamaguchi of Nippon Steel Pipes. . . . During the lunch, few speak. . . . After coffee, the members listen to Ogawa's presentation. The meeting ends after about an hour. The official name of the Monday Club is the General Session of the Market Policies Committee. It was organized in 1958 and since then has served as a point of contact between MITI and the industry.

Vice President Ohashi is responsible for coordinating the industry view. Twenty years ago [circa 1960] the current president of the Japan Federation of Economics Organization [Keidanren], Mr. Inayama, now the chairman of New Japan Steel, had the job [which Mr. Ohashi now holds]. Among the ranks of the senior directors of the major steel firms are former MITI officers who "descended" to these firms. Japan Steel Pipe's Counselor Matsuo (former MITI vice minister); Sumitomo Metal's President Kumagai (former MITI vice minister); Kobe Steel's Vice President Kamatsu (former MITI vice minister). . . . *[Nihon keizai, Jan. 7, 1981]*

A representative of the FTC, for example, carefully understated the effectiveness of "implicit" guidance:

> The essence of cartels is an agreement among businessmen. This means that even an "implicit understanding" is an agreement. If so, when a government agency indicates to the industry leaders what prices are considered appropriate by the agency and the industry raises their prices to that level or negotiates prices at that level (indicated by the governmental agency), this too is an agreement based on implicit understanding. When administrative guidance is conducted in this fashion, it easily leads to effective cartels. [Iyori 1975, pp. 61-62].

At this point, let me present a more analytical perspective, which I believe is useful in gaining insight into the reasons for all of these policies, in understanding why the effective government-business cooperation was achieved in pursuit of the policy goal, and in providing a basis for the next section of this paper (see chap. 4). As I have stressed, the most fundamental reason for the rapid growth of the Japanese economy was a continued large capital investment. Of course, its leaders were the large firms in major industries that had a long way to go in catching up with the West's productive efficiency. As they continued to invest in newer technology, taking advantage of its ready availability, their total productive capacity continued to increase rapidly. This meant that these firms were constantly faced with the economic reality that the fruit of investment in new technology—reduced unit cost—could be realized only by producing and selling more.

That is, by producing more (i.e., by making the best use of the newly adopted technology), each firm could achieve more rapid cost reduction and gain a competitive edge over other firms in the same industry that were slower in increasing output and sales. Producing more, then, meant more sales and profit. Or, maximizing one's market share also maximizes one's profit. These two are indistinguishable when a firm faces a negatively sloping long-run average cost curve, resulting from a successive adoption of "lumpier" new technology.[6]

Maximizing market share to maximize profits, however, is not a strategy that can be pursued by all firms in a market. If they all choose to maximize their market share, the total productive capacity of the industry and the quantity of products supplied to the market will quickly exceed the demand and some firms will be forced to drop out of competition by being absorbed or bankrupted. Economists would call such a market unstable, meaning that there is no market mechanism capable of preventing bouts of competition that would create a monopolist who has outproduced all others.

However, even in a market economy, there is a way to let all large firms

---

6. As stated in chapter 4, this analysis is valid provided no new entry occurs. Given the policy, no new entry occurred during this period into any of the major innovative industries. Of course, before a series of liberalization measures were adopted by the Japanese government in the late sixties and early seventies, no foreign entry was possible or profitable into these industries because of various Japanese policies and administrative procedures.

grow profitably with a minimum of risk to their investment: it is the "arrangement" with a "coordinator" to arbitrate the race for investment and market share competition with an appropriate carrot and stick. Dictated by prewar tradition, the Japanese had no doubt as to what such an arrangement might be or who would be the coordinator. MITI quickly began to guide the firms to coordinate their investment plans. The goal was to increase the capacity of each large firm roughly proportionally to its current market share. Among those firms selected to join the investment race, usually by virtue of their current size, none was to grow so rapidly as to bring confusion to the market. "Orderly growth," assuring everyone's steady growth and profits, was the catchword of the day. Executives of the largest firms, for whom cooperation with MITI was a well-practiced habit that had been acquired in working closely with the predecessor of MITI in the prewar years, were generally most cooperative and eager to follow MITI guidance. After all, this enabled them to achieve profitable and rapid growth with little risk of unnecessary and possibly ruinous competition (for more on these points, see Johnson 1975; Yamamura 1975; Kumagai et al. 1970, vol. 2; Kumagai 1973, 1974, 1976; Misono 1960).

With their past experience, MITI officials were no novices at guidance. MITI made it known, as noted, that the amount of investment each firm was guided to make was determined by the current market share of each firm. This of course encouraged all the firms to compete by using their current capacity to the hilt, absorbing or acquiring smaller competitors,[7] and, perhaps most important, offering better products (often by improving currently used technology, designs, product performance, and the like) and/or better services (quicker delivery date, providing better aftercare, etc.).[8]

Note that the more effective MITI guidance was in promoting the investment race, the more active firms would be in market share-maximizing competition; this necessarily increased individual firms' incentive to engage in price competition. This incentive can be quite strong when demand grows more slowly than rapidly growing productive capacities or during a "recession." Stated differently, the more effective the guidance, the more frequently the firms tended to have excess capacity (as demand, more often than not, failed to grow rapidly enough to keep pace with the growth of capacities), and the more risk there was for price competition. However, if MITI was to help the industries achieve an orderly investment race, the

7. Yamamura 1975 presents data on mergers. The total number of mergers rose steadily during the sixties and the number of mergers in 1970 was nearly three times that of 1960.

8. Although no discussion of this point can be presented here, as numerous examples described by many specialists of such efforts attest, Japanese firms often improved upon newly licensed technology by devising numerous small (at times major) ways to reduce costs or to produce superior products. Large firms were also fiercely competitive in marketing and in providing all forms of services to their customers in Japan and abroad. This explains much of the competitiveness among the large firms, a crucial élan that energized the Japanese economy.

price competition needed to be minimized. This was the principal reason why MITI pursued a procartel policy.

It is important to emphasize that the industries that were wishing to form "recession" cartels must first "convince" MITI (and the FTC) of the desirability of preventing "unwholesome" potential competition or of ending the price competition that might have already begun. Convincing MITI was often not difficult, as the steel, shipbuilding, chemical, and other industries found, because MITI was anxious not to retard the pace of the orderly and rapid growth of industrial capacities that was deemed essential to increase Japan's competitive ability. In short, for the MITI guidance to succeed in coordinating the investment race, cartels limiting or preventing the most unwelcome risk—price competition—had to be an integral part of the policy. And, to minimize this risk, MITI was not reluctant to be flexible in judging what constituted a "recession" (or "rationalization") that merited legal and extralegal cartels.

It should be emphasized, however, that even with these cartels and the widely practiced price leadership of the largest firms in several industries, it is not argued here that price competition did not exist or that all cartels were effective. Price competition, at times intense, did occur, and even cartelized and administered prices were often reduced to reflect the increasing productivity of Japanese industries. What is argued, therefore, is that cartels were quite prevalent and generally effective in reducing or even preventing price competition in "recessions" that threatened both profits and the pace of the investment race.

With guidance to coordinate investment and the ability to resort to cartels, the firms competed to maximize market share, to develop new products that performed better than competitors', and to offer better services. As new technology was adopted and productive efficiency rose steadily, even with a succession of cartels, the prices of the products of large innovative firms continued to decline, thus enabling them to capture an increasing share of the international market.[9]

The policy was succeeding admirably. The guidance, accompanied by the procartel policy and enjoying close cooperation with the industry, played a significant role in achieving rapid growth. Continuing large investment kept the economy buoyant, increased productivity, and raised real wages.

MITI policy also was extremely important in aiding rapid growth in other ways. I believe the following is most significant among them and merits a brief discussion. That is, the MITI guidance was an important, and perhaps even a decisive, factor that encouraged large firms to employ labor on a "lifetime" or "permanent" basis much more widely than in the prewar period. Being able to engage in an investment race and pursue the market

9. Often prices in a market declined step-wise and at the same time because of cartels. All specialists agree that a principal factor contributing to the rapid growth of Japanese exports was the increasing competitiveness of most of the Japanese products. See, for example, Nakamura 1978, pp. 182-87.

share-maximizing strategy with minimum risk, the large firms' policy to steadily increase the number of permanent employees (in effect incurring a large and increasing fixed cost) was not surprising. As the growth of the firms' productive capacity and market share continued to increase, they were certain that they could continue to make the best use of the increasing number of permanent employees, and rapidly growing fixed costs presented little problem. Indeed, any employer, faced with the same circumstance, would be motivated to follow a similar employment policy because, so long as continued growth in capacity and market share is reasonably certain, a minimum turnover in the labor force is preferred.[10]

Minimum turnover meant that the firm's employees were spared the anxiety of job security and were better motivated to work, since they identified their interests with those of the firm. Japanese employees had no reason to object to the adoption of productivity-increasing new technology, even though it was labor saving. They had all the reasons to do their best in devising ways to improve the quality of the firm's products and services. And they were also less inclined to engage in bitter and prolonged labor disputes. Of course, not all the motivation of employees and seemingly smooth labor-management relations during this period can be explained by the adoption of the permanent employment system by the large firms, but few could deny that the latter played a very large part.

Aided by the permanent employment system and what it implied, and by numerous policies pursued by other ministries,[11] MITI's guidance and procartel policies enabled Japan to grow rapidly. The growth steadily increased the real income of most Japanese and dramatically transformed the economy from what it was in 1945.

Before moving on to the decade of the seventies, however, we should note that this seemingly successful policy was beginning to encounter several problems by the mid-sixties. And most of them were a direct result of the policy's success. Consumer complaints against cartels, which were first heard in the early sixties, were growing louder. The large differential between domestic and exported prices of television sets, which angered Japanese consumers, was only the tip of the iceberg.[12] With cartels and a more oli-

10. Of course, in times of slack demand, the large fixed labor cost became an added motivation for the firms to pursue the market share-maximizing strategy even more vigorously. Also, there are institutional and sociocultural dimensions of the Japanese employment system that are relevant to the points made in the text. See Murakami's essay in this volume for further discussion of employment practices.

11. Most significant among them are the policies designed to increase flow of low-cost capital to the large innovative firms—the policy to maintain the exchange rate that undervalued yen, and the slow and deliberate course the government chose in liberalizing international trade and inflow of foreign capital.

12. The consumer movement against the effectively cartelized domestic price of television sets, which was found to be nearly three times that of the export price, was nationwide. From the early sixties on, such movements increased gradually and were organized against high cartelized prices of various industrial products and the high prices

gopolistic market structure, many Japanese undoubtedly realized that they
were sharing less and less of the gains being realized by the large innovative
firms. Economists had no difficulty showing that prices of products of
highly oligopolistic markets had grown more rigid and less responsive to the
supply and demand in many markets (see Yamamura 1975, sources cited in
his notes 27, 39). The small proportion of the government budget allocated
for welfare and health programs became a target of increasingly vocal criticism, as did the pollution of air and water.

By the mid-sixties, it was becoming evident, even to the industries, that
MITI policies were about to bequeath them a major problem. As the technological level of Japanese industries caught up with that of the West one
after another, it was becoming obvious that the investment race no longer
promised increased efficiency but held a distinct danger of excess capacity.
Thus, it was no accident that journalists began to speak of a "structural
problem"—mainly excess capacity—in several, mostly technologically advanced, industries.[13] Japan was beginning to realize that no economy can
continue to grow by increasing its industrial capacity 15 percent per year
(see Bronfenbrenner 1975, pp. 523-53).

As more industries reach the frontier of technology, the rapid pace of
investment at nearly 30 percent of GDP—the principal reason for the rapid
growth—could be maintained only with increasing difficulty. There was less
old machinery to be replaced by new. The appearance of structural problems
was an unmistakable warning that the investment race could not be continued indefinitely. That Americans and others, seeing the rapidly accumulating trade surplus of Japan, were now expressing serious concern about
the increasing share of Japanese products in their markets was another
warning of the impending difficulty. But, as I shall discuss in the next
section, the policies that had served so well were difficult to reverse or dis-
card. MITI, at the end of the sixties, still continued its guidance, and the
number of cartels was increasing, and more mergers—now primarily among
the largest firms—were occurring.[14]

THE DECELERATED GROWTH PERIOD

As the seventies progressed, the Japanese were soon made aware that the
international and domestic conditions that had sustained rapid growth

---

for agricultural and dairy products, pegged significantly above the world price level. Also
see Kirkpatrick 1975, pp. 234-46.

13. MITI, of course, argued that no such structural problem began to exist. See, for
example, Hoshida 1965, pp. 8-12.

14. Even the merger between the largest and the third largest steel producers was
permitted in 1969 to create the giant New Japan Steel, although both firms were already
internationally competitive and the domestic market share of the newly merged firm in
many submarkets would range between 30 and 55 percent. For a discussion of this
merger characterizing the policy of the period, see Yamamura 1975, pp. 81-83.

ceased to exist. The "Nixon shock" of August 1971 made it clear that Japanese exports to the United States could not go on increasing while Japan accumulated large trade surpluses and contributed to the weakening of the dollar. The shock, however, turned out to be only a harbinger of more serious changes. The Smithsonian agreement of December 1971 put a formal end to the export-promoting undervalued yen and the flexible exchange rate system was adopted, further raising the value of the yen. Then came the oil crisis. In the fall of 1973, the Japanese, who import virtually all of the oil they use, literally panicked. The economy reacted by registering negative growth of 1.8 percent for 1973-74.

These developments demonstrated, more clearly than the Japanese ever expected to see, how much the postwar growth had owed to a sustained increase in productive capacity that was encouraged in crucial ways by the rapid growth of exports and availability of cheap raw materials. The 1973-77 recession that followed the oil crisis caused the structural problems to worsen and spread to more industries. Worse still, for many firms in such industries as specialized steel, chemical, paper, shipbuilding, and several others, the problems now threatened to be long-lasting. The period of rapid growth had ended, and the end had come sooner than hoped or predicted because of the oil crisis and the subsequent recession.

These developments in the early seventies made it even more obvious to many critics of MITI that the policies of coordinating investment and reducing risks of investment by cartels had become counterproductive. Those who had been demanding a major change in these policies now had more reasons to accuse MITI of continuing an outdated policy. But before turning to an examination of MITI policy, let us first describe developments in the seventies.

As the recession deepened, the number of legally permitted recession cartels rose sharply. In 1974, nineteen industries were being allowed to form such cartels (Fair Trade Commission 1980). The illegal cartels also multiplied visibly. The FTC chose to prosecute sixty-nine cartels in 1973 and sixty in 1974, many more than the around thirty that were prosecuted each year during the late sixties. Unlike in earlier years, virtually all these illegal cartels were price-fixing cartels (see also Shibata 1978). But what shocked the public most was the disclosure that wholesalers of petroleum products were engaged in 1973 in large-scale price fixing to take advantage of OPEC actions. The mass media and the Diet hearings uncovered how extensively and systematically prices had been fixed, using secret codes and taking elaborate precautions to prevent detection by the FTC (*Asahi Shimbun*, Aug. 18, 1980, p. 9).

Under the circumstances, the LDP had little choice but to indicate it was willing to consider a re-examination of the Antimonopoly Act to prevent recurrence of such flagrant violation. Given this, the FTC, which had for some time been aware of the increasing need to tighten the act, pro-

posed in 1974 a series of amendments.[15] They were far from stringent
and were only intended to cope with such specific problems as the FTC's
inability to prevent the recurrence of illegal cartels, the continuing accumulation of market power in a small number of the largest firms, and various
forms of ongoing unfair trade practices.[16] No changes regarding the legal cartels were suggested and other proposed revisions also reflected the FTC's
recognition of what would be politically possible. Most of the amendments
were severely criticized by many economists and lawyers as being too limited
or too lenient (see Baba 1975; Kazunori 1974; Imai 1975; Imai, Imamura,
and Komiya 1975; Komiya 1973; Komiya, Sanekata, and Uekusa 1975;
Sanekata 1975, 1976), but they immediately came under a barrage of
criticism from industry, MITI, and many persons within the ruling party.
The criticisms clearly indicated that those who had been benefiting from, or
pursuing, the procartel policies tenaciously held to their fundamental view
that the policies would continue to contribute to growth. And, in a nutshell,
they opposed the FTC amendments on the grounds that (1) the Japanese
economy was sufficiently competitive; (2) Japan must continue to face
strong international competition; and (3) the Japanese economy should not
be exposed to added disadvantages when it already suffered from near-total
dependence on imported petroleum and other raw materials.[17]

The debate continued during the 1974-77 period. But finally the amendment, in a significantly modified version of the original FTC proposal,
passed the Diet in 1977, principally because of the earlier political commitment made by the leadership of the ruling party, now under an increasingly
potent political opposition. The extent of the major modifications are obvious in comparing some of the amendments as originally proposed by the
FTC with those that were actually made (for a comparison of revisions and
those proposed, see Shibata 1978).

15. For the original FTC proposal, see *Ekonomisuto*, March 19, 1974. This is a
special issue on the proposed revisions.

16. It is very revealing that, because of the inability to issue permanent injunctions
against cartels, a large number of the orders issued to cease collusive conduct were against
repeat offenders. The ratio of repeat offenders were (in percentages) 36.4 (1970), 43.2
(1971), 26.7 (1972), 48.5 (1973), and 56.5 in the first six months of 1974. From Fair
Trade Commission, *Annual Reports*, respective years.

17. Amaya 1974. In this article appearing in a widely read magazine, Amaya, who
was one of the highest ranking MITI officers until summer 1981, also argued that

the Occupation Forces unilaterally imported the American method of surgery which was designed
to deal with the American-type monopoly disease. Thus, the so-called original Antimonopoly Act
was enacted. Some say the revision of this Act has been a regrettable process that weakened the
Act. Is this true? One view can certainly be that it is quite intolerable to apply to humans the surgical
method that has been successful for mice. [P. 38] . . . The antimonopoly policy of Japan naturally is
a subsystem of the Japanese economic policy system which must remain cognizant of the reality of
the Japanese economy and the unique international environment in which Japan is placed. Therefore,
before we make any reference to the original Antimonopoly Act of 1947 or to the American antitrust
statutes, we must assiduously evolve a theory of an antimonopoly policy befitting Japanese society. If
not [any view advanced] could not be expected to be persuasive. [P. 45]

The FTC proposal was to penalize illegal cartels by imposing a fine calculated by multiplying the amount of total shipment by the amount of price increase (above the price that prevailed before price fixing) made by the colluding firms. The intent was to eliminate all incentives for illegal price fixing. The amendment actually passed imposes a fine of 2 percent of the total sales made during the price-fixing cartel.[18] (Note, in passing, that in Japan there is virtually no likelihood of the officers of convicted firms being incarcerated for illegal price fixing and, unlike in the United States, private antitrust actions—especially consumer class-action suits—are extremely difficult to initiate, let alone win. Unlike in the United States, no provision exists for triple damage penalties for illegal price fixing.)

The 1977 amendment also failed to include an FTC-proposed provision empowering it to order price-fixing industries to reduce prices to precollusion levels. The FTC must, therefore, rely only on the penalty to prevent price fixing from recurring.[19] This is an indication of the leniency of the amendment as well as of the continuing passiveness of the policy against illegal cartels.

And, to deal with seeming parallel price increases (or the cases of apparently effective price leadership), the FTC proposed that it be given the right to examine company books to ascertain whether or not price increases were justified by cost increases. Instead, the Diet chose to rely on moral persuasion and the amendment passed mandated the industries to submit "explanations" for their price increases to the FTC, which forwarded them to the Diet. But explanations only had to be submitted if the largest three firms of the industries involved had a joint market share in excess of 70 percent and if the industries had a total annual shipment value in excess of 30 billion yen (about 150 million dollars) (for discussions of the weaknesses of these limitations, see Baba 1975; Kazunori 1974; Imai 1975; Imai, Imamura, and Komiya 1975; Komiya 1973; Komiya, Sanekata, and Uekasa 1975; Sanekata 1975, 1976). Although the precise scope depends on the specific definition used in determining what constitutes an industry or a market, the restricting clauses in the amendment leave the FTC powerless to deal with many cases of price increases and leadership.[20]

Even toward the end of the 1973-77 recession, the economy continued to grow slowly by Japanese standards and to face serious structural problems in a dozen or so major industries. Indicating that the procartel policy had

18. The penalty for price fixing is 1 percent for retailers and .5 percent for wholesalers.

19. See the data on repeat offenders in n. 16. Although a judgment must be withheld until we are able to examine the total effect of the amendments on illegal cartels in the coming years, one could not but ask: given the penalty that can be imposed, will not illegal price fixing by more than 2 percent continue to be profitable?

20. In November 1977 the FTC issued a guideline to be used in defining a "market." An examination of the guideline clearly shows that the FTC fully anticipates extreme difficulties ahead in deciding upon an operating definition of a market in many industries. FTC, pp. 153-55.

not changed in any fundamental sense, the Japanese Diet enacted in 1978 the Designated Recession Industries Stabilization Act. In the words of MITI, the act (to be in force until June 30, 1983) was necessary because

many industries are suffering from factors inherent in the industrial structure, such as increased costs for energy and raw materials and the prolonged slump in domestic demand resulting from slow economic growth. These structurally depressed industries are now facing an increasingly serious situation with large portions of their production facilities sitting idle. The objective of the Law is to improve the structure of these industries by encouraging the disposal of excessive facilities: the basic and common ailment of these industries.[21]

Its principal objective is to assist four specific industries (aluminum refining, synthetic fibers, shipbuilding, and steel by open-hearth and electric furnaces) and any other industry with excess capacity "designated" as "depressed" by MITI. When an industry is so designated, a plan for stabilization is drawn up for the industry by the cabinet minister with the relevant jurisdiction (MITI). The plan would contain the amount of capacity to be reduced, the method of reduction, the length of time for accomplishing the reduction, restrictions on new capacity expansion, and specified procedures to change the product mix of the firms in the industry. To reduce capacity, the act will help the industry to obtain loans necessary by providing a loan guarantee from the Credit Fund for the Designated Recession Industries created for this purpose. (The loans are necessary because the capacity is usually used as collateral for bank loans.) And, among other provisions, the act authorizes the minister to order the formation of a cartel, provided that capacity reduction cannot be implemented voluntarily without one. The total amount of the Credit Fund is ten billion yen.[22]

As of the summer of 1978, fourteen industries were designated. The industries and the proportion of the total capacity (percent) to be scrapped (or sealed) were as follows: steel by open-hearth and electric furnace (14); aluminum refining (32); nylon filament (20); polyacrylnitrile staple (17); polyester filament (11); polyester staple (17); ammonium (26); urea (45); phosphoric acid by wet process (20); cotton (6); wool (11); ferrosilicon (21); liner and corrugating medium for container board (15); shipbuilding (35). As anyone familiar with postwar cartels readily recognizes, these were the industries allowed to form cartels repeatedly in the past.[23]

We should also note that MITI continued to take the initiative in enacting new laws to encourage rationalization. The most important was the July 1978 Law for the Promotion of Designated Machinery and Information

21. A MITI memo entitled "Outline of the law concerning provisional measures for specific depressed industries" (n.d.) that was made available to the author by the ministry.

22. From the act as passed on May 5, 1978.

23. A MITI memo entitled "Conditions of the application of the law concerning provisional measures for specific depressed industries" (n.d.) that was made available to the author by the ministry. Also see FTC 1980, for these industries' past history of cartel information.

Industries (to remain in force for a period of seven years, until 1985). The law provides loans at specified interest rates (lower than the market rate) from the government-controlled Japan Development Bank and others, as well as tax incentives for investments made to produce "high performance machinery equipped with computers and other electronic devices." As in the earlier laws, the stated goal is to "promote rationalization and technological advancement of the industries" so they can "contribute to the sound development of the economy as well as to the qualitative improvement of national life."[24]

To be sure, because of the 1977 amendment to the Antimonopoly Act, industries can now be prevented from forming repeated illegal cartels and can be penalized by larger fines. But no substantive change has occurred in the procartel policy as cartels are still permitted under the Antimonopoly Act (especially the recession cartels authorized during the most recent recession), the provisions of the 1978 Designated Recession Industries Stabilization Act, and other special laws (industry-specific and others). Indeed, for MITI, the industries, and some in academia, there was little necessity to change, let alone offer apologies for, the procartel policy. On the contrary, they argued that it is more effective in facing current economic ills than those adopted (or not adopted) elsewhere and is one of the important reasons the continuing performance of the Japanese economy is envied by other industrialized nations. For example, an executive of a large Japanese shipping firm observed that

in Japan, an emergency Act to stabilize designated industries in a recession was passed last year. Under the Act, if an industry is designated to be in recession, it is exempt from the Antimonopoly Act. This means that the industry can form cartels and members of the industry can talk to each other openly. Through such cooperation, it is possible to limit output by means of less than full capacity operation or by scrapping a part of existing capacity. The shipbuilding industry's ability to cooperate in adopting its rationalization measure comes from this Act. Everyone knows that output limitations in aluminum and ammonium sulphate are being done under the terms of this Act. That is, among the advanced nations, Japan is the first to make such a rationalization method.

In the West, the Antitrust laws are stringent and no such method can be adopted and they are still wasting time. . . . Especially in the United States where the Antitrust laws are sacrosanct, no such method, let alone recession cartels, is possible. We in the shipping industry know how tough the American Antitrust laws are. [Ariyoshi 1979, p. 228]

Or, in the words of a highest-ranking official of MITI:

The increase in cartels seen in Japan since 1970 was a phenomenon resulting from the very economic characteristics that are prone to excessive competition. These cartels did not result from Japan's becoming non-competitive because the Japanese economy ceased to be in the stage of maturity and began to show the symptoms of old age, as in the case of Western economies. The basic character of the contemporary Japanese econ-

24. See articles 1 and 5 of the act.

omy, I judge, is definitely still excessively competitive when compared to the economies of the West. [Amaya 1974, p. 40]

Here, let us highlight the fundamental changes that had occurred in the Japanese economy in the seventies and answer such questions as, Why does MITI continue to pursue a procartel policy? (Why did it oppose the FTC-proposed amendments to the Antimonopoly Act, but initiate the 1978 Act to stabilize the designated recession industries?) What are the costs of continuing the procartel policy?

One unquestioned fact is that by 1970 many Japanese industries had caught up with the West's productive efficiency. Some technologically more advanced industries had done so by the mid-sixties and many more reached or surpassed it in the late sixties and early seventies. In short, readily available borrowable technology had been exhausted and many Japanese industries in the seventies could no longer hope to increase their productive efficiency by adopting new technology. Or, in contrast to the rapid growth period, the long-run average cost curve faced by most Japanese industries in the seventies was no longer declining; with a few exceptions, a reduction in unit cost of production could no longer be realized by increasing capacity and production. An increasing number of large firms could remain profitable only by reducing costs as much as possible and by finding new ways to increase their efficiency. The market share-maximizing strategy no longer promised more profit. As in the case of most American firms, the Japanese firms now also had to be keenly concerned with current fixed costs. The short run had to take precedence over the long run. To maximize profit, capacity needs to be as close as possible to the optimum operating level. Large fixed costs, such as interest on large long-term debts and wages for permanent employees, must be trimmed as much as feasible. Price competition must be avoided because it cuts sharply into profit.[25]

Thus, more and more Japanese firms in the seventies engaged in an "operation scale-down" that consisted of cost-saving campaigns (no frills and maximum economizing), encouraging older employees to retire before the mandated retirement age, eliminating redundant employees, hiring a minimum of young entrants, devising ways to use less energy, and reducing accustomed debts from the banks if at all possible (articles in English on this development are Rohlen 1979; Nakamura 1980). At the same time, more industries sought to prevent price competition (even resorting to illegal price fixing) and competed vigorously in product development and services. Research and development expenditures too began to rise visibly (Economic Planning Agency 1976; MITI 1974).

All of the above made it clear that, in the seventies, MITI could no longer justify its procartel policy. There was no more need for a coordinator to assure rapid adoption of new technology. What the MITI policy accomplished now, by promoting cartels, was to limit price competition that could

25. See chapter 4 for a more analytical discussion of the observations made in this paragraph.

force the firms in structurally depressed industries (designated as well as others) to reduce excess capacity. Note that, in the seventies, an industry could be structurally depressed if it had excess capacity due to a change that had occurred in the composition of domestic and international demand, if the competing firms in the newly developing nations (NICs) began to out-compete the Japanese firm, and/or if it continued to have excess capacity due to what proved to be an overinvestment.

Why did MITI continue the same policy? Simply because it found it virtually impossible to do otherwise. The ministry, in effect, was trapped because MITI policies are, by nature, self-perpetuating and extremely diffi-cult to reverse for two reasons. One is that the structural problem (aggra-vated by the recession of the mid-seventies) being faced by many industries was to a significant extent a creation of past MITI policy. MITI had actively encouraged rapid growth of productive capacity and was not in a position to betray the industries that had followed the earlier MITI guidance. The other reason was less direct though no less obvious. Because of MITI policy, the industries continued to delay taking necessary measures to reduce their ca-pacity (or even increase it) in anticipation of an increase in demand that would result, they hoped, from economic growth and/or recovery from the recession. They had come to expect that MITI would run to the rescue by providing guidance, enacting new legislation, or battling the FTC, if their problems intensified.

These two reasons for MITI's inability to reverse its policy have been noted frequently by many scholars and evidence supporting their analysis is readily available. For example, Imai, in his study of the Japanese steel in-dustry found that

when a cartel to limit output is in effect, prices recover and excess profits are obtained, causing internal reserves to increase. Also, in a recession, interest rates decline and the in-dustries with large fixed costs borrow as much as possible in long-term funds in order to reduce the burden of fixed costs for years to come. That is, for the industries having large fixed costs, low interest rates act as an especially strong incentive to make capital invest-ments. When the demand begins to recover and a supply shortage begins to be expected, investment becomes active, drawing on internal reserves and taking advantage of the still-low interest rates. Competition to increase capacity resumes. The amount of capacity increase is now relatively larger (than that achieved in the last round); thus as the new capacity is used, supply gradually exceeds demand. Furthermore, in the high fixed-cost industries, increased output uses capacity more fully and reduces unit cost. A result of this is a keen price competition which reduces the profit rate. The ground is again pre-pared for the formation of another cartel.

As seen above, the industries having large, fixed costs are characterized by a pro-nounced phenomenon of a cycle consisting of cartel formation, cartel collapse, and refor-mation of the cartel. A fact which should not be neglected is that the ability to form a cartel in each recession leads these industries to readily compete to increase their respec-tive capacities. [Imai 1974; quoted in Sanekata et al. 1975, p. 131]

Imai's analysis is applicable to many other major industries. Although there is not sufficient space to present a great deal of data, it is not difficult to demonstrate, industry by industry, how one cartel led to another. To cite only two examples, the polyvinyl chloride resin industry was authorized to form recession cartels eight times between November 1958 and August 1978, and the stainless steel producers were permitted to practice five recession cartels between November 1965 and June 1973 (for other examples, see Fair Trade Commission 1980). And one is correct, I believe, in viewing the Designated Recession Industry Stabilization Act of 1978 as a direct consequence of the procartel policy. In the words of a Japanese economist: "Put simply, there has been a policy commitment, and in a real sense, the economy has not been *laissez-faire*. At this juncture, the industries cannot be suddenly told, 'do the best you can' by ignoring the historical background of the policy commitment" (Takeuchi 1978, p. 18).

Of course, that "cartels beget more cartels" was recognized as early as 1966 by Bronfenbrenner when he wrote (the following is what he thought Japanese business executives would be saying to themselves under MITI's procartel guidance policy):

> We know there is too much output and capacity in our industry. That is the reason we call our industry excessively competitive. So why do we increase our own output and capacity? Primarily, because we expect the government to protect our profits before very many of us fail. MITI, or some other agency, will step in, set minimum prices, allocate output, apportion imported raw materials or the foreign exchange with which to buy them in such a way that business becomes profitable again. In such a control scheme, the larger our share of our industry's capacity or output, the larger our share of the market will be under controls, and the better off we are likely to be in the long run. This is why it is good business to expand the way we do, accepting losses at the margin to increase our share of the market! [Bronfenbrenner 1966, p. 124]

And nearly fifteen years later, Bronfenbrenner's observation was echoed by Japan's leading daily newspaper, *Asahi Shimbun:*

> The postwar industrial policy, based on the cooperation of bureaucracy and business, contributed in strengthening the heavy and chemical industries of Japan and in promoting the international competitiveness of our industries. However, it allowed, gradually and unperceived, an increased involvement and guidance of the government; the industries became accustomed to working with the government and accepted the assistance of the government, even in the failures resulting from entrepreneurial misjudgment. [*Asahi Shimbun*, Aug. 25, 1980, p. 9]

The above quote suggests only one of several problems—costly to the economy as a whole—caused by the continuing MITI policy. Most serious among them is that it inevitably leads to further involvement and even abuse of bureaucratic power in the economy. The following quotes are but a small sample of observations that attest to this.

Criticizing the serious problems inherent in the procartel guidance policy, *Asahi Shimbun* wrote:

> The electric furnace industry [steel producers using electric furnaces] has been permitted to organize a cartel eight times since September 1975 in order to limit the output of small steel rods. And, the price too was cartelized beginning in August, 1977. But the cartels authorized under the Antimonopoly Act cannot be continued for an extended period of time and the cartels also could not force "outsiders"—those firms unwilling to

participate—to join the cartel. This was the reason why 52 firms organized the National Small Steel Rod Industry Association and, since October 1977 have engaged in a cartel authorized under the Small-Medium Enterprises Trade Association Act.

After the formation of the Industry Association, the Association and the Ministry engaged in a skillful cooperation. The Association asked the Ministry to force "outsiders" to join the cartel [as can be done for the cartels organized under the Small-Medium Enterprise Trade Association] and MITI chose to issue an order to the "outsiders" to join the cartel as it could under Article 56 of the Small-Medium Enterprises Trade Association Act. The order stated "cut the output by 35 percent" and that, if the order was not obeyed, a fine of 300,000 yen would be imposed.

One outsider, confident that he could successfully reduce his costs and compete, initially refused to be coerced to join the cartel and association, but the pressure brought upon him was extremely strong:

The indignities suffered [in 1978] are still fresh in the memory of Masanari Ikeya, president of Tokyo Steel, which was not a member of the Association. At that time, he was doing his utmost to resist MITI's efforts to coerce him to join the cartel. "I heard that an order to join the cartel might be issued if I continued to resist. First I thought 'they wouldn't dare,' then, I really got angry. After I reached the conclusion that I had no alternative but to join the cartel, I felt totally defeated."

For those managing the "outsider" firms, the fine was no more than pocket money. But the principle involved was great. "Though the industry is supposedly suffering from a structural recession," Mr. Ikeya observed, "our firm was healthy. Can a healthy person be forcibly hospitalized? Can this occur in a free enterprise economy? I thought a constitutional issue was involved." The firms considered appealing the issue to the court and consulted with an attorney. But, they came to the conclusion that the chance of winning a case against the government was slim and finally decided to accept the MITI order against their will. [Ibid.]

Commenting on the bureaucratic way the Designated Recession Industries Stabilization Act of 1978 was implemented, one Japanese scholar noted that

when excess capacity is scrapped [benefiting from the Credit Fund], all of a company's capacity, namely that of the least efficient companies, cannot be scrapped. What typically happens is that, as is seen in the chemical fertilizer industry, the newest and most efficient capacity of the firms is scrapped. From the economic point of view, a best way of scrapping is not adopted. In reality what happens is that scrapping is done proportional to the capacity [of the firms in the industry]. [Takeuchi 1978, p. 21]

And, on the same 1978 act, Saxonhouse, who is critical of its basic rationale, noted, "The setting up or continuation of a cartel by itself seems a strange way to deal with long-term structural problems. The successful cartel is designed to raise product prices by restricting competiton among firms in an industry. Given the presence of secular supply-demand gaps in structurally depressed industries, such a policy would retard rather than encourage the removal of excess capacity" (1979, p. 306).

Another significant and already visible problem is what one may call a decreasing margin of policy error. That is, the bureaucracy is forced to be more and more involved in rectifying and coping with problems it created, the slowly growing economy can no longer absorb or tolerate policy errors. Increasingly costly errors to the economy include miscalculating future demand, misguiding industries on the best technology to adopt, or "picking wrong winners" as targets for future growth.[26] Earlier, an overestimation of future demand resulted only in a longer duration and/or in the reauthorization of recession cartels (as in steel and other industries) (Imai 1974; Fair Trade Commission 1980). Correct technology could be adopted in the next round of expansion (as happened in the soda industry) and a winner not selected or even discouraged by MITI could still be a winner (as was Sony) (see also Namiki 1979, p. 57). The tasks now facing MITI officers have become far more difficult. Their errors demand, more quickly and visibly, correction and further involvement in the economy.

Yet another problem of the prolonged procartel policy is that it has created an atmosphere where collusive conduct among firms was not regarded by some business leaders, even in principle, as morally or socially reprehensible. This is not a surprising development. On this subject, a Japanese scholar went so far as to argue that "Cartels, created by a group of many, constitute a dangerous power and are conspiracies to monopolize markets. In modern societies of citizens, that cartels are criminal acts is common sense. An image associated with cartels is evil deeds being agreed upon in the dark of night. The reality of the Japanese economy today is that such cartels have become a common custom" (Sanekata et al. 1975). A leading economist, more moderately perhaps reflecting the view of many of his colleagues observed that "among business leaders of major enterprises, the notion that 'cartels are evil' has not yet been accepted. While tax evasion and causing pollution are considered shameful acts, being prosecuted for illegal cartels is not so considered. We find many names of prominent business leaders in sections of the recently published Annual Report of the Fair Trade Commission of 1973 which describes indictments and decisions concerning the cartel cases" (Komiya 1974, p. 14).

The difficulty of accepting the notion that "cartels are evil" per se can be readily seen in numerous articles carried by the major dailies. Let me quote only the following:

According to the Fair Trade Commision, the Antimonopoly cases first showed a tendency to decline in number following the revision of the Act [in 1977]. . . . However, the numbers began to rise again from the end of 1978 and rose to 103 during 1980. . . .

26. "Picking winners" too will be extremely difficult in the coming decades. As the economy grows more slowly, Japan will experience the same problems faced by the United States. Fallows (1980, p. 50) reports a conversation with Charles Schultze, former chairman of the Council of Economic Advisers:

Schultze recently obtained a list of the twenty products and industries that grew fastest during the 1970s—the "winners." Of those twenty, perhaps five look "predictable" in retrospect: various forms of plastics, oil and gas drilling equipment, semiconductors, small cars. (The car makers, of course, say this last item was unforeseeable, even though it was the fastest growing product on the list.) But what about "utility vehicles," number 2 on the list? Vacuum cleaners (9)? Construction glass (13)? Cheese and tufted carpets (18 and 19)? "And where have you had the highest productivity increase in the past generation?" Schultze asks. "Poultry and turkey rearing. Who was going to pick that as a 'winner'?"

The petroleum wholesalers' illegal cartel organized by twelve firms which fixed and raised prices together went so far as to mark its secret price-fixing document with a [graphic design of a] small bird signifying "beware of the Fair Trade Commission." The spirit of the Antimonopoly Act was being ignored and the means adopted to violate the Act have grown skillful. [Asahi Shimbun, Aug. 18, 1980, p. 9]

And,

On the 15th [December 1980] the Fair Trade Commission issued a notification to the industries in question and to MITI that the concerted output limitation undertaken— "the output reduction by industry initiative"—from July to September by the steel ingot, small steel frame, ethylene, polyvinyl chloride, and paper industries "can constitute an Antimonopoly Act violation unless care is taken." It was discovered that the information concerning current market conditions was exchanged among firms using their respective trade associations and these industries engaged in joint reductions in output. The FTC requested MITI to take extreme care not to promote illegal conduct by means of providing information or administrative guidance. [Ibid., Dec. 16, 1980, p. 9]

The problems described above are not, however, all of the ones created by MITI policy. The latter also has been and can continue to be detrimental in achieving smooth economic relationships with Japan's major trading partners. Let me briefly summarize only the most significant among these problems.

First, MITI policies have constituted an important reason for the export drive of Japanese firms, as many knowledgeable Japanese economists (and even businessmen) readily recognize. It is not difficult to see why this can continue to occur. As I have already discussed, one result of the MITI policies was to increase an industry's capacity beyond what would be prudent.[27] And, today, when the cushion of a cartel still exists, the reduction in total excess capacity will be slower than when no collusion is permitted. This means that the firms have constantly had a great incentive to increase exports to make full use of the industry's large capacity and absorb the burden of high fixed costs.[28]

This is only part of the reason for what the Japanese aptly refer to as a "concentrated downpouring of exports" (shūchū gōteki yushutsu). This occurs because new technology tends to be adopted at about the same time by all firms in an industry (often aided by MITI). The desire to increase exports also matures around the same time for all the firms in an industry. The more extensive the policy inducements—subsidies, low-cost loans, effective guidance cartels, or specific laws—the stronger and more pronounced the export drive will be. Of course, domestic recessions cannot but intensify

27. That is, it is "rational" for businessmen to engage in an investment race if they can continue to rely on recession cartels being formed.

28. This also can be a factor motivating Japanese firms to compete for market share in the foreign markets even if such competition leads to competitive offering of discounts and other methods of reducing prices to below what is agreed upon by the cartel authorized under the Export-Import Trade Act. This may be desirable for American consumers, but this became (and can continue to be) a factor contributing to U.S.-Japan trade conflicts.

this as does misjudgment (typically overestimation) of the growth of domestic demand by MITI and industries.[29] The periods of sudden, and at times sustained, Japanese export drives into the United States and other markets can easily be identified. Beginning with the "dollar blouses" of the mid-fifties, an influx of radios, tape recorders, television sets, various products of the steel and chemical industries, and many other goods had occurred during the past thirty years.

One must, however, be aware that not all industries engage in export drives, induced directly or indirectly by MITI. A rapid increase in exports can take place independently of any policies. The point here is that the Japanese policy, in a sense, accentuates product cycles and can continue to do so. One salient fact is that any export drive in the eighties, which can occur unless the policy is fundamentally changed, cannot but severely strain economic and political relations between Japan and her major importers much more than in the past.

Second, the lax antimonopoly policy has provided Japanese industries with a relative advantage in international competition vis-à-vis American and other Western industries. Many segments of Japanese export-oriented industries—steel, shipbuilding, chemical, machinery, and several others—have been shielded from the vagaries of the market forces by sanctioned collusion.

In contrast, the firms in the United States, where antitrust statutes are enforced more vigorously, cannot seek such refuge in times of a recession. And, in making investments, they cannot enjoy the reduced risks of co-ordinated investment and other activities under the guidance of governmental agencies. Thus the advantages gained by Japanese firms can be substantial, in periods of both rapid and slower growth. In the former, capacity increases were achieved more quickly, knowing that the effects of excess capacity could be cushioned. Once an industry achieves higher productivity and larger capacity, it is easier for it to retain its competitive ability and to improve it further, especially if the government becomes increasingly involved to this end.

Other international competitive advantages are even more obvious. In the extreme, a Japanese industry protected by a cartel can immediately rebound in the international market as soon as market conditions have improved. The same industry in the United States may succumb to the recession (go bankrupt or be forced to reduce productive capacity too rapidly to re-enter competitively in the international market). This was precisely the advantage MITI officials have used and, in effect, are using to justify their procartel policy. In earlier years, the recession and guidance cartels were justified on the grounds that such cartels prevent the "loss of productive capacity that is needed for international competition." And, the MITI officials included basically the same argument, among others, in successfully advocating the Designated Recession Industries Stabilization Act of 1978.

---

29. For the case of the steel industry, see *Asahi Shimbun*, Aug. 25, 1980. In this case, MITI readily acknowledged its error in estimating future demands.

As noted earlier, in the 1950s and even in the 1960s, such a policy was easy to justify. The advantage enjoyed by the protected industries also helped the Japanese economy to grow, benefiting many in the economy. However, today we should ask, Why are such cartels still needed to protect some industries while Japanese industry as a whole is so successful in world markets? And, why should the Japanese continue to permit cartels that, in effect, provide subsidies from the national coffer and consumers so that selected recession industries can compete internationally?

Third, the current policies cannot but contribute to increasing the involvement of Japanese exporters in public and private antitrust and dumping litigations in importing nations, especially the United States.

In most instances, private litigants and various U.S. governmental agencies have had little difficulty obtaining what they believed to be evidence of domestic cartels in Japan; of collusive price fixing or market share agreements in American markets under the aegis of the export cartels legally formed by trade associations or created by MITI guidance; of significant differences between domestic and export prices that were difficult to explain in terms of differences in costs of marketing, demand elasticity, and other valid reasons.[30]

Even large price differentials in two markets do not, by themselves, show that dumping occurred. Nor does a domestic cartel, even in those instances where price fixing has been in effect, need to be considered to provide sufficient evidence that a rapid increase in exports resulted from dumping. The point is simply that the conduct of Japanese firms in domestic and American markets (and also in European and other markets) has been such that the data and observations that serve as evidence have been obtainable. It is naïve to believe that the existence of such evidence—sufficient to merit litigation, investigation, or even conviction in some instance—is totally unrelated to the Japanese policies.

Some may say that the prosecution of firms is not more than legal harassment by competing American firms or is due to the protectionist policies that have colored the standard of legal or administrative procedures adopted by the American courts and government. Or that the conduct of Japanese firms has in no way been affected by Japanese policies. I believe this is as unjustified as saying that the successes of Japanese firms in American markets could not have been achieved were it not for their "unfair" tactics.

Last of all, MITI policies did and still do, to a less degree, contribute to creating a climate conducive to business and bureaucratic practices that limit imports and cause foreigners to believe that Japan limits access to its

---

30. The best-known case involving an "unexplainable" price differential between domestic and export prices was the color television sets exported to the United States. MITI had to order an investigation into the price differential because the minister found the industry explanation unconvincing. See *Yomiuri Shimbun*, Nov. 10, 1966. This case is fully analyzed in Komiya et al. 1977.

own market by various nontariff barriers. This is a familiar and extensively argued point of contention between the Japanese and the Americans. Even after the substantial changes made during the past two decades by policy makers and the industries to liberalize the economy and reduce nontariff barriers, criticisms remain. For example, as late as 1981, the binational group (the so-called Wisemen) concluded after their careful and even-handed study of the economic relations between Japan and the United States that "The protectionism of the earlier period has left important legacies, both in foreign perceptions of the Japanese market by those whose experiences with Japan were formed in the earlier period and in Japanese bureaucratic orientations and regulatory and administrative survivals of the earlier era which still inhibit market access." And, that "Japan is not yet as 'open' as the United States to foreign imports, capital, and influences" (Japan and U.S. Economic Group 1981, pp. 55-56), despite the significant efforts since the early 1960s to reduce tariffs and quota restrictions, and so forth. Thus, the group concluded that, despite that "Japan appears to be generally meeting its international obligations," it must "strive to substantially improve access to her market and society" for the sake of "its own national interests and in the interest of a more harmonious American-Japanese economic relationship" (ibid., p. 55).

The group justified this general assessment by presenting its analysis of Japan's foreign exchange controls and foreign investment; standards, inspection and approval procedures, the government procurement system, the distribution system, and other business practices all tend to impede imports. And most significantly, in the context of this essay, the group, after warning against the false and misleading image of Japan Inc., noted that "Most Japanese, however, do acknowledge the existence of government reliance on administrative guidance, usually describing the informal means by which the government attempts to influence business without resorting to legislative or regulatory measures as would be the case in the United States." And, "Administrative guidance often serves a legitimate function in the Japanese economy, and its constructive use should not be condemned. What is important in the context of American-Japanese relations is that it should not be used in ways that discriminate against foreign interests. We believe that when administrative guidance is exercised, it should be exercised in a publicly visible, transparent fashion, and the rationale should be explained, even *post facto*" (ibid., pp. 61-62).

Given the very nature of administrative guidance, its past history, and one of its central goals—to develop and maintain the international competitiveness of Japanese industries—the critical questions that still remain are, Can the guidance, if continued at all, not discriminate against foreign interests? And, given the nature and characteristics of the guidance, which I described earlier, can it be made "transparent"?

CONCLUSION

MITI policy was successful in accomplishing its goals for nearly two decades.

Taking full advantage of expanding world trade and availability of advanced technology, MITI effectively guided the investment race to increase industrial capacity, productivity, and exports. Cartels, legal and de facto, minimized price competition, thus reducing one of the major risks of adopting large-scale new technology rapidly. Understandably, the industries cooperated with MITI policy most willingly and pursued their profitable market share-maximizing strategy, investing more and more to ensure that their capacity and productivity would continue to grow.

Principally because of the sustained large investment, the economy continued to grow steadily, increasing Japanese real income at a fast pace. As long as the economy was growing at more than 10 percent year after year, the policy makers were duly rewarded; the LDP repeated its electoral victories and MITI officers enjoyed power and prestige. All the problems created by MITI policy seemed insignificant compared to its accomplishments. Political opposition and critical economists could be ignored. Even the effectiveness and virtues of cartels were openly praised. The Antimonopoly Act was only a minor irritant, and its effects minimized by revisions and nonenforcement.

However, the honeymoon ended. The conditions that were necessary for the continued success of the MITI policy began to disappear in the mid-sixties. And it became clear in the early seventies that readily borrowable technology had been exhausted, structural problems had surfaced, and Japan's trading partners no longer welcomed a continuing flood of Japanese exports. The prices of petroleum and other raw materials took a sudden and steep climb. These developments marked the end of both the rapid growth period and the success of MITI policies.

As the growth rate suddenly decelerated, the problems and consequences of this policy that had long been ignored or tolerated grew in magnitude. It was no longer possible to deny that cartels beget more cartels, and that an increasing number of them were having a negative effect on the economy. But MITI could not and did not reverse its policy. It continues to permit and encourage cartels, even though these cartels now not only rob the vitality of the economy, but also impose costs on consumers and taxpayers. Also, MITI policy, directly and indirectly, continues to magnify frictions between Japan and its major trading partners.

My intent is to stress that the Japanese guidance and procartel policy, which was once effective under the unique conditions of the 1950s and 1960s, is no longer justified. Worse still, it cannot but be detrimental to the interest of the economy when most Japanese industries have reached the frontier of technology and exports can no longer grow as rapidly as they once did.

These facts are extremely significant because they mean that the United States must neither emulate "the highly rational and sophisticated" Japanese economic policy, nor create, in effect, an American MITI. Those who advocate that we follow the Japanese model obviously have only an inadequate understanding of both the unique set of economic (and political) conditions that made the MITI policy successful and the costs of the policy. This criticism applies not only to those who are promoting their own narrow self-interest but also to the scholars who specialize in the study of Japan.

To cite an example, Ezra Vogel, the author of *Japan as Number One,* has in effect urged Americans to create a MITI of their own. Though long, the following excerpts from his book are perhaps not out of place here:

> The ministry that takes the greatest initiative in guiding industrial growth is MITI. MITI officials are so persistent in their efforts to look after the welfare of Japanese industry that they are dubbed by their countrymen as *kyōiku mana,* over-anxious mothers who hover over their children and push them to study. They endeavor to push the pace of modernization ahead of market forces by setting high standards for modernization of plants and equipment and by promoting mergers of companies that lack the capital to meet those standards. They boldly try to restructure industry, concentrating resources in areas where they think Japan will be competitive internationally in the future. . . .
>
> MITI officials consider it their responsibility to assist companies in declining industries to merge or go out of business while encouraging new ones to move into the localities and employ the personnel who were laid off. If conditions are not serious enough to shut down a whole industry, they work out a "depression cartel"; agreement among companies in a depressed sector to reduce production capacity, with the reduction distributed relatively equally among the companies. . . .
>
> MITI relegates to itself the right to enunciate very detailed rulings about what companies can and cannot do, but it does so only with a broad base of support from leading firms in an industrial sector. . . . it is allowed to form depression and modernization cartels, albeit with some counterpressures from the Fair Trade Commission; it controls some research expenses; and it grants approval to licensing agreements and to companies that affiliate with foreign companies. But overwhelmingly the success of the ministry is derived not from statutory rules but from its efforts at administrative guidance and from the voluntary cooperation of the business community. [Vogel 1975, pp. 72-73]

In light of the arguments presented in this essay, the fundamental misconception and naïveté involved in Vogel's observations are painfully evident. He failed to realize that the virtues and strengths of MITI, which he so unqualifiedly praised, were like a potent drug that is effective only at the cost of serious and lasting side effects, one of which is inevitable addiction. Vogel only described the positive effects seen during the fifties and sixties and ignored the serious and already visible consequences of addiction to guidance and cartels. In short, for Vogel to suggest that we emulate the Japanese was advising Americans to take the wrong medicine at the wrong time.

I would also like to add a few brief comments on several "strengths" and the "uniqueness" of the Japanese economy admired by many "experts." First, the most frequently mentioned of such "superior" qualities is the close cooperation between government and business. And this cooperation, already clearly inferred by Vogel, is invariably contrasted to the "adversary" (and presumably inferior) relationship that is thought to prevail in the United States.

It should be noted that this is basically the same cooperation that many criticized as Japan Inc. only a decade earlier and that existed in the rapid growth period because under the existing conditions, the industries had every reason to welcome MITI's coordination of the investment race.[31] But, as I stressed, by the seventies the economic conditions had changed. MITI must now preside over the painful process of reducing productive capacity in many industries, and must wield its power to guide reluctant firms to join a cartel. MITI's carrot has become distinctively less palatable and its stick more visible. Under present circumstances, cooperation is more forced than willing, and signs of discord between MITI and industries have already appeared. To suggest that we emulate the Japanese cooperativeness is to fail to see both why it existed and why it has become much more difficult to achieve.[32]

Second, it is frequently argued that Japanese management, in contrast with its American counterpart, takes a far-sighted view of business, that is, it invests with future profits instead of a quick gain in mind; and that given the long gestation period required of successful large industrial ventures, the Japanese management is superior to that of most American firms.[33] In making such an observation, few note that for the large firms that had long been engaged in a guided investment race with minimum risk, it was only rational (profitable) to make far-sighted business decisions. They were able to take advantage of the declining long-run cost curve by successively adopting large-scale new technology and, with the MITI coordination and cartels, they could maximize their market share and profits by making long-term decisions that had little risk of turning out to be "wrong" decisions. Now, however, most Japanese firms facing economic conditions increasingly similar to those in the United States, are being forced to shorten the time horizon of their decision making. I should also add here that the oft-made statement that "Japanese maximize market share and not profit" is based on the failure to understand that the market share-maximization strategy was also profit maximizing during the rapid growth period.[34]

Third, the loyal employees of large firms can no longer be expected to remain as seemingly docile and motivated as before. Their jobs are no longer as secure as they were. As the investment race has ended, firms are reluctant to be saddled with large fixed costs, and many are now forced to

31. It is interesting to note that one former high ranking officer of MITI acknowledged that Japan in the past was Japan Inc. and the U.S. government-business relationship is adversary. In his words, "It is more accurate to view the relationship between the government and private enterprise [in the United States] in general as an adversary one. Such a relationship is no more desirable than the extremely close relationship which prevailed in the past within Japan Inc." (Namiki 1979, p. 26).

32. I am aware that in discussing the government-business relationship in Japan historical and cultural factors need to be considered. However, my view is that such factors tend to be overemphasized.

33. Fallows 1980, pp. 44-45, for example, quotes American executives and Senator Bentsen, who in effect argue the point made in the text.

34. This statement is made most frequently by American business executives.

engage in an "operation scale down" even if it means to fundamentally alter or gradually abandon the permanent employment system. Indeed, no careful observer can deny that it is being quietly transformed, along with its corollary "seniority wage" system.[35] It is too early yet to predict whether or not these developments will in time change the Japanese labor-management relationship and make it more similar to that found in Western nations.[36] This is a complex subject that needs to be analyzed carefully, with various political and sociocultural characteristics of each nation being taken into consideration.

What we can say is that the Japanese economy, which now closely resembles ours (i.e., it is growing slowly, forced to create its own frontiers of technology, facing uphill battles to promote exports, required to make riskier managerial decisions, and more concerned with short-run profits than long-run market share, etc.) will increasingly face problems familiar to Americans, although for many reasons they will not be identical.

Most of Japan's policies and managerial practices that once contributed to rapid growth cannot serve as a guide to U.S. economic policy or business executives. It is possible that some of them could be emulated to our advantage, but speaking broadly, we must be extremely cautious not to delude ourselves that the adoption of Japan's past policies would benefit the United States of the 1980s.

Here, I should emphasize that the most dangerous course would be to redefine our antitrust policy as some have suggested—that is, to weaken the antitrust acts by allowing legislative exemptions or by lax enforcement—with the hope of achieving the Japanese success of the fifties and sixties.[37]

35. See Murakami's essay in this volume for a further discussion of the observations made here.

36. Also note that real wages no longer rise rapidly and the effect of such developments has already injected and is expected to increase serious difficulties in the labor-management relationship in Japan.

37. To cite only a few examples, Givens and Rapp (1979, p. 104), a business consultant and a banker, wrote:

Our antitrust laws, and our interpretations of them, have been a major constraint for American companies competing for global market share. What began basically as economic theory has taken on a moral dimension. We tend to see these things in moral terms, as if government-business cooperation were somehow immoral and conspiratorial. If you think about it, there is absolutely no moral issue here at all. There is nothing moral or immoral about any particular degree of government-business cooperation, or lack thereof. Our adversary relationship between business and government is artificial, not natural.

A former secretary of transportation argued (Goldschmidt 1981, p. 9) that "As a matter of national priorities, for a specific period of time, we should focus our efforts and our capital first on preserving our industrial base and our jobs. [To do so,] *re-define our anti-trust laws*. Historically, we have defined the automobile market as national or even regional. Today, the source of competition is an international market. We must, therefore, re-focus our anti-trust laws so that we are not unwittingly hamstringing our domestic companies by refusing to recognize the international rules by which the competition plays." See also Thurow 1980, p. 146.

The most important lesson to learn from the Japanese experience is that a weak antitrust policy is more likely to rob the competitive vitality of the economy than to revitalize it. Nor should we hastily accept Vogel's prescription that the American antitrust legislation be "adjusted to encourage" both government-business cooperation and "flexible administrative procedure" in dealing with "monopolies and oligopolies." To follow such advice would lead us to emulate the Japanese administrative guidance with all the problems and consequences that I have stressed in this essay.

Furthermore, in redefining our antitrust statutes for the sake of increasing the competitive ability of American firms in the international market, there are additional questions we must ponder. What will occur in the trade relationship between the United States, with its redefined antitrust statutes, and Japan, which, in effect, has already redefined its antimonopoly policy to increase the international competitive ability of its firms? Will the competition between the two nations be on a more equal footing, thus desirable for the Americans, or for both parties? Should we not seriously consider the desirability of the world's two economic superpowers *not* adopting policies explicitly designed to increase the competitive ability of their firms? Will not the interest of both economies be better served if the United States redefines its antitrust statutes most cautiously, respecting the long-established spirit of these statutes, and Japan discontinues her procartel policies?

It will be unfortunate indeed if we see, in the coming decade, a Japan that fails to change its current procartel and proexport policies and a United States with its "MITI" and an antitrust statute redefined solely to increase exports. With today's troubled bilateral economic relations, one thing we do not need is the specter of two aggressive proexport policies, each guided by its own MITI, colliding in the Pacific. I raise these questions here hoping they will receive their due attention from those interested in revitalizing the American economy, and in economic harmony between Japan and the United States.[38]

I believe a desirable decision is for Japan to discontinue all administrative guidance that now restricts domestic competition and contributes to international trade conflicts. So long as guidance is practiced, even with its legally required reporting to the FTC, competition is likely to be restricted and strongly worded FTC warnings against bureaucratic guidance, which in effect promote price fixing (and maintain trade barriers), will continue to be issued.[39] Ideally, Japan can also go one step further and revise the Anti-

38. One question that must also be considered is, What would be the effects, political and economic, of a Japanese-style U.S. proexport policy toward the newly industrializing nations?

39. On February 5, 1981, the FTC warned that the problems of the principle of the Antimonopoly Act are involved when the administrative guidance "limits economic activities of the firms and restricts competition in markets." Accompanying the warning were the following explicit statements regarding the administrative guidance being made

monopoly Act to provide realistic opportunities for private (including consumer class-action) suits against illegal collusion, rigorously delimit the scope
of activities in which trade associations can engage, and adopt several provisions of the 1974 FTC proposal that failed to be incorporated in the 1977
revisions.

I do not underestimate the political and economic difficulties involved
in adopting these suggestions. However, collective resolve and political
courage to this end will result in significant dividends. The changes would
not only contribute to reducing domestic problems and the detrimental effects of current policies, but also be most useful toward eliminating or
decreasing the political and economic frictions between Japan and the
United States as well as European and other countries. Of course, I should
hasten to add that if we ask that such changes be made in Japanese policies
and practices, we must also endeavor to quickly minimize and eliminate
many of our own that are correctly regarded by the Japanese as protectionist.

Finally, I must stress that I am in no way arguing that the Japanese
policies discussed in this essay are the only important reasons for the enviable accomplishments of the postwar Japanese economy. They would not
have been possible were it not for Japan's industrious population, able business leaders, and numerous effective and foresighted policies. How significant a role the MITI policies played in Japan's growth is difficult to measure
because of the complexity of their effects and, in the final analysis, any such
estimate must contain the subjective judgment of each analyst.[40] Some would

---

"without legal foundations": (1) the administrative guidance made on price and output
to the trade associations tends to foster cartels and cannot be permitted under the Antimonopoly Act; (2) the same applies to the guidance issued to individual firms; and (3)
cartels, if they are to be permitted, must be authorized under the provisions of the Antimonopoly Act (such as recession cartels), *Asahi Shimbun*, Feb. 5, 1981, p. 1. *Asahi Shimbun* noted, on p. 9, that this warning is directed not only to MITI, but also to the Ministry of Welfare and the Ministry of Forestry and Fisheries that issue similar guidance to
drug manufacturers and the food industry, respectively.

40. As Hugh Patrick pointed out, in commenting on the original draft of this essay
at the symposium, this subjective judgment can be made more objective by undertaking a
careful quantitative study of the effects of the procartel policy. Such an undertaking will
be extremely difficult because of the analytical and empirical problems involved in
identifying and defining these effects, and because of the substantial difficulties that must
be faced in an effort to obtain pertinent information and data relating to extralegal
guidance cartels and to numerous cartellike behavior encouraged under the policy.
Despite these difficulties, such a quantitative study yet remains to be undertaken (as
is stressed in chap. 4).

Readers interested in a useful English source that made an important initial effort to
undertake a quantitative study of the effects of cartels are referred to the work of Caves
and Uekusa 1976. Although the authors' quantitative analysis was limited (vis-à-vis the
broader issues raised in this essay), they concluded their study of the government policy
toward industry by observing that "In the 1960s legal cartels covered about one-fifth of
Japanese manufacturing" and that:

argue, in both Japan and the United States, that these policies played virtually no role in the postwar economic success of Japan. These persons too are entitled to their views. If they believe this, however, there is all the more reason for the Japanese to abandon these policies as soon as possible and for the Americans not to emulate them.

---

competition is also sharply restricted in many important industries by the "administrative guidance" provided by the competent ministries, chiefly the Ministry of International Trade and Industry. Through a clandestine bargaining process, MITI pursues various goals related to market structure and performance: promotion of large scales in Japanese plants and firms, encouragement of the dissemination of new technology and minimization of its cost when purchased abroad, the overall expansion of certain industries, and the protection of Japanese producers from foreign competition and oligopolistic rivalry with one another. These goals are served, directly or obliquely, by MITI's promotion of collusive arrangements among oligopolistic sellers—especially in the installation of new capacity. Clearly, MITI has reduced the cost of new technology and may have speeded its dissemination. Our evidence suggests that its efforts to enlarge plant scales have been overdone, but some gains may have been obtained. Significant cost have been incurred in increased collusion and its consequences—allocative inefficiency, price inflexibility, and diversion of rivalry into nonprice channels. [P. 154]

REFERENCES

Ackley, G. and Ishi, H. 1976. "Fiscal, Monetary and Related Policies." In *Asia's New Giant: How the Japanese Economy Works*, ed. H. T. Patrick and H. Rosovsky. Washington, D.C., Brookings Institution.

Amaya Naohiro. 1974. "Dokkinhō kaisei shian ni hanron suru" [A rebuttal to the proposed revision of the Antimonopoly Act]. *Ekonomisuto* (November), pp. 36-45.

Ariyoshi Yoshiya. 1979. "Usagi no koya kara mita kokusai keizai" [International economics as seen from a rabbit hutch]. *Chūō kōron* (June), pp. 220-30.

Baba Masao. 1975. "Dokkinhō kaisei no kinkyūsei o uttaeru" [An appeal for the urgency of changing the Antimonopoly Act]. *Shūkan tōyō keizai*, February 12, pp. 20-26.

Bronfenbrenner, Martin. 1965. "Economic Miracles and Japan's Income Doubling Plan." In *The State and Economic Enterprises*, ed. W. W. Lockwood, pp. 523-53. Princeton, Princeton University Press.

——. 1966. " 'Excessive Competition' in Japanese Business." *Monumenta Nipponica* 21:114-24.

Campbell, John C. 1976. *Contemporary Japanese Budget Politics*. Berkeley and Los Angeles, University of California Press.

Caves, Richard, and Uekusa, Masu. 1976. *Industrial Organization in Japan*. Washington, D.C., Brookings Institution.

Economic Planning Agency. 1976. *Keizai hakusho* [White Paper on the economy]. Tokyo, MOF Printing Office.

Fair Trade Commission (FTC). See Kōsei Torihiki Iinkai.

Fallows, James. 1980. "American Industry: What Ails It, How to Save It." *Atlantic* (September).

Fukui Haruhiro. 1970. *Party in Power: The Japanese Liberal-Democrats and Policy-Making*. Berkeley and Los Angeles, University of California Press.

——. 1972. "Economic Planning in Postwar Japan: A Case Study in Policy Making." *Asian Survey* 12 (April):327-48.

Givens, William L., and Rapp, William V. 1979. "What It Takes to Meet the Japanese Challenge." *Fortune*, June 18.

Goldschmidt, Neil. 1981. "The U.S. Automobile Industry, 1980." A letter of transmittal to the president, January 18.

Henderson, Dan Fenno. 1973. *Foreign Enterprise in Japan: Laws and Policies.* Durham, University of North Carolina Press.

Hoshida Seiji. 1965. "Kyoku nōryoku kajō-ron o haisu" [A refutation of the excess capacity view]. *Tōyō keizai,* July 2, pp. 8-12.

Imai Ken-ichi. 1970. "Sangyō soshiki" [Industrial organization]. In *Kindai keizaigaku* [Modern economics], vol. 2, ed. H. Kumagai et al. Tokyo, Yuhikaku.

———. 1974. "Tekkō" [Iron and steel]. In *Nihon no sangyō soshiki,* ed. H. Kumagai, vol. 2.

———. 1975. "Dokkin kyōka de daikigyō taisei no henkaku o" [Toward the reform of the big business system by strengthening the antimonopoly policy]. *Ekonomisuto,* Feb. 11.

———, Imamura, N., and Komiya, R. 1975. "Dokkinhō kaisei seifu sōan no mondaiten (shinpojiumu)" [Problems in the tentative proposals to amend the Antimonopoly Act as presented by the government—a symposium]. *Kikan gendai keizai,* no. 17.

Iyori Hiroshi. 1975. "Sangyō seisaku gyōsei no rekishiteki hyōka to nokosareta kadai" [A historical evaluation of, and the remaining issues in, the industrial policy and administration]. *Kikan gendai keizai,* no. 20 (Winter), pp. 61-62.

Japan-U.S. Economic Relations Group. 1981. *Report of the Japan-United States Economic Relations Group* (January).

Johnson, Chalmers. 1975. "Japan: Who Governs? An Essay on Official Bureaucracy." *Journal of Japanese Studies* 2, no. 1:1-28.

Kazunori Echigo. 1974. "Dokkinhō kaisei shian no kihonteki nanten" [The basic weaknesses in the proposed revision of the Antimonopoly Act]. *Kigyō keiei kenkyū* (November).

Kirkpatrick, Maurine A. 1975. "Consumerism and Japan's New Citizen Policies." *Asian Survey* 15 (March): 234-46.

Komiya Ryutaro. 1974. "Dokusen kinshi-hō kaisei no kihon mondai" [The fundamental problems concerning the revision of the Antimonpoly Act]. *Kikan gendai keizai,* no. 17 (Winter), p. 14.

———, Sanekata, K., and Uekusa, M. 1975. "Dokkinhō kaisei no igi to kongo no hōkō (zadankai)" [The significance of and the future perspective on the revision of the Antimonopoly Act: A forum]. *Keizai hyōron* (May), pp. 6-38.

——— et al. 1977. "Kaden sangyō" [Electric home appliances industry]. *Kikan chūō kōron keiei mondai* (Summer).

Kōsei Torihiki Iinkai [Fair Trade Commission]. 1951-69. *Nenji hōkoku* [Annual reports].

———. 1971. Annual Report of 1970. Tokyo, FTC.

———. *Fukyō karuteru seido to sono unyō ni tsuite* [The recession cartel system and its use]. Tokyo, FTC.

Kumagai, H., ed. 1973, 1974, 1976. *Nihon no sangyō soshiki* [Industrial organization in Japan], vols. 1, 2, 3. Tokyo, Chūō kōronsha.

——— et al., eds. 1970. *Kindai keizaigaku* [Modern economics], vol. 2. Tokyo, Yuhikaku.

Misono, H. 1960. *Nihon no dokusen* [Monopolies in Japan]. Tokyo, Shibundō.

Ministry of International Trade and Industry (MITI). 1974. *Kenkyū kaihatsu oyobi gijitsu kōryū ni kansuru hōkokusho* [Report on the survey concerning research and development and the exchange of technology]. Tokyo, MITI.

Nakamura Takafusa. 1978. *Nihon keizai: Sono seichō to kōzō* [The Japanese economy: Its growth and structure]. Tokyo, Tokyo University Press.

———. 1980. "An Economy in Search of Stable Growth: Japan since the Oil Crisis." *Journal of Japanese Studies* 6, no. 1:155-78.

Namiki Nobuyoshi. 1977. "Gyōsei shidō no shūen—Nihon no seifu to minkan" [The end of the administrative guidance—the government and the private sector in Japan]. *Kikan gendai keizai,* no. 27 (Summer), p. 57.

Namiki Yoshinobu. 1979. "Nihon keizai no katsuryoku wa yomigaeruka?" [Will the vitality of the Japanese economy revive?]. *Ekonomisuto,* May 8, pp. 20-27.

Niino Kojiro. 1981. "Seichō seisaku no kōzai" [Success and failure of the progrowth policies]. *Ekonomisuto*, March 17, pp. 96-102.

Patrick, H. T., and Rosovsky, H., eds. 1976. *Asia's New Giant: How the Japanese Economy Works*, Washington D.C., Brookings Institution.

Pechman, J. A., and Kaizuka, K. 1976. "Taxation." In *Asia's New Giant: How the Japanese Economy Works*, ed. Patrick and Rosovsky. Washington, D.C., Brookings Institution.

Pempel, T. J. 1974. "The Bureaucratization of Policymaking in Postwar Japan." *American Journal of Political Science* 18 (November):63-79.

——, ed. 1977a. *Policy Making in Contemporary Japan*. Ithaca, N.Y., Cornell University Press.

——. 1977b. "Japanese Foreign Economic Policy: The Domestic Bases for International Behavior." *International Organization* 31 (Autumn):723-74.

Rohlen, Thomas. 1979. " 'Permanent Employment' Faces Recession, Slow Growth, and an Aging Work Force." *Journal of Japanese Studies* 5, no. 2:235-72.

Sakakibara Eisuke, and Noguchi Yukio. 1977. "Ōkurashō-Nichigi ōchō no bunseki" [An analysis of the dynasty of the Ministry of Finance—the Bank of Japan]. *Chūō kōron* (August), pp. 96-150.

Sanekata Kenji. 1975. "Dokkinhō kaisei mondai no hōritsuronteki sōkatsu" [A survey of legal views expressed on the problems relating to the revision of the Antimonopoly Act]. *Tōyō keizai*, July 26, pp. 43-47.

——. 1976. "Honenuki dokkinhō kaisei seifuan ni igiari" [Objections to the toothless government amendment proposal of the Antimonopoly Act]. *Tōyō keizai*, May 22, pp. 82-93.

—— et al. 1975. "Karuteru no tetteiteki kenkyū" [A comprehensive study of cartels]. *Kikan chūō kōron keiei mondai* (Fall).

Sato Kazuo, ed. 1980. *Industry and Business in Japan*. White Plains, N.Y., M.E. Sharpe.

Sato Seizaburo, Kumon Shumpei, and Murakami Yasusuke. 1977. "Datsu-hokafu jidai no tōrai" [The arrival of the post-Conservative vs. Progressive period]. *Chūō kōron* (February), pp. 64-95.

Saxonhouse, Gary. 1979. "Industrial Restructuring in Japan." *Journal of Japanese Studies* 5, no. 2: pp. 79-101.

Shibata Shohei. 1978. "Kaisei no ikisatsu to gaiyō" [A summary and background of the amendment of the Antimonopoly Act]. In *Kaisei dokusen kinshi-hō chishiki* [A guide to the amended Antimonopoly Act], ed. FTC. Tokyo, FTC.

Stockwin, J. A. A. 1975. *Japan: Divided Politics in a Growth Economy*. New York, W. W. Norton.

Takeuchi Hiroshi. 1978. "Kōzō fukyō hōan no hamon" [The effects of the Structural Recession Industries Act]. *Ekonomisuto*, March 7, pp. 16-25.

Thayer, Nathaniel B. 1973. *How the Conservatives Rule Japan*. Princeton, Princeton University Press.

Thurow, Lester. 1980. *The Zero-sum Society*. New York, Basic Books.

Uekusa Masu. 1977. "Nihon no dokusen seisaku—sono kaiko to tenbō" [The Japanese antimonopoly policy—a review and survey]. *Kikan gendai keizai*, no. 27 (Summer), pp. 112-31.

Ueno Hiroya. 1975. "Wagakuni sangyō seisaku no hassō to hyōka" [The reasons for, and an evaluation of, the industrial policy of Japan]. *Kikan gendai keizai*, no. 20 (Winter), pp. 6-38.

Vogel, Ezra F., ed. 1975. *Modern Japanese Organization and Decision Making*. Berkeley and Los Angeles, University of California Press.

——. 1979. *Japan as Number One*. Cambridge, Harvard University Press.

Wallich, H. C., and Wallich, M. I. 1976. "Banking and Finance." In *Asia's New Giant: How the Japanese Economy Works*, ed. Patrick and Rosovsky. Washington, D.C.,

Brookings Institution.

Yamamura Kozo. 1967. *Economic Policy in Postwar Japan.* Berkeley and Los Angeles, University of California Press.

——. 1975. "Structure Is Behavior: An Appraisal of Japanese Economic Policy, 1960-72." In *The Japanese Economy in International Perspective,* ed. Isaiah Frank, pp. 67-100. Baltimore, Johns Hopkins University Press.

A Technical Note on

Japanese Firm Behavior and Economic Policy

YASUSUKE MURAKAMI

KOZO YAMAMURA

THIS NOTE, which was originally written as a technical appendix to Mura-kami's and Yamamura's respective papers (chapters one and three), presents hypotheses concerning the basic rationale for the behavior of postwar Japanese firms and economic policies adopted by the Japanese government. After the symposium, we expanded the original version slightly for two reasons. One is that we believe the revised discussion as presented below can also provide useful background for reading Imai's and Noguchi's essays (chapters two and four). The second reason is that we wish to state more explicitly what further research is needed to better understand, within an analytically consistent paradigm, the behavior of Japanese firms and policies—the subjects of constant debate in American and Japanese efforts to minimize the trade frictions between their two nations.

AN ANALYSIS OF THE BEHAVIOR OF JAPANESE FIRMS

In examining the Japanese economic policies and performance and especially in evaluating the behavior of Japanese firms (or often both policies and firm behavior, i.e., the "unique" behavior patterns of Japanese firms in "Japan Inc.," etc.), it is frequently argued that the Japanese firms are "excessively" competitive because they maximize their respective market share (and not profits as such). Indeed, many Japanese government officials and business leaders and some economists (along with some American journalists and non-academic economists) explain the Japanese policies and firms behavior by offering an analysis that accepts or assumes that the Japanese firms maximize market share.

Thus, the purpose of this section is to establish analytically what explains the seeming market share maximizing (MSM) behavior of the Japanese firms and then to examine this behavior in the cases in which an industry is facing two different long-run average cost situations, that is, decreasing and increasing.

THE BASIC HYPOTHESIS CONCERNING MSM BEHAVIOR

Leaving a discussion of what motivates a firm to maximize market share to the next section, let us first specify analytically what we understand MSM behavior to mean. We believe that the MSM means that a firm maximizes its output subject to a minimum rate of profit (π) that it hopes to maintain, that is, max. output (X) subject to $(pX - wL - rK)/X = \pi$ where L is labor input; K, capital input; p, price of output; w, wage rate; r, rental cost of capital; and $X = f(L,K)$. Put differently, X is maximized subject to $p = (wL + rK)/X + \pi$ or average cost plus mark-up that we shall call "modified average cost" (or simply MAC).

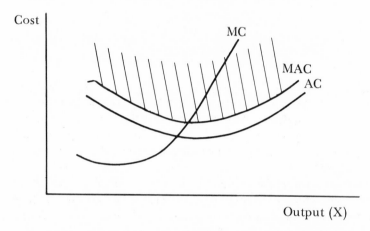

Fig. 4.1

In terms of figure 4.1, the above means that MSM is for a firm to produce its output on or above MAC. Of course, if K is fixed, MAC can be regarded as a short-run modified average cost curve (SMAC) and if K is variable, then MAC, as drawn, is a long-run modified average cost curve (LMAC). LMAC, of course, is an "envelope" of SMAC. The shaded area above MAC can be regarded as a supply zone for a firm pursuing the MSM strategy.

THE CASE OF INCREASING LONG-RUN AVERAGE COST

To better understand the implications of the MSM behavior, let us first examine and discuss the implications of the behavior in a situation where an industry faces an increasing long-run average cost. When long-run average cost is increasing, the relevant short-run average cost is also increasing. That is, both costs are rising and the distinction between long-run and short-run costs are immaterial. Thus, we believe, it is possible to deduce the following proposition:

As shown in figure 4.2, firms in an industry where costs are rising, that is, operating on a rising segment of MAC, the aggregate supply function of the

industry can be obtained by adding up individual firms' MAC curves hori-
zontally, provided that there is no entry into the industry. An equilibrium
within an industry where firms are pursuing MSM can be established at an
intersection (point Q) of a demand function (D) and the aggregated MAC
curve (ΣMAC). Furthermore, the equilibrium thus attained is stable.

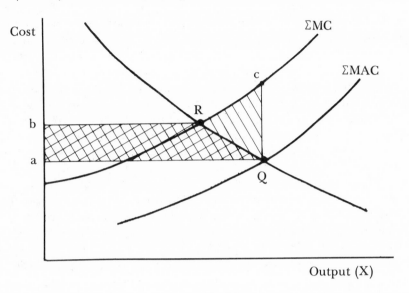

Fig. 4.2

Note that R is an equilibrium point when firms are maximizing profits
instead of market share. The area $bRcQa$ is the amount of the producers'
surplus reduced, and $bRQa$ is the amount of consumers' surplus increased,
both because of the MSM strategy. Thus, we are in effect advancing additional propositions: (i) *the total output under the MSM regime without*
entry is greater at the equilibrium than that resulting at the equilibrium
attained among the firms deciding their respective output based on profit-
maximizing strategy; and (ii) *the consumers' surplus is larger under the MSM*
regime and the producers' surplus is smaller than its counterpart under the
profit-maximizing regime.

An important observation to be stressed in the preceding is that when
MAC is increasing, the firms following the MSM strategy behave differently
from those maximizing profit in the observable ways just described.

The Case of Decreasing Long-Run Average Cost

Similarly, when firms are operating on the decreasing long-run average cost
curve (i.e., decreasing long-run AC, thus also decreasing long-run MAC), we
can also show that the aggregate industry supply consists of a sum of long-
run MAC curves of individual firms pursuing the MSM strategy. However, a
crucial fact to be noted is that an equilibrium reached can be an unstable one.

Furthermore, it is not difficult to see that in this case, *both the firms following MSM strategy and those pursuing profit maximization strategy will behave in the same manner.* This is so simply because, when average cost is falling and the market price of output is given, an individual firm can increase its profit by increasing output. A result is that all firms are anxious to supply output that is greater than the quantity they are now producing, provided that an increase in output can be obtained anywhere above the AC curve. This is to say, when AC curves are "added" up, we obtain the amount that all the firms in the industry wish to produce collectively. This simply means that *when faced with decreasing long-run average cost, both the profit-maximizer and the MSM firms behave in a virtually identical fashion and there is no need to distinguish the difference in their respective motivations. In both cases, the equilibrium reached will be unstable,* as expected of any decreasing cost industries. The point we wish to emphasize here is that profit-maximizing firm behavior is indistinguishable from MSM behavior.

POLICY IMPLICATIONS OF THE ANALYSIS

If we are correct in making the above analysis, its implications are significant in evaluating the Japanese economic policies and in analyzing the Japanese performance and policies vis-à-vis those of most other industrial economies, and especially those of the United States. To begin with, since we can reasonably argue that most manufacturing industries of Japan, during the period of rapid economic growth (the 1950s and most of the 1960s) faced a decreasing long-run average cost, the Japanese firms' behavior in these industries, while appearing to follow MSM strategy, was in fact following a profit-maximizing behavior. That is, their MSM strategy was a variant or a surrogate of profit-maximizing strategy.

Why, then, were the Japanese firms not only perceived to follow MSM strategy, but observed by many to have unique behavior because they behaved as if their primary goal was MSM and profit was secondary? The answer, we believe, is evident from our preceding analysis. The Japanese firms, during the period of rapid growth, continued to face a situation in which they could assume that the long-run average cost curve would continue to decline; thus they could behave as if MSM was their primary goal while maximizing their profits as well.

Their assumption of the decreasing long-run cost curve was justified for most industries during the period of rapid economic growth because Japan could continue to catch up with Western firms by taking advantage of readily available foreign technology. But the existence of borrowable technology was a necessary condition for the assumption. Sufficient conditions justifying the assumption included the rapid growth of domestic demand from the low 1945 level, the rapid expansion of world trade that was capable of absorbing Japanese output, and other favorable conditions, such as a sufficient quantity of trained or readily trainable labor, a high savings rate, a reliable supply of raw materials from abroad, and so forth.

And, no less significantly—we argue as a part of a "sufficient" condition for the assumption—the policies adopted by the Japanese government were important in reducing the remaining risk for firms of assuming that the long-run cost curve would be a decreasing one and adopting the MSM strategy. The administrative guidance and the policy to permit cartels acted as a useful coordinator of the firms' MSM strategy, thus preventing the unstable equilibrium from getting out of hand. Under the policy in effect, no firm would "bust" the market open for cutthroat price competition unduly and aggressively aggrandize one's relative market share in an industry by ignoring guidance or investment (why invite potential bankruptcies?). Note also, because of the policies adopted, legal and extralegal cartels (especially recession cartels) were effective in making necessary adjustments when collective errors were made (i.e., adopting too vigorous an MSM strategy, thus getting too far ahead of the demand). Furthermore, the policies relating to the market structure, capital market, monetary policy, and so forth, were also significant in enabling the firms to pursue the MSM strategy.

The analytically necessary assumption of "no entry" condition, too, was generally met during the period of rapid growth. Under MITI guidance and the policy adopted by the monetary authority, the already established large Japanese firms participating in the investment race were to be encouraged to grow as rapidly as possible. This meant that the policy to delay the liberalization measures was adopted to prevent imports to Japan from increasing too rapidly and also to discourage foreign entrants from adding productive capacity and/or output within the Japanese markets.

The foregoing raises an important question. Was the de facto intervention in the market by the Japanese government justified? (Or, did the policies, some of which we described above, contribute on balance more gains to the society than losses?) If we are to answer this question from the limited perspectives of economic analysis and the two decades following the end of the war, our answer is affirmative. During the period of rapid growth, the policies, we judge, enabled the Japanese firms to pursue, as rapidly as possible but in an orderly fashion, the gains that could be realized by "tracing" the respective decreasing long-run average cost curves of many major industries. The policies adopted effectively prevented the inherent instability of equilibrium from jeopardizing the orderly growth of innovative large firms. Thus, these policies were crucial, we believe, in helping the economy achieve rapid growth, a continued increase in real income, and a steady gain in productive efficiency that manifested itself in a steadily declining trend of the unit cost and price of output of the manufacturing industries during the period of rapid growth. We, of course, realize that this is a very broad assertion that needs to be qualified.

Two obvious qualifications immediately come to mind. One is that, as briefly discussed in both Murakami's and Yamamura's essays, the Japanese policies caused some foreigners, especially Americans, to perceive the Japanese economy as an effectively "coordinated" economy—Japan Inc.—that could aggressively market its products abroad. This perception continues to impose a significant political cost on Japan's efforts to achieve harmonious trade relationships with her trading partners, even well after the effective co-ordination has ceased to exist and Japan has liberalized her trade policies as much or more than some of her trade partners. This must be regarded as a cost of the Japanese policy pursued during the rapid growth period.

When we realize that such a perception is created in the minds of foreigners mainly because of the highly visible downpour of exports— spurts of rapid increases in Japanese exports, especially when Japan was suffering from periodic large excess capacity (often because of a recession)—we are led to conclude that the Japanese policies encouraging the MSM strategy need to be seen as a factor giving rise to such a perception.

The reason for this can be readily seen in figure 4.3. When the Japanese

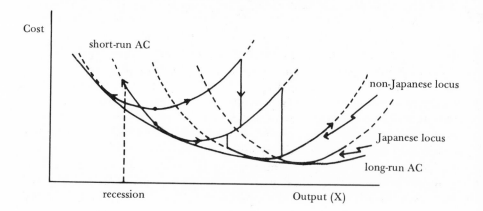

Fig. 4.3

firms find themselves having large excess capacity (because of recession or demand for the industry not rising as rapidly as anticipated), these firms tend to experience a rapid increase in average cost in comparison with less ambitious or more cautious non-Japanese firms that are not benefiting from a similar policy. To ease the pains (of reduced profits or even loss) of sharply rising average cost, the Japanese firms often resorted to both recession cartels and export drives, with the latter causing foreign competitors to make the accusation of Japan Inc.

The other qualification is what one may call the "legacies" of the policies that tend to remain after the policies are no longer pursued as before (and the difficulties involved in reversing or discontinuing them as Yamamura argued in his essay).

Returning again to our general assessment of the policies, we should stress that our evaluation of the policies differs sharply if and when the industries are facing a rising long-run average cost curve, because Japan caught up with the West, or because technological changes are not forthcoming. Even if new technology is available, the firms in an increasing number of industries may not be able to take advantage of new technology, if it is "lumpy" (and requires a sizable increase in output to realize cost reduction) and if, at the same time, demand is increasing only slowly because of a reduced growth rate of the domestic economy and/or international political reaction against the continuing growth of Japanese exports.

In this situation, policy intervention is unnecessary (as well as undesirable) because the equilibrium in an increasing long-run average cost case is stable, and because it will be far less likely for the Japanese firms to pursue the MSM strategy. In short, the policies that were once justified—controlled capital market, lax antitrust policy, and other policies along with administrative guidance—are no longer justifiable when the long-run average cost is increasing.

In light of the foregoing, we should indicate, in passing, one disagreement with the recent argument made by Amaya Naohiro, Iida Tsuneo, and others to the effect that some cartels (especially recession cartels) and generally lax antimonopoly policy continue to be needed because the Japanese firms are either excessively competitive or more competitive than firms in other nations for cultural and economic reasons. We believe such an argument is not based on an analytically sound understanding of the changing economic condition, that is, a shift from decreasing to increasing long-run average cost curves facing an increasing number of industries (Amaya Naohiro, "Dokkinhō kaisei shian ni hanron suru" [A rebuttal to the proposed revision of the Antimonopoly Act], *Ekonomisuto*, Nov. 19, 1974, and Iida Tsuneo, *Nihon-teki chikarazuvosa no saihakken* [A rediscovery of the Japanese strength] [Nippon keizai shimbunsha, 1979]).

A final interesting question remains. How correct are we in arguing as if the firms in other industrial nations, which must have faced similar decreasing long-run average cost curves, did not behave as did the Japanese firms (i.e., act as if they were following the MSM strategy)? Perhaps, in answering this question we should separate the United States and other Western nations.

Broadly stated, in the United States, the decrease that American firms could confidently expect in the long-run average cost curve was significantly more limited than for Japan, which was able to borrow new technology until very recently. Many American industries were near or at the frontier of technology until sometime in the 1960s (the timing depends on the industry, of course). No less important, even if the long-run average cost was decreasing, the U.S. firms did not have a coordinator in the form of MITI or any other agency to stabilize the market (i.e., to minimize errors made by MSM firms). And, any concerted self-policing of the collective MSM strategy would come into conflict with the much more stringent American antitrust statutes. Furthermore, the United States had no monetary policy encouraging established firms to expand capacity, her markets were wide open for foreign entrants and imports, and so forth. For the Americans, it was more rational not to assume the existence of decreasing long-run average cost and not to engage in an MSM strategy. Put differently, the above meant that the American firms were in effect facing, at any given time, a short-run increasing cost curve as shown in figure 4.4, and not a decreasing long-run average cost curve. Under the circumstances, there is little reason not to follow the profit-maximizing strategy.

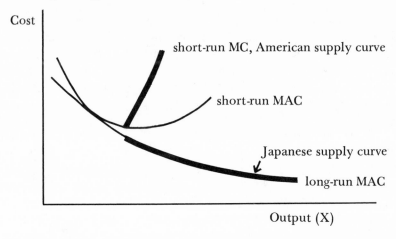

Fig. 4.4

Though only a speculation (due to our limited knowledge of Western European economies), we think that the Western European nations, especially West Germany, were closer to Japan than to the United States in economic conditions, especially vis-à-vis the expectation concerning the decreasing long-run average cost curve. (There is evidence that West Germany followed the economic policies that were much closer to those adopted by Japan than those of the United States, and the German firms were apparently more market-share conscious than were American firms.)

AGENDA FOR FURTHER RESEARCH

In writing our respective essays, and after discussing differing views held by Murakami and Yamamura in the symposium, we were made aware that numerous questions remain to be investigated. We will summarize some of these questions with the hope that they will receive the attention of interested specialists.

Among the many empirical studies needed, most directly pertinent and important in better supporting (or refuting) the analyses and observations contained in this note include: Can we empirically establish the hypothesized causal relationship between the degree and rapidity with which the average long-run cost could be reduced for an industry and the intensity with which firms in that industry pursued the MSM strategy? What criteria was in fact used in permitting a recession cartel? (Murakami's discussion in his paper tends to argue that these cartels were permitted in recessions. For him, such cartels were not seen in booms and came into being only in situations when the short-run average cost was rising rapidly for the firms in industries practicing such cartels. But in contrast, Yamamura argues that such cartels tended to be formed more liberally to stave off unprofitable price competition even when the industries in question were not necessarily experiencing a rapid increase in short-run average cost, i.e., not in a genuine recession [and this is the reason why the latter places quotation marks on the word recession].)

And how extensively did the MITI guidance and cartels of all types affect the behavior of the firms when measured quantitatively, for example, in terms of total output of the affected industries as a proportion of the total national industrial output? The answer to this question is crucial in determining the significance of the roles the policy played in enabling the firms to engage the MSM strategy as well as assessing the validity of the general tones apparent in Yamamura's paper and to a lesser extent in Murakami's (thus the differences in their views and the differences evident in the views expressed by Noguchi in his paper vis-à-vis especially those expressed in Yamamura's paper).

Finally, the only justification for presenting this note is to stress that an economic analysis such as attempted here is useful in elucidating the behavior of the Japanese firms and the reasons for the Japanese policies, and that noneconomic explanations for them should not be substituted for economic analysis in explaining what is essentially and primarily explainable in economic terms. All too often noneconomic analysis can be easily abused to misinterpret the reasons for the behavior of economic actors, and to justify the policies that no longer serve the interest of the majority of the population. And we are all familiar with the unnecessary burdens that are often imposed by frequently used, facile, noneconomic analysis on the American and Japanese efforts to reduce economic friction between their two nations.

The Government-Business Relationship in Japan:

The Changing Role of Fiscal Resources

ALTHOUGH THE GOAL of this essay is to examine the future of the government-business relationship in Japan, a considerable part deals with its past. I included this history because the view presented here is significantly different from the conventional one, and the difference is certainly relevant to prospects for the future.

One of the most popular views (especially among foreign businessmen) concerning the government-business relationship in Japan is that Japan as a whole is like a corporation (Japan Inc.), with the government serving as headquarters and each enterprise acting as a corporate division. According to this view, Japan's economic policy has been purposefully and skillfully administered through some sophisticated master plan formulated by elite bureaucrats of the central government. The followers of this view regard the above structure as the secret source of Japan's miraculous success in economic growth.

Also influential is the Marxist thesis of the "state-industrial complex," that the government is nothing but an organ established by capitalists to secure benefits for themselves. Thus its basic function is to exploit the people by means of heavy taxes and to serve the capitalists by providing funds for big enterprises.

Although advocated by entirely different groups of people, these theses are essentially the same in that they emphasize the close relationship between the government and large private enterprise and the existence of a deliberate conspiracy to control the economy. My basic point is that neither

I am grateful for the constructive comments given by participants of the conference, especially by Professors Kozo Yamamura (University of Washington) and Yasusuke Murakami (University of Tokyo).

the close relationship nor the deliberate conspiracy alleged by these views exists or has existed in Japan.

First, there is no group of able bureaucrats or greedy capitalists contemplating a comprehensive plan to manage the economy. The essential character of governmental decisions is anonymity, that is, decisions are the results of organizational processes.[1] It seems that most governmental decisions in Japan can be explained by the Cyert-March organizational model or Wildavsky's disjointed incrementalism model (Campbell 1977; Noguchi 1979; Noguchi et al. 1979), which emphasize the suboptimal nature of organizational decisions—such things as sectionalism, persistent inertia, and short-sightedness. Thus Allison's remark (1971) that many governmental decisions that cannot be explained by the classical rational model *can* be explained by the Cyert-March-Wildavsky model also applied to Japan.

Second, in decisions where political pressure is effective, it works in favor of rural areas and low-productivity sectors such as agriculture, small-scale firms, or declining industries. There are two interrelated reasons for this bias: most politicians find a firm base for their votes in rural areas and small-scale firms and these regions or industries need political assistance. Advanced sectors of the economy are able to grow through their own efforts, and government intervention is usually an obstacle to their growth, after a self-sustained growth process takes place. Thus, resource allocation in the General Account of the national budget has been heavily biased toward rural areas and low-productivity sectors of the economy. This is strong evidence against the "Japan Inc." and "state-industrial complex" views.

My concern is with the government-business relationship from a macro point of view. Specifically, I shall discuss the magnitude and composition of the resources allocated by governmental decisions. In a broad sense, such allocation is not only direct (i.e., allocation of resources raised by the government through such measures as taxes, social security contributions, and public borrowing) but also indirect (i.e., private resource allocations affected by various government controls and regulations that are *not* accompanied by subsidies or preferential government loans). It is on the direct allocation that I shall concentrate.

It may be argued that this approach overlooks an important aspect of the government-business relationship in Japan. In particular, it may disregard the administrative guidance (*gyōsei-shidō*) conducted by MITI (Ministry of International Trade and Industry) and other agencies. In response, I wish to point out that although administrative guidance may have been important in the early stages of rapid growth, it lost its importance or even

---

1. In this respect ex-premier Kakuei Tanaka, who many people believe to be the person behind all political decisions in Japan, has made a very interesting statement. In a recent interview he stated that no matter who becomes president of the Liberal Democratic party (LDP), there will be little difference in its decisions because these are made not by individuals but by the organization as a whole. See S. Tawara's interview with Kakuei Tanaka in *Bungeishunjū*, Feb. 1981.

became nonexistent in the sixties.[2] This is especially true for the import quota, which was abolished in the early sixties. Some administrative guidance still exists, but its importance is limited to rather special industries such as iron and steel.

If government regulations are to be discussed, one should consider regulations and controls in the financial sector (restrictions in the capital market and in foreign exchange transactions, and regulation of banks' operations). Although their importance will diminish in the future due to liberalization in the capital market and in foreign exchange transactions, the importance of government regulations in the rapid economic growth era should never be dismissed. However, this topic is not discussed in this essay.[3]

THE ROLE OF PUBLIC FINANCE IN THE RAPID GROWTH ERA

THE GENERAL ACCOUNT BUDGET

Immediately after World War II, the national budget played a straightforward role in the reconstruction of the economy by providing subsidies to basic industries. In fiscal year 1946, approximately 20 percent of the national budget was allocated to industry-related expenditures, including subsidies to commercial banks for their reconstruction. In 1947, the so-called Priority Production Policy *(keisha seisan hōshiki)* was initiated, whereby reconstruction of such strategic industries as coal, electric power, and iron and steel were given top priority. To implement this policy, the national budget subsidized the difference between the regulated product price and actual cost. Since the difference amounted to 30 to 40 percent of the total cost, the amount of the subsidy became enormous, almost one quarter of the total budget in fiscal year 1947. The policy was successful in that basic industries achieved remarkable reconstruction, but at the same time, it caused hyperinflation in the economy. The basic role of public finance in this period was therefore exactly that envisioned by Marxist doctrine: to provide resources to strategic industries by raising funds from the public through taxes and inflation.

The public finance system was changed drastically in 1949 when the "Dodge line" was introduced. In accordance with a policy recommendation by an American banker, Joseph Dodge, the Allied forces impelled the Japanese government to terminate subsidies to industries and to balance the budget. The immediate objective of the Dodge line was to bring inflation under control, but the adoption of a tight budget policy had the effect of reformulating the basic fiscal-monetary framework of the Japanese economy. Since that time, direct provision of funds from the national budget to

2. A symbolic event was the abortion of the law for promoting specific industries (usually called *tokushinhō)* in 1963.

3. For recent related developments, see the essays by Hamada and Makin included in this volume.

leading industries has been terminated, and the financial sector has taken over this role. The national budget began providing aid to low productivity sectors and regions that could not keep up with the rapid expansion of the economy.[4]

This can be seen in the figures of table 5.1. The major expenditures of

TABLE 5.1

MAJOR EXPENDITURES OF THE GENERAL ACCOUNT BUDGET
(Share in percentage)

	1955	1965	1970	1975
Grants-in-aid to local governments	15.8	19.3	21.6	16.3
Defense	13.3	8.2	7.2	6.6
Public works	14.4	18.7	16.2	14.3
Industry related	6.0	8.5	11.8	11.6
(agriculture)		(3.5)	(5.0)	(4.4)
Social security	13.6	17.0	15.8	21.7
Government employees' pension	8.5	4.2	3.6	3.6
Education	12.5	12.8	11.4	12.6

SOURCE: Ministry of Finance 1980

the General Account of the national budget since 1955 have been grants-in-aid to local governments *(kofu-zei)*, social security, and public works. These expenditures can be regarded as direct or indirect subsidies to low productivity sectors or rural regions.

Grants-in-aid is a direct measure for equalizing regional income differences by distributing a certain percentage of the central government's taxes to local governments according to their fiscal needs. The percentage, which was 20 percent in 1955, was raised repeatedly to the rate of 32 percent in 1968. The share of this expenditure rose continuously throughout the rapid growth era. Table 5.2 shows the interregional redistribution through grants-in-aid and national subsidies.[5] For urban regions such as Kanto, Tokai, and Kinki, the amount of grants-in-aid and national subsidies is less than the national tax revenue raised in the region. The situation is reversed for rural regions.

Social security expenditures are a direct measure for equalizing individ-

4. Special treatment *(sozei tokubetsu sochi)* in corporation taxes can be regarded as a subsidy to industries. However, the amount of tax revenue reduced by the treatment was not large; in fiscal year 1955 the amount was 15.9 percent of the corporation tax, or 3.1 percent of the total budget. The amount decreased significantly after the mid-1960s and is almost nil in recent years.

5. Corporation tax is excluded from the figures in column A. This adjustment is made to see the "net" redistribution effect of the grants-in-aid system. Similar adjustments are made in columns D and F.

TABLE 5.2

Interregional Redistribution through Grants-in-aid and National Subsidies

(In thousand million yen and %)

Regions	National Taxes (A)	Local Taxes (B)	Total (A)+(B)=(C)	Grants-in-aid (kofu-zei) (D)	Grants-in-aid (joyo-zei) (E)	National Subsidies (F)	Total (D)+(E)+(F)=(G)	(G)/(A)
Fiscal year 1970								
Hokkaido	1,318	1,345	2,672	852	68	1,441	2,361	179.1
Tohoku	2,183	2,438	4,666	2,013	176	2,676	4,865	222.9
Kanto	18,372	14,363	32,735	1,572	200	4,005	5,777	31.4
Tokai	5,327	4,901	10,228	575	113	1,611	2,299	43.2
Hokuriku	652	904	1,556	395	42	656	1,093	167.6
Kinki	9,700	7,724	17,424	909	151	2,590	3,650	37.6
Chugoku	2,437	2,234	4,671	834	114	1,414	2,362	96.9
Shikoku	696	915	1,611	679	59	943	1,681	241.5
Kyushu	2,517	2,628	5,145	1,924	163	3,032	5,119	203.4
Total	43,201	37,507	80,708	9,752	1,087	18,369	29,208	67.6
Fiscal year 1975								
Hokkaido	3,073	3,177	6,250	2,389	208	3,993	6,590	214.4
Tohoku	5,077	5,707	10,784	5,289	376	7,340	13,005	256.2
Kanto	38,814	31,258	70,072	4,324	525	11,557	16,406	42.3
Tokai	10,677	10,083	20,760	1,617	259	5,156	7,032	65.9
Hokuriku	1,490	1,934	3,424	1,053	88	1,741	2,882	193.4
Kinki	18,373	15,737	34,110	2,793	329	7,656	10,778	58.7
Chugoku	4,800	5,010	9,810	2,200	225	4,303	6,728	140.2
Shikoku	1,808	2,110	3,918	1,792	120	2,977	4,889	270.4
Kyushu	5,989	6,533	12,522	5,717	351	9,533	15,601	260.5
Total	90,101	81,548	171,649	27,174	2,482	54,258	83,914	93.1
Fiscal year 1980								
Hokkaido	4,693	4,959	9,652	2,683	300	6,190	9,173	195.9
Tohoku	7,578	9,023	16,610	5,644	526	11,391	17,561	231.7
Kanto	56,280	47,220	103,500	5,550	865	17,537	23,952	42.6
Tokai	15,506	14,990	30,496	2,453	421	7,411	10,285	66.3
Hokuriku	2,163	2,877	5,040	1,249	121	2,599	3,969	183.5
Kinki	24,842	22,617	47,459	3,967	513	11,417	15,897	64.0
Chugoku	6,890	7,163	14,053	2,815	303	6,554	9,672	140.4
Shikoku	2,622	3,232	5,856	2,026	163	4,596	6,785	258.8
Kyushu	9,228	10,279	19,507	6,239	492	14,710	21,441	232.3
Total	129,801	122,371	252,172	32,626	3,704	82,405	118,735	91.5

ual income differences, and the share of this expenditure increased remarkably in the early sixties and seventies. The following points should be noted,
however. First, if expenditures for government employees' pensions *(onkyū)*
are included, their share of the total budget stayed almost at a constant
level until the early seventies. That is to say, the share of social security
expenditures in a broader sense did not show remarkable increase during the
rapid growth era. Second, almost one half of the social security expenditures
were for medical expenses, reflecting the heavy bias of Japanese social
security benefits toward medical care.[6] Third, although the system has improved, actual payments stayed at a relatively low level due to the im-
maturity of pension programs and the age structure, which is tilted toward
younger segments. Income differences caused by the unbalanced growth of
industries in the rapid growth era have been equalized, not by social security
programs but by industry-oriented subsidies, which will be mentioned later.

Public works expenditures do not directly aim at equalizing income differences, but since allocations to public works were relatively concentrated
in rural regions, there was also the effect of equalizing regional income
differences. Table 5.3 shows the regional allocation of public works. Both

TABLE 5.3

REGIONAL ALLOCATION OF PUBLIC WORKS
(In 10,000 yen)

Regions	Per Capita Government's Investment			Per Capita Subsidy for Local Public Works		
	1970	1975	1978	1970	1975	1978
Hokkaido	8.2	21.9	32.8	1.6	3.7	6.6
Tohoku	5.4	16.6	27.4	1.2	2.9	5.1
Kanto	5.8	13.9	18.7	0.6	1.3	2.1
Tokai	5.5	12.7	17.8	0.7	1.7	2.9
Hokuriku	6.4	17.2	25.2	1.3	3.0	5.0
Kinki	5.9	14.5	18.2	0.8	1.7	2.7
Chugoku	5.1	15.0	23.0	1.0	2.6	4.5
Shikoku	5.8	15.5	24.0	1.1	3.0	5.7
Kyushu	4.8	14.0	22.4	1.0	2.8	5.0
Average	5.7	14.8	21.2	0.9	2.1	3.5

in terms of per capita government investment and per capita subsidy for
local public works, the figures for rural regions such as Hokkaido, Tohoku,
and Hokuriku are significantly higher than those for Kanto, Tokai, and Kinki.

Industry-related expenditures share about 10 percent of the total budget.
Unlike the years before the Dodge line, however, most of this expenditure

6. In recent years, social pension expenditures have increased rapidly. As a result,
the share of medical expenses has become less than 50 percent (it was 43.7 percent in
fiscal year 1980).

is in subsidies to low productivity sectors such as agriculture and small-scale firms. It should be noted that the relative share of agricultural subsidies has increased since the late sixties, when the productivity difference between agriculture and manufacturing became apparent and the agricultural population began to decrease rapidly. Since industry-specific subsidies are concentrated and "visible," they were important in maintaining social stability by diminishing the gap between the modern leading sector and the traditional low productivity sector, at least politically and psychologically.

To summarize, the basic function of the national budget in the rapid growth era was not in fostering economic growth but in adjusting distortions caused by the imbalance of the rapid growth. Funds were supplied to leading industries not through the national budget but through the financial sector. That is, savings of the household sector were channeled into the modern industrial sector through the workings of the financial mechanism. The macroeconomic conditions that enable this type of resource allocation to occur are large and spontaneous savings in the household sector, and a government sector that is not operating under a deficit.

This second condition is equivalent to saying that the total government expenditure (the sum of government investments, government consumption, and transfer payments) does not exceed *current* government revenue (the sum of tax revenue and social security contributions). After adopting a balanced budget policy in 1949, the basic character of the Japanese fiscal sector continued along this line until the mid-seventies. The General Account of the national budget followed the balanced budget policy strictly until 1964. It has been under a deficit since fiscal year 1965, but the average deficit/expenditure ratio remained at a relatively low level of 10.4 percent between 1965 and 1974, as seen in table 5.4.

The main factor in creating a low expenditure level was the light burden of social security and defense expenditures. I have already remarked that the social security system in Japan has not reached maturity. Reflecting this, the ratio of transfer payments to national income was 5.8 percent in Japan, compared to 11.1 percent in the United Kingdom and 15.5 percent in West Germany (fiscal year 1970).[7] Defense expenditures were also very low. The ratio of defense expenditures to GNP was 0.9 percent in Japan, far lower than the United States with 5.0 percent and West Germany with 3.4 percent (fiscal year 1979).

THE FILP

As has been argued above, the major role of the General Account Budget in the rapid growth era was assisting the low productivity sector of the economy to adjust income discrepancies caused by economic growth. A con-

---

7. In recent years, the gap has been decreasing. In fiscal year 1976, the ratio was 10.6 percent in Japan, 13.5 percent in the United Kingdom, and 20.4 percent in West Germany.

TABLE 5.4

DEFICIT/EXPENDITURE RATIO OF THE GENERAL
ACCOUNT OF THE NATIONAL BUDGET

Fiscal Year	Ratio (%)
1966	14.9
1967	13.8
1968	7.7
1969	5.9
1970	4.2
1971	12.4
1972	16.3
1973	12.0
1974	11.3
1975	25.3
1976	29.4
1977	32.9
1978	31.3
1979	35.4
1980	33.5
1981	26.2

siderably different role has been performed by the Fiscal Investment and Loan Program (FILP), a unique system of government-operated financing. Although the FILP is a fairly complicated program, its basic function is providing financing through the Trust Fund (Unyōbu Shikin) to various government-affiliated agencies, such as the Japan National Railways (JNR), the Japan Highway Corporation, the Japan Development Bank (JDB), the Export-Import Bank of Japan (EIBJ), and the Small Business Finance Corporation (today more than forty agencies receive Trust Fund financing). The main sources of the Trust Fund are postal savings and the reserve funds of pensions. In fiscal year 1980, the increment in the fund, the amount newly allocated to these agencies, was 14.9 trillion yen, or about one-third of the General Account Budget.

In the years before World War II, these funds were accumulated in the Deposit Fund (Yokinbu) and were used mainly for the purchase of government bonds. Because government bonds were not issued in postwar decades, it was possible to allocate the funds directly to various government-affiliated agencies, most of which were established in the fifties. In this sense, the balanced budget policy of the General Account Budget was the basis of the FILP.

The Trust Fund financing played a strategic role in the rapid economic growth, especially in the fifties. First, it provided preferentially low-interest funds to heavy industries and export industries through such government-affiliated banks as the JDB and the EIBJ. Table 5.5 indicates that in the early stage of rapid economic growth, almost 30 percent of funds supplied to

TABLE 5.5

SOURCES OF FUNDS TO INDUSTRIES
(Percentage share)

	1952-55	1956-60	1961-65	1966-70	1971-75
All Industries					
Capital market	11.9	21.6	17.8	11.2	12.2
Private banks	59.8	60.7	66.4	73.7	74.2
FILP	28.3	17.7	15.8	15.1	13.7
JDB	13.3	4.6	4.2	3.9	3.6
Others	15.0	13.1	11.6	11.2	10.0
Four Basic Industries					
Capital market	6.5	24.9			
Private banks	56.3	53.8			
FILP	37.2	21.3			
JDB	24.1	10.4			
Others	13.1	10.9			

SOURCE: Ishikawa and Gyoten 1977

industry came from the FILP. In the four basic industries (electrical power, shipping, coal, iron and steel) the share was as high as 40 percent, most of which was loans from the JDB. Aside from such quantitative importance, these funds helped extract loans from private banks, because in the early stage of economic growth when risks were high, loans from the government-affiliated banks served as guarantees. Second, the Trust Fund financed the construction of infrastructures that formed the basis for economic growth. This was done by such government-affiliated agencies as the JNR and the Japan Highway Corporation.

It is interesting to note the different function of the General Account Budget and the FILP. The FILP fostered growth while the former made the political "distortion-adjustment." One reason for this differentiation can be found in the different decision-making processes. As in other countries, the General Account Budget is subject to the Diet's approval, which implies that it is sensitive to political pressures. Since political pressures usually work in favor of rural areas and low productivity industries such as agriculture and small-scale firms, rather than in favor of urban areas and big corporations, the heavy bias in the General Account Budget reflects such pressures. On the other hand, the FILP was not subject to the Diet's approval until 1972, which was one of the reasons it was able to foster growth.

It was argued in the previous section that the General Account Budget fostered growth only in the sense that by restricting the size of the budget it created a macroeconomic environment that favored growth. It must be noted that there were virtually no judgments concerning individual firms at the government level. These judgments were left to the private sector. A similar situation existed in the FILP. The judgment made at the govern-

ment level—that is, the allocation of the Trust Fund to various agencies—
was fairly broad, and detailed judgments were left to such agencies as the
JDB or the EIBJ. It might be argued that some kind of administrative
guidance was given by MITI and other agencies, or even that the JDB or
the EIBJ are nothing but a part of government in its broad definition. An
important point is that in spite of the above, it is true that the system is
characterized by decentralization of decision-making. In an environment
where fundamental conditions are stable, such a system can be regarded as
ideal because it is best suited to making fine adjustments to small changes in
the environment. However, once basic conditions begin to change, it per-
forms badly due to an inability to alter its basic character. In the next section we will see that this is in fact happening.

THE CHANGING STRUCTURE

Deficit in the General Account

Although the basic feature of the General Account of the national budget
was its small size, a fundamental change has been taking place in recent
years. Since the oil crisis, the General Account has been suffering from a
huge deficit. The deficit as a proportion of total government expenditures
has been continuously above 25 percent since fiscal year 1975.

Some people argued that the deficit was only cyclical and would automatically disappear if economic activities returned to the normal level. This
has turned out to be untrue. In spite of a recovery in economic activities in
recent years, the deficit remains large. Still other people attribute the deficit
to expansionary fiscal policies aimed at helping the economy recover from
the depression caused by the oil crisis. This is not valid either; the deficit
developed before an expansionary fiscal policy was adopted in fiscal year
1977. Although it is true that the expansionary policy has increased the
deficit, its contribution was quite marginal.[8]

The deficit must therefore be regarded as a reflection of a more fundamental structural change. In my view such a change was caused by easy
fiscal management in the years preceding the oil shock. Reflecting vigorous growth of the economy, tax revenue grew remarkably rapidly in the
early seventies, as is apparent in the rise in the ratio of tax revenue to GNP
(fig. 5.1). The continued favorable fiscal condition considerably loosened
budgetary decisions. In particular, there were remarkable advances in the
social security system. Many new programs were introduced and the payment levels in various programs were substantially upgraded. Examples are
the initiation of a children's allowance (1971) and free medical services for
the elderly (1972), improvement in medical insurance benefits (1973),
initiation of allowances for expensive medical services (1973), improvement
in the old-age pensions (1973).

8. There are disputes as to whether the expansionary policy was effective. Here I
am not discussing such macroeconomic problems.

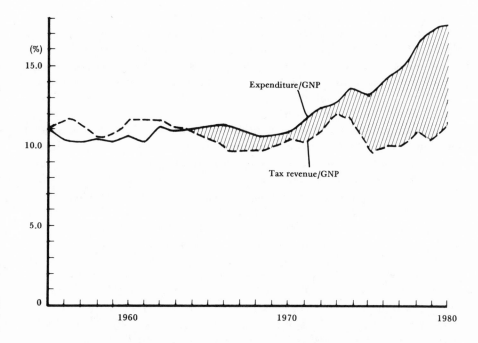

Fig. 5.1. Tax revenue and expenditure of the General Account Budget

Needless to say, budgetary authorities are usually cautious in allowing increases in expenditures, especially true for social security expenditures because they are irreversible—that is, it is virtually impossible to abolish programs once initiated or to downgrade payment levels once upgraded. Thus a decision to improve the social security system is made only if fiscal conditions are expected to be favorable for the foreseeable future. In the early seventies, many people believed that such a condition existed.[9]

Ironically enough, the oil shock came immediately after such decisions were made. Due to a depression caused by the oil shock, tax revenue fell drastically in fiscal year 1975, which increased the deficit. It is important to note, however, that in terms of the ratio of tax revenue to GNP, figures after the oil shock are not necessarily lower than those in the sixties (see fig. 5.1). Figures for the early seventies should be regarded as abnormal from a long-run point of view. In this sense, the decisions may be regarded as shortsighted.

In principle, there are two alternatives for reducing a deficit. One is to cut expenditures, the other to increase tax revenues. The first is an off-

9. An analysis presented in Noguchi (1980a) shows that increases in expenditures in the General Account Budget can be explained by a variant of Friedman's permanent income consumption function, where the rate of growth of each expenditure is explained by a weighted average of fiscal surpluses in past years.

setting strategy, or a choice to maintain a small government. The second may be termed an accommodating strategy, or the way toward big government. It seems that we have already proceeded in the latter direction.[10]

In 1978 the report of the Tax Council (Zeisei Chōsakai) had already concluded that to reduce the deficit a substantial tax increase was inevitable, and it proposed introduction of a general sales tax (a variant of the Value Added Tax of European countries).

Of course the road to tax increases is not an easy one. In the general election in 1979 the LDP suffered a serious defeat because of its sympathetic attitude toward the government's proposal of introducing a general sales tax. This is not surprising, however, because "a new tax is always a bad tax." Thus this election result does not necessarily deny the possibility of tax increases.

This was proved in the budget for fiscal year 1981; although no new taxes were introduced, considerable tax increases were made within the existing tax structure (the major increases were in the corporation income tax and stamp duty). Moreover, it was decided that no adjustments would be made to the income tax system, which has been unchanged since fiscal year 1977. Because of the progressive structure of the income tax, this in effect implies a considerable increase in tax revenue. As a result, the ratio of deficit to total government expenditures has fallen to 26.2 percent from the previous year's level of 33.5 percent.

That public opinion does not exhibit strong resistance to tax increases can be confirmed by opinion surveys I conducted with the assistance of the Nihon Keizai Kenkyū Sentā (Noguchi et al. 1980b). Surveys were taken twice (November 1979 and December 1980) of the following groups: (a) all members of the Diet, (b) executive businessmen, (c) economists, both academic and nonacademic, and (d) bureaucrats.

Table 5.6 summarizes the answers to a question that asks the pros and cons of tax increases. Most remarkable is that answer 3 (an unconditional "no" to tax increases) represents an apparent minority. If answer 2 is interpreted as a "conditional yes," about 90 percent of the people have affirmative (or at least nonnegative) attitudes toward tax increases. Note that

10. It may be argued that recently there has been some sign of change. One of the most notable developments is the establishment of the Council for Reorganizing Government Activities (Rinji gyōsei Chōsakai). The council will check every aspect of government activities and is expected to recommend abolishment of outdated subsidies and agencies. Prime Minister Suzuki is reported to have declared that reorganization of government activities (gyōsei kaikaku) is the most important political task of his administration and that he will stake his political life on a successful implementation of the council's recommendation.

It is difficult to judge at this stage whether the council could make any substantial recommendation and whether it could be implemented at all in the real world. However, one can say almost for certain that although a successful implementation of the recommendation might reduce government expenditures to some extent, no radical reformulation of the present public policies would be undertaken.

TABLE 5.6

PUBLIC OPINION ON TAX INCREASES
(Percentage shares)

	November 1979					December 1980				
	A	B	C	D	T	A	B	C	D	T
1	7.5	5.1	25.1	50.8	18.0	8.8	6.3	30.2	59.1	21.3
2	57.9	87.7	65.7	44.8	68.9	77.4	86.9	62.7	39.2	71.1
3	32.7	5.6	8.0	3.8	11.7	10.6	6.9	5.9	1.8	6.6
4	1.9	1.5	1.1	0.5	1.4	3.2	—	1.2	—	1.0

Answers: 1, "Should be done as soon as possible"; 2, "Inevitable, but must be examined with caution"; 3, "Should never be done"; 4, No answer
Groups: A, Members of the Diets; B, Executive businessmen; C, Economists; D, Bureaucrats; T, Total

no hostile attitudes can be observed in businessmen's answers. A comparison of the recent result with the previous one reveals another interesting fact: an apparent shift toward tax increases. The most significant change is observed among the politicians. By examining another question that asks for an interpretation of election results, it can be concluded that the change is mainly attributable to the defeat of the LDP in the fall 1979 election and the unexpected victory of the LDP in the spring 1980 election.

These results must of course be interpreted with great caution; they do not imply that the deficit can be easily diminished.[11] First, there is considerable diversification in answers to a question on increasing specific taxes (general sales tax, income tax, corporation tax, and others). Thus, although a consensus exists at a general and abstract level, there is none at a realistic level. Second, although the conditional affirmative answer 2 has been interpreted as representing an affirmative attitude, there could be a different interpretation if one emphasizes its conditional rather than affirmative part. In fact, cross-examination with another question reveals that those who chose answer 2 in this question strongly urge radical re-examination of present expenditure as a prerequisite to tax increases. Thus it may be concluded that unless there is significant rationalization of present expenditure, which is far from an easy task, no substantial tax increase can be realized. Third, even if a new tax (probably some version of a broadly based indirect tax) can be successfully introduced, it is probable that a reduction in income tax would be inevitable. If such a reduction is large, the deficit will not be diminished significantly.

In spite of these remarks, it is almost certain that the present structure of

11. In addition to what is mentioned in the text, it must also be noted that there is a significant bias in the sample in the sense that it consists of the elite of society. Their opinions may be different from those of the general public.

public expenditures will remain intact. As a result, expenditures will not be reduced even in terms of the ratio to GNP. In fact, a recent report of the Tax Council states that the target of medium-term fiscal management would be to maintain the ratio of General Account expenditure to GNP at the present level (it points out that even this would require considerable effort due to automatically increasing expenditures, such as interest payments on bonds and social security). This implies, in effect, that the ratio of General Account expenditure to GNP will increase by more than 50 percent compared to the level during the rapid growth era. (The ratio was in the range of 10 to 12 percent in fiscal years 1950 through 1973. In fiscal year 1980, the figure was 17.2 percent.)

It may be argued that an increase in the share of public expenditure is desirable from the point of view of the macrobalance, because it offsets the decline in the expenditures in the private sector, especially business fixed investments. It is true that if public expenditure is allocated to such areas as urban development, it will certainly improve the over-all resource allocation and will help the industrial structure change from its present export orientation to a domestic demand orientation. However, the present public expenditure is not structured in such a way and it is difficult to expect a radical change.

It may also be argued that even with this increase, the share of public expenditure to GNP is still lower than that of European countries, so that it is not the object of a hot debate. On the surface this is true, but the important point here is that policies adopted in the past remain intact, that we have chosen to increase the government's share without making any serious re-examination of the fiscal structure that was formed in the rapid growth era. The implication is quite profound if one takes into account inevitable future increases in social security expenditures.

SURPLUS IN THE FILP

At the very moment when the General Account Budget was suffering from a huge deficit, the FILP had a huge surplus. In fiscal year 1978, only 70 percent of the total planned expenditure was actually used within the fiscal year. The remaining 30 percent was either carried over into the next fiscal year or canceled.

One reason for this phenomenon is that the functions performed by the agencies included in the FILP do not meet the recent needs of the society. For example, JDB lending is not strategic in changing the industrial structure but is directed to the same areas as commercial bank lending, and considerable friction is occurring because of the competition. In this sense, the huge surplus in the FILP is a reflection of the inability of large organizations to respond flexibly to changing needs of society. Thus, although superficially quite different, both the deficits in the General Account and the surplus in the FILP stem from the same pathology of large organizations.

The second reason for surplus in the FILP is that the basic condition necessary for Trust Fund lending to function as preferential financing has been lost. This can be seen in the diminishment of the discrepancy between the Trust Fund lending rate and the long-term prime rate to about 1 percent, whereas it was greater than 3 percent in the early 1960s.

It can be argued that the existence of such discrepancies is abnormal and that the system is returning to normal. Note that the General Account provides no aid for the operations of the Trust Fund. Both the Postal Savings Special Account and the Trust Fund Special Account are operated on a self-paying basis—that is, operating expenses are paid out of interest revenue. Thus, if the combination of these two special accounts is regarded as a bank, it has performed a miracle function of collecting deposits at commercial rates and lending funds at preferential rates on a self-paying basis. (It is true that the General Account provides subsidies to the Employees' Pension [kōsei nenkin] Special Account and the People's Pension [kokumin nenkin] Special Account. But since the Trust Fund pays the same interest on deposits as on Postal Savings, the Trust Fund operation remains a miracle.) Several reason could be offered for this (i) the operations of Postal Savings and Trust Funds are tax exempt; (ii) because the agencies that receive Trust Fund finances are relatively few in number and less risky due to their public nature, the cost of lending is lower than that for commercial banks; and (iii) post offices are a nationwide network.

These reason, although not totally deniable, cannot explain the miracle function completely. For example, if lending costs could be lowered for loans to government-affiliated agencies, it is strange that commercial banks did not choose them as their customers. The fundamental reason could be found in the controls in financial markets. Because the number of banks was severely limited, and because most interest rates were artificially fixed to enable marginal financial institutions to survive, surplus profits must have existed in banks. The preferential financing by the Trust Fund has thus been made possible by taking advantage of this surplus profit. In this sense, the FILP, which has played a strategic role in fostering rapid economic growth, could exist only on the premise that the private financial sector is strictly controlled. Therefore the diminishing discrepancy between the Trust Fund lending rate and the long-term prime rate reflects the growing competitiveness in the banking business due to liberalization of interest rates and internationalization. If such reasoning is valid, the basis for the FILP is lost and preferential financing in the future will be impossible without explicit subsidies from the General Account.

THE PATH TO BIG GOVERNMENT

Even after Japan attained remarkable economic growth, it was customary to regard Japan as a less-developed country in terms of social welfare. This view is common among both foreigners and Japanese. Thus when Nakagawa argued that Japan is a super-welfare state (1980), the general reaction was that he was exaggerating. In fact, he was not. He compared the old-age pension benefits in various countries and claimed that the Japanese level exceeds that of most European countries. Table 5.7 shows the corresponding recent figures, which basically validate Nakagawa's point.

TABLE 5.7

OLD AGE PENSION BENEFITS
(Per month, per couple)

	Benefit (yen)	Ratio to average salary (in percentages)
Japan (1979)	107,858	(50.3)
(Employees' pension)		
United States (1978)	83,338	(39.9)
United Kingdom (1978)	55,303	(42.8)
West Germany (1979)	118,925	(56.2)
(Employees' pension)		
France (1977)	51,191	(37.4)
Sweden (1978)	75,089	(41.9)
(Basic benefit)		

SOURCE: Ministry of Health and Welfare 1980

It is of course necessary to evaluate the figures in the table with some caution. First, the Japanese figure is that of a "model benefit," the amount provided to a hypothetical recipient who satisfies certain conditions. Thus the actual average benefit of ¥85,939 is considerably lower than that of West Germany (although, it is still higher than that of other countries). Second, as has been remarked before, the public pension system in Japan has not reached maturity. Because of the nature of the pension program, forty years must elapse after the establishment of the system before fully qualified recipients appear. Still more time must pass before all the recipients become fully qualified. Because the Employees' Pension was established in 1942 and the People's Pension in 1961, the former matures around 2000 and the latter as late as 2020. Third, the percentage of elderly people in Japan has been considerably lower than that in the Western countries, as is seen clearly from the figures in table 5.8.

As has been remarked before, the latter two reasons explain the low ratio of transfer payments to national income in the rapid growth era (although the ratio is rising, it was still 12.6 percent in fiscal year 1979). Thus Nakagawa's claim should be that Japan is *potentially* a super-welfare state.

At the same time, it is important that the above conditions are destined to change in the future. The pension program will inevitably mature as time passes, and demographic conditions will also change dramatically in a relatively short span of time (see projected figures in table 5.8). When such changes occur, the potential will become reality. According to an estimate by the Ministry of Welfare, the ratio of the number of contributors to pen-

TABLE 5.8

PERCENTAGE OF PEOPLE OVER 65

Country	Year	Percentage of total population
Japan	1970	7.06
	1980	8.88
	1990	11.01
	2000	14.26
United Kingdom	1976	14.2
France	1976	13.5
West Germany	1976	14.7
Sweden	1976	15.3
United States	1976	10.7

SOURCE: Ministry of Health and Welfare, 1980

sion recipients is now 23:1 for the Employees' Pension and 8.6:1 for the People's Pension, but will fall by the year 2010 to 3.6:1 and 4:1 respectively. Although public pensions in Japan use (modified) reserve-fund financing methods, the situation cannot be managed without increasing the contributions significantly.

According to a more recent estimate by the Ministry of Welfare, the ratio of social security contributions to national income must be increased to 12.35 percent in the year 2000 from the present level of 5.35 percent (1977). Other sources of funds must also be increased (table 5.9). Note that no improvements over the present system are assumed in the above estimate. All the increases will occur automatically through maturing of the pension system and demographic change.

TABLE 5.9

ESTIMATED INCREASE IN SOCIAL SECURITY

	Current (A) (1977)	Projected (B) (2000)	Percentage Increase (B/A)
Social security (total)	10.72%	18.82%	1.76
By type of funds			
social security contributions	5.53	12.35	2.27
subsidy from the General Account	4.27	5.12	1.20
local governments	0.93	1.35	1.45
By type of benefits			
old-age pensions	4.05	11.13	2.75
medicare	4.94	5.96	1.21
others[a]	1.74	1.73	0.994

SOURCE: Ministry of Health and Welfare 1978

[a]Public assistance, allowance for children, and unemployment benefit

In principle, an over-all increase in the financial burden is not totally unavoidable. First, downgrading the benefits or other conditions of payment (such as raising the eligible age) may be considered. Second, if it is possible to cut expenditures that are not urgent, it will be possible to accommodate the increasing social security expenditures without significantly increasing the burden. Third, if it is possible to discontinue some of the present FILP programs, the resulting surplus may be allocated to purchase bonds issued by the General Account Budget, which would also prevent an increase in the burden. The problem is whether such radical changes could be made to the present fiscal structure. The preceding arguments suggest that it is extremely difficult.

It might be argued that although the burden increase is significant, the resulting level would roughly be the same as or even lower than that of European countries, so that it does not imply a doomsday. This is true as far as the preceding discussion is concerned, but the following must be noted. First, the estimate of social security expenditure is very likely an underestimate, especially for medical expenses. As has been mentioned before, the estimate reflects only demographic changes. Other factors also increase medical expenses, such as improvement in medical treatments or relative increases in medical costs. Thus the income elasticity of medical expenses is higher than unity. The average income elasticity of medical expenses in recent years has been about 1.05. If the same elasticity continues, the ratio of medical expenses to national income in the year 2000 will be 13.4 percent, assuming 10 percent annual growth in income. Thus it is not unrealistic to suppose that the ratio of social security expenditure to national income will be above 25 percent in the year 2000.

Second, there are still other factors that inflate public expenditure. One is defense. As I remarked earlier, the present level of defense expenditure is extremely low compared with other countries, especially in its ratio to GNP. Thus it would not be surprising, at least from the international comparison of such macrofigures, if defense expenditures were increased twice or even thrice from the present level in the near future. The other factor is economic cooperation. Although Japan's aid to developing nations has improved remarkably in recent years not only in absolute amount but also in ratio to GNP, it is still regarded as insufficient in terms of the latter measure (in 1978, Japan's figure was 0.23 percent, far lower than the official objective of 0.7 percent).[12] Thus, again it would not be surprising if a considerable increase took place in the near future (the Ministry of Finance has recently agreed to double such aid within the next five years).

If all these factors are taken into account, it is possible that the burden of tax and social security contribution as measured by the ratio to national income will increase to around 50 percent. It is important to note that most

12. It must be noted that most countries' figures are below the DAC objective. The figures in 1978 were 0.27 percent for the United States, 0.38 percent for West Germany, and 0.48 percent for the United Kingdom.

of the factors that contribute to inflating the government's share are already present in the existing fiscal structure.

CONCLUSION

What are the implications of the increase in the government's share discussed in the previous section? First, the government-business relationship will no longer be peaceful. As mentioned, the present relationship is not full of tension—businessmen seem to accept, although not unconditionally, increases in taxes. Such a peaceful relationship cannot be expected to continue if tax and social security contributions are increased to the level mentioned. Thus, attempts to increase taxes will certainly meet strong opposition, and if they fail, deficits will again increase, and this might bring inflationary pressures into the economy. If taxes are successfully increased, the private sector's vigor will be considerably weakened.

Second, the principle of self-reliance will be lost and attitudes of depending on government for everything will become popular. If this atmosphere prevails, it will destroy the vitality of Japanese society in a fundamental fashion.

Third, it will continue to be extremely difficult to allocate public resources to new areas of social demands, such as urban development and redevelopment. As is frequently pointed out, Japan's level of social overhead capital in large cities is considerably lower than that of the Western countries.[13] It is quite probable that this situation cannot be improved in the future.

The future as presented here is admittedly a gloomy one. My basic reason for choosing this gloomy picture is the strong inertia in the making of decisions in large organizations and their inability to adapt to a changing environment. It may be argued that the societal structure is much more adaptive and that some kind of negative feedback certainly works at some stage to prevent society from running off in a dangerous direction.[14] I do not necessarily deny such a possibility, but I am not sure if such a mechanism would in fact work in the near future.

Finally, I wish to consider international aspects of the above discussion.

13. There are several reasons for this. First, urbanization is a rather recent phenomenon in Japan. Thus, unlike in Western countries, there has not been enough time for constructing urban infrastructures. Second, as mentioned earlier, over-all resource allocation in the rapid growth era was biased toward private investment rather than public investment. Third, public investment was concentrated in rural rather than in urban areas, as shown in table 5.3.

14. Establisment of the Council for Reorganizing Government Activities may be regarded as an example of such a feedback effect. However, as was mentioned in n. 10, it is difficult to expect a radical reformulation of the present public policies.

Another possibility may be found in a radical decentralization of government activities to local governments, which presently are nothing but passive attachments to the central government. Although not a perfect solution, this would enhance flexibilities in the over-all public performance. Of course there are many obstacles against such transformation.

It might be argued that this paper deals only with domestic problems, so that it has almost no implication for the Japan-U.S. relationship. This is, in my view, superficial. As I have suggested, it is most important for public finance in Japan that the present public policies be re-examined and a way found to reallocate resources for new areas of social needs, such as urban development. This is virtually the only area in which substantial new domestic demand will be found in the future.[15] Without realizing this demand, it would be difficult to change the Japanese industrial structure from its export orientation to domestic demand orientation. If substantial resource reallocation can be realized in this respect, there will be important implications for Japan's future industrial structure and its export performance.

Furthermore, it can be argued that the international competitiveness of Japanese exports is supported by the poor living standard of workers (a variant of the social dumping thesis). In fact, although nominal wage has been increased remarkably, its purchasing power of housing has been reduced. If such a situation is to be improved, huge amounts of investment must be made in urban infrastructures, and if such reallocation of resources were realized, Japan's export performance would change significantly.

15. Actually, Shin Nihon Seitetsu, the largest iron and steel company in Japan, is eager to find opportunities for expanding its business to urban redevelopment.

REFERENCES

Allison, G. T. 1971. *Essence of Decision: Explaining the Cuban Missile Crisis*. Boston, Little, Brown.

Campbell, J. C. 1977. *Contemporary Japanese Budget Politics*. Berkeley and Los Angeles, University of California Press.

Cyert, R. M., and March, J. G. 1963. *A Behavioral Theory of the Firm*. Englewood Cliffs, Prentice-Hall, Inc.

Ishikawa, A., and Gyoten, T. 1977. *Zaiseitōyūshi* [The FILP]. Tokyo, Kinyū Zaisei Jijō.

Ministry of Finance. 1980. *Zaisei tōkei* [Financial statistics]. Tokyo, Government Printing Office.

Ministry of Health and Welfare. 1980. *Kōsei hakusho* [White paper on welfare]. Tokyo, Government Printing Office.

Nakagawa, Y. 1980. *Chō senshinkoku Nihon* [A super advanced country Japan]. Tokyo, Kodansha.

Noguchi, Y. 1979. "Decision Rules in the Japanese Budgetary Process." *Japanese Economic Studies* 7, no. 4:51-75.

—— et al. 1979. *Yosan nensei ni okeru ishikettei katei no kenkyū* [A study of public decision making processes in budgeting]. Research Monograph no. 33. Economic Research Institute, Economic Planning Agency.

Noguchi, Y. 1980a. "A Dynamic Model of Incremental Budgeting." *Hitotsubashi Journal of Economics* 20, no. 2 (February):11-25.

—— et al. 1980b. *55 Nendo yosan ni taisuru teigen* [A proposal to the 1980 budget]. Tokyo, Nihon Keizai Kenkyū Sentā.

Patrick, H., and Rosovsky, H. 1976. "Japan's Economic Performance: An Overview." In *Asia's New Giant*, ed. Patrick and Rosovsky, pp. 1-61. Washington, D.C., Brookings Institution.

Wildavsky, A. 1964. *The Politics of the Budgetary Process*. Boston, Little, Brown.

Japan's Savings and Internal

and External Macroeconomic Balance

KAZUO SATO

THE SAVINGS RATE in postwar Japan, particularly household savings, has been remarkably high. It increased swiftly, enabling Japan to grow rapidly with minimal strain on the economy through the sixties when the annual growth rate was above 10 percent. However, rapid growth came to an end early in the seventies as Japan entered an era of moderate growth. While the demand for capital formation registered a substantial drop, the private savings rate remained high. Consequently, there emerged an excess of savings over investment in the private sector. The government's deficit spending absorbed this excess, preventing Japan from plunging into a deep recession. From the viewpoint of macroeconomic balance, a high savings rate is no longer the virtue it used to be.

This point is not well appreciated outside of Japan, particularly by Americans who have been suffering from a savings shortage. For some time, American politicians, scholars, columnists, and people on the street have unanimously praised and envied Japan's high rate of savings. However, they are concerned with only one side of savings, the supply of investable funds, and pay little attention to oversavings being as undesirable as undersavings in keeping the macroeconomic balance on an even keel.

The main concern of this paper is that Japan's savings will remain in excess supply for some years to come. How to balance it in the domestic economy will be a pressing problem for Japan's policy makers. Why can't Japan export its excess savings overseas where the savings shortage is a chronic constraint to economic growth, for example, in many developing countries? In its January 1981 *Report to the President of United States and the Prime Minister of Japan,* the Japan-United States Economic Relations Group stated: "Because savings in Japan seem likely to remain relatively high compared to domestic investment demand, it is likely that Japan will have a long-run tendency to run a current account surplus and thus be a capital exporter" (p. vi). (See also Trezise 1980 for a similiar view.)

The view, however, is unrealistic in two ways. First, it neglects the reality of the world market. A surplus can appear on the current account when exports are larger than imports. Japan's imports, mostly essentials for the nation's survival, will grow at about the same rate as its GNP. As long as Japan grows faster than other nations, its exports will also grow faster. The outcome is the recurrence of trade friction, especially because Japan's exports are heavily concentrated in a few technology-intensive products. The surplus on the current account can only be moderate.

Second, of the advanced nations, Japan has been the least open to international capital flows, both into and out of the country. The insularity is most apparent with direct investment. Unless Japanese firms become far more willing to move their operations abroad, Japan's capital exports cannot be expected to be large, particularly in the crucial field of productive investment. A workable solution is urgently needed if Japan's savings are to be effectively utilized abroad.

JAPAN'S SAVINGS AND THE MACROECONOMIC BALANCE

The fundamental proposition in macroeconomics is the equality of investment (I) and savings (S) for the economy as a whole. For individual sectors. this equality does not necessarily hold and lending-borrowing relations emerge among them. A sector lends the excess of its savings over its investment to the other sectors, that is, NL (net lending = S - I. Following the system of national income and product accounts (NIPA), I distinguish four sectors, the household (H), the business (B), the government (G), and the external (E). Households include not only worker households but also farmers and nonfarm proprietors (plus, sometimes, nonprofit institutions serving households). The business sector consists of corporations, both financial and nonfinancial. The government sector covers the central government, the prefectural/local government, and the social security fund. The external sector refers to all foreign transactions on the current account.

The investment-savings equality is given by[1]

$$(S_H - I_H) + (S_B - I_B) + (T - G) = (X - M - R) \quad \text{(A)}$$
$$NL_H + NL_B + NL_G = NL_E \quad \text{(B)} \tag{1}$$

Table 6.1 quantifies (1.B) for the seventies, with all items expressed as percentage of gross domestic product (GDP) in purchasers' values. We can note the following major features: (1) The net lending for households, which are net creditors in the economy, displayed little tendency to increase or decrease through the decade. (2) In contrast, corporations' demand for external funds decreased sharply in the late seventies. (3) Clearly, the private

---

1. Notations: S = savings net of capital consumption; I = investment net of capital consumption; T = government's total receipts; G = government's total disbursements; X = exports of goods and services including factor income; M = imports of goods and services including factor payments; R = net transfers to the rest of the world; NL = net lending. Subscripts: H = households; B = corporate business; G = general government; E = external.

TABLE 6.1

Net Lending by Sector, in Percentage of
GDP in Purchasers' Value, 1970-79

	1970	1971	1972	1973	1974	1975	1976	1977	1978	1979
Households	6.8	8.7	11.5	8.0	9.9	9.6	10.6	9.9	9.8	8.4
Corporations	-7.7	-7.4	-9.5	-8.7	-11.3	-6.9	-6.2	-4.6	-2.0	-5.0
Nonfinancial	-8.6	-8.7	-10.9	-10.5	-12.4	-7.8	-6.8	-4.9	-2.8	-6.0
Financial	.9	1.3	1.4	1.7	1.1	.9	.6	.3	.8	1.0
Government	2.3	.9	.4	1.4	-.2	-3.5	-3.6	-4.2	-5.3	-4.2
Central	.4	-.9	-1.1	-.0	-1.7	-4.1	-4.4	-5.4	-6.1	-5.5
State and local	-.2	-.7	-.9	-1.0	-1.1	-2.0	-1.4	-1.4	-1.5	-1.2
Social security funds	2.1	2.4	2.4	2.3	2.6	2.6	2.3	2.7	2.4	2.6
External	1.0	2.5	2.2	-.0	-1.0	-.1	.6	1.5	1.7	-.9

SOURCE: Economic Planning Agency (Japan) (hereafter cited as EPA) 1981

domestic economy provided more funds than it could absorb by itself in the second half of the seventies. The excess was drawn into the general government, particularly the central government. (4) The external balance fluctuated considerably. Deficits in 1974-75 and 1979 were due to the oil shocks that sharply raised payments for imported fuel. On the average, however, Japan's current account surplus was positive at a moderate level.

The over-all picture is clear. In the seventies Japan massively redirected its flow of funds. While households continued to supply funds with undiminished intensity, corporations sharply reduced their borrowing and the excess of domestic private savings was absorbed mostly by the central government through its deficit spending and slightly by the external sector.

THE SECTORAL INVESTMENT-SAVINGS BALANCE: A REVIEW

The Household Sector

Japan's high savings rate is due to high household savings. The level of households' net lending throughout the seventies is the most striking feature of table 6.1. Households' savings and investment behaviors deserve a careful review.

The household sector is heterogeneous within itself. It consists of farmers and nonfarmers, including individual proprietors and worker households, working and retired. The number of farmers has steadily declined in the last three decades to a very small fraction of the household sector (table 6.2). Nonfarm proprietors, mainly in retail trade and services, have been a relatively constant fraction of the sector and will probably remain so in the foreseeable future.

Household savings rates are reported in table 6.3 and illustrated in figure 6.1. The series are given for all households (new and old NIPA series) and for worker households *(Family Income and Expenditure Survey)*. The savings

TABLE 6.2

SELF-EMPLOYED HOUSEHOLDS: NUMBER AND INCOME

| | Percentage of All Households | | | Percentage of National Income | | | |
| | | | | Proprietors' Income | | | |
Year	Total	Farm[a]	Nonfarm	Total	Farm[a]	Nonfarm	Employee Compensation
1955	48.3	29.0	19.3	37.1	20.5	16.6	49.6
1960	42.2	24.0	18.2	26.5	12.7	13.8	50.2
1965	33.8	18.2	15.6	23.4	9.4	14.1	56.0
				21.9	8.8	13.2	55.6
1970	29.7	13.6	16.1	17.5	5.0	12.5	53.0
1975	26.4	11.2	15.2	17.3	4.3	13.0	63.0
1980	22.1	7.2	14.9	13.9[b]	3.3[b]	10.6[b]	67.4[a]

SOURCES: Japanese Census of Population, various issues; EPA 1978, 1981

[a] Agriculture, forestry, and fisheries
[b] 1979

rate is defined as the ratio of savings to disposable income, which is equal to the sum of final consumption expenditure and savings. The two series are not strictly comparable as definitions differ between them.[2]

2. Definitions of income, consumption, and savings differ between the two sources as follows: The NIPA figures are adjusted for imputed rent and capital consumption. Final consumption and income of the NIPA figures include imputed rent for owner-occupied dwellings. As some 60 percent of houses are owner-occupied this adjustment is sizable. The ratio of house rent to total consumption excluding rent is 3 percent in the Budget Survey and 15 percent in the NIPA. In the NIPA, the addition of imputed rent to income is accompanied by the subtraction of capital consumption on reproducible fixed assets of households covering dwellings owned by households and business fixed assets owned and used by unincorporated businesses. Household savings in the NIPA are net of capital consumption.

To make the savings rate computed from the Family Budget Survey comparable with the NIPA savings rate, these differences must be adjusted for. A crude adjustment we have tried has raised disposable income by less than 5 percent but reduced savings substantially, resulting in a reduction of the worker-household savings rate by some six percentage points (e.g., from 20.3% [1970] and 23.0% [1975] to 14.3% and 16.8% respectively).

Since the average income and savings of all households are the weighted averages over worker households and proprietor households, we can conjecture from tables 6.2 and 6.3 that the average proprietor household has an income about double the average worker household and that the former probably saves about twice as much of his income as the latter (i.e., about 30% as against 15%). We can also conjecture that proprietors' average savings rate must have moved almost pari passu with workers' average savings rate over the last three decades as proprietors' total income has become steadily smaller as the share of total household income. This observation brings us to our final conjecture that both worker and proprietor households have been under the same set of influences on their respective savings decision.

HOUSEHOLD SAVINGS RATES AND HOUSEHOLD DISPOSABLE INCOME, 1951-80

	Savings/Disposable Income			Disposable Income per Household						
	All households		Worker households (3)	All households		Worker households (6)	All households		Worker households (9)	Implicit deflator (10)
Year	new series (1)	old series (2)		new series (4)	old series (5)		new series (7)	old series (8)		
	Percentage of income			¥000 in current prices			¥000 in 1975 prices			1975=100
1951	—	—	2.0	—	—	179	—	—	685	26.1
1952	—	10.3	4.4	—	278	228	—	1007	826	27.6
1953	—	7.8	5.8	—	290	277	—	980	935	29.6
1954	—	9.6	7.4	—	322	299	—	1033	959	31.2
1955	—	13.4	9.2	—	355	311	—	1146	1003	31.0
1956	—	13.7	11.8	—	377	330	—	1208	1056	31.2
1957	—	15.6	12.5	—	412	360	—	1275	1107	32.3
1958	—	15.0	12.6	—	425	382	—	1321	1186	32.2
1959	—	16.7	13.9	—	461	410	—	1410	1252	32.7
1960	—	17.4	14.9	—	517	453	—	1526	1335	33.9
1961	—	19.2	16.5	—	586	502	—	1633	1398	35.9
1962	—	18.6	16.2	—	655	563	—	1724	1482	38.0
1963	—	18.0	16.2	—	739	589	—	1815	1447	40.7
1964	—	16.4	17.1	—	818	659	—	1924	1549	42.5
1965	15.8	17.7	17.2	924	913	715	2036	2010	1575	45.4
1966	15.1	17.4	17.6	1019	1000	781	2216	2175	1698	47.6
1967	15.5	19.0	18.4	1144	1134	865	2292	2273	1733	49.9
1968	16.7	19.7	18.6	1289	1284	965	2451	2441	1835	52.6
1969	17.4	19.2	19.2	1454	1425	1078	2639	2586	1957	55.1
1970	18.2	20.4	20.3	1647	1624	1244	2777	2738	2097	59.3
1971	18.2	20.7	20.1	1786	1784	1372	2826	2823	2170	63.2
1972	18.6	21.7	21.6	2013	2011	1520	3022	3020	2283	66.6
1973	21.2	25.1	22.5	2449	2459	1811	3328	3340	2461	73.6
1974	23.9	25.7	24.3	2988	2974	2254	3334	3319	2516	89.6
1975	22.5	25.1	23.0	3353	3426	2586	3353	3426	2586	100.0
1976	22.7	24.3	22.6	3693	3745	2802	3391	3426	2573	108.9
1977	21.3	—	22.8	3982	—	3076	3415	3439	2638	116.6
1978	21.1	—	23.0	4289	—	3244	3513	—	2657	122.1
1979	18.9	—	22.3	4518	—	3436	3580	—	2723	126.2
1980	—	—	22.1	—	—	3667	—	—	2714	135.1

SOURCES: Cols. 1 and 4: 1965-69, from Organization for Economic Cooperation and Development (hereafter cited as OECD) 1980, covering households only; 1970-79 from EPA 1981, col. 1 for all households plus nonprofit institutions serving households and col. 4, for all households; the number of households from Japanese Census of Population, various issues, interpolated between census figures available every five years. Cols. 2 and 5: EPA 1978; cols. 3 and 6: Statistics Bureau 1977; col. 10, implicit deflator of private consumption expenditure, EPA 1978, 1981; cols. 7, 8, and 9 are cols. 4, 5, and 6 divided by col. 10.

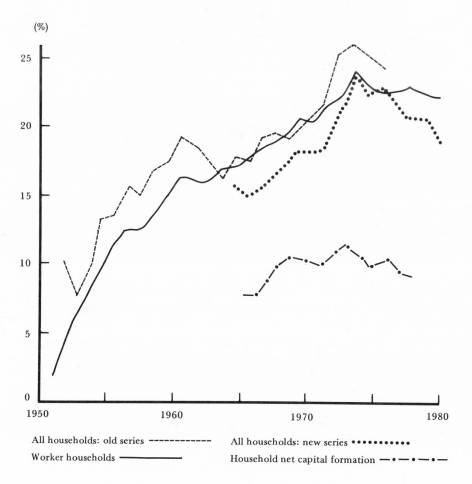

Fig. 6.1. Household savings rates as percentage of household disposable income

The over-all trend in the savings rate over the last three decades is quite clear. There was a sharp rise through the fifties, a moderate increase in the sixties, another surge to the mid-seventies, and some decline since then.

The household savings behavior in the fifties is easy to explain. Real income of households, particularly workers, was reduced sharply below the subsistence level after the end of World War II. In the meantime, inflation raged and the price level rose one hundred times. Households' financial assets were destroyed. However, by 1951, inflation was brought under control and real income began to rise. Households were able to build up their wealth. Thus, through the fifties, the household savings rate continued to rise. It was expected at that time that the savings rate would stop rising once normalcy was attained (see, e.g., Shinohara 1959).

The betrayal of this prediction was the surprise of the sixties. The savings rate continued to increase albeit at a modest rate and with some fluctuation.

This puzzled economists, who put forth a number of alternative hypotheses (see, among others, Komiya 1966; Blumenthal 1970; Mizoguchi 1970; Boltho 1975, p. 84; Komine 1980, p. 95). Some attributed the continued increase in the high level of worker household savings to Japan's bonus system, insisting that workers considered their seminannual bonuses as transitory income and saved most of them. With steady increases in the size of bonuses relative to workers' regular earnings, workers' savings rate should rise. In this author's opinion, this still popular hypothesis belongs to folklore (see Komine 1980, p. 95; however, Shinohara [1981], a foremost authority on Japanese personal savings behavior, maintains that this hypothesis is still valid). Others used to point out that Japanese households had to save a high percentage of their income because of the underdeveloped social security system. The system has improved substantially in the seventies, but households have continued to save at a high rate.

It was also noted that households were strongly motivated to save for their childrens' educations, acquisition of dwellings, and provisions for retirement. However, strong saving motives imply equally strong dissaving motives later on and it is necessary to weigh the two before assessing their net effect. A most theoretical hypothesis refers to the delayed adjustments of consumption to income. Consumption is subject to strong inertia and when real income rises rapidly, households tend to fall behind in raising their level of consumption, inadvertently increasing savings (see, e.g., Ohkawa 1970). The hypothesis may have been plausible in the rapid growth period but its validity is suspect in the seventies (e.g., 1974). We are still in search of appropriate hypotheses.

Before presenting my own view, let me conduct an exercise in accounting. Households' wealth or net worth (W) consists of reproducible tangible assets (R), land (L), financial assets (F), and debt (D). Real assets and land are evaluated at the current market prices, P_R and P_L, respectively. Japanese households hold most of their financial assets in fixed-price types, and so F and D are given in nominal terms. The wealth identity is thus

$$W = P_R R + P_L L + F - D \qquad (2)$$

Household savings add to household wealth so that

$$S = P_R \Delta R + P_L \Delta L + \Delta F - \Delta D \qquad (3)$$

Note that in (3) intrasector transactions are canceled out; sales of used houses and land from one household to another do not show. Therefore, ΔL is purchases of land and ΔR is households' purchases of houses and proprietors' purchases of plants, equipment, and inventory, all from outside the sector. As savings are the net of capital consumption allowance (CCA), so is ΔR, that is, $\Delta R = GCF - CCA = NCF$ where GCF and NCF are gross and net capital formation. These real-asset transactions involve changes in households' financial positions either within the household sector (which do not appear in (3)) or with the other sectors. Households' net lending is equal to $\Delta F - \Delta D$.

The gross accumulation (GA) account in the NIPA records these components of saving. The relation is expressed as follows:

$$S + CCA + CTR = GA = GCF + \Delta L + \Delta F - \Delta D + SD \qquad (4)$$

or,

$$S + CTR = NCF + \Delta L + NL + SD \qquad (4)'$$

where new symbols are CTR, a small item standing for net capital transfers received and SD, a sometimes sizable entry, statistical discrepancy. Table 6.4 shows these components in percentage of disposable household income.

TABLE 6.4

THE GROSS ACCUMULATION ACCOUNT:
THE HOUSEHOLD SECTOR, 1965-79
(% of household disposable income)

Year	S (1)	CCA (2)	CTR (3)	GA (4)	GCF (5)	ΔL (6)	SD (7)	NL (8)	ΔF (9)	$-\Delta D$ (10)	NCF (11)
1965	15.8	4.6	—	—	11.7	—	—	—	—	—	7.1
1966	15.1	4.7	—	—	11.8	—	—	—	—	—	7.2
1967	15.5	4.9	—	—	13.1	—	—	—	—	—	8.2
1968	16.7	5.0	—	—	14.3	—	—	—	—	—	9.3
1969	17.4	5.1	—	—	14.7	—	—	—	—	—	9.6
1970	18.2	5.1	-.4	22.9	14.6	-4.4	2.0	10.7	21.8	-11.1	9.5
1971	18.2	5.3	-.5	22.8	14.3	-6.3	1.6	13.2	23.0	-9.8	9.0
1972	18.6	5.4	-.7	23.2	15.5	-7.5	-2.1	17.3	29.7	-12.4	10.1
1973	21.2	5.2	-.6	25.8	16.3	-8.3	6.1	11.7	27.1	-15.3	11.1
1974	23.9	5.1	-.4	28.6	15.1	-3.5	3.1	13.9	20.8	-7.0	10.0
1975	22.5	5.4	-.4	27.4	14.4	-2.2	2.2	13.0	23.6	-10.6	9.0
1976	22.7	5.7	-.4	28.0	15.0	-1.5	.1	14.3	23.1	-8.8	9.3
1977	21.3	6.0	-.4	26.9	14.2	-1.1	.2	13.5	21.9	-8.3	8.2
1978	21.1	6.2	-.4	26.8	14.2	-.1	-.8	13.5	22.1	-8.7	8.0
1979	18.9	6.5	-.4	25.0	14.6	-1.5	.2	11.7	20.6	-8.9	8.1

SOURCES: EPA 1981; OECD 1980. 1965-69 cover households (including unincorporated businesses); 1970-79 cover households plus nonprofit institutions serving households. (1) S = saving; (2) CCA = capital consumption; (3) CTR = capital transfers received, net; (4) GA = gross accumulation; (5) GCF = gross capital formation; (6) ΔL = purchase of land; (7) SD = statistical discrepancy; (8) NL = net lending; (9) ΔF = increase in financial assets; (10) $-\Delta D$ = decrease in debt; (11) NCF = net capital formation = (5)-(2)

An important economic question is how these variables in (4) or (4)' interact with themselves. For instance, suppose that an increase in GCF is financed by a decrease in ΔF and/or an increase in ΔD. Total savings, S, is unaffected. In this case, we are studying savings as a whole, not their separate components. But an increase in GCF may be accompanied by an increase in S; capital formation may have to be matched by savings. Then, we are studying the components of savings first, and are adding them up to get the total. A statistical test suggests that *NCF* is probably wholly passed on to *S* but ΔL is not,[3] implying that *NCF* and *NL* may be studied more or less separately except for the intervention of ΔL.

When households accumulate physical assets and financial assets (net of debt), they probably have some idea about how much they want to accumulate. Their aspirations may be guessed from the actual record of wealth-income ratios computed for different types of assets in households' wealth portfolio. Table 6.5 gives their time series for 1969-79 in percentage of disposable household income.

Reproducible tangile assets. The ratio rose sharply until 1973, partly because of a rapid rise in the relative price, P_R/P_Y (where P_Y is the implicit GNP deflator). Since then, the ratio has remained stable (its rise in 1979 was again due to a rise in P_R/P_Y). It seems plausible that the ratio had been on the rise through the two decades preceding the seventies for the following reasons. Of the two components of these assets, proprietors' business assets may have become a smaller part of disposable household income as proprietor households became a smaller fraction of the sector, but owner-occupied dwellings must have continued to increase up to the early seventies. As shown in table 6.6, the housing investment/GNP ratio continued to rise until the early seventies, and 60 to 70 percent of the dwellings in Japan are owner-occupied. There has been a strong demand for housing capital formation: in the fifties it was to restore or replace houses demolished

3. Let us set up the following relation:

$$S = \underline{b}_1 (Y - NCF - \Delta L) + \underline{b}_2 NCF + b_3 \Delta L$$

$(Y - NCF - \Delta L)$ is the total resources at households' disposal after paying for capital formation; the coefficient $\underline{b}_1$ is the propensity to accumulate financial assets, which should be a small, positive fraction. $\underline{b}_2$ is unity if *NCF* is fully matched by *S* and less than unity if part of it is financed by reducing financial assets and/or increasing debt. For $\underline{b}_3$, note that households have been net sellers of land ($\Delta L < 0$). If proceeds are wholly invested in financial assets, there is no effect on *S* and $\underline{b}_3 = 0$. If they are partly consumed as households cannot resist the temptation of spending what is readily at hand, we have $1 > \underline{b}_3 > 0$.

Rearranging terms and deflating by *Y*, we get

$$\frac{S}{Y} = \underline{b}_1 + (\underline{b}_2 - \underline{b}_1)\frac{NCF}{Y} + (\underline{b}_3 - \underline{b}_1)\frac{\Delta L}{Y}$$

A regression is run for 1965-79. Although $\Delta L/Y$ is not available for 1965-69, it is known that the variable was at a comparable level to the later one, so a dummy variable *D* (= 1 for 1965-69 and 0 thereafter) is added. The regression is

$$\frac{S}{Y} = .112 + 1.225\frac{NCF}{Y} + .531\frac{\Delta L}{Y} - .515\,D, R^2 = .7664$$
$$(.520)\qquad\quad (.223)\qquad (.102)$$

yielding $\underline{b}_1 = .112$, $\underline{b}_2 = 1.34$, and $\underline{b}_3 = .64$.

TABLE 6.5

THE RATIOS OF HOUSEHOLD WEALTH (YEAR END)
TO HOUSEHOLD DISPOSABLE INCOME, 1969-78
(In percentages)

Year	$P_R R$	$P_L L$	F	D	F-D	W	$\dfrac{HDY}{GDP}$	P_R/P_Y
	(1)	(2)	(3)	(4)	(5)	(6)	(7)	(8)
1969	.60	2.79	1.43	.61	.83	4.22	.64	.97
1970	.62	2.80	1.43	.59	.85	4.27	.64	.96
1971	.65	2.88	1.50	.62	.89	4.41	.65	.93
1972	.76	3.30	1.59	.64	.95	5.00	.66	1.12
1973	.84	3.27	1.54	.64	.90	5.01	.68	1.15
1974	.81	2.62	1.44	.59	.86	4.29	.71	1.05
1975	.80	2.46	1.50	.63	.87	4.13	.74	1.00
1976	.84	2.32	1.56	.61	.95	4.12	.74	1.02
1977	.85	2.29	1.65	.67	.98	4.12	.73	.99
1978	.87	2.41	1.73	.70	1.04	4.31	.72	.98
1979	.97	2.70	1.82	.75	1.07	4.73	.72	1.07

SOURCE: EPA 1981. (1) Real assets, excluding land; (2) Land; (3) Financial assets; (4) Debt; (5) Net financial assets; (6) Net worth = (1) + (2) + (5); (7) Household disposable income/gross domestic product; (8) The household fixed assets deflator/GDP implicit deflator

TABLE 6.6

HOUSING INVESTMENT/GNP, QUINQUENNIAL AVERAGE
(In percentages)

Period	Private	Government	Total
1952-54	2.9	.3	3.2
1955-59	3.3	.4	3.7
1960-64	4.5	.3	4.8
1965-69	6.0	.4	6.4
1970-74	7.1	.5	7.6
1975-79	7.0	.5	7.5

SOURCE: EPA 1978, 1981

during the war; in the sixties and early seventies it was to provide adequate shelter for the population moving to cities from rural areas and to upgrade the quality of housing to be commensurate with the rising standard of living.

The ratio (particularly in real terms) reached a plateau in the late seventies because the strong demand abated. On the one hand, business investment demand was weakened, and on the other, the demand for new houses was depressed because population migration had now reached its limits, the growth of real income became very moderate, the prices of new dwellings and land continued to rise, and mortgages became less readily available.

Let $P_R R/P_Y Y = \underline{b}$. Then, we have an identity relation for the ratio of NCF to household disposable income:

$$\frac{P_R \Delta R}{P_Y Y} = \underline{b}\left(\frac{\Delta Y}{Y} + \frac{\Delta P_Y}{P_Y} - \frac{\Delta P_R}{P_R}\right) + \Delta \underline{b} \qquad (5)$$

The identity can be turned into a behavioral equation if $\underline{b}$ can be regarded as a decision variable. My argument suggests that economic factors kept $\underline{b}$ rising until the mid-seventies and then stabilized it. This behavior of $\underline{b}$ governed the observed behavior of NCF in the period under study.

Land. The land-income ratio fluctuated considerably in the seventies because unusual market conditions made increases in land price unsteady. Over the last quarter of a century, the urban land price rose some thirty times while the implicit consumption deflator rose only a little over four times. During the same period, total real household income rose about six times. Hence, the increases in the land-income ratio in current values must have been small, if not zero. However, the inequality in landownership has no doubt been magnified by the sharp increase in land price (even though two-thirds of dwellings are built in owners' lots) (see Takayama 1981). Nonetheless, since land is the most illiquid of assets, increases in the land price per se probably did not have too noticeable an effect upon household savings except when part of the land was actually sold.

Financial assets net of debt. A well-known feature of the net financial position of Japanese households is that they keep most of their financial assets in fixed-price assets (currency and bank deposits), which are vulnerable to inflation (see table 6.7 for a breakdown of these assets). We saw in

TABLE 6.7

HOUSEHOLDS' FINANCIAL ASSETS AND DEBTS IN
RELATION TO HOUSEHOLD DISPOSABLE INCOME
(In percentages)

	1969	1979
Financial assets	1.43	1.85
Currency and deposits	1.04	1.39
Long-term securities	.10	.16
Equities	.10	.04
Life insurances	.18	.24
Others	.01	.02
Debt	.61	.76

SOURCE: EPA 1981

table 6.5 that the ratio, except for a dip in 1973-74, maintained an upward trend through the seventies, most plausibly as an extension of the trend prevailing since the early fifties.

Let $(F - D)/P_Y Y = a$. We have then another identity:

$$\frac{NL}{P_Y Y} = \frac{\Delta F - \Delta D}{P_Y Y} = \underline{a} \left(\frac{\Delta Y}{Y} + \frac{\Delta P_Y}{P_Y} \right) + \Delta \underline{a} \qquad (6)$$

As simple as relation (6) may be, it is powerful in explaining Japan's household behavior of net financial savings or net lending. Imagine that households as a whole have a certain target level for this ratio $\underline{a}$. To realize this ratio, they must acquire financial assets (net of debt) according to (6) when their nominal income grows. If so, this rate of household savings responds equally to real income growth and inflation. What happens is that inflation erodes the real value of households' fixed-price financial assets and households must accumulate financial assets to compensate for the depreciation.[4] Nominal income rose rapidly in the sixties and seventies, either because of real growth or inflation; this increase helped raise households' net lending ratio in these decades.

In addition, there has been a steady increase in the target ratio $\underline{a}$ (of equation (6)) itself. This increase kept the net lending ratio on an upward trend until the mid-seventies. It is clear that, if we wish to understand Japan's household savings behavior, we must explain why the ratio continued upward for so long. For this, we have to look at more basic factors, including demographic changes, among other things.

Predicting Japan's household savings behavior has been a baffling experience, primarily because the period had drastic changes in not only economic but also social, cultural, and demographic conditions. While household capital stock satisfies households' current and relatively near future needs for capital services, it is reasonable to presume that households acquire financial assets (beyond the transactions demand for money) principally for meeting more distant needs, say, retirement. Such needs change as life-cycle factors change. And the latter changed profoundly over the last three decades. Let us note six of these factors that are of particular importance to household savings behavior.

Migration from farms. The massive migration of labor reduced the labor force in agriculture sharply. Its share in the total labor force fell from 48 percent in 1950 to 31 percent in 1960, 16 percent in 1970, and 10 percent in 1980. The traditional structure of a farm family has been a three-generation family. Life-cycle saving was probably not the dominant motive for

---

4. In 1973 and 1974, the oil shock brought double-digit inflation. Since the inflation was largely unanticipated, the ratio was temporarily depressed below the trend as the accumulation could not fully make up for the deleterious effect of inflation. When inflation was brought under control, the ratio was restored.

farmers' saving. Thus, as the population moved out of farms, the need to save for postretirement must have risen.

The increase in the number of nuclear families. One of the most sweeping societal changes that was brought into postwar Japan was the weakening, if not the collapse, of the traditional concept of the *ie* or family. The almost universal mode for first sons was the three-generation family. They were obligated to maintain the unbroken lineage of the *ie*. They supported their parents in old age and expected to be supported later in turn by their children. The expectation is no longer automatic. The number of nuclear families (couples without parents living together) has been increasing (from 63% in 1960 to 72% in 1975 and 74% in 1980 of all kinship families). Those who cannot expect much financial help from their offspring must depend on self-help. The generation now going into retirement is in a double bind because it began with a social contract to support its elders and yet cannot expect the same support from the younger generation. In this social environment, this generation cannot help being frugal.

Population aging. People used to die young. In 1950, life expectancy was 58.0 years for males and 61.5 years for females. By 1979, it rose to 73.5 and 78.9 years, respectively. But employment opportunities have not been expanded commensurately. When the social security system was very much underdeveloped, saving for old age had to take its place. Even now, the mandatory retirement age in large companies is being raised from 55 to only 60 and strong savings needs for retirement still remain unless sufficient employment opportunities are provided for workers over age 60.

Erosion of the seniority-related wage system. Under the seniority-related wage system that promises automatic incremental increase in wages for workers with continued service, the burden of wage cost tends to rise as there are more older workers in the work force, even though workers retained past age fifty-five are paid only something like two-thirds of their peak pay. It has become necessary for large firms to reduce the size of automatic increments, and the age-wage profile has been made much flatter. Similarly, the lump-sum retirement allowance paid at the time of retirement has been decreasing for quite some time. Since regular employees of large companies counted on saving a large part of their pay as well as their retirement allowance shortly before their mandatory retirement, this means that they have to realign their lifetime consumption-savings plans in light of the new working environment. This again is likely to raise the average savings rate of working households.

The spread of the social security system. Earlier, it was popularly asserted that one, probably powerful, reason why Japanese households saved so much was that there was almost no social security system except for the old-age pension for civil service. A rather liberal system has developed: the Employee Pension System (Kōsei nenkin) pays its participants, after age sixty, average monthly benefits equivalent to some 60 percent of the final pay (excluding bonuses) if the contributory period has been long enough. If individuals are rational, there should be a yen for yen exchange between the expected social security benefits and current savings of workers as Feldstein (1974) and others insist for the United States. In Japan, however, it is difficult yet to detect any appreciable effect of the social security system upon private savings because other things have not been kept unchanged.

Future consumption needs. After all these considerations, what remain as fundamental determinants of life-cycle savings are the duration of living in retirement and the level of consumption hoped to be maintained in that period. Given the former, the current savings rate must be raised if the anticipated consumption level is increased. During the sixties when real economic growth was rapid, the savings rate had to be increased for households to enjoy the higher level of living that would prevail when retirement finally came. This increase was feasible without much strain on household budgeting because real income was rising at a rapid rate. In the seventies, especially after 1973, economic growth slowed down and inflation took over. Just to realize the desired real level of living in retirement, households had to maintain a high rate of financial savings to compensate for depreciating financial assets.

Household savings are the outcome of careful consumption-savings planning, which is upset only in the short run when unanticipated events intervene. It can be explained in economic terms even though we may have to refer to extra-economic factors.

THE BUSINESS SECTOR

In the business sector, a substantial decline took place in capital accumulation since 1974 in the wake of the first oil shock. Table 6.8 reports quinquennial averages of the sector's gross accumulation account. Gross capital formation, inventory investment, and purchases of land all fell in the latter

TABLE 6.8

THE GROSS ACCUMULATION ACCOUNT:
THE BUSINESS SECTOR, IN PERCENTAGE
OF TOTAL GDP IN PURCHASERS' VALUE, 1970-79

Period	S (1)	CCA (2)	CTR (3)	GA (4)	GFCF (5)	INVI (6)	ΔL (7)	SD (8)	NL (9)
1970-74	4.7	9.8	.6	15.1	19.6	2.0	3.3	-1.2	-8.9
1975-79	1.2	8.2	.6	10.0	15.2	.6	.1	-.9	-5.0
1970-79	3.0	9.0	.6	12.6	17.4	1.3	1.7	-1.0	-6.9

SOURCE: Computed from EPA 1981. (1) Corporate savings; (2) Capital consumption allowance; (3) Capital transfers received, net; (4) Gross accumulation; (5) Gross fixed capital formation; (6) Changes in stocks; (7) Purchases of land; (8) Statistical discrepancy; (9) Net lending.

half of the seventies, their sum total dropping from 25 percent to 16 percent of GDP. The decline in corporate gross savings was less marked and consequently, the sector's net borrowing shrank from 9 percent to 5 percent of GDP.

It is easy to explain ex post facto the capital formation proportions when we note that net capital formation expands capital stock. The well-known capital growth identity is

$$\left(\begin{array}{c}\text{gross capital}\\ \text{formation/}\\ \text{GDP in}\\ \text{current}\\ \text{value}\end{array}\right) = \left(\left[\begin{array}{c}\text{growth rate}\\ \text{of net capital}\\ \text{stock}\end{array}\right] + \left[\begin{array}{c}\text{depreciation}\\ \text{ratio}\end{array}\right]\right) \times \left(\begin{array}{c}\text{net capital}\\ \text{stock/GDP}\\ \text{in current}\\ \text{value}\end{array}\right) \quad (7)$$

The depreciation ratio is about 10 percent per year for plant and equipment and 0 for inventory and land. Table 6.9 shows relevant data for the seventies, which can be used to verify the validity of (7).

TABLE 6.9

CAPITAL-OUTPUT RATIOS AND GROWTH RATES:
THE BUSINESS SECTOR, 1969-79

	Capital-Output Ratio[a]		
	1969	1974	1979
Fixed capital stock	.63	.97	.94
Inventory stock	.27	.28	.24
Land	.64	.73	.77
Total	**1.54**	**1.97**	**1.95**

	Growth Rate (1969-79)		
	Nominal	Real	Deflator
Business			
Fixed capital stock	.180	.101	.072
Inventory stock	.119	.057	.059
Land	.149	—	—
Economy			
GDP	.135	.054	.076
Land	.145	—	—

SOURCE: Computed from EPA 1981

[a]The ratio of net stock (year end) to the economy's GDP, both in current value

It follows from (7) that, when the economy's growth rate falls, the capital formation proportions decline in proportion unless the capital-output ratio is allowed to rise. That is what happened in the late seventies.

On the savings side, gross accumulation consists of capital consumption allowance (*CCA*), corporate profit retention or net savings (*S*), and capital transfers received (*CTR*). *CCA* has been a relatively stable fraction of GDP, hovering around 8 to 10 percent. *CTR* was also very stable at about 0.6 percent of GDP. In contrast, corporate net savings were quite volatile. To explain this component, we may look at a simplified corporate income account summarized by

$$P = DT + DIV + S$$

$$\underbrace{\begin{pmatrix} \text{corporate} \\ \text{income net} \\ \text{of CCA} \end{pmatrix}}_{} \quad \underbrace{\begin{pmatrix} \text{direct tax} \end{pmatrix}}_{} \quad \underbrace{\begin{pmatrix} \text{dividends} \end{pmatrix}}_{} \quad \underbrace{\begin{pmatrix} \text{corporate} \\ \text{savings} \end{pmatrix}}_{} \quad (8)$$

The elements of (8) as well as *CCA* are shown in table 6.10 in quinquennial averages as percentage of corporate net fixed capital stock (*NFK*) in current values for the seventies.

TABLE 6.10

CORPORATE INCOME IN PERCENTAGE OF
CORPORATE NET FIXED CAPITAL STOCK (YEAR END),
BOTH IN CURRENT VALUES, 1970-79

Period	CCA	P	of which			$\dfrac{DT}{P}$	$\dfrac{NFK}{GDP}$
			DT	DIV	S		
	(1)	(2)	(3)	(4)	(5)	(6)	(7)
1970-74	12.1	15.1	5.4	3.4	6.2	40.0	82.2
1975-79	8.9	8.6	4.7	2.5	1.3	56.0	92.3
1970-79	10.5	11.8	5.1	3.0	4.8	48.1	87.2

SOURCE: EPA 1981. (1) Capital consumption allowance; (2) Corporate income = (3) + (4) + (5); (3) Direct tax; (4) Dividends; (5) Corporate savings; (6) Col. 3/col. 2; (7) Corporate net fixed capital stock (year end)/total GDP, both in current values.

From table 6.10, we find that *CCA/NFK* ratio was around 9 to 10 percent; *P/NFK* was depressed in the late seventies because of poor business conditions. Dividend payments, however remained very stable at about 2.5 percent of *NFK*. Direct taxes varied from year to year but averaged about 50 percent of corporate income. Net corporate savings were very much depressed in the late seventies.

THE GOVERNMENT SECTOR

When Japan's rapid growth period ended with the 1973-74 oil shock, its private sector had a substantial excess of savings over investment. Government deficits, which matched this excess, expanded sharply to as much as 4 to 5 percent of GDP (see table 6.1). Obviously, without this convenient accommodation of government finances, the Japanese economy would have faced a serious and prolonged recession in the late seventies. How did this fiscal situation emerge? Was it a brilliant action of stabilization policy? Before looking at this question from the perspective of macroeconomic policy, let us first examine what happened in the government account.

Internationally compared, Japan's government sector occupied a relatively modest position in relation to the economy. In the late seventies, the share of government final consumption expenditure in GDP was 10 percent in Japan vis-à-vis 18 percent in the United States, 21 percent in the United Kingdom, 15 percent in France, 20 percent in Germany, and 28 percent in Sweden, thanks largely to Japan's small defense expenditure (0.8 percent of GDP in Japan vis-à-vis 5.4 percent in the United States). The share of government current receipts in GDP was 24 percent in Japan as compared with 32 percent in the United States, 40 percent in the United Kingdom, 43 percent in France and Germany, and 60 percent in Sweden.

However, the fiscal scale has been expanding very rapidly in Japan, as seen in table 6.11; if the trend is extrapolated, "Big Government" is already

TABLE 6.11

THE GENERAL GOVERNMENT ACCOUNT,
IN PERCENTAGE OF GDP

	1965-69 (1)	1970-74 (2)	1975-79 (3)	Change (4)=(3)-(1)	U.S. 1976-78 (5)
Current receipts					
Indirect tax	7.1	7.0	6.9	-.2	8.7
Direct tax	7.4	9.2	9.4	2.0	14.3
households	3.8	4.8	5.1	1.3	10.5
corporations	3.6	4.4	4.3	.7	3.2
Social security contributions	4.0	4.7	6.8	2.8	7.6
Property income receivable	.7	1.0	1.4	.7	1.2
(A) **Total**	19.4	22.1	24.7	5.3	32.1
Current disbursements					
Government final consumption	7.7	8.2	9.9	2.2	18.4
Social security benefits	3.2	3.9	6.9	3.7	7.6
Social assistance grants	1.4	1.4	2.1	.7	3.3
Subsidies	.9	1.2	1.3	.4	.4
Property income payable	.5	.8	1.9	1.4	2.7
(B) **Total**	13.9	15.6	22.5	8.6	32.6
(C) Savings = (A)-(B)	5.5	6.5	2.3	-3.2	-.5
(D) Fixed capital consumption	.5	.4	.5	—	1.4
(E) = (C)+(D)	6.0	6.9	2.8	-3.3	.9
(F) Gross accumulation	—	6.7	2.4	—	1.3
(G) Gross capital formation	4.5	5.2	5.7	1.2	1.7
(H) Purchases of land	—	.7	.8	—	.2
(I) Total disbursements	18.4	21.5	29.0	10.6	34.5
(J) Net lending	—	1.0	-4.2	—	-.4

SOURCE: EPA 1981, OECD 1980. (A) = Sum of listed items + casualty insurance claims receivable + compulsory fees, fines, and penalties + unfunded employee welfare contributions imputed + current transfers n.e.c. received from other resident sectors and the rest of the world + statistical discrepancy; (B) = Sum of listed items + net casualty insurance premiums payable + current transfers to private nonprofit institutions serving households + unfunded employee welfare benefits + current transfers n.e.c. paid to other resident sectors and the rest of the world. (F) = (E) + capital transfers received, net, from other resident sectors and the rest of the world; (I) = (B) +(G)+(H); (J) = (E)-(G)-(H)-statistical discrepancy.

in sight. The expansion is more pronounced for government spending (see item (I) in table 6.11), particularly in social security benefits and government final consumption. The social security system has improved significantly in Japan. Its benefits amounted to 6.9 percent of GDP in 1975-79, a figure quite comparable to 7.6 percent in the United States and 6.7 percent in the United Kingdom, even though behind France (17.0%), Germany (10.9%), and Sweden (14.6%). The rise in government consumption is mostly due to the rise in the government wage bill, which in turn is attributed to a more rapid increase in the average earnings of government employees than those of private industry employees and to a relative expansion of government employment.

On the revenue side, the increase is for the most part accounted for by increases in social security contributions and direct taxes. As participation in the social security system spread swiftly, the social security funds maintained a sizable surplus in the seventies (table 6.1). The increase in direct taxes, particularly on households, was due to the suspension of tax-rate reductions, which used to be annual events in the rapid growth period. Japan maintained relatively low taxes, with personal income taxes particularly low when compared to those of other countries.

Thus, the increase in total government disbursements was more secular than countercyclical. Government deficits have appeared since 1975 because government revenue could not match the increase in spending. When the government contemplated a revenue increase in 1975, it met with strong resistance from both management and labor, which had not recovered from the oil shock. A special public-finance law was passed by the Diet to allow the national government to issue "deficit" bonds so that it could meet the shortfall of revenue. (Until then, the only bonds the national government could issue were construction bonds for financing public construction projects.) Since that year, nearly one-third of the national government expenditure has been financed by new bond issues.[5] The outstanding balance of public debt as a percentage of GDP has risen from 6 percent in 1971 to 29 percent in 1980 (end of the fiscal year), which is quite close to the current U.S. ratio, 35 percent in 1980 (see Uchihashi 1981 for the political background of this development).

THE EXTERNAL SECTOR

As equation (1) shows, the excess of domestic savings over domestic investment is equal to the surplus of exports over imports on the current account of the balance of payments. When savings exceed investment in the domestic economy in the ex ante sense, aggregate demand is not enough to fully absorb aggregate supply at full employment. In an open economy like Japan, which is aggressive in sales promotion abroad, a strong push for

5. Outstanding bonds have been held largely by the central bank and the consortium of financial institutions, which were "asked" by the government to purchase these bonds.

the export drive emerges. When this push is successful, a surplus appears on the current account, indicating that the excess of domestic savings has been exported abroad. However, there seems to be a fairly low upper limit on the current account surplus permissible to a large country. For the United States, for instance, it was only 0.6 percent of GNP in the early sixties when the surplus was considered significant.

In the floating exchange rate system, exchange rates are supposed to fluctuate to bring the balance of payments into a reasonable equilibrium position for individual countries unless there are strong external factors that stand in the way. A powerfully disequilibrating force has been OPEC. As OPEC maintained a huge export surplus, the rest of the world was forced into current account deficits. However, Japan and also Germany succeeded in keeping the current account in surplus when the seventies are taken as a whole (1% of GDP).

The situation is quite a change from the period before the mid-sixties. In the earlier period, Japan's exports were more in light manufactures, which were not very world-income-elastic. Thus, when Japan's domestic growth accelerated, imports of crude materials and fuels tended to expand sharply in excess of exports. This balance-of-payments disequilibrium put a brake on growth. From the mid-sixties onward, Japan has been highly internationally competitive in machinery, transport equipment, and other technology-intensive products. Since exports of these products have grown rapidly, Japan has maintained a reasonably high rate of increase in its exports; its world market share has continued to rise. On the other hand, Japan's demand for imports of crude materials has not been so intense that its domestic economic activities have been shifting toward the tertiary sector. The demand for oil has been successfully checked through concerted efforts at energy conservation and energy-saving technical change. On the merchandise account, therefore, exports tend to surpass imports by a substantial margin. The service account, however, tends to be in deficit (close to 1% of GDP), while factor income and receipts are small and in balance because foreign investment in and out of Japan is still small compared to the size of the economy. Altogether, Japan ends up with a surplus on the current account unless sharp oil price increases make Japan's oil bill soar temporarily as in 1973-74 and 1979.

Nonetheless, the current account surplus has not been a major factor in achieving the macroeconomic balance of savings and investment in Japan. And the prospect is not very bright that it will serve as such. For that, Japan must expand its merchandise exports. But the strong resistance displayed by policy authorities of the United States and the European Community against Japan's invasion of their markets in automobiles and other technology-intensive products makes it clear that the possibility is limited.

JAPAN'S SAVINGS AND THE FUTURE OF THE JAPANESE ECONOMY

High savings are more desirable than low savings in that the economy is potentially capable of sustaining a high rate of capital accumulation. However, when the desire to accumulate is significantly weakened, potentially high savings may largely go to waste. Aggregate demand cannot match potential output. Productive capacity is left idle, workers are unemployed.

The miracle of Japan's economic growth up to 1973 was that private savings kept perfect pace with rapidly expanding capital formation but it has come to an end. Private investment has declined but private savings remain high.

This situation is likely to continue in the eighties. Economic growth has declined permanently. Private investment demand will be held low. Private savings, on the other hand, may remain strong so long as individuals have strong needs for savings. These needs will increase as the concentration of elderly in the population rises at a rapid rate, pushing up the dependency ratio to a level incomparably high among advanced nations. As private savings will exceed private investment, the government must be prepared to absorb the excess by its deficit spending.

Based on the review in the preceding section, the following exercise will help present my hypothesis about the aggregate demand-supply gap.

Economic growth. The rate of economic growth (GNP) averaged at 3.8 percent per annum between 1973 and 1980. This rate will continue into the eighties, or perhaps be even lower. The decline in growth is attributable to Japan's entry into the postindustrial stage. The share of the secondary sector in the labor force has been falling since 1973. The primary sector's share has fallen to as low as 10 percent. Productivity growth is characteristically low in the tertiary sector and the over-all growth rate for the economy as a whole is bound to fall.

Inflation. The rate of inflation is a crucial determinant of household savings. Yet it is impossible to predict the course of inflation. There are, however, at least three factors in favor of moderate inflation in Japan. First, Japanese labor has been moderate in its demands for higher wages in recent years. Second, when savings respond positively to inflation, there is a self-correcting mechanism that will keep inflation within bounds. Third, the Japanese yen will remain strong as exports tend to exceed imports and this will keep import prices low in Japan. From 1975 to 1980, the GNP deflator and the private consumption deflator rose at 4.4 percent and 6.2 percent per annum respectively. Barring unforeseen drastic disturbances, these rates may perhaps continue into the eighties.

Household sector. Social security contributions must be increased to pay for benefits expected to expand as many more people qualify for benefits, but this is a redistribution of income within the sector. Excluding social security benefits, government disbursements are expected to continue climbing steeply through the eighties. If government revenue is to catch up with government spending, the tax burden must rise—from 24 percent of GDP at present to, say 30 percent ten years hence (including social security contributions). Subtracting this increase in the tax burden, households' disposable income will grow at 7.5 percent per annum nominally if total nominal GDP is to grow at 8 percent per annum (3.8% real and 4.4% inflation).

Excluding land sales to the other sectors, household savings consist of net capital formation and net financial savings. As a predominant component of capital formation, housing investment is likely to decline in percentage of disposable income for the reasons noted earlier. Suppose that this component will fall from 8 percent of household disposable income at the end of the seventies to, say, 6 percent, judging from available economic projections for the eighties.

Households' net financial savings were as high as 13 percent of disposable income in the late seventies. Is this high rate going to continue? Among other things, this depends on where the target ratio of net financial assets to disposable income is set. The actual ratio has been rising in a trend; it reached 1.07 at the end of 1979. Will this ratio continue to increase?

The act of saving is a tug of war. There is always a desire to improve one's standard of living. This desire was satisfied in the rapid growth period through the continued rise in real income. Both rising consumption and expanding savings were made compatible. Now that real income growth has become modest, consumption can be expanded only at the expense of reduced savings. How high savings will be depends largely on how strict Japanese households can be in controlling consumption. In the period of demographic transition when uncertainties of the future will remain quite large, the desire for increased consumption may have to be suppressed. The population is rapidly aging. The expected extension of the mandatory retirement age is not sufficient to provide enough employment opportunities for persons beyond the age of sixty. At the same time, there is a strong anticipation of the debasement of social security such as starting benefits at age sixty-five instead of the current sixty for the sake of averting bankruptcy of the social security funds or avoiding an intolerable increase in the level of contributions.

If the ratio of net financial assets to disposable income remains at its recent level and if nominal income growth is 7.5 percent, households will save a little over 8 percent of their disposable income or a little above 6 percent of GDP in the form of financial assets (net of debt). This is likely to be the bottom line.

Adding the two components together, the household savings rate comes to 14 percent of disposable income or a little above 10 percent of GDP.

Business sector. Equation (7) can be applied to estimate the business demand for gross capital formation consisting of fixed capital formation and inventory investment.

For fixed capital formation, we note that the capital-output ratio was a little over 0.9 in the late seventies. This ratio is not likely to rise for three reasons. First, the capital-goods deflator may lag behind the GNP deflator as the latter becomes more strongly influenced by service prices, which tend to rise fastest. Second, the tertiary sector, which will become more important over time, has a substantially lower capital-output ratio (about 0.7) than the secondary sector. Third, the capital-output ratio was raised substantially in the early seventies when fixed capital formation was sustained at a high level while output expansion was not very large. Any further increase in the ratio will depress the rate of profits on capital.

Thus, assuming the fixed capital-output ratio will remain at around 0.9 and that net capital stock will grow at the same rate as real GDP (4.4%), we obtain the gross fixed capital formation proportion that is 13 percent of GDP (with the depreciation ratio of 10%). For inventory investment, our estimate is 1.5 percent of GDP.[6] Hence, total gross capital formation of the business sector comes to 14.5 percent of GDP.

As for business savings, capital consumption will remain at the stable level of 9 percent of GDP, which is historically observed. According to historical data, corporate gross income will be about 12 percent of GDP when firms operate at full capacity. By subtracting the direct tax (50% of gross income) and the dividends (25% of gross income), we arrive at retained profits, which will be 25 percent of gross income or 3 percent of GDP. Net capital transfers received is 0.6 percent of GDP as historically observed. The business sector's gross accumulation is thus 12.5 percent of GDP, which is the sum of fixed capital consumption (9%), retained profits (3%), and net capital transfers received (0.6%).

Putting investment and savings together, we find that the business sector will be nearly self-sufficient with its net borrowing as low as 2 percent. This means that internal funds are nearly enough to finance business investment. Corporations need no longer depend so much on bank loans. Needless to say, this estimate is on the low side. If business investment unexpectedly picks up or business profits are not as good as assumed, the business sector must borrow more. But the estimate here of the household sector's net lending is also on the low side.[7] For the private economy as a whole, savings will be in excess of investment by 4 percent of GDP.

The government sector. The government has been under extremely strong pressure for fiscal expansion since 1975 with the greatest pressure placed on government final consumption, social security benefits, and debt servicing.

The increase in government final consumption will be due to the increasing expense of government services because of high labor content and external pressure, particularly from the U.S. administration, for increasing Japan's defense expenditure.

We have noted many times the inevitable and imminent increase in social security benefits. In addition, interest payments on the public debt are in-

6. The inventory deflator increased faster than the GDP deflator by 2.6 percent per year in the seventies. To keep the inventory-GDP ratio constant in current value (at .25), the inventory stock must grow at 3.8 + 2.6 = 6.4 percent. The inventory investment/GDP ratio implied here is 1.6 percent.

7. When corporations increase capital formation, their purchases of land tend to be expanded. This adds to business spending on investment. Households' sales of land to corporations seem to reduce household savings to some extent because their consumption is stimulated. This is one element that may reduce the investment-savings gap in the private sector.

creasing. With the outstanding balance of public debt at 30 percent of GDP and the interest rate close to 10 percent, interest cost takes an additional 2 percent of GDP. Moreover, the redemption of "deficit" bonds will begin soon, as their maturity is ten years.

The situation has been deemed a "fiscal crisis." Government revenue must be increased at an even faster rate than government expenditure if the present gap between the two is to be closed and new issues of "deficit" bonds are to be brought to zero within the next few years. The Medium-Term Perspective of Public Finance, released by the Minister of Finance in January 1981, describes a plan to meet this challenge. A high-powered government commission has been at work to map out an extensive set of recommendations for radically reforming and restructuring public finance. The success of this attempt at "reconstruction" of public finance will be seen in the future.[8]

Despite the valiant try to keep Japan's government small, some expansion in the fiscal scale seems to be unavoidable. Furthermore, whether the government deficits that have prevailed for several years can be eliminated or not depends on the balance of saving and investment in the private sector.

The external sector. Japanese exports are almost wholly manufactured goods with a heavy concentration in technology-intensive products. As the domestic demand for these goods has been sluggish, the export drive has been strong, particularly toward the American market. Trade friction has occasionally erupted: every time some protective measures were imposed upon Japanese exporters—"voluntary" quotas on textiles and automobiles or the trigger price mechanism on steel. Nonetheless, Japanese exports have been increasing in market share in world trade slowly but steadily. Japan's share of manufactured exports from major industrial nations has risen from 6.2 percent in 1960 to 10.7 percent in 1970, and 13.3 percent in 1980.

Japan's import requirement was kept at bay through the seventies despite the well-known heavy dependence of Japan upon foreign supplies of resource products—often virtually complete dependence on imported fossil fuels, which now account for 40 percent of Japan's merchandise import payments. This performance is attributed to Japan's successful adaptation of techniques for energy saving, to the shift of its demand away from manufactured goods and toward services in the postindustrial stage, and the strong yen.

Since world income is not growing at the rate it used to, Japan's exports can be kept growing at a rate commensurate with its domestic output growth only by enlarging its world market share. With the rising mood of protectionism in the world economy, there must be a limit on how fast Japan can in-

8. Over the last fifteen years there has been a trend for better government wages and a larger civil service. The government is now trying to enforce a reduction in government employment via a hiring freeze in the next few years and a less-than-full compliance with the Personnel Agency's annual recommendations for an across-the-board wage raise of civil servants (particularly in prefectural and local governments).

crease exports. Considering this limitation, it does not seem that Japan can expand the surplus on the current account much beyond the historical level that averaged 1 percent of GDP from 1965 to 1980.

Summing up. According to my hypotheses, net lendings (in percent of GDP) will be 6 percent from the household sector, 2 percent from the business sector, and 1 percent in the external sector. To establish the macroeconomic balance of equation (1), the government must remain a net borrower of funds at the level of 3 percent of GDP.

While estimates like these are subject to a large margin of error and must be taken with a grain of salt, there is little doubt that private savings will be in excess supply in Japan for some years to come. A new era has already opened and will continue for some time.

JAPAN'S SAVINGS AND EXTERNAL ECONOMIC RELATIONS

JAPAN AS A CAPITAL EXPORTER

If, contrary to what we have maintained, Japan will be able to raise the surplus on the current account substantially above 1 percent of GDP, will Japan be a capital exporter as the Japan-United States Economic Relations Group's Report asserted? The answer is "not necessarily," if capital exports are confined narrowly to long-term capital outflows.

Between the current account and the capital account of the balance of payments, there is a well-known identity relation:

$$\begin{matrix} \text{current account} \\ \text{surplus} \end{matrix} = \begin{matrix} \text{net capital} \\ \text{outflow,} \\ \text{long-term} \end{matrix} + \begin{matrix} \text{net capital} \\ \text{outflow,} \\ \text{short-term} \end{matrix} + \begin{matrix} \text{change in} \\ \text{official reserve} \\ \text{position} \end{matrix} \quad (9)$$

A surplus on the current account may very well go into outflows of short-term capital or accumulations of foreign currency and foreign exchanges. These are unstable and mobile components of capital flows. If capital exports are to help other nations suffering from shortages of capital, they should take the form of long-term capital flows. Such flows are direct investment in real physical assets or portfolio investment in long-term securities. Long-term investment requires deliberate decisions on the part of investors—individuals and corporations—to undertake it. Thus, even if a current-account surplus is expanded, it may not go into long-term capital flows unless there are those who are willing to tie up their capital abroad for a long time.

Table 6.12 shows major items on the current and capital accounts in percentage of GDP, averaged for 1976-79, for the eight nations most prominent in international capital investment. A few features are notable.

(i) Surpluses on the current account are on average within ± 1 percent of GDP except for small countries like the Netherlands and Switzerland (as verified for the entire decade of the seventies).

(ii) Regardless of their current-account positions, these countries (with the exception of Canada) were net exporters of long-term capital. When

TABLE 6.12

CURRENT ACCOUNT AND CAPITAL ACCOUNT BALANCE,
IN PERCENTAGE OF GDP, 1976-79 AVERAGE

Country	1979 GDP ($bn)	Current account surplus	Capital Account[a]						
			STKO (1)	LTKO (2)	DI (3)	of which (out-flow) (4)	(in-flow) (5)	PI (6)	OT (7)
Japan	782	.79	-.25	.80	.27	.28	-.01	-.04	.55
U.S.	2350	-.30	.40	.75	.49	.80	-.31	.08	.18
U.K.	401	-.42	.29	.87	.74	1.47	-.73	-.08	.21
Germany	591	.52	-.29	.17	.34	.54	-.20	-.05	-.12
France	442	.35	-.27	.47	-.09	.39	-.47	-.07	.63
Canada	176	-2.02	-.62	-1.80	.42	.79	-.37	-2.32	.10
Netherlands	115	.23	-1.37	1.93	.87	1.40	-.53	-1.03	2.09
Switzerland	69	5.09	-3.04	13.27	–	–	–	8.06	5.21

SOURCES: International Monetary Fund 1980; OECD 1981. (1) Short-term capital flow (net); (2) Long-term capital flow (net); (3) Direct investment; (4) Direct investment abroad; (5) Direct investment into the country; (6) Portfolio investment; (7) Others

[a]Outflow is + ; inflow is –.

there are deficits on the current account, this means that they borrowed short and lent long. A surplus on the current account does not ensure that country to be a long-term capital exporter.

(iii) As for direct investment, two-way flows were involved. While domestic capital is exported, foreign capital is imported. The exception is Japan; very little foreign capital flowed in—it is a virtually one-way flow. Moreover, Japan's gross outflow was internationally low. In percentage of GDP, it was the lowest among the eight countries—as low as one-fifth of the British and Dutch levels and one-third of the American and Canadian levels. The insularity of Japan with respect to direct investment flows is a well-known feature that is verified for a longer period from 1965 to 1980 in table 6.13. We may note that the outflow of direct investment was not influenced by rapidly changeable short-run positions of the current account, short-term adjustments finding ways mostly in short-term capital flows and the Bank of Japan's foreign exchange reserves.

These observations indicate that the appearance of a surplus on the current account is neither a necessary nor a sufficient condition for Japan to become a long-term capital exporter. It is obvious that a fundamental change is needed to make the Japanese perspective look outward. Without that change, however much Japan's savings may be in excess supply, they will not be exported abroad.

JAPAN'S ECONOMIC RELATIONS WITH THE UNITED STATES

The position of Japan's savings will have a great deal to do with Japan's

TABLE 6.13

JAPAN'S CURRENT ACCOUNT SURPLUS
AND DIRECT INVESTMENT IN JAPAN AND ABROAD,
AS PERCENTAGE OF GDP, 1965-80

Year	Current Account Surplus	Direct Investment Abroad	In Japan
1965	1.12	.08	.05
1966	1.30	.10	.03
1967	-.04	.10	.04
1968	.81	.14	.05
1969	1.29	.12	.04
1970	1.02	.17	.05
1971	2.52	.15	.09
1972	2.25	.24	.06
1973	-.01	.46	-.01
1974	-.96	.44	.04
1975	-.10	.35	.05
1976	.67	.36	.02
1977	1.55	.24	.00
1978	1.73	.24	.00
1979	-.87	.29	.02
1980	-.97	.22	.03

SOURCES: EPA 1981; Bank of Japan 1981

economic relations with the United States. First of all, the United States is the largest importer of Japan's manufactured goods, currently buying up as much as one-quarter of Japan's exports to the world. It is at the same time an important supplier of foodstuffs and crude materials to Japan, providing 18 percent of Japan's total imports (in 1979). However, that Japan sells more to than it buys from the United States has been a persistent source of tension between the two countries over the last fifteen years. The issue is brought into the political limelight whenever the United States runs heavily into a global deficit on its merchandise account. When the export drive is initiated by Japanese manufacturers to compensate for weak domestic aggregate demand, the first place they direct the drive is toward the American market. Trade friction appears and tension deepens between the two nations. This scenario has become familiar by repetition. And we can anticipate its rerun a few more times as long as Japan's surplus savings find a way into promotion of exports.

As for international capital flows, we can anticipate increasing interchanges in financial flows across the Pacific now that capital transactions are completely liberalized in Japan. Flows are two way. Japanese capital is attracted to the U.S. capital market by high interest yields, while American capital comes to Japan because of the appreciating yen and equity values.

However, important here are long-term capital flows, particularly direct investment. Foreign investment, intimately connected with multinational corporations, has long been dominated by the United States, the United Kingdom, and a few other early comers to the field. Japan and Germany have come onto the scene in earnest only in the seventies.

Though its history is young, there are distinct features in Japan's direct investment. It is not surprising that about one-fourth of it is in developing petroleum and mineral resources. This area of activity is essential for Japan's national security in ensuring an uninterrupted supply of strategic materials in the event of emergencies. Direct investment in manufacturing has largely been directed to less developed countries, particularly in Southeast Asia (including Taiwan and Korea) and Latin America. Japanese manufacturers engaged in such industries as textiles have been declining in Japan and losing international competitiveness because of high labor intensity. These manufacturers were strongly motivated to move abroad to make use of manual workers at low wages and/or bypass trade restrictions imposed on imports from Japan. To advanced countries like the United States and those in Western Europe, Japan's direct investment has been heavily in trading and finances as Japan's general trading firms and major banks have been developing their world network of business.

Over-all, one-third of Japan's direct investment is in manufacturing but only 20 percent goes to this field in the United States. In this regard, Japanese firms differ considerably from direct investors from other nations—40 percent of their direct investment in the United States is in manufacturing.[9]

When the United States held a supreme position in the world economy, it dominated the field of foreign investment. The flow was one-way out of the United States. The seventies witnessed a marked change in that there has emerged a sizable reverse flow, even though the inflow is still about 40 percent of the outflow (0.29 vis. 0.79 of GDP, 1974-79). Some of the major factors for this change are the undervalued dollar that makes investing in the United States a profitable proposition, the high cost of funds in the United States that forces foreign firms located in the United States to get funds from home, growing lags of American firms in technology, and so on. At the same time, the American public has become much more receptive to foreign firms investing in the United States. A foreign firm setting up manufacturing plants in the United States is seen to create new jobs, an event very much welcomed by the local community. Workers in American firms competing with foreign imports are relieved because their job security is improved. On the other hand, foreign manufacturers can now avert trade friction by pro-

9. When we compare the balance of direct investment in manufacturing between the United States and Japan, we find that at the end of 1979, the American balance in Japan was about four times the Japanese balance in the United States.

ducing in the United States. The U.S. administration will be pleased as its balance-of-payments problem is given a partial solution.

Now that Japanese steelmakers and automobile manufacturers are said to have overtaken American firms in technology—some claim that the lead is as much as ten years—they can set up plants in the United States competitively, thereby averting the stigma of trade friction. Japan's excess savings will also be exported by this action. It is beneficial to United States-Japan economic relations. How much can we expect here?

As we noted, the outflow of Japan's direct investment was less than 0.3 percent of its GDP in the late seventies. One-third was directed to the United States, amounting to less than 0.1 percent of Japan's GDP or 0.03 percent of American GDP. This is only one-tenth of all direct investment flowing into the United States in this period. Thus, despite much talk on the subject lately, Japan's activity in foreign investment has only been minuscule compared to the American market size.

If Japan's direct investment is to claim a meaningful existence in United States-Japan economic relations, the over-all level of Japan's direct investment outflow ought to be raised at least to the present American level, namely, three times to 0.8 percent of GDP.[10] Also, a much higher proportion of Japan's direct investment in the United States should go into manufacturing (from the current level of 20% to at least 40%, which is the average for all investors).

Are there any special circumstances that stand in the way of such an expansion in the United States by the Japanese? A number of factors have been cited in the literature on the subject, for example, the difficulty of securing reliable subcontractors who supply parts and components; the scarcity of qualified and dependable workers; and especially, the difficulty of adapting managerial practices to local conditions.

On the last point, there has been much talk in the popular press about the success of Japanese-style management as symbolized in paternalism, familism, and the spirit of *wa* or harmony. The excellent performance of Japanese business is attributed to it. It follows, then, that the Japanese business success will collapse as Japanese-style managerial practices—such as lifetime employment, seniority-related wages, and the no-layoff policy that ensures employee loyalty—become unmaintainable. It must be for this reason that some Japanese firms express their intention to keep these policies even in the their subsidiaries overseas. Whether they have succeeded or not is hard to ascertain at this point because known cases are still very few. It is unknown

10. At the end of 1979, the American balance of direct investment overseas was 8 percent of the American GDP, while the balance of foreign direct investment in the United States was 2 percent of the American GDP. (Japan's balance of direct investment in the U. S. was 0.14% of the American GDP in 1979, a small fraction, albeit a significant increase from the level of 0.01% held in 1973.) For data, see *Survey of Current Business,* December 1980. The Japanese balance of direct investment overseas was less than 3 percent of its GDP in the same year.

if Japanese-style management can be transplanted abroad in an alien socio-cultural environment (see Shishido 1980, chaps. 4 and 5). This is a challenging problem that must be resolved by Japanese managers when they go abroad. Unless that challenge is overcome in one way or another, Japan's direct investment cannot prosper.

Exporting Japan's savings is not a simple problem of numbers alone.

REFERENCES

Bank of Japan. See Nihon Ginkō.

Blumenthal, T. 1970. *Saving in Postwar Japan.* Harvard East Asian Monograph no. 35. Cambridge: Harvard Asian Research Center.

Boltho, A. 1975. *Japan: An Economic Survey, 1953-1973.* London: Oxford University Press.

Economic Planning Agency. See Keizai Kikakuchō.

Feldstein, M. 1974. "Social Security, Induced Retirement, and Aggregate Capital Accumulation," *Journal of Political Economy* 82 (September/October):905-26.

International Monetary Fund. 1980. *Balance of Payments Yearbook,* vol. 31 (December).

Japan-United States Economic Relations Group. 1981. *Report of the Japan-United States Economic Relations Group.* Washington, D.C. and Tokyo: The Japan-United States Economic Relations Group.

Keizai Kikakuchō. 1978. *Kokumin shotoku tōkei nempō* [Annual report on national income statistics, 1978]. Tokyo: Government Printing Office.

———. 1981. *Kokumin keizai keisan nempō* [Annual report on national accounts, 1981]. Tokyo: Government Printing Office.

Komine, T. 1980. *Nihon keizai tekiōryoku no tankyū* [The adaptability of the Japanese economy]. Tokyo: Tōyō keizai shimpōsha.

Komiya, R. 1966. "The Supply of Personal Savings." In *Postwar Economic Growth in Japan,* ed. R. Komiya, pp. 157-81. Berkeley and Los Angeles: University of California Press.

Mizoguchi, T. 1970. *Personal Savings and Consumption in Postwar Japan.* Tokyo: Kinokuniya.

Nihon Ginkō. 1981. *Kokusai shushi geppō* [Balance of payments statistics monthly].

Ohkawa, K. 1970. "Chochikuritsu no chōki hendō—kojin chochikuritsu o chūshin to suru daiichiji sekkin" [Changes in the long-term savings rate—a first approximation, focusing on the personal savings rate]. *Keizai kenkyū* 21 (May):129-36.

Organization for Economic Cooperation and Development (OECD). 1980. *National Accounts of OECD Countries, 1961-1978.* Paris.

———. 1981. *National Accounts of OECD Countries, 1961-1979.* Paris.

Prime Minister's Office, Statistics Bureau (Japan). See Sōrifu Tōkeikyoku.

Shinohara, M. 1959. "The Structure of Savings and Consumption in Postwar Japan," *Journal of Political Economy* 67 (October):589-603.

———. 1981. "Chochikuritsu no nazo" [The riddle of the savings rate]. *Chochiku jihō,* no. 127 (March), pp. 2-12.

Shishido, H., et al. 1980. *Nihon kigyō in USA* [Japanese enterprise in the United States]. Tokyo: Tōyō keizai shimpōsha.

Sōrifu Tōkeikyoku. 1977. *Katei shukyu to chusho no yoran, 1963-1975* [Family income and expenditure survey, 1963-1975]. Tokyo: Government Printing Office.

———. *Kokusei chōsa* [Census of population] various issues. Tokyo: Government Printing Office.

Trezise, P. H. 1980. "The Evolution of United States-Japan Relations." In *Japan and the*

United States: Economic and Political Adversaries, ed. L. Hollerman, pp. 147-60. Boulder, Colo.: Westview Press.

Uchihashi, K. 1981. "Zaisei hatan no 'hannin' o tsuiseki suru" [Pursuing the culprit of financial ruin]. *Bungei shunjū* 59 (February):220-35.

Oil Crises and Stagflation in Japan

YOICHI SHINKAI

ANYONE WITH A CASUAL INTEREST in the Japanese economy is aware that its macroeconomic performance since the Iranian revolution of 1979, which brought about the second oil crisis, has been markedly different from the performance after the first oil crisis of 1973. The 1973-74 inflation was the worst in more than twenty years and in 1974 the economy experienced the first negative growth rate since the end of the Second World War. The growth rate of the economy after the second crisis, though low compared with that achieved during the sixties, has been no worse than the average growth rate of the seventies. Inflation too has virtually disappeared, when measured in terms of the GNP deflator.

The Japanese experiences after the two oil crises seem to belie the notion that there is a trade-off between price stability and vigorous growth. Also called into question is the conventional wisdom that severe stagflation is inevitable when oil prices are raised sharply, as occurred in 1979. I am not implying that the second oil crisis has left the Japanese economy unscathed; inflation, measured in terms of the cost of living, has been far from negligible, and the current account balance of payments in 1980 posted a deficit of around 10 billion dollars, that is, worse even than the 1979 deficit of 8.8 billion dollars. What I shall argue in this paper is that with a proper monetary policy and reasonable wage demands made by organized labor, it is possible (as it has been in Japan) to avoid severe stagflation after an oil crisis.

Japanese economists are unanimous in attributing this avoidance of severe stagflation to the lessons learned from the first oil crisis. Policy makers learned the importance of monetary restraint, labor unions of wage

An earlier version of the paper (ISER Discussion Paper No. 110, November 1980) was presented at the U.S.-Japan Economic Relations Conference and at several seminars in Japan and the United States. I am indebted to the participants for many useful comments.

restraint, and consumers and producers of the folly of the panic buying that
fueled inflation in 1974. Japan certainly learned more lessons from the
1973-74 experience than other countries. It seems to me, however, that the
macroeconomic framework in which the lessons can be profitably applied
is not well understood. An oil price increase may sometimes cause a demand-
pull inflation (even in the absence of speculative buying) in manufactured
goods and there is reason to believe that the Japanese economy was in
danger of having such an inflation in 1979. But the restrained monetary
policy and the reasonable wage demand were instrumental in averting a
demand-pull inflation accompanied with a decline in production, that is,
a stagflation.

Another conventional wisdom is that inflation hurts export competitiveness. Economists may think differently and be inclined to the view that inflation is neutral in this respect because (nominal) exchange rates move in the
long run to preserve a purchasing power parity. After both oil crises, the
quantity of Japanese exports increased fairly rapidly. This implies that inflation per se has little to do with Japanese competitiveness, but that the
purchasing power parity theory of exchange rate is not applicable to Japan
after an oil crisis, either. The final subject discussed in this paper will be why
Japanese export competitiveness seems to improve after an oil crisis.[1]

THE JAPANESE ECONOMY AFTER THE SECOND OIL CRISIS

What happened to prices and output in Japan after the second oil crisis,
and how does this compare with the developments after the first crisis? Or,
why did we observe a macroeconomic performance in 1979 and 1980 that
was in sharp contrast with that of 1974? I shall attempt to answer these
questions and I shall also try to show here, and following, that the movements in several price ratios and the money supply are of key importance in
understanding the effects of oil price increases on the Japanese economy.

Some readers might have considered the statement that inflation was
virtually nonexistent in 1979 an exaggeration. They must certainly have
remembered the news that the Japanese wholesale price index (WPI hereafter) was registering inflation rates of 20 percent for April 1979 through the
same month of 1980. But the Japanese WPI, being heavily biased toward
imported materials and fuels, often gives a misleading impression of the inflation scene. To remedy the bias let me present a graph from the *1980
Economic White Paper* (Economic Planning Agency 1980a).

Figure 7.1 compares the movements of several price indexes before and
after the two oil crises. The left panel of figure 7.1 traces Consumer Price
Index or CPI (all inclusive), WPI (all inclusive), and Import Price Index.
The right panel shows how the average WPI is broken down into three broad

---

1. It must be noted at the outset that the last topic will be dealt with concisely to
save space. I have written another paper that discusses the topic fully in the context of
U.S.-Japan trade relations. See Shinkai 1981.

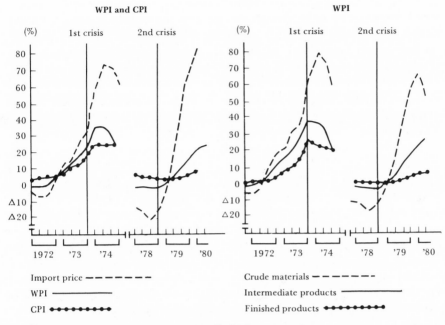

SOURCE: Economic Planning Agency 1980, fig. I.1.7

Fig. 7.1. Movements in several price indexes (in percentage of rate of change over a year)

categories: crude materials, intermediate products, and finished products. One can see that during the first oil crisis, prices had been rising before the quadrupling of the oil price, with finished-product WPI and CPI more or less paralleling the other indexes. In the second oil crisis, on the other hand, prices were stable when the crisis hit and while the import price or crude materials price increase'd as rapidly as in 1974, CPI and finished-products WPI have remained fairly stable.

These observations suggest the following: demand management by the authorities before 1974 left something to be desired; there are two categories of commodities, those with prices tending toward volatile movements and those with prices less liable to change; and we cannot therefore speak of *the* price level in Japan, but should analyze several price ratios (or relative prices). The first point will be taken up later, so suffice it here to introduce table 7.1 and note that the money supply behaved in a markedly contrasting manner between 1972-73 and the period since 1974. Points one and two are elaborated below.

It is probably well known that agricultural and mineral products, including crude fuels, are traded in an "auction market," while most manufactured products are sold in a "customer market" (this distinction is emphasized in Okun 1975). Auction market prices make large, frequent changes, reflecting changes in demand and/or supply. In a customer market, prices tend to be

TABLE 7.1

MONEY SUPPLY, PRICES, AND REAL GROWTH RATE IN JAPAN
(Annual rates of change, in percentages)

	M_2+CD	CPI	GNP Deflator	Real GNP
1972	26.5	4.5	4.7	9.5
1973	22.7	11.7	10.9	10.0
1974	11.9	24.5	20.1	-0.5
1975	13.1	11.8	8.6	1.4
1976	15.1	9.3	5.6	6.5
1977	11.4	8.1	5.6	5.4
1978	11.7	3.8	3.9	6.0
1979	11.5	3.6	2.0	6.0
1980[a]	10.1	7.7	0.6	5.9

SOURCES: Bank of Japan 1980; Economic Planning Agency (hereafter cited as EPA) 1980b

[a]The first half of 1980

"sticky," but the price of manufactured goods can change significantly relative to those of primary good prices. As is mentioned in the appendix, the relative price movements after the first oil crisis are too large to ignore when discussing the stagflation problem in Japan. Figure 7.1 shows a wide divergence between the finished products price and the price of imported crude materials (fuel included) after the second oil crisis. This implies a large deterioration in the Japanese terms of trade, as in figure 7.2.

Figure 7.2 traces two important price ratios. One of the two, the terms of trade (export price index divided by import price index) referred to above roughly measures the impact of the oil crises. In Japan, an oil crisis is summarized as a large increase in the oil price relative to the price of manufactured goods. This shows up in the terms of trade because Japan exports manufactured goods and oil is about 40 percent of Japan's imports. If the world price of manufactured goods increased fairly rapidly after an oil crisis, inflation would increase but the real cost of the OPEC action to industrial economies would be small. However, the present situation is that an oil price rise means a relative price change and exerts a real economic impact.[2]

I discuss the nature of this impact below, but to see beforehand how Japanese wages behaved in the fact of deteriorating terms of trade, figure 7.2 shows another important price ratio, the price of manufactured goods relative to the efficiency wage rate. The latter is simply the *shunto*[3] wage

2. This formulation of an oil crisis is from, among others, Solow 1980. As Solow notes, the price of manufactured goods does not rise fast enough because of the monopoly power on the part of OPEC as well as the customer market nature emphasized in the text.

3. *Shunto* or spring wage offensive is a unique Japanese phenomenon (perhaps

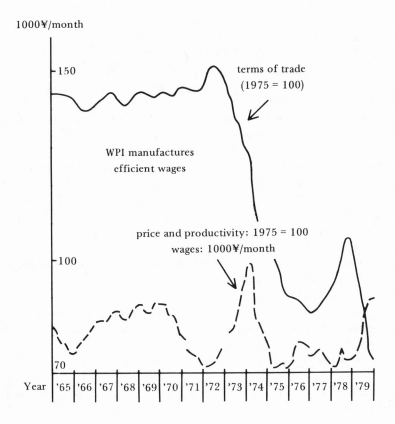

1000¥/month

150 ─

terms of trade
(1975 = 100)

WPI manufactures
efficient wages

price and productivity: 1975 = 100
wages: 1000¥/month

100 ─

70

Year ’65 ’66 ’67 ’68 ’69 ’70 ’71 ’72 ’73 ’74 ’75 ’76 ’77 ’78 ’79

Fig. 7.2. Two important price-ratios

rate, an equivalent of the straight wage rate in other countries, divided by
the labor productivity index. This ratio measures (in reverse) the real wage
cost to manufacturing firms. Figure 7.2 also shows that the real wage cost
decreased (the relative product price increased) markedly during 1979,
while it sharply increased after the first oil crisis.

THE ECONOMICS OF OUTPUT DECLINE AFTER AN OIL CRISIS

We have seen that the Japanese economy experienced a severe recession after
the first oil crisis but the output growth slowed down only moderately, if
at all, after the second crisis. The two price ratios, the relative price of oil
and the relative wage (adjusted for productivity), seem to have played important roles in determining the developments in manufacturing output.
This section will provide an economic background to the recession induced
by higher oil prices.

_____

the wage-round in West Germany is comparable); it will be briefly explained in a later
section.

The idea that a recession is inevitable when oil prices are raised steeply is based on three lines of economic reasoning. The easiest to understand is that the government resorts to an excessively restrictive policy measure to deal with the cost-push pressure and the trade-balance deficits due to an oil price rise. It seems to me that the world-wide recession of 1975 can be explained to a large extent by this line of argument (Black 1977). Further discussion of this topic will be presented later. The other two lines of reasoning are an excise-tax effect and a profit-squeeze effect.

It is well known that the OPEC-induced increase in oil prices works as an excise tax on an essential good, transferring the purchasing power from oil-importing countries to OPEC countries (see Gordon 1975 for one of early explanations). Since oil exporters are unlikely to spend all the transferred income, the result will be a decrease in the demand for manufactured goods produced by the oil-importing countries. In Japan, this shortfall in demand has been calculated as 3 percent of GNP after the first oil crisis and 1.5-2 percent after the second. The calculation may overstate or understate the true impact, but the basic message of the excise tax view is clear: the nominal (or money-value) demand for manufactured goods declines, and given the downward rigidity of their prices, so does real demand. The demand management policy should therefore aim at expansion, to the extent that the excise-tax effect will be offset.

The profit-squeeze view, popular among economists, arrives at the opposite conclusion (Solow 1980; Bruno and Sachs 1979; see also Gordon 1975 for a balanced appraisal of the issue). A sharp increase in the relative price of oil, which is what an oil crisis is, squeezes the manufacturing profit that uses oil as input. Unless the real wage cost per unit of output is reduced, the profit must be recovered either by laying off some of the labor or by putting employees on shorter hours. Either way, the supply of manufacturing output is decreased, which to an outside observer may be indistinguishable from a demand-constrained decline in output. Actually, the situation is one of supply constraint, and to stimulate demand in this case would only lead to a demand-pull inflation.

Which of these three lines of economic reasoning about the cause of actual or potential stagnation applies to Japan? Although it is difficult to identify the cause of a particular situation, let us here look at figure 7.3 and discuss the two episodes of 1974 and 1979 with the help of hindsight. The upper panel of figure 7.3 traces the quarterly values of the jobs-offered to jobs-wanted ratio[4] (scaled upside down), a measure comparable to the unemployment rate of other countries. The lower panel is a demand-supply gap index computed by the forecasting team of the Japan Economic Research Center (JERC 1980; since I interpret the figure liberally, JERC should not be held responsible for what follows). Both the job measure and the gap

4. Compiled by the Ministry of Labor. Needless to say, a rise in the ratio corresponds to a fall in the unemployment rate.

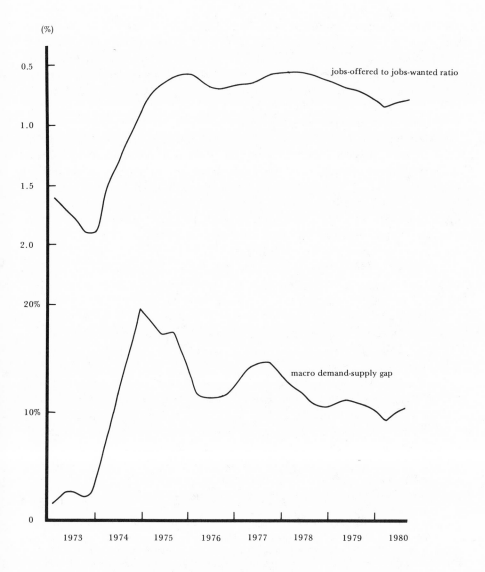

Fig. 7.3. Two cyclical indexes

index indicate that the economy was overheated before the first oil crisis. The 1979 situation is more controversial, but I submit that the Japanese manufacturing sector on the whole was near the full-employment, full-capacity point through 1979. It is generally agreed that the first quarter of 1980 was a period of prosperity, and the two measures of figure 7.3 put the average of 1979 not far from that for this period of 1980.

The nearly 20 percent decline in manufacturing output in 1974, then, may be explained either by the restrictive policy or by the profit squeeze.

The excise-tax effect could explain a small portion of the decline, as I have indicated. One might perhaps argue that the demand management policy in 1974 and 1975 was too restrictive. But a milder policy could have only slightly alleviated the recession. Figure 7.2 shows that the real wage cost in 1975 was no lower than in 1972, a mild recession year, and with the steeply increased cost of oil, the supply constraint would have prevented manufacturing output from recovering rapidly.[5]

What happened, or more properly, what did not happen in 1979? The price of oil nearly doubled. This translated to a 30 percent increase in the price of crude materials (including fuel). With the real wage cost per unit of output unchanged, the profit squeeze would have decreased the supply of manufactured goods by about 13 percent. This number, whose derivation is discussed in the appendix, is of course subject to a wide margin of error. It seems certain, however, that the supply constraint would have outweighed any excise-tax effect on the demand side.

The fact is that output did not decline.[6] In my opinion, the single most important factor that contributed to this outcome was a 15 percent decline in the real wage cost per unit of output during 1979. As figure 7.2 shows, the relative price of manufactured goods, in terms of efficiency wage rates, increased by about 15 percent. This is the value calculated in the appendix as necessary to prevent the manufacturing supply from declining in the face of a 100 percent increase in the oil price.

The 1979 episode may be summarized as follows. The Japanese economy was not far from a full employment situation when the second oil crisis hit. The monetary policy turned mildly restrictive, but not excessively so, and contributed to averting a demand-pull inflation without depressing demand. The profit-squeeze effect, which could have decreased the supply of manufactures by as much as 13 percent, was prevented because of a substantial cut in the real wage cost. A recession did not materialize, and, moreover, the oil-induced inflation has been largely avoided.

5. Richard Cooper pointed out that in view of the fairly rapid increase in Japanese real exports in the ensuing years, there must have been room for stimulative policies after the first oil crisis. I concede the force of his argument so far as real output and relative prices are concerned. I have one reservation though: that export increase and stimulative policies may have had different effects on inflation, which must be examined empirically in a future study.

6. Ryutaro Komiya, Hugh Patrick, and Richard Cooper, among others, expressed their doubt as to my contention that the Japanese economy was near full-employment output around 1979. Since I cannot provide a solid number on the potential output, I must concede (as I did in the text) that my argument here is subject to qualifications. There can be little doubt, on the other hand, that since the second half of 1980 Japan has had a mild recession of the demand-constraint type. One could argue that this is an aftermath of the second oil crisis, though I am inclined to attribute it to the somewhat restrictive monetary policy.

OIL INFLATION, WAGES, AND THE MONETARY POLICY

I have emphasized the importance of price ratios, but the reader may wonder how a change in the real wage cost, for example, occurred in such a way to contribute to the performance of the Japanese economy following the second oil crisis. The real wage cost consists of at least three elements: nominal wage rate, productivity, and product price. If we ignore productivity here for the sake of simplicity, are not nominal wage and product price set more or less independently? It is the purpose of this section to focus on price and wage levels and address ourselves directly to the problem of inflation.

Let me first deal with the conventional view that a steep rise in oil prices inevitably leads to substantial inflation.[7] While I concede that the result depends on the choice of countries and/or time periods, the Japanese experience in the last several years establishes the opposite position. As the *Economic White Paper* notes (see fig. I-3-10), the period of 1976-79, when the monetary policy was mildly restrictive, saw the inflation rate in GNP deflator steadily moderating, while the import price index posted a sharp increase after 1978. I have calculated how price levels in Japan are influenced by the import prices, and summarize the results in table 7.2.

TABLE 7.2

EFFECTS OF IMPORT PRICES ON THE GENERAL PRICE LEVELS
(In percentages)

	GNP Deflator	Total Demand Deflator	WPI, Manufacturing Goods
Import price, average	-0.01[a]	0.065[b]	
Import price, crude materials	-0.01[a]		0.069[b]
Terms of trade	-0.03[a]		

[a]Statistically undistinguishable from zero

[b]Statistically significant

GNP deflator may be interpreted as the price of domestically produced goods and services or as the price of wages and profits (the value-added deflator). It is one of the representative inflation measures, and table 7.2 shows

7. This view is widely held in Japan as well as in the West. A leading Japanese monetarist, Seiji Shimpo, says that the elasticity of import price on GNP deflator is about 0.1, see Shimpo 1979, p. 138. Michael Bruno, in his study of several OECD economies, calculates that the elasticity of import price on the CPI is more than 0.4, see Bruno 1978.

that the effect of import prices on it can be ignored.[8] Total demand deflator is computed as the weighted average of GNP deflator and import price (average). The Japanese weight on the latter is about 0.1, and the estimated value of 0.065[9] in table 7.2 is consistent with the definition of total demand deflator and the zero import-price effect on GNP deflator. The effect of the price of imported crude materials on manufactured goods WPI is also small. There is reason to suspect, however, that this effect has been estimated with a large margin of error. Moreover, the possibility remains that an imported inflation in this index will be transmitted to the GNP deflator later on. Hence my reservation above that different time periods may lead to different conclusions on the importance of inflation induced by high oil prices.

How serious this inflation can be depends largely on the behavior of nominal wages.[10] If the annual wage increase is heavily influenced by movements in the CPI, as in many Western countries, the real wage in terms of the CPI can be regarded as sticky (see Branson and Rotemberg, 1980; Sachs 1979; it appears that Japan is classified into the same group). This implies that the nominal wage rate must rise as fast as the manufactured good price because the latter constitutes a large portion of the CPI.[11] Even a moderate rise in the manufactured good price due to an oil crisis can be translated in this case into a serious wage-price spiral.

The Japanese wage did rise steeply after the first oil crisis. During the 1974 *shunto*,[12] labor, alarmed at the 25 percent CPI inflation, demanded and obtained a stunning 32 percent pay raise.[13] As time passed, however, labor had to learn that a large increase in the nominal wage rate was not

8. Hendrick Houthakker pointed out correctly that Japan could enjoy this independence of GNP deflator because its domestic production of oil can be ignored. In a country such as the United States where domestic production of oil is substantial, it will be difficult to isolate GNP deflator from imported oil price.

9. The estimated standard error is 0.025.

10. This is in fact the main point of the Western economists. See Solow 1980, Gordon 1975, Bruno 1978, and Bruno and Sachs 1979.

11. I abstract here from the problem raised by the usual inclusion of imported manufacturers in the CPI. The problem becomes important when one is interested in the relationship among oil-importing countries. See, for example, Branson and Rotemberg 1980.

12. As Sachs 1979 notes, the Japanese unions are organized almost exclusively at the enterprise level, but wage settlements are synchronized through the annual spring wage offensive that involves virtually all unions. Nonunion wages are also revised annually at about the same time as *shunto;* of the manufacturing sector establishments more than 80 percent annually revise the standard wage between April and June. See Ministry of Labor 1980, appendix, p. 60.

13. This is in terms of the *shunto* wage rate. Because of the prevalent bonus system as well as of nearly routine overtime, the Japanese nominal wage is somewhat more flexible than the *shunto* rate. This can be seen by comparing the first and second columns of table 7.3. My point here, however, is that the *shunto* rate itself has been flexible recently.

necessarily to its advantage. True, the real wage and labor's share in the national income went up (see table 7.3), but CPI inflation continued well into 1977 in spite of the restrictive monetary policy. Worst of all, the profit squeeze meant a severe recession, with the resulting deterioration in employment rates.

TABLE 7.3

SOME WAGE-RELATED INDEXES

(In percentages)

Wage Rate, Rate of Change

Fiscal Year	shunto[a]	ML index, nominal	ML index, real	Labor's Share in the Firms' Value-added
1970	18.5	17.3	9.5	53.1
1971	16.9	13.7	7.5	56.9
1972	15.3	16.5	10.7	56.9
1973	20.1	21.9	4.8	53.3
1974	32.9	29.1	6.0	58.4
1975	13.1	12.4	1.8	66.6
1976	8.8	11.8	2.2	64.2
1977	8.8	8.1	1.3	65.7
1978	5.9	5.9	2.4	59.7
1979	6.0	7.4[a]	3.7[b]	—
1980	6.7	—	—	—

SOURCES: Ministry of Labor 1980; EPA 1980c; Ministry of Finance 1980

[a]Private sector

[b]Manufacturing sector

The lesson of the first oil crisis has led labor to "rationalize" its wage demand in subsequent *shuntos*. As seen in table 7.3, the rate of increase in *shunto* wages has moderated considerably. Especially noteworthy are the two last *shuntos*, when the nominal wages increased by less than might be expected from a low unemployment figure (1979) or a high expected CPI inflation (1980). In fact, the 1980 *shunto* result was so low that the real wage in terms of the CPI has been declining since February of 1980.

How was labor's moderation rational? First, it has brought about a decline in the real wage cost, as discussed earlier. This decline was instrumental in preventing a severe recession from materializing, which would have cost labor many jobs. Second, it helped avert a wage-price spiral, from which no one would benefit. That labor understood the implications of a moderate wage demand can be seen from the following quotation from a representative "offensive" white paper: "Our wage demand is based on our assessment of the impact of oil price increases and the growth prospect, and aims at a real wage increase lower than the real GNP growth; in setting the 1980 wage demand we have given due consideration to restraining inflation, as we have done in the past."[14]

With such rational behavior on the part of labor,[15] it should not be too difficult to avoid an oil inflation if the monetary policy is mildly restrictive, as it has recently been in Japan. We have already seen in table 7.1 that the money supply has been stable since 1977, with annual rates of increase at about 10 percent. In the face of the second oil crisis, the Bank of Japan did a good job of controlling the money supply; it neither slackened the reins[16] as it did in 1972-73, nor did it slam on the brakes as in 1974-75. The result has been the conspicuous absence of what has come to be described in Japan as "homemade inflation."

There is another reason why a steady monetary policy is recommended in the face of an oil crisis. I have assumed that the economy was near a full-employment situation in 1979 and argued that the supply constraint was in force after the oil price increase. However, it may be more reasonable to concede the difficulty of identifying which constraint is in force. A steady monetary policy is recommended then because the two worst cases can be avoided—stimulating demand when supply is a constraint and depressing demand when a demand constraint is effective.

I think the Bank of Japan has been successful in pursuing this course of monetary management. It is why the bank is largely credited with turning the lesson of 1972-73 into profit in 1979. Trade unions are successful in the same sense. If the lesson of the first oil crisis is remembered by the parties concerned, as I think it will be, then one can conclude that a severe stagflation is not likely to plague Japan in the coming years.

THE JAPANESE EXPORT PROSPECTS
IN THE INTERNATIONAL PERSPECTIVE

If a severe stagflation is unlikely to plague Japan, the price level will be stable and productivity will continue to increase. Does this imply that the Japanese export competitiveness is going to improve, or will the bright outlook for Japan be clouded when examined in the international perspective? The

14. See Zen-Nippon Rōdōsōdōmei 1980, pp. 7-8. Rōdōsōdōmei is a federation of major private-sector unions that shares the control of *shunto*s with Sōhyō, a stronghold of public employee unions. The word *control* should not be interpreted too literally. As Komiya pointed out, Japanese wages may be more influenced by bargains at individual firms than by the union federations.

15. In this paper I have maintained that labor has learned a lesson from the first oil crisis. It is possible, however, to interpret the whole *shunto* history in terms of a value-productivity theory of wage determination. That is to say, one can argue that the *shunto* wage bargains have been mainly dependent on the product price adjusted for input materials price and on labor productivity. See Koshiro 1980; Shinkai 1980a. See also my paper, "The Effect of Terms of Trade on Wage Determination and Foreign Exchange Rates" (mimeograph).

16. The excise-tax interpretation of the crisis would have recommended that money be eased somewhat.

answer to either question is, in my view, yes. However, I shall only give an
outline of my views on this problem, due to space limitations.

Two conflicting forces are at work: one that encourages Japanese exports and another that discourages them. The former is a likely improvement
in Japan's export competitiveness, which I shall discuss under three head-
ings: export-biased growth in productivity, a fall in the terms of trade, and
nonprice competitiveness. The latter force is concerned with the stagflation in Japan's trading partners and financing their oil deficits. One would
need a lengthy paper to examine these issues adequately, so I shall have to
be brief.

Let us begin with export-biased growth. I have shown elsewhere (Shinkai
1980b) that productivity growth in the Japanese export sector has been
faster than average but that no such pattern is observed for the United
States. An implication of the disparate productivity movements between the
two countries is that purchasing power parity (PPP), with respect to a
general price level, does not neutralize the Japanese edge in export competitiveness. A slower inflation in Japan than in the United States will be neu-
tralized by appreciating the yen/dollar exchange rates. A PPP with respect to
the general price level, however, results in lower export prices on Japan's
part because of said patterns of productivity.

What, then, if the PPP holds with respect to traded-goods prices? In this
case, given a country's terms of trade, there is no reason why export competitiveness should improve. But do the terms of trade remain unchanged,
especially after an oil crisis? I have already suggested that the Japanese
terms of trade worsen after an oil crisis. A more satisfactory discussion of
this phenomenon would have to include the analysis of major determinants
of the yen exchange rates, which I cannot attempt here. Suffice it to point
out that the U.S. terms of trade worsen after an oil crisis, too, but that the
deterioration will be less than for Japan. Thus the U.S.-Japan bilateral
terms of trade will move against the latter nation.[17]

Shinkai 1981 contains a discussion of nonprice competitiveness. Such
factors as the larger share of new products among Japanese exports, the
larger share of those goods for which world demands grow fast, and export
promotions that seemed to contribute to an improved nonprice competitiveness are mentioned. The list can be enlarged, perhaps to include such
items as the reliability of products. Since the United States is trying to improve on this front, however, it is difficult to judge whether the Japanese
relative competitiveness will improve or not.

Turning to factors that may discourage Japanese exports, perhaps the
stagflation in Japan's trading partners is easier to deal with. The inflation
part of stagflation has just been discussed. That the stagnation part will lead

17. My calculation of a version of the bilateral terms of trade (actually the Japanese
export-import price ratios with the bilateral trade as weights) indicates that there is a
trend movement against Japan on the order of 30 percent between 1965 and 1980, and
that two sharp declines are observed after the two oil crises. See Shinkai 1981.

to poor demands for Japanese exports needs no explanation. What is difficult to forecast is how likely stagflation is in those countries. Unfortunately, one cannot forecast it with any certainty. I can only conjecture that if oil crises continue to plague the world economy, other countries will be less successful than Japan in avoiding the resultant recessions.

My last point is concerned with financing the trade deficits that will result from future oil crises. This is a complicated subject and I find no easy way to work through its ramifications. One possible projection would be that future oil deficits will be shared mostly by less developed countries, and those countries will tend to find it increasingly difficult to finance these deficits. Since the bulk of Japanese exports are marketed in these countries, it is entirely possible that Japan's export growth will be hampered by the oil deficit problem.

CONCLUSION AND SOME POLICY IMPLICATIONS

In examining Japanese stagflation, I have found that Japan's performance was good, seen in isolation, and prospects not bleak. When seen in an international perspective, however, Japan cannot expect only good fortune. Japan's trading partners are more likely than not to suffer from stagflation, implying a sagging demand for Japanese exports. Even Japanese export competitiveness, which I contend is likely to improve after oil crises, may be a cause for trade conflicts. While one can speculate almost anything about the coming decade in Japan, I am inclined to conclude that the future cannot be bright when the rest of the world is expected to suffer from recurrent oil crises.

Apart from this view, what lessons can one draw from the recent Japanese experience? One is the importance of monetary restraint in avoiding inflation. The first oil crisis hit Japan when inflation, caused by the easy-money policy of 1972-73, was well under way. The 25 percent CPI inflation of 1974 testifies that the combination of easy money and oil crisis can push prices beyond control. The second oil crisis showed that a stable monetary policy can prevent inflation in the GNP deflator from materializing in the face of even doubled oil prices.

But monetary restraint may lead to a severe recession if labor makes inflexible wage demands. Another lesson drawn from the recent Japanese experience is that the nominal wage should rise less, proportionately, than labor productivity when the price of imported oil rises sharply. In other words, the real wage in terms of product price (adjusted for productivity increase) must fall to compensate for the rise in the real price of imported oil. This real adjustment is necessary anyway when there is a sharp increase in the real oil price and must be in the form of nominal wage moderation if stagflation is to be avoided.

A third lesson is mostly for Japanese policy matters. After two oil crises, the Japanese economy could overcome aggregate demand deficiency or excise-tax effect largely through sharp increases in export quantity. This was realized by large declines in its terms of trade, not only vis-à-vis OPEC countries but also vis-à-vis the United States and other oil importing countries. I would not say the Japanese authorities engineered terms of trade declines deliberately. However, the Japanese should keep in mind that the export-oriented solution of the demand constraint problem is not available to all oil importing countries. For the mutual terms of trade cannot decline for all these countries, and the aggregate trade balance of these countries must be negative against the oil exporting countries.

Policy implications presented here thus seem to be the following. There are a few measures that individual countries can implement, such as a stable money supply. There is a lesson organized labor can learn, that a nominal wage moderation is important in avoiding stagflation in the face of an oil crisis. But when one views the world economy as a whole, the demand deficiency problem remains to be solved, and this solution may not be easy if the real price of oil continues to rise rapidly.

APPENDIX 1. TECHNICAL NOTES

Discussion here is to allow the technically oriented reader to make critical assessments of some of the points raised in the text.

A Comparison of Price Indexes

In the text, I referred to the distinction between an auction market and a customer market, and suggested that some prices are considerably more variable than others. To see the extent to which price volatility differs among various indexes, I have calculated their mean absolute rates of change (monthly). The result is given in table 7.4, together with the maximum and minimum rates of change. The abbreviations used there are: **WPGEN**: WPI all commodities; **WPMFG**: WPI manufacturing products; **WPNMF**: WPI nonmanufacturing; **WPPUB**: utility rates; **WPPRD**: WPI producer goods; **WPCAP**: WPI capital goods; **WPCON**: WPI consumer goods; **WPINV**: WPI investment goods; **CPGEN**: CPI all items; **CPMFG**: CPI industrial products; **CPTER**: CPI general service; **CPSER**: CPI personal service; **PEXAV**: export price, all commodities; **PEXMF**: export price, heavy and chemical industry products; **PIAVE**: import price, all commodities; **PIFOO**: import price, foodstuffs; **PIMAT**: import price, raw materials and fuels; **WPDOM**: WPI domestic products; **WPEXP**: WPI export goods; **WPIMP**: WPI import goods; **WAGE**: *Shunto* wage rate.

Table 7.4 confirms my contention that manufactured goods prices are more stable than primary goods prices. This implies, because of the commodity contents of the Japanese foreign trade, that import prices are far more volatile than export or domestic prices. Some items of table 7.4 are misleading. The utility rates index, for example, may appear fairly variable, with the average absolute change of 1.28% and the maximum monthly increase of 61%. Utility rates are subject to government regulation, and change rarely, but when they do change, due to oil-price increase, say, they can jump steeply.

I also argued in the text that the Japanese export prices can move somewhat differently from the general trend, resulting in improved export competitiveness. In this respect, it may be of some interest to calculate the correlation coefficients among various price indexes. A selection is shown in table 7.5. One can see that though exports consist almost exclusively of manufactured goods, their prices diverge considerably from domestic prices or manufacturing WPI. The coefficient between WPMFG and PIMAT is rather

TABLE 7.4

VARIABILITIES OF PRICE INDEXES
FEBRURARY 1970 TO MARCH 1980
(In percentages)

	Mean Absolute	Minimum	Maximum
WPGEN	0.76	-0.95	7.12
WPMFG	0.66	-0.79	7.58
WPNMF	1.36	-2.73	12.95
WPPUB	1.28	-8.50	61.15
WPPRD	0.99	-1.33	9.40
WPCAP	0.42	-0.57	5.45
WPCON	0.53	-0.72	4.52
WPINV	0.64	-0.74	6.95
CPGEN	0.88	-1.16	4.47
CPMFG	0.84	-1.64	5.02
CPTER	0.79	-0.15	4.51
CPSER	0.91	-0.20	10.60
PEXAV	0.96	-3.21	7.91
PEXMF	1.01	-3.18	8.03
PIAVE	1.99	-6.54	16.55
PIFOO	1.98	-6.88	10.66
PIMAT	2.36	-6.84	24.12
WPDOM[a]	0.48	-0.46	1.92
WPEXP[a]	1.09	-3.67	3.62
WPIMP[a]	2.16	-6.15	7.61

[a] February 1975-March 1980

TABLE 7.5

CORRELATION COEFFICIENTS
AMONG SELECTED PRICE INDEXES, RATE OF CHANGES,
FEBRUARY 1975 TO MARCH 1980

	WPEXP	WPMFG	CPGEN
WPEXP	1.00		
WPMFG	0.63	1.00	
CPGEN	0.66	0.19	1.00
WPDOM	0.45	0.95	0.25
PIMAT	0.76	0.82	0.06
WPPUB	0.25	0.38	0.30

high at 0.82, my assertion in the text that their ratio plays an important role notwithstanding. If I include the first oil crisis period, the coefficient comes down to 0.64.

Determinants of Manufacturing Output

In the text I argued that manufacturing outputs can decline because of a supply constraint as well as due to demand deficiencies. Japanese empirical studies (and Western studies, for that matter) tend to focus their attention on one of the two constraints. It seems to be the case, however, that at certain periods a supply constraint of the profit squeeze type was in effect (see the discussion on pp. 181-84), while at other times demand deficiencies determined the output level. (I argued elsewhere that during the 1974-78 period, manufacturing production did not respond to relative price changes; see Shinkai 1979.) To estimate the effects of supply and demand factors on the output level in this situation, a statistical technique for markets in disequilibrium would be an appropriate tool.

I have assumed that output in the manufacturing sector, given the stock of capital, depends on WPMFG/PIMAT and WPMFG/WAGE, where wage denotes *shunto* rate, in supply-constrained periods; and that when output is demand-determined, real public investments, real private investments, and real money supply (distributed lags with a priori weights) are the strategic variables. A rationale for the supply constraint specification was given in the text. The specification for the demand-constraint period will be controversial; real exports were omitted on the grounds that exports are endogenous (dependent strongly on terms of trade), and real private investments could have been excluded on the same grounds.[18] In any case, I readily concede that the specification here is at best tentative.

Perhaps more controversial is the way in which the whole period is divided into the demand-constrained and supply-constrained subperiods. If the specification discussed above was correct, one could apply a maximum likelihood method to estimate the subdivisions simultaneously with the coefficients on the explanatory variable. As it is, I feel it is safer to use a priori information on the macro demand-supply gap, the jobs-offered/ jobs-wanted ratio, and overtime hours. The result reported in table 7.6 is based on subdivisions according to the macro demand-supply gap, but there is no compelling reason why other indicators could not have been employed.

TABLE 7.6

MANUFACTURING OUTPUTS/CAPITAL STOCK AS
DETERMINED BY SUPPLY AND DEMAND FACTORS

Subperiods	Factors	Elasticity	t-value
Supply constrained	WPMFG/WAGE	0.232	6.4
	WPMFG/PIMAT	0.452	6.0
	MONEY/WPMFG[a]	0.127	0.4
Demand constrained	INVPU/WPMFG[b]	0.452	2.4
	INVPR/WPMFG[c]	0.516	4.4

$\bar{R}^2 = 0.89$ D.W = 0.58   1966 I ∿ 1979 IV

[a]Real money supply, distributed lags: $0.2M + 0.3M_{-1} + 0.3M_{-2} + 0.2M_{-3}$

[b]Real public investment

[c]Real private fixed investment

The estimated output equation in table 7.6 leaves something to be desired. A low value for the Durbin-Watson statistic indicates that the t-values may have been overestimated. Some may question the plausibility of the first two elasticities. If one as-

18. I am inclined to regard private fixed investments as more or less autonomous. I know that few economists will agree, but I should remind the reader of an assertion by Keynes to the effect that such investments are based on economic calculations "only a little more than an expedition to the South Pole."

sumes that the underlying production function is of a two-level CES type (see Bruno and Sachs 1979, p. 36), the elasticity of substitution between capital and labor should be 0.06 and the partial elasticity of substitution of materials and fuels with respect to capital, 0.79.[19] The labor elasticity appears a little too low but it is possible that labor is more like a fixed factor of production in Japan. A high elasticity for materials and fuels is not surprising in view of the well-known energy savings realized since the first oil crisis (see, for example, Economic Planning Agency 1980a, pt. 2, chap. 2, and MITI 1980, chap. 3).

The numbers in table 7.6 can be translated into a graph as in figure 7.4. Output/

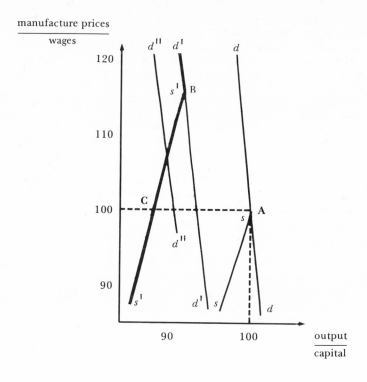

Fig. 7.4. Changes in real demand and supply due to an oil price rise

capital is measured on the horizontal axis and WPMFG/WAGE on the vertical axis, both as indexes. Point A is supposed to be a full-employment equilibrium where demand (d—d, drawn downward sloping[20]) and supply (positively sloping s—s) are equal. A 30% increase in PIMAT, given WPMFG, will shift s—s leftward by 13.6% (0.452 x 0.3). A full-employment output should decrease slightly to B, say, so that the heavy line s'—B—d' shows how output is determined after a 30% rise in PIMAT as a function of WPMFG/WAGE. At this moment output is supply constrained, and the unchanged demand d—d would imply an excess demand at whatever real wages. If the real wage can be reduced so that WPMFG/WAGE is about 115, d'—d' would be optimum. If WGMFG/WAGE can increase only to 105, say, demand must be reduced to d''—d''.

19. Based on the approximate labor share value of 0.7 and the materials and fuels share in gross outputs of 0.1.

20. Perhaps because a rise in labor's share will increase ceteris paribus real demand, a factor ignored in table 7.6. What follows does not depend on this slope of d—d.

An Oil-Induced Inflation

I want to argue that the effect of import prices on GNP deflator is negligible when the money-supply effect is taken into account. Monetarists now maintain that money supply affects nominal income with long lags, and few economists would object. The division of nominal income changes into price changes and real GNP changes is a matter of controversy, but I want to circumvent it here by treating real GNP as given. Thus I shall estimate price equations of the form:

$$\Delta p = -\alpha \Delta y + \beta \Delta M + \gamma \Delta pm$$

where Δy is real GNP changes, ΔM distributed lags of money supply changes, and Δpm distributed lags of import price changes. A select result is presented in table 7.7.

TABLE 7.7

SOME PRICE EQUATIONS, 1975 II - 1980 I

General Prices	Real GNP	Money/Real GNP in Almon lags	Money[a]	Import[a] Prices Average	PIMAT[a]	s.e. D.W.
GNP	-0.194		0.437	-0.013		0.0049
deflator	(1.47)		(5.9)	(0.4)		1.94
GNP	-0.198		0.440		-0.015	0.0049
deflator	(1.5)		(5.9)		(.6)	1.95
GNP		0.603		-0.049		0.051
deflator		(8.0)		(1.4)		1.80
Total						
demand	-0.070		0.376	0.065		0.0039
deflator	(0.7)		(6.4)	(2.6)		2.02
WPMFG		0.451			0.069	0.0058
		(5.2)			(2.1)	0.92

t-ratios in parentheses. Estimated without intercepts.

[a] Almon lags of 4 to 8 quarters, 2nd or 3rd degrees.

The coefficients on import prices were already discussed in the text (table 7.2). Otherwise, table 7.7 is self explanatory, and I point out only that the coefficients on money supply are considerably smaller than unity, implying money is not neutral. This particular result may reflect what is actually happening or it may be due to some fault in the estimation.

APPENDIX 2. RECENT PRICE STABILIZATION POLICIES

In the face of the second oil crisis, Japanese policy authorities resorted to various measures, one of which was the Bank of Japan's monetary restraint referred to in the text. What follows is a list of the measures taken by the central government.[21]

Measures Agreed on in February 1979

On February 26, an eight-item precautionary measure was agreed upon, and included: carefully watching the demand and supply conditions of important commodities; preventing unwarranted price-hikes of oil-related goods; and being strict on the regulation

21. Taken from the Economic Planning Agency's 1980 price report.

of utility rates. In addition, it was decided to slow down the number of contracts awarded for public investment projects in the first half of fiscal 1979.

Measures Agreed on in November 1979

To cope with a fairly steep rise in WPI (all inclusive), a new eight-item program was decided on November 27, which emphasized promoting an adequate supply of perishable foodstuffs. In addition it was decided on Jan. 11, 1980, that 5 percent of the public investment budget for fiscal 1979 would be frozen.

Measures Taken in March 1980

As the new year unfolded, it was the CPI that threatened to rise with a possible impact on the coming *shunto*. The government decided, on March 19, on a seven-item program, planning to: restrict public investments; promote supplies of various commodities that show signs of price rises; take measures that help stabilize food prices; and promote energy savings.

REFERENCES

Bank of Japan. See Nihon Ginkō.

Black, Stanley W. 1977. *Floating Exchange Rates and National Economic Policy*. New Haven, Yale University Press.

Branson, William H., and Rotemberg, Julio. 1980. "International Adjustment with Wage Rigidity." *European Economic Review*, vol. 13 (May).

Bruno, Michael. 1978. "Exchange Rates, Import Costs, and Wage-Price Dynamics." *Journal of Political Economy*, vol. 86 (June).

——, and Sachs, Jeffrey D. 1979. "Supply versus Demand Approaches to the Problem of Stagflation." Working Paper, National Bureau of Economic Research.

Economic Planning Agency. See Keizai Kikakuchō.

Gordon, Robert J. 1975. "Alternative Responses of Policy to External Supply Shocks." *Brookings Papers on Economic Activity*, no. 1. Washington, D.C., Brookings Institution.

Japan Economic Research Center. See Keizai Kenkyū Sentā.

Keizai Kenkyū Sentā. 1980. *Shihanki keizai yosoku* [Quarterly economic forecast], no. 45 (June).

Keizai Kikakuchō. 1980a. *Nenji keizai hōkoku* [Annual economic report, or Economic White Paper]. Tokyo, Government Printing Office.

——. 1980b. *Nippon keizai shihyō* [Japanese economic index]. Tokyo, Government Printing Office.

Koshiro Kazutoshi. 1980. "Dainiji sekiyukiki kano chingin kettei" [Wage determination into the second oil crisis]. *Nippon rōdōkyōkai zasshi*, vol. 254 (May).

Ministry of Finance. See Ōkurashō.

Ministry of Labor. See Rōdōshō.

MITI. See Tsūshō-sangyōshō.

Nihon Ginkō. 1980. *Keizai tōkei geppō* [Monthly report of economic statistics], October.

Okun, Arthur M. 1975. "Inflation: Its Mechanics and Welfare Costs." *Brookings Papers on Economic Activity*, no. 2. Washington, D.C., Brookings Institution.

Ōkurashō. 1979. *Hōjin kigyō shikihō IV 1978* [Quarterly report on corporate enterprises]. Tokyo, Government Printing Office.

Rōdōshō. 1980. *Rōdō hakusho Fiscal 1980* [White Paper on labor]. Tokyo, Government Printing Office.

Sachs, Jeffrey D. 1979. "Wages, Profits, and Macroeconomic Adjustment: A Comparative Study." *Brookings Papers on Economic Activity*, no. 2. Washington, D.C. Brookings Institution.

Shimpo, Seiji. 1979. *Gendai Nippon keizai no kaimei* [Explanation of the modern Japanese economy]. Tokyo: Tōyō keizai.

Shinkai, Yoichi. 1979. "Producers' Responses to Changes in Terms of Trade and Sales." Discussion Paper no. 105 (November), Institute of Social and Economic Research, Osaka University.

——. 1980a. "Spillovers in Wage Determination." *Review of Economics and Statistics*, vol. 62 (May).

——. 1980b. "Patterns of American and Japanese Growth and Productivity." *Japan Quarterly*, vol. 27 (July-September).

——. 1981. "U.S.-Japan Trade Relations—an Economic Perspective." Paper presented at the Rutgers University Conference on U.S.-Asia Economic Relations, April 16-18.

Solow, Robert A. 1980. "What to Do Macroeconomically When OPEC Comes?" In *Rational Expectations and Economic Policy*, ed. Stanley Fischer. Chicago, University of Chicago Press.

Tsūshō-sangyosho. 1980. *Tsūshō hakusho* [White Paper on external commerce]. Tokyo: Government Printing Office.

Zen-Nippon Rōdōsōdōmei. 1980. *Chingin seisaku tōsō hakusho* [Report on wage policy disputes].

INTERNATIONAL ECONOMIC POLICIES

The Political Economy of

United States–Japan Trade in Steel

HUGH PATRICK

HIDEO SATO

THE FOCUS OF THIS PAPER is U.S.-Japan bilateral trade and trade policy in steel products during 1975-80. These were years of worldwide recession, excess capacity in steel, an increase in the import share in the U.S. market, and the American imposition, suspension, and reinstatement of a trigger price mechanism (TPM) that set a de facto floor price on steel. During this period, notably in 1977, steel trade became highly politicized.

There are six main actors: the American steel industry; the Japanese steel industry; the American government; the Japanese government; the European steel industry; and the European Communities (EC), national and supra-national governmental organizations. No single actor is homogeneous, of course. It is a story without beginning or end. The antecedents lie in the quite different histories of the steel industries in the United States, Japan, and Western Europe since World War II. The American industry modernized somewhat without greatly expanding capacity, the European industry expanded capacity considerably and modernized somewhat, while Japan built a very large, modern industry comparable in size to that of the United States. Consequently, comparative advantage shifted from the United States to Japan,[1] and continues to do so. The bit actors, with larger future roles, are the industries in Canada, Australia, and particularly in a number of develop-

We express our appreciation to Tae-dong Kim for research assistance, to those many Japanese and American policy makers and specialists whom we have interviewed and whose anonymity we respect, and to the Luce Foundation for financial support.

1. In the last five years there have been a number of government, industry, security analysis, and academic studies of the changing competitive position of the American steel industry vis-à-vis Japan and Europe, and to a lesser degree the other steel-producing nations. See Federal Trade Commission (1977), Council on Wage and Price Stability (1977), Office of Technology Assessment (OTA 1980), General Accounting Office (GAO 1981), American Iron and Steel Institute (AISI 1980), the Putnam, Hayes, and Bartlett studies (1977 and 1978) for AISI, Marcus and Kirsis (*World Steel Dynamics* 1979),

ing countries where labor costs are low and industrialization is well under way.

The primary issue is how the American steel industry has responded to substantially enhanced competition in the American market and how Japanese steel producers have entered that market. One important response by the American industry has been to seek protection by restriction of imports. It has been successful in obtaining protection because it is large, powerful, politically well organized, and because it is generally considered to be an important basic industry. At the same time it is constrained by major steel users, who are also politically powerful and want prices kept competitive, especially as their products, such as automobiles, face increasing competition both abroad and at home.

Import restrictions harm users by raising prices and increasing the rate of inflation (important since steel input cost increases are often passed on by users). In the long run they reduce the competitive stimulus for the steel industry (management and labor) to keep costs in line. The result is socially inefficient allocations of capital and labor. And particularly in the case of steel, import restrictions invite retaliation. The benefits of import restrictions are more jobs and higher wages for steelworkers, higher salaries for management, and higher profits for stockholders. If such a redistribution is desired, import restrictions are a particularly clumsy and inefficient way of achieving it.

Much of the recent story involves the TPM, an American political solution to some of the economic problems confronting its steel industry. In the remainder of this section we outline American antidumping legislation and administration, and the import control system of the late sixties and early seventies. We then discuss the evolving structure and competitiveness of the American and Japanese steel industries in a world context. In the following sections we briefly describe the TPM and consider the political and economic circumstances that led to its creation. Its suspension and reinstatement in 1980 are treated next, followed by an evaluation of the TPM. Finally, we speculate on future prospects for U.S.-Japan steel trade and trade policy.

THE ANTIDUMPING LAW

One of the tasks of trade policy has been to define unfair competitive practices such as predatory pricing, dumping, and export subsidization, to establish criteria for determining their occurrence, and to provide mechanisms (such as antidumping or countervailing import duties) to offset demonstrable injury to domestic producers of import-competing products. In steel the main trade issue in recent years has revolved around American industry allegations of foreign dumping in the U.S. market. Two criteria are basic in an

---

reports by Charles Bradford of Merrill Lynch, Pierce, Fenner and Smith (*Steel Industry Quarterly Review*, various issues), the numerous studies by Kawahito and Mueller (see references), and Crandall (1980a, 1980b, as well as his forthcoming Brookings Institution study).

antidumping case: imports must have been sold at "less than fair value" (dumped); and this dumping must have caused material injury to domestic producers.

The U.S. Antidumping Act of 1921 defined three alternative measures of less than fair value, in descending order of application. First was comparison between domestic prices in the exporting nation and export prices—export prices less than home prices are unfair. Second, if there were insufficient home-market sales, comparison was made with prices of exports to third-country markets. Third, if neither set of price comparisons should be made, export prices were compared with a "constructed value" based on costs of production including overhead (fixed) costs of at least 10 percent of direct costs plus an 8 percent profit margin. This final measure was not frequently used because price data were usually available. Note the first criterion allowed marginal cost pricing abroad if also done at home.

The 1974 Trade Act fundamentally altered the use of these criteria, substantially increasing the degree of import protection for industries subject to strong cyclical recessions or persistent excess capacity. Essentially it has eliminated the possibility of marginal cost pricing for exports, substituting instead some measure of average production cost in making the comparison with export prices. It made antidumping suits more attractive since the constructed-value criterion for determining less than fair value could be applied. In recessions, producers in industries with high fixed costs will sell at prices below average cost because small losses are preferable to large. Now they run the risk of antidumping suits if they practice this in pricing exports to the United States.

This new definition of dumping above all emphasizes cost of production in recessions, and, as the TPM experience indicates, costs are extremely difficult to measure. Moreover, it poses an administrative nightmare (Crandall 1980a). Unfortunately, this definition has spread: the EC adopted a similar dumping code in December 1979.

Nonetheless, antidumping suits are not a panacea for import-competing firms and industries. The information gathering and legal costs, time lags in implementation, and uncertainty as to final determination make it expensive. However, if dumping and injury are found, a preliminary antidumping duty is assessed, subject to a final determination of the amount of the duty. Imports that clear customs after the preliminary determination are subject to the duty at the (unknown) rate to be set in the final determination. As a consequence, imports of the affected product virtually cease during the approximately six-month period between preliminary and final determination—a draconian solution.

PREVIOUS IMPORT CONTROL EFFORTS

Satisfied with the large, prosperous domestic market, the U.S. steel industry—like many other American industries—remained complacent about export markets for many years. As others became stronger and the competition grew, the industry was forced to struggle with smaller shares of the home market. Since 1959, when there was a major domestic steel strike and imports exceeded exports in volume for the first time, the share of imports in domestic consumption increased steadily from about 5 percent at the beginning of the sixties to 17 percent in 1968.[2] As imports increased, so did domestic protectionist efforts. Until the late sixties, the government had maintained a rather antagonistic position toward the domestic industry, underscored by the 1962 confrontation over prices between President Kennedy and Roger M. Blough, then chairman of US Steel. The situation was considerably different in 1967-68.

In 1967 the steel industry mounted a major anti-import campaign, focusing largely on lobbying Congress to pressure the executive branch. This led to the introduction of an omnibus bill providing for mandatory import quotas on a number of products, including steel. Regarding such legislative moves as too protectionist, the State Department negotiated a three-year voluntary export restraint (VRA) with Japanese and European steelmakers. It went into effect January 1, 1969, and was extended in 1972 for another three years.

While American producers were more or less content with VRAs, which limited imports and allowed them to raise domestic prices, consumer groups in the United States were unhappy. In October 1972 the Consumers Union brought an antitrust suit against the State Department, the domestic steel industry, and foreign steel producers, charging they had violated the Sherman Act by conspiring to restrain foreign commerce. The U.S. Court of Appeals upheld the State Department's authority to negotiate the agreement and dismissed an expression by the U.S. District Court suggesting that there was an antitrust violation. The antitrust issue had been withdrawn from the case by agreement of counsel because it would have required protracted litigation. Nonetheless, this case has led most observers to believe that there are antitrust risks in a VRA not entered into under foreign governmental direction or specific U.S. legal authority. The VRA was allowed to expire in 1975, partly for this reason.

In July 1975, American specialty steel (alloy and stainless) producers, backed by the United Steelworkers of America (USW), filed a petition for relief from imports under the escape clause provision (sect. 201) of the 1974 Trade Act. In January 1976, the International Trade Commission (ITC) ruled in favor of the industry, recommending import quotas for a five-year period on a product-by-product basis. Upon receipt of this recommendation, President Ford instructed his Special Trade Representative (STR) Frederick B. Dent to negotiate intergovernmental VRAs, called orderly marketing agreements (OMAs), that would not risk antitrust violations with principal exporting countries. While Japan was willing to accept an OMA, the EC and Sweden refused, so Ford imposed three-year quotas on specialty steel imports (Adams and Dirlam 1979, pp. 98-101).

Meanwhile, the Europeans had persuaded the six major Japanese producers to limit voluntarily shipments of general steel products to the EC.

---

2. Apparent consumption $\equiv$ apparent supply $\equiv$ production + imports - exports, that is, inventory change is not taken into account.

The U.S. industry reacted immediately by filing in October 1976 a section 301 complaint with the office of the STR. The 301 provision of the 1974 Trade Act is specially intended to deal with foreign practices and policies harmful to the U.S. economy, including trade distortions resulting from foreign government arrangements. The suit charged that the Japanese producers' restraint agreement unfairly diverted steel from Europe to the United States. Although the Ford administration did not seriously act on the suit and it was later dismissed for lack of sufficient evidence, the case prepared the ground for a new round of steel-trade politics under the Carter administration (Sato and Hodin 1980, pp. 8-13).

THE AMERICAN AND JAPANESE STEEL INDUSTRIES IN WORLD PERSPECTIVE

Steel of given specifications does not differ from producer to producer, but the term steel refers to an enormous variety of products. The American Iron and Steel Institute (AISI) classifies thirty-two product categories, and many products within each category. Each product is further distinguished by grade, size (width and length), other specified qualities (such as coating, finish, tolerance, packaging), and other special conditions entering into the price. In general, steel refers to basic carbon steel. Stainless and alloy (specialty) steels are sufficiently different with specialized producers, to have had a separate trade policy in the seventies, as noted above.

Most steel is produced in integrated mills where economies of scale are significant, and optimal scale is very large. About 85 percent of American steel is produced by integrated producers (Office of Technology Assessment [OTA] 1980, p. 10). The proportion in Japan is comparable. A limited range of products—mainly rods, angles, and bars—are efficiently produced from scrap in electric furnaces in mini-mills. Such plants can be located near markets.

The world steel industry has gone through a remarkable transformation since World War II—in technology, in total capacity, and in production location. Demand in the United States has not grown substantially since the mid-fifties, especially relative to capacity. Between 1955 and 1979 U.S. production increased by 11 percent; European, 108 percent; and Japanese, 1,080 percent. During this period world steel trade grew, as did the role of all the Western European nations and Japan; their shares of the 139 million tons exported (excluding intra-EC trade) in 1979 were 33 and 29 percent, respectively (Organization for Economic Cooperation and Development [OECD] 1980a). The steel industry has reflected the dynamics of evolving comparative advantage and some countries have successfully pursued infant industry protection in steel. Japan has become the low-cost producer. However, costs both of building efficient integrated mills and of operating them are now lower in developing countries due to low wage rates even relative to productivity (Crandall 1980b, p. 144). The excess capacity in world steel since 1974 will continue well into the eighties. The major new integrated plants will probably not be built in Western Europe, the United States, or Japan.

Detailed analyses of production costs, pricing, market structure, technology, and other characteristics of the industry are provided elsewhere (see n. 1). A brief summary follows.

MARKET STRUCTURES

Economies of scale mean the steel industry in any country is oligopolistic. Competition across national boundaries is impeded by substantial transport costs and various trade barriers. The Japanese industry is most concentrated, followed by the United States and then the EC. US Steel, the largest American producer, has relatively old plants specializing in carbon sheets (Crandall 1980a, p. 19). Much of the American import problem is a US Steel problem: in 1955 its U.S. market share was 31 percent, imports were negligible; by 1979 US Steel's share had declined to 18 percent, and imports increased to 15 percent (Bradford 1980, pp. 13-14). More discussion of the structure and problems of the American industry can be found in Lynn (1980) and Woolcock (1980).

The Japanese industry has ten integrated producers. It is dominated by the Big Six (Nippon Steel, Nippon Kōkan, Kobe, Kawasaki, Sumitomo, and Nisshin). Nippon Steel, the largest producer in the world, exercises considerable leadership among the Big Six. Since late 1977 they have all been regarded as the world's most efficient, cost competitive, integrated steel producing firms. Some American and European mills are, however, as efficient, and Japanese firms are not the minimum-cost producers of all steel products. For more detail see Kawahito's various studies, Imai (1975), and Watanabe and Kinoshita (1970).

The steel industry in the EC is more heterogeneous and less concentrated, not surprising since it includes firms, some state-owned, in all the member countries. There are national differences in industry and government attitudes and policies, and in degree of competitiveness. A number of new, large modern plants have been built at deepwater sites, but many obsolete facilities have yet to be modernized or scrapped.

More than fifty developing countries have some type of steel production, but only nineteen have integrated steelmaking capacity (Kawahito 1980b, p. 68). Since optimal scale for an integrated facility is now on the order of six million tons annual capacity, developing countries, not surprisingly, build electric furnaces and fabrication facilities until domestic market size makes an integrated plant economical. Thus they import some steel products and export others.

PRICING BEHAVIOR

Price and service (assured supplies, early delivery dates, technical assistance) are the main means of competing. American firms have had a policy of friendly competition since 1910, when US Steel was established (Adams 1977, p. 88). The industry engages in what the Federal Trade Commission (FTC) study (1977) terms "barometric price leadership." In Japan, Nippon Steel has been the main price leader since it was established in 1970 by the merger of Yawata and Fuji. Woolcock (1980, p. 5) describes European pricing practices as imperfect collusion.

List prices are the starting point for the pricing of steel products. They are changed infrequently, but are in practice only a reference point. Actual market prices reflect short-run demand and supply conditions. Price variability is considerably greater than price indexes suggest; comprehensive data are difficult to obtain.

It appears that in a recession U.S. producers are reluctant to shift far from administered (average cost plus markup) pricing strategies toward marginal cost pricing. Japanese producers apparently are somewhat more willing to do so, in both domestic and export markets. Thus Japanese (and European) steel firm pricing practice is a substantial constraint upon the market power of the American industry. Kawahito has considered Japanese domestic pricing arrangements in various studies.

TECHNOLOGY

Substantial innovation has taken place in steel production over the past thirty years in both product and process technologies. This has affected the various national industries very differently. Japan, with all its capacity established since the fifties, has been able to take advantage of new technologies. Almost all current American integrated steel capacity was built prior to 1950. The optimum size of integrated mills has increased, but American firms have had to bear higher costs in introducing new technologies to its relatively small plants.

It is estimated that at least one-fifth of American steel facilities are obsolete (OTA 1980, p. 129).[3] It is too expensive and inefficient to modernize most of this obsolete capacity. Europe has had a similar problem. Thus, while the same "best" technologies are embodied in the efficient modern mills in Japan, the United States, and Europe, the technological level is generally lower in the United States and the EC. The 1980 OTA study stresses that the U.S. lag in product technologies is not serious but is in process technologies. American management has also been conservative and slow.[4]

Steel is often regarded as capital intensive. In fact, it is in the middle range as measured by the proportion of gross value added by labor, similar in the United States to bakery products and costume jewelry. By this meas-

3. Father W. T. Hogan, a well-known economist specializing in the steel industry, has suggested only 70 to 75 percent of the U.S. capacity consists of good, modern equipment (speech before the Japan Society, New York, November 29, 1979).

4. Lynn has done an excellent study of the differential diffusion rate of the blast oxygen furnace (BOF) in replacing the open hearth in Japan and the United States. By 1960 it was clear the BOF technology was superior: it costs less both to build and to operate. Since then no new open hearth furnaces have been built in Japan or the United States. BOF was developed in the early fifties; its superiority was not initially evident since there were many technical problems and high pollution. However, during the crucial introduction period, 1954-60, Japanese firms selected the BOF process in six of nine cases of investment, and American firms in four of twelve (Lynn 1980, p. 51).

ure it is substantially less capital intensive than industrial inorganic chemicals or petroleum refining (Crandall 1978).

Costs of Production

Considerable research has been done in the United States over the past five years concerning the comparative costs of production of the American steel industry and its major competitors, since these estimates provide the basis for evaluating allegations of dumping. The FTC and Council on Wage and Price Stability studies of 1977 were of great importance in changing perceptions. Japanese firms were no longer seen simply as dumpers but as the most efficient, low-cost producers and the competitive difficulties of the American industry came to be seen more as problems of controlling its own costs and slowness in technological innovation and diffusion. It was generally concluded that even after transport costs Japanese average (and presumably marginal) costs were below domestic American costs though how much was unclear. Moreover, Japanese costs were not subsidized by the government. Besides newer plants, Japan's relative cost advantage has several other aspects. The decline in ocean transport relative to land transport costs means the United States and Germany no longer have the advantage of relatively cheap domestic raw materials (Crandall 1980b). In addition, American steelworker wages have risen not only absolutely but also relative to all manufacturing wages; it is now considerably above the ratio in Japan.[5] Table 8.1 provides comparisons of American and Japanese labor and raw material costs.

Capital costs are more difficult to compare. Short-run marginal costs are about two-thirds and fixed costs one-third of total average costs at normal (90 percent) capacity utilization rates. A major difference in capital costs between the United States and Japan lies in company financing structure. Generally, the respective debt/equity ratios are 40:60 and 80:20. Accordingly, Japanese firms pay more interest and earn less profit per ton of steel. It is not clear that it makes a great deal of sense to compare average rates of profit (return on equity) in the United States and Japan since the variance among firms is substantial, particularly in the United States (see OTA 1980, p. 122). It is a remarkable indication of Japanese industry cost competitiveness that they have operated profitably in the past three years at only 70 percent capacity utilization; in part this is due to an upgrading of steel product mix.

5. The premium of steelworker wages over those in all manufacturing, about 30 percent in 1970, had risen to 75 percent by 1980. This has been in large part the consequence of the union contract that since 1974 has incorporated the Experimental Negotiating Agreement, by which unions have pledged not to strike in exchange for real wage increases and a cost of living clause. If the United States had the 1978 Japanese ratio of steelworker wages to all manufacturing of 32 percent, hourly labor costs in 1978 would have been $2.28 lower, and the cost per ton of steel lower by $22.89. By 1980 the attendant per ton cost differential was $30 to $40 (GAO 1981, pp. 7-13).

TABLE 8.1

UNITED STATES AND JAPAN:
LABOR AND RAW MATERIALS UNIT COSTS
PER TON OF STEEL MILL PRODUCTS
(Dollars per metric ton)

Year	Unit Labor Cost[a] U.S.	Japan	Basic Material Cost[b] U.S.	Japan	Total U.S.	Japan	Gap[c] (Japan-U.S.)
1956	54.67	26.66	56.17	93.17	110.84	119.83	8.99
1960	71.83	23.01	48.35	62.07	120.18	85.08	-35.10
1965	65.06	22.11	47.93	54.27	112.99	76.38	-36.61
1970	80.81	23.22	56.42	54.83	137.23	78.05	-59.18
1975	132.87	49.93	137.40	109.33	270.27	159.26	-111.01
1976	136.42	49.64	151.12	112.29	287.54	161.93	-125.61
1977	148.58	60.53	146.24	115.32	294.82	175.85	-118.97
1978	154.33	75.25	151.46	121.79	305.79	197.04	-108.75
1979	168.21	66.10	175.62	133.80	343.83	199.90	-143.93

SOURCES: Federal Trade Commision (hereafter cited as FTC) 1977 for pre-1976. For 1977-79, the FTC series has been updated using the same method and sources, except as noted. Underlying sources are: FTC 1977, for pre-1976, 1977-79; American Iron and Steel Institute (hereafter cited as AISI); Japan Iron and Steel Federation (hereafter cited as JISF); U.S. Department of Commerce

NOTE: Substantial date problems exist for comparisons of capacity as well as some inputs; such figures are indicative rather than precise.

[a]The total man-hours for U.S. was taken from AISI, *Annual Statistical Report.* The total number of employees for the Japanese steel industry was obtained from JISF, *Steel Statistics Survey.* The total man-hours for Japan is calculated by using monthly hours worked per worker from JISF's *Monthly Report.* The U.S. labor cost for 1976 is a FTC revision of a projection in FTC 1977. For U.S., the total employment cost per hour was taken from AISI, *Annual Statistical Report.* For Japan, monthly earnings per worker and employee taken from JISF, *Monthly Report,* were converted to hourly figures.

[b]For Japan, the quantity of electric power purchased by the steel industry for each of the years 1977-79 was computed from the percent purchased in 1975-76. Producer price indexes have been used for extending the FTC 1977 series except for labor costs (see note a), and Japan iron ore, scrap, coking coal, and fuel oil, where extensions of the series in the FTC's sources are used. Also, includes iron ore, scrap, coking and noncoking coal, fuel oil, electric power, and natural gas

[c]There has been considerable debate on the average cost differential; much depended on assumptions regarding yield, Japanese labor subcontracting, and the use. The estimates ranged from $61 (COWPS) to $120 (FTC), with Crandall initially at $65-70, Bradford at $85-97, and Mueller–Kawahito $97. See Kawahito 1978

GOVERNMENT POLICY

Governments treat steel differently from most other industries. Steel is regarded as a basic input for industrial activity. Thus it is encouraged through both domestic and foreign trade policies. About 30 percent of non-Communist world capacity is government-owned. There is no government ownership in the United States or Japan, but there is substantial ownership in Europe, except for West Germany. Government ownership has been linked to subsidy, expecially in recessions. At the same time steel is an oligopolistic industry with considerable market power. Price increases become inflationary signals. It is also an industry that generates much pollution. These lead to government regulatory efforts.

Until the early seventies the Japanese industry was protected from imports or direct investment in Japan. Over-all, the Japanese government has been very supportive of the industry. U. S. government policy toward the American steel industry has been more ambivalent, reflective of the general ambivalence toward industrial policy. The industry blames its difficulties on the government, yet there is little evidence the industry used the 1969-75 and 1978-80 periods of import restraint to accelerate its restructuring and modernizing efforts.

THE WORLD STEEL RECESSION, 1975-80

The world steel industry faces two broad problems: structural and cyclical. There are two interrelated structural problems: the shift in comparative advantage from the United States and Europe to Japan and some developing countries; and the large world excess capacity that has emerged since 1975 as a consequence of world recession and excessively optimistic expansion programs begun in the mid-sixties by European, and to a lesser extent, Japanese firms. Excess capacity is more than a cyclical problem, though the cyclical recession has exacerbated it.

Steel continues to be a troubled industry. Prospects are poor until world demand catches up with world supply. The American industry has a vested interest in forecasting future shortages to justify government support now. The general view is that serious shortages of more than a temporary nature are unlikely within five years, probably longer (see OECD 1980b; a summary of various projections appears in OTA 1980, pp. 145-50). This issue is considered further in the final section.

SUMMARY COMPARISON OF AMERICAN AND JAPANESE STEEL INDUSTRIES

Contrasts between the American and Japanese steel industries are substantial. The Japanese industry is modern, large scale, efficient, low cost; the American industry is a mixture of these characteristics and a substantial (20 to 25 percent) obsolete capacity. The Japanese average technological level is higher, especially in process technology where diffusion has been more rapid. Japanese wage rates are lower, absolutely and relative to wages in all manufacturing. Japanese capital costs are lower, due mainly to a financial system that tolerates high debt/equity ratios. Many American firms are vertically integrated; the industry relies mainly on domestic coal and iron ore. Japanese firms import all iron ore and coal; they have profited from the development of new low-cost foreign sources of supply, often based on long-term contracts, and sharply reduced relative costs of ocean transport by giant carriers. The Japanese industry is located at deepwater ports, minimizing transport costs. The bulk of the U.S. industry is located in the Midwest, near traditional markets but distant from growing markets in the South, Southwest, and on the West Coast.

The Japanese industry benefited from rapidly growing domestic demand in the 1955-73 period, making profitable the building of new, large-scale efficient mills. Demand has not grown substantially in the United States, especially relative to existing capacity. The Japanese industry has long had a global strategy that took into account export opportunities in planning production and capacity expansion; the American industry has focused on the U.S. market, with little attention to possible export opportunities. Japan exports over 30 percent of its production; the United States, less than 3 percent, and it has been a net importer since 1959. The Japanese industry appears to have engaged relatively more in marginal cost pricing in recessions, in both domestic markets and abroad.[6] In addition, it has been helped by somewhat more favorable government policies than those affecting American industry.

The industries also have important similarities. They are big, and have large domestic markets. They both have high technological capabilities for research and development, and for innovation. Both industries are mature: neither is likely to add substantially to capacity, and any additions are likely to be in expansion of existing facilities and electric furnace mini-mills.

CREATION OF THE TRIGGER PRICE MECHANISM

This section deals with the political-economic processes leading to the creation of the TPM in the United States.[7] The TPM was a way to provide import relief to domestic industry while avoiding a trade war and political confrontation with major steel exporting countries, particularly those in Europe. Imports from Japan, however, were the first target of the steel lobby in 1977. The Carter administration immediately came under strong pressure from the domestic steel industry. Both the companies and the steelworkers union emphasized limiting imports from Japan, which were 37 percent higher than in 1975. Vice President Mondale on his Tokyo visit in early February expressed concern but stopped short of proposing any specific measures. Nevertheless, this was a sufficient signal for the Japanese steel industry. On February 5, Eishiro Saito, president of Nippon Steel, and seven other executives proposed to International Trade and Industry (MITI) Minister Tatsuo Tanaka intergovernmental negotiations to reach an orderly marketing agreement (OMA). Indeed, the Japanese industry had been more or less will-

---

6. Given the oligopolistic structure of steel industries, pricing under such circumstances was below "normal" average cost but probably not often so low as short-run marginal costs.

7. Unless otherwise noted, this section is a summary of the 1980 Sato and Hodin paper (see references).

ing to restrain exports ever since the issue first arose with the United States in 1967.

Why is steel less resistant to export restraint? Four reasons are usually given by experts in Japan: (1) the interdependent nature of the industry, (2) its sense of indebtedness *(on)* to the United States for earlier assistance, (3) profitability of quantitative export restraint, and (4) fear of losing a large and stable market share in the United States. Of course, relative emphasis given to these factors varies. Nippon Steel Chairman Yoshihiro Inayama, known as "Mr. Cartel" for his strong belief in the importance of export restraint and orderly markets, singles out the second factor as most important.

GILMORE FILES AN ANTIDUMPING SUIT

While Japanese steelmakers did not particularly mind their American countterparts calling for an intergovernmental agreement to restrain their exports to the United States, they abhorred another action, that is, the antidumping suits. Gilmore Steel, a small firm in Portland, Oregon, filed an antidumping suit against five major Japanese steelmakers in February 1977, charging that their sales of carbon steel plate for seventy-seven dollars below the average U.S. domestic price per ton was dumping. Finding Gilmore's documentation in order, the Treasury Department began an investigation on March 29. Although Gilmore was a small company, an affirmative determination could affect all Japanese carbon steel plate exports to the United States. Japanese steelmakers were also disturbed by what they regarded as a peculiar definition of dumping under the 1974 Trade Act. They feared being forced either to stop exports altogether or to raise prices sufficiently to avoid further allegations, thereby losing their competitive edge.

Meanwhile, the AISI and the steelworkers union were organizing major nationwide campaigns to enlist support. Their strategy included efforts to achieve quantitative import control (through an OMA or an appeal under the 301 provision of the 1974 Trade Act) or limiting imports through antidumping suits. Their ultimate goal has been a multilateral sectoral agreement to regulate steel trade under the auspices of the General Agreement on Tariffs and Trade (GATT) along the lines of the Multifiber Arrangement (MFA) on textiles.

The AISI commissioned a report (Putnam, Hayes and Bartlett 1977) that charged foreign suppliers (including Japanese) were practicing discriminatory pricing between home and export shipments; that various types of direct and indirect government aid had led to large-scale capital expansion; and that pressures existed to export at prices below full-unit costs to help pay for this substantial investment. Finding the AISI allegations fraught with factual errors and misrepresentations, the Japan Iron and Steel Exporters Association prepared a formal rebuttal (JISEA 1977), which appeared in July. In addition, because Japanese industry leaders interpreted the AISI move as indicative of a serious intent by the U.S. industry to seek import control, they renewed their call for intergovernmental negotiations to work out an OMA. However, MITI preferred to await a formal U.S. government request.

It soon became known that US Steel was preparing an antidumping suit against all major Japanese steel exporters. Because European steelmakers were less efficient than the Japanese and therefore more likely to have dumped steel, one may wonder why the focus was on Japan. It appears that Edgar B. Speer, chairman of US Steel, and others were effectively using Japan as a scapegoat. There was a growing climate of opinion critical of Japan because of the enormous bilateral trade imbalance beginning in 1977. Also, an image of unfair Japanese trading practices had been emphasized in political speeches and news reports. The general lack of knowledge about Japan in the United States and the Japanese reticence to respond made such allegations seem even more credible.

There was no consensus within the Carter administration on how to cope with the problem. However, having just concluded an OMA with Japan on color television imports, there was a reluctance to handle steel with quantitative restrictions. The industry was an oligopoly and such restrictions would only mean an opportunity to raise prices. On the other hand, many in the executive branch who normally would have opposed protection were reluctant to because of their greater concern for successful completion of the multilateral trade negotiations (MTN). They were willing to allow some assistance to steel in exchange for steel's support for the MTN. Considering it inflationary, those opposed to quantitative import control eventually held sway.

The first sign of confrontation between the governments of the United States and Japan on steel surfaced in late July when the Japanese steel industry refused to submit production cost data to the Treasury Department for the Gilmore case investigation. The Japanese agreed to provide price data but refused to submit product-by-product costs. Industry leaders saw the suit as a pretext to obtain production secrets. The Japanese government also opposed submission of cost data and advised noncompliance.

The Japanese industry was caught in a dilemma. To clear themselves of the dumping charge Japanese firms felt they had to cooperate with the Treasury Department. If they did not, the Americans could say the Japanese had admitted their guilt. Moreover, without the cost data, the Treasury Department would depend on less reliable figures available in the United States, including data submitted by Gilmore.

MITI officials were sandwiched between the Japanese industry, which wanted voluntary export restraint through an OMA, and the United States government, which opposed such approaches. Under these circumstances, Naohiro Amaya, MITI's director of the Heavy Industries Bureau, visited the United States in August. It became clear from these talks that the U.S. government was more inclined to support a price-oriented approach. Amaya reported this to Inayama, but Inayama refused to believe him, saying the U.S. government would definitely push for a quantitative approach.

THE RAGING FIRESTORM AGAINST IMPORTS

Still unable to obtain any government support for import restrictions, U.S. industry and labor leaders escalated their anti-import campaign. This well-orchestrated effort coincided with some bad news about the domestic industry. Youngstown Sheet and Tube (Youngstown, Ohio) announced it would severely cut back operations, permanently furloughing five thousand production workers. Bethlehem and Armco announced closings that eliminated eight thousand jobs. Some of the closings may have been announced intentionally to put pressure on the government.

On September 19, 1977, US Steel filed an antidumping suit against the six largest Japanese steel companies, alleging that they were dumping their excess steel products at distress prices (23 percent below costs). Just the day before, Inayama had stated in a press conference that the Japanese industry was prepared to resort to unilateral export restraint. Again there was a problem of perception: eagerness for voluntary restraint was interpreted by some Americans as an admission of guilt.

With no particular solutions emanating from the Carter administration, the steel lobby stepped up pressures on Congress. This resulted in the formation of steel caucuses in the Senate and House. Congressional mobilization in support of the steel lobby's position was seen by the administration as a preview of congressional "stonewalling" on the MTN agreement if influential lobbies such as steel were not satisfied.

Further encouraging the anti-import campaign, the Treasury Department ruled on Gilmore's suit that carbon steel plate from Japan was being sold in the United States at less than fair value, with a dumping margin estimated at an average of around 32 percent. Thus, as of October 3, importers of Japanese steel plate were required to post a bond equivalent to 32 percent of the declared value of new shipments to pay the higher duties if deemed necessary by the final determination. This itself was a deterrent to new shipments. Japanese industry leaders were surprised by the preliminary ruling and attributed it to the Japanese refusal to provide cost data (see Mueller and Kawahito 1979b, p. 9).

The ruling on the Gilmore case encouraged similar suits against European steelmakers, particularly after President Carter gave his blessing to the anti-dumping approach in his October 13 meeting with domestic industry representatives. Initially, antidumping suits under the 1974 Trade Act seemed a reasonable solution, certainly preferable to quantitative restrictions on steel imports. However, the Carter administration had not really thought through how to cope with a large number of antidumping cases and began to panic when it became clear that it did not have the staff to handle such a load.

A more serious policy concern was how to avoid a major political confrontation with Europe. Many U.S. officials had come to realize (from the FTC and Council on Wage and Price Stability studies) that the Japanese were indeed the world's most efficient producers and that their dumping, if any, would not be widespread. At the same time it became increasingly clear that European firms had been engaged in large-scale dumping. Japanese imports leveled off in volume and even declined as a share of total imports partly in response to the U.S. antidumping actions. From around August 1977, European imports exceeded the Japanese.

In September 1977, Carter asked Treasury Under Secretary Anthony Solomon to produce a plan that would defuse the domestic political crisis in steel—to convince the industry the administration was serious about helping it. The plan was to address all of the industry's problems—modernization, environmental regulations, and trade. In early November there were press reports the Solomon task force would propose that imported steel could be sold in the United States at or 5 percent below a price based on production costs of Japanese steel companies.

Meanwhile, Japanese and Common Market officials were being briefed on the emerging price-oriented mechanism to regulate imports. In effect, the administration was establishing a system that discriminated in favor of the Europeans, a conscious political choice. By using Japanese production costs, the system allowed most Europeans to continue to sell in the American market below average costs without retaliation. But the Japanese were not particularly bothered; the system would not cost them a great deal and would give them what they wanted—peace and higher prices. Still, it took a face-to-face meeting between Solomon and Inayama to dispel some uncertainty on the part of the Japanese industry.

In a meeting with Treasury Department officials in Washington on November 18, Hachio Iwasaki, director of MITI's Iron and Steel Division, was informed Japan should submit average cost data for the Big Six Japanese firms for the purpose of determining reference price for imports. Iwasaki promised to comply within six weeks, and the Japanese companies subsequently agreed.

The announcement of the TPM on December 2, 1977, had an immediate effect. Industry and congressional outcries against the Japanese (and European) steel producers quickly subsided, and the highly politicized U.S.-Japan steel issue of 1977 almost died out. But this was not the end. Concern by US Steel over renewed imports in a softening market in late 1979 led to new antidumping suits and a suspension of the TPM in March 1980, and its resumption in October only after intense negotiations.

TRIGGER PRICE MECHANISM

Trigger prices were first announced in January 1978 but did not take effect until May 1, 1978, to provide a grace period for import contracts already signed and to give importers and foreign producers time to adjust. The TPM has the following general features: (1) the average cost of production in dollars of the most efficient foreign steel producer is determined and becomes the trigger price; (2) all steel imported at or above the trigger price, plus transport costs, is not subject to government-initiated antidumping investigations and can enter freely; (3) steel imports at below the trigger price automatically initiate investigation. If dumping (using the constructed value definition) and injury are evident, countervailing duties are applied to all shipments from that foreign producer so that its average cost of production (higher than the trigger price) becomes the effective minimum price for its exports to the American market.

The TPM involved important assumptions. First, it was to be a substitute for antidumping suits initiated by the steel companies, as well as for any use of quantitative import restrictions. While the steel companies could not be denied their legal right to initiate antidumping suits, it was made clear that if they did so to any substantial degree the government would terminate the TPM. At the same time the government informed the Europeans they did not have an unlimited license to dump.

Second, the TPM was viewed as temporary, until the gradual increase in world demand eliminated the excess capacity, thus lowering world prices (Solomon report 1977, p. 20). While only implicit in the Solomon report, the October 1980 resumption of the TPM made it clear that the American and European industries would be expected to scrap or modernize obsolete facilities and become fully efficient. The TPM was to last no longer than five years from the fall of 1980, with the possibility of termination after three years should the U.S. industry not make adequate progress in rationalization.

The decision to use the TPM brought on a number of immediate practical problems. How were costs to be estimated? How would the system be administered? Considerable effort has gone into resolving these issues. Determination of the average cost of production of the most efficient (i.e., lowest cost) producer has been a central concern. At the plant or firm level such data are regarded as proprietary and highly secret. The agreement of MITI and the Japanese steel industry to provide average production cost data for the Big Six has been essential to the TPM.

The initial estimates of Japanese production costs had to be made within three weeks. Initial Japanese estimates appeared low to the American officials, in part because of different assumptions concerning steel yields and fixed costs. While there was apparently no explicit, politically determined minimum reference price based on current U.S. prices, it was understood by the Solomon task force that the average cost of Japanese production plus transport had to be within politically acceptable limits (say 5 to 10 percent below U.S. prices) or the TPM would not be a feasible solution. Fortunately the American estimates were within an acceptable range; the continued appreciation of the yen during the fall of 1977 fortuitously helped make that possible.

Estimation of production costs is difficult because it involves conceptual and definitional as well as measurement problems. All the evidence indicates the Japanese have been scrupulously honest in providing the basic data; this has never been a serious source of contention. Most conceptual controversies tended to evaporate as the Japanese industry came to realize it would benefit more from high rather than low cost estimates. Kawahito and Mueller have argued in a series of technical papers that costs have been overestimated in the trigger price calculation; not surprisingly the American steel industry has suggested underestimation. Regardless, the data used are an upward-biased approximation of lowest foreign production costs, since Japanese firms are not equally efficient in all products and since other foreign mills may produce specific products more cheaply.

The cost structure for the trigger price formula contains the following main elements: raw materials, direct and indirect labor costs and output per man-hour, steel yield rates from raw steel, and capital costs. Iron ore and coal costs are estimated directly in dollars, the unit for import contracts; about one-third of the costs to Japanese integrated producers are denominated in dollars (Treasury *News*, May 15, 1979, p. 4).

The capital costs involve two controversial issues: the appropriate operating rate (capacity utilization) for averaging depreciation, interest costs, and other fixed costs per ton of steel, and the appropriate profit rate. The higher the capacity utilization rate, the lower average production costs. MITI at first proposed an 85 percent rate, the twenty-year historic average. The TPM administrators have instead used the most recent five-year average, initially using 1973-77 annual data and then, beginning in 1980, quarterly data on the justification that this represented the business cycle. The average rate has typically been above the actual operating rate.

The Japanese permanent employment system adds some fixity to labor costs. In its cost calculations, MITI assumed labor costs were 100 percent fixed, disadvantageous when utilization rates were declining but advantageous when actual rates were less than the average rate used, as has typically been the case. The TPM administrators have regarded both labor costs and other expenses as 50 percent fixed, 50 percent variable. Depreciation is 90 percent fixed, interest costs 75 percent fixed (Treasury *News*, July 20, 1978).

The profit rate is mandated under the 1974 Trade Act, so has not been a matter of contention. The tax profit rate is set at 8 percent of operating costs (raw materials, labor, and other expenses). There is little economic rationale for this method, much less for the specific profit rate used. The U.S. government has suggested (Treasury *Notice*, July 20, 1978) that 8 percent translates into a 13.1 percent pretax return on total steelmaking assets and regarded this as reasonable. Applying the ratio of fixed assets to equity from AISI's 1978 annual statistical report result in a pretax return on net worth in the United States of 14.5 percent. However, since Japanese steel firms are highly leveraged, an 8 percent pretax profit on current costs implies a far higher return on net worth.

Japanese cost data, except for imported raw materials, are estimated in yen. One burdensome issue has been what exchange rate to use in an era of floating rates, especially since sales contracts are typically signed several months before shipment and delivery. The TPM administrators used the sixty-day average prior to announcement of the trigger price for the coming quarter—rates prevailing some four to seven months prior to the actual landing of steel in the United States. The yen/dollar exchange rate fluctuated widely between late 1977 and early 1980. That had not been anticipated, and added an element of price fluctuation undesired by an industry in which list prices change relatively infrequently. Because of the time lag, when the yen was appreciating the trigger price underestimated the actual dollar cost and made Japanese firms less competitive, and the reverse when the yen was depreciating. The Japanese industry complained bitterly about this aspect of the TPM formula. When the TPM was reinstituted in the fall of 1980, it was revised to use an average exchange rate for the latest thirty-six-month period.

Table 8.2 provides the U.S. government estimates of Japanese steel-making costs, and the trigger price in effect each quarter. The TPM formula has a flexibility band (± 5 percent) to allow for temporary, short-term disturbances; while not used since late 1980 it remains in effect in principle. It was used in 1979 to moderate the swings in Japanese cost estimates due to exchange-rate fluctuations. Adjustments were also made in the first quarter of 1980, despite the negligible change in Japanese costs in dollar terms, apparently to placate the American industry at a time when US Steel was threatening to file its antidumping suits.

Establishment of the quarterly trigger price for steel is only the first step. There is also an adjustment for prices of specific steel products, and the determination of transport costs. The trigger price is in terms of basic steel produced by integrated producers. Separate trigger price estimates have been made for steel products produced by electric furnaces.

As already noted there are many different steel products, each with its own well-defined characteristics. Production cost and market price differ for each product. Accordingly, trigger prices have to be set not simply for steel but for a large number of steel products. The initial 1981 quarter *Trigger Price Mechanism Price Manual* contains 268 pages of trigger prices by product, port, and extra specification.

The Japanese production cost estimates, provided by MITI, do not include the shipping costs to U.S. ports: ocean freight, insurance, interest, and unloading charges must be added. The major component is ocean freight; its cost is typically between 6 and 18 percent of the trigger price, depending on the product and the port. Steel (and other commodities) enters the United States through ports on the Pacific, Atlantic, and Gulf coasts, and on the Great Lakes. Shipping costs from Japan are lowest to the Pacific, and increasingly costly to the Gulf, Atlantic, and Great Lakes ports; the difference between Pacific and Great Lakes ports is typically $20 to $30 per ton. These transport costs significantly affect the competitiveness in different regions of the United States among American producers and importers. Thus Europe's historic markets are the Great Lakes and Atlantic Coast, Canada's industry is located close to the Great Lakes markets, and Japan has been particularly competitive in the Pacific and Gulf markets.

TABLE 8.2

JAPANESE STEELMAKING COSTS AND THE TRIGGER PRICE

(As estimated by the U.S. government in dollars)

		Basic Raw Materials	Other Raw Materials	Labor	Other Expenses	Depreciation	Interest	Profit	Yield Credit	TOTAL per metric ton	TOTAL per net ton	TOTAL % change	TRIGGER PRICE dollars/net ton	TRIGGER PRICE % change	Trigger/Cost Gap (%)	Yen Value Used
1978	Second Quarter[a]	113.17	63.66	73.14	26.48	21.49	21.30	22.11	(9.81)	331.54	300.76	—	300.76	—	—	240
	Third Quarter	116.20	67.60	80.86	28.12	22.82	22.62	23.42	(10.31)	351.33	318.73	6.0	318.73	6.0	—	226
	Fourth Quarter	116.20	71.06	85.02	29.56	23.99	23.78	24.14	(10.57)	363.12	329.42	3.4	329.42	3.4	—	215
1979	First Quarter	116.20	81.70	97.75	33.99	27.58	27.34	26.37	(11.34)	399.59	362.51	10.0	352.53	7.0	-2.8	187
	Second Quarter	119.03	72.21	94.07	28.65	29.72	25.96	25.12	(10.82)	383.94	348.31	-3.9	352.53	—	+1.2	197
	Third Quarter	124.68	67.10	91.08	26.62	27.62	24.12	24.82	(10.79)	375.97	341.08	-2.1	347.54	-1.4	+1.9	212
	Fourth Quarter	132.99	65.55	89.68	26.01	26.98	23.56	25.14	(11.05)	378.86	343.70	0.8	347.54	—	+1.1	217
1980	First Quarter	139.23	62.66	87.19	26.75	26.58	23.10	25.27	(11.15)	379.63	344.40	0.2	358.31	3.1	+4.0	227
	Fourth Quarter	161.36	77.23	92.57	32.68	36.19	26.62	29.11	(12.93)	442.83	401.73	16.6	401.73	12.1	—	223
1981	First Quarter	161.94	77.93	93.69	33.07	36.71	26.98	29.33	(13.02)	446.63	405.18	0.9	405.18	0.9	—	221
	Second Quarter	168.08	83.77	104.13	30.47	33.99	28.66	30.92	(13.80)	466.22	422.95	4.4	422.95	4.4	—	218

SOURCES: U.S. Department of Treasury; U.S. Department of Commerce

NOTES: Assumes 8% profit margin on sum of the costs of all raw materials, labor and other expenses categories. Production costs are averages for the six major Japanese integrated steel producers. The trigger price mechanism was suspended in the first quarter of 1980, and reinstituted from the fourth quarter.

[a]Revised—original cost and trigger price was $328.26 per metric ton and $297.80 per net ton.

Accordingly, the trigger price consists of the basic price for steel as given in table 8.2, cost adjustments for each product, plus shipping costs. This price is then compared with the actual import price, adjusted where necessary for unloading and handling costs. The trigger prices are revised quarterly. As this description of the procedure implies, substantial administrative and technical effort has been required to implement TPM and make it work effectively.

Another complication is that some efficient producers can deliver certain products to certain ports at prices below the TPM but not below their average cost of production. This competitiveness is further enhanced when the yen (and hence the TPM) appreciates relative to the importer's local currency. Such firms can request an investigation of their production costs and obtain preclearance to sell at specified minimum prices below the TPM. This clearly enables them to outcompete all other exporters subject to the trigger price. The four Canadian steel producers sought and obtained preclearance on their steel exports to the Great Lakes markets, thereby expanding exports to the United States.

SUSPENSION AND REINSTATEMENT OF THE TPM

The TPM was suspended in March 1980 when US Steel brought a massive antidumping suit against European producers. This sudden turn of events created new uncertainty in international steel trade and threatened to cause a trade war with America's European allies, the avoidance of which was the primary U.S. motivation behind the establishment of the TPM in the first place. In this section, the interaction of political and economic processes involving the suspension and the eventual reinstatement of the TPM in October 1980 will be examined.

There were several factors peculiar to this second phase of the steel trade issues. First, Europe—rather than Japan—was the main target. Second, administrative jurisdiction over the TPM and antidumping (as well as countervailing duty) enforcement had been transferred from the Treasury to the Commerce Department in January 1980. Third, two new steel-related institutions (one domestic, the other international) had come into existence: the Steel Tripartite Advisory Committee (STC) created in the United States in July 1978 to coordinate steel-policy discussions among government, industry, and labor; and the OECD Steel Committee established in October 1978 as a forum for exchanging views on steel industry and trade among member countries.

US STEEL CHALLENGES THE ADMINISTRATION

Under the TPM, Japanese steel exports to the United States dropped sharply in 1978 (see table 8.3). Japanese producers were selling in the U.S. market slightly above the trigger prices partly because the dollar value rose as the yen appreciated vis-à-vis the dollar. Moreover, Japan's Big Six were resorting to self-imposed cutbacks to make sure Japanese imports would not alarm

TABLE 8.3

AMERICAN IMPORTS OF STEEL MILL PRODUCTS

(Thousands of net tons; semiannually to coincide with TPM composition from May 1978)

	Total Imports			From Japan			From E. C.			From Canada			From Others		
	Amount	% change one year earlier	% of U.S. apparent supply	Amount	% of total	% change one year earlier	Amount	% of total	% change one year earlier	Amount	% of total	% change one year earlier	Amount	% of total	% change one year earlier
May-Oct. 76	7,368	52.0	14.1	4,136	56.1	71.4	1,669	22.7	2.0	632	8.6	35.8	931	12.6	277.1
Nov. 76-April 77	7,374	22.7	15.0	3,779	51.2	12.3	1,886	25.6	48.7	820	11.1	27.7	889	12.1	21.0
May-Oct. 77	10,868	47.5	19.1	4,108	37.8	-0.7	4,219	38.8	152.8	939	8.6	48.6	1,602	14.7	72.1
Nov. 77-April 78	11,946	62.0	21.1	4,044	33.9	7.0	4,415	37.0	134.1	1,104	9.2	34.6	2,383	19.9	168.1
May-Oct. 78	9,825	-9.6	16.7	2,773	28.2	-32.5	3,556	36.2	-15.7	1,206	12.3	28.4	2,290	23.3	42.9
Nov. 78-April 79	8,149	-31.8	14.3	2,821	34.6	-30.2	2,343	28.8	-46.9	1,141	14.0	3.4	1,844	22.6	-22.6
May-Oct. 79	9,563	-2.7	15.9	3,314	34.7	19.5	3,299	34.5	-7.2	1,224	12.8	1.5	1,726	18.0	-24.6
Nov. 79-April 80	8,496	4.3	16.1	3,449	40.6	22.3	2,194	25.8	-6.4	1,163	13.7	-5.0	1,690	19.9	-8.4
May-Oct. 80	7,477	-21.8	17.5	2,744	36.7	-17.2	2,009	26.9	-39.1	1,130	15.1	-2.8	1,594	21.3	-7.6

SOURCES: AISI, *Annual Statistical Report*; idem, *Selected Steel Industry Data*

the U.S. industry again. They believed that such self-restraint, on top of the TPM, would be necessary to help the U.S. industry revitalize itself.

The U.S. industry, however, did not get much respite from imports—although it was able to raise domestic prices because of the TPM depreciation of the dollar—as European steel imports declined less rapidly, and imports from Canada and third-world countries actually rose. Moreover, US Steel's new chairman, David M. Roderick, shared with the rest of the domestic industry the conviction that Carter's domestic programs to help the industry did not go far enough; government tax and environmental regulations were still too rigid to permit sufficient capital formation and investment for revitalizing the industry. Under these circumstances, US Steel decided to spearhead a major campaign seeking further improvements in the government's steel-industry relief program. US Steel persuaded the AISI to devote considerable effort in 1979 to the preparation of an industry position paper (AISI 1980) referred to as the Orange Paper, published in January 1980. While evaluating the TPM as "an innovative attempt to help deal with wholesale dumping," the paper called for substantial changes in the mechanism (p. 56). However, most of the paper argued for stronger government support for the industry's modernization and revitalization program.

While the Orange Paper was being put together, US Steel was preparing to file antidumping complaints against European producers. In fact, the Orange Paper was prepared in part to set the stage. US Steel executives apparently concluded that large-scale antidumping suits against European producers would act as a useful political device to force the administration to pay more serious attention to the plight of the industry—precisely because the United States wanted to avoid a major political confrontation with Europe.

The U.S. media started reporting on the impending US Steel suits in November 1979. In early December interagency discussions began at both staff and high-policy levels within the administration on how to head off the suits and, in case this failed, on what to do with the TPM. US Steel seemed determined to go ahead. In early February 1980, Commerce Secretary Philip M. Klutznick and U.S. Special Trade Representative Reubin Askew tried to work out a compromise whereby US Steel would limit its antidumping complaints. But the company would have none of that because it wanted to maximize the political effect of its antidumping action. Finally, well before the actual US Steel action, the decision was made to maintain the TPM in the absence of antidumping suits but to suspend it as soon as a single major complaint was made (Gordon 1980, p. 558).

At first, the Europeans did not take seriously the rumor of the US Steel suits, believing the threat was directed mainly at the U.S. government. As one person interviewed said, "It must be Roderick's ploy to squeeze concessions on government regulations." But as the possibility of the suits became more real, EC officials became anxious and wanted to head them off. Japanese officials and industry leaders were also apprehensive about the chaos antidumping complaints might bring to steel trade, which they thought had been relatively well-managed under the TPM. They were also concerned about what they considered a lack of serious U.S. efforts to revamp the domestic industry.

On March 19, 1980, the Commerce Department, after considerable delay, announced that the trigger price would not be increased for the second quarter and made a last-minute attempt to forestall the antidumping complaints by repeating the threat to suspend the TPM if US Steel went ahead with the suits. Two days later, however, US Steel filed a massive antidumping suit against sixteen steelmakers in seven European countries (France, West Germany, Belgium, Luxembourg, Italy, Britain, and the Netherlands), all of which had problems of steel overcapacity and unemployment. US Steel charged that steel products accounting for 75 percent of the $1.5 billion in European steel shipped to the United States in 1979 were dumped.

Why did US Steel choose this particular time for filing the suit? European imports—declining since late 1979—were reaching a nadir. There are several possible explanations. It may simply have taken several months to prepare the seventy-two boxes of documents for the complaints. Perhaps US Steel waited because the Commerce Department was considered more receptive than the Treasury Department to industry interests. Moreover, the action may have been timed to produce maximum pressure on Carter's reelection campaign. The Commerce Department's preliminary determination on the antidumping petitions filed March 21 would be due by October 17 at the latest, two weeks before the presidential election.

On April 10, the Commerce Department announced it had found "sufficient evidence" to start antidumping investigations. Mindful of the strong European frustration over the US Steel action and the TPM suspension, administration officials emphasized that the United States would make its utmost effort to reinstate the TPM. The administration was anxious not to antagonize European allies at a time when the United States was accumulating a large trade surplus with the EC—at an annual rate of $20 billion—and was energetically seeking cooperation in regard to the hostage crisis in Tehran and the Soviet invasion of Afghanistan.

THE ITC ISSUES A PRELIMINARY DETERMINATION

US Steel survived the first major test of its antidumping action May 7 when ITC ruled three to two that there was "reasonable indication" of injury. Within the administration as well as outside of it, there had been efforts to persuade the ITC to dismiss the complaints. In hearings leading up to the ruling, the Justice Department contended imports were not the cause of US Steel's troubles because imports actually dropped from 18 percent in 1978 to 16 percent in 1979 relative to domestic steel consumption. The Council on Wage and Price Stability joined the Justice Department in arguing that US Steel's problems "had more to do with domestic competition than foreign imports."

On May 22, Lewis W. Foy, chairman of Bethlehem Steel and the AISI, said, "We want to avoid a trade war," adding that a compromise might be possible if the TPM could be improved to reflect faithfully the production costs of both Japan and the EC. But the Europeans were averse to the idea of setting higher trigger prices for the EC than for Japan. This approach was never seriously considered even by Commerce Department officials because its administration would be too cumbersome. Department officials at one point suggested using European instead of Japanese production costs for the TPM, but the idea was strongly opposed by Japan for fear of being priced out of competition. Moreover, as one official put it, "European cost data are not very reliable and may create all sorts of confusion in the course of TPM enforcement."

Japanese industry leaders resented repeated dumping allegations by US Steel, since they were the basis of the TPM. They also pointed out what they considered a gross inconsistency in the behavior of the American steel industry. They said certain American companies were negotiating to sell South Korean and Southeast Asian mills hot-rolled coils at prices 10 to 20 percent below the trigger price of $285 (F.O.B.) per ton for the 1980 first quarter. Nonetheless, the threat of antidumping suits restrained any aggressive Japanese selling in the American market during this period.

After the bitter experience of being made scapegoats in 1977, the Japanese industry realized the need to speak up against accusations. This feeling was particularly strong among younger industry executives and staff. An Overseas Public Relations Committee had been created within the JISEA to counter foreign allegations and disseminate correct information about the Japanese steel industry. This committee brought up the subject of U.S. dumping in a paper put out June 10 to rebut US Steel's criticism of Japanese dumping (Takano 1980).

SOME PROGRESS TOWARD TPM REINSTATEMENT

The European steelmakers fully cooperated with the Commerce Department's antidumping investigations by submitting detailed sales and production cost data. They had little other choice. Unless they submitted their own data, the United States would automatically use domestically available data, including that supplied by US Steel. Besides, any incentive to protect production secrets was weaker than that of the Japanese, given the state of their industry. To verify the data the U.S. government sent inspectors to Europe. It was feared the data might not be reliable—not necessarily because of cheating but because the EC Commission did not necessarily have enough authority to obtain full cooperation. Moreover, methods of calculating production costs vary from company to company.

By late July, the Commerce Department had collected substantial information on the European steel industry. As a result, there was a real possibility of having to impose substantial antidumping duties on most

European steel imports covered by the US Steel suits. Accordingly the opposition of some ranking administration officials (including Kahn, Miller, and Schultze) to the TPM reinstatement gradually weakened in interagency discussions for fear of triggering a major political confrontation with the Europeans. In talks in Washington in July, the EC's Etienne Davignon drove home the seriousness of the situation by implying that if the TPM was not reinstated by late September the EC would be forced to reexamine its entire trade policy with the United States. Another relevant development was that the EC Commission had become more serious about reducing steel-producing capacity in member countries and restructuring the European steel industries.

The STC also played a part in the resolution of the steel-trade issue. Composed of representatives from government, industry, and labor, the STC was created by President Carter on July 26, 1978, to serve "as a mechanism to ensure a continuing cooperative approach to the problems and prospects of the American steel industry" (STC 1980). The STC's role was crucial in developing recommendations for industry revitalization acceptable to both the industry and the administration. US Steel Chairman Roderick, himself a member of the committee, was generally pleased with its work, for much industry data were utilized by the STC, including the AISI's Orange Paper, which Roderick insisted the committee use as a basis for analyzing modernization and capital formation (STC n.d., p. 5). In August 1980 he publicly voiced his view that he would consider withdrawing US Steel's petitions for dumping relief if it received "equivalent protection."

The international trade section of the report recommended "the TPM should be reinstated in a restructured form that would remedy the defects, asserted by industry, in the previous TPM and, during the period of industry modernization, the U.S. market should not be disrupted by excess volumes of imports" (STC 1980, p. 13). On September 15, the administration's cabinet-level Economic Policy Group chaired by Treasury Secretary Miller approved the substance of the report and forwarded it to the president for final approval.

Meanwhile, Commerce Secretary Klutznick had not been able to persuade Roderick to accept the specifics of the government proposal for reinstating the TPM—though MITI had been advised in mid-August that a broad framework of agreement had been reached. The administration proposed an antisurge provision. Specifically, the government would initiate investigations if aggregate foreign imports increased beyond 15.2 percent of domestic consumption when the domestic industry was operating below 85 percent of capacity. Roderick wanted the activation of the antisurge provision even if the industry were operating above 85 percent and a trigger-price increase well over the government proposal of 10 percent. The compromise reached in late September was to raise the trigger price 12 percent, and the antisurge provision would be activated if the industry operated below 87 percent. The Commerce Department could have prolonged the negotiations but the administration was eager to settle the issue before October 17, the deadline for the department's preliminary determination on the US Steel antidumping suit.

The TPM Is Restored

On September 30, President Carter announced the reinstatement of the TPM and the withdrawal of the US Steel antidumping petitions. There was also a broad package of domestic programs proposed earlier by the STC. The president recommended an amendment to the Clean Air and Water Acts allowing an individual steel mill an extension of up to three years for compliance. In addition, the rate of depreciation for equipment (which accounts for the 85 to 90 percent of the steel industry's fixed capital) would be about 40 percent greater than permitted under current law, and there would also be a full 10 percent regular investment tax credit for all new equipment with more than a one-year life, along with an extra 10 percent credit for capital investment (White House Press Release 1980, pp. 5, 9).

Effective for steel shipped after October 21, the trigger prices would still be based on Japanese production costs and the exchange rate would be calculated according to a thirty-six-month rolling average. The TPM would be in effect for a maximum of five years. If the industry were judged to be making adequate progress toward modernization at the end of three years, the TPM would remain in effect for the full period. Otherwise, it would be terminated.

A Comparative Analysis of the First and Second Political Phases

During the first phase, the steel issue escalated and led to the firestorm of the fall of 1977—despite the willingness of the Japanese government and industry to cooperate. The principal reason was that American officials did not understand the seriousness of the issue, a result of the ignorance of the new administration, and of the low profile of the issue early on. Insufficient government response to calls for import relief in 1977 made industry and labor leaders attack imports (particularly Japanese) even more vociferously, linking trade problems to unfair practices of foreign firms and their governments. Hence the politicization of the issue.

During the second phase, by contrast, intensification of the issue triggered by US Steel's antidumping complaints was avoided because the administration moved quickly—even before the complaints were actually filed—in trying to work out a compromise with US Steel and the EC. The administration was more receptive, and the industry did not feel the need to launch a massive lobbying campaign.

What explains this difference? First, the industry's anti-import campaign in 1977 (particularly before September) was multifaceted and did not focus on antidumping actions on which the administration was legally bound to act within a specified time period. In 1976-77, the industry was more interested in the traditional quantitative restriction approach. The section

301 complaint filed in October 1976 by the AISI did not require the administration to come up with a decision within a limited time; yet the industry could also have filed for relief under section 201 of the 1974 Trade Act, which has deadlines for action. But the industry chose not to, apparently because it was not certain of winning an affirmative ITC decision. Among Carter aides there was much opposition to the quantitative approach, both for fear of adding fuel to inflation and because of its inferiority to price-oriented mechanisms of import restraint. Consequently, the administration delayed action. In contrast, US Steel's antidumping action in March 1980 was a well-focused and carefully prepared move that politically (as well as legally) forced the administration into an immediate response.

Second, the steel issue was allowed to escalate in 1977 because Japan, not Europe, was the main target. Making Japanese steelmakers scapegoats was politically useful in winning public sympathy; it was difficult for U.S. officials to be sensitive to Japanese interests, especially in light of Japan's huge bilateral trade surplus. On the other hand the EC, which became the target of the 1980 US Steel antidumping action, had been piling up a large trade deficit, and the U.S. political climate was not conducive to the berating of Europe, despite the open secret that the TPM enabled the Europeans to dump steel. Moreover, American policymakers feared the Europeans might retaliate by launching their own antidumping and other actions against such major U.S. exports as soybeans, synthetic textiles, and petrochemicals. A related factor was the growing realization among U.S. officials in 1977 that the Japanese were not dumping as extensively as the Europeans, if at all. It was only after major antidumping complaints were filed against the Europeans in the fall of 1977 that the administration became serious about developing the TPM.

Third, unnecessary escalation of the issue was avoided in 1980 because, unlike 1977, the administration was more sensitive to both domestic and European (as well as Japanese) steel interests through the STC and the OECD Steel Committee. By the time the US Steel action was brought against the Europeans, eight months after the STC had started working, government representatives on the STC, including Commerce Secretary Klutznick and U.S. Trade Representative Askew, were well informed of industry demands. Without the comprehensive industry revitalization program that the STC recommended in September, US Steel would not have withdrawn its antidumping complaints and the issue would have become enormously more difficult to resolve. Also, the STC provided a regular forum where industry and labor leaders could speak their minds before ranking administration officials in closed sessions, reducing the necessity of politicizing the issue through lobbying in Congress and media campaigns as had been done in 1977.

Finally, American officials were united in efforts to work out a compromise. At the highest level, Klutznick negotiated directly with Roderick, and Askew with Davignon. This cooperative relationship was in part a consequence of the transfer of administrative jurisdiction over antidumping and countervailing duties from the Treasury to the Commerce Department in January 1980. The Treasury Department has been known to be more free trade oriented than either the Commerce Deparment or the Office of the Special Trade Representative. Also in 1977, Special Trade Repesentative Strauss and Treasury Secretary Blumenthal did not get along well.

AN EVALUATION OF THE TPM

THE ECONOMIC RATIONALE

With regard to the TPM, two U.S. government objectives stand out: to help the American industry by restricting imports; and to prevent a major confrontation with the EC. Relations with Japan were also a concern, but since the Japanese industry was indeed efficient and not subsidized, it was not the central issue. Given these policy aims, what then was the most efficient approach? The policymakers (Blumenthal, Solomon, Bergston, Cooper) realized that price mechanisms were preferable to quantity restraints. Antidumping suits and investigations were neither politically desirable nor administratively feasible, as the administration quickly realized when it went that route in the fall of 1977. Nor was the imposition of a tariff possible; it could be subject to retaliation, would be directly counter to the intent of the MTN that were under way.

The TPM can be viewed either as simply a technique for more efficient administration of antidumping laws, or as a way of setting a minimum price for steel in the U.S. market. Either way it is an instrument of protection against imports. The real culprit is not the TPM per se, but the protectionist provision in the 1974 Trade Act that defines fair value in terms of average rather than marginal production costs.

Koo (1979) provides a good analysis of the TPM as a minimum price mechanism. While tariffs and quotas are equally efficient under perfect domestic and international competition, this is not the condition the steel industry operates under in the United States, Japan, or Europe; where industries have oligopolistic market power, tariffs impose less social cost than quotas (Morkre and Tarr 1980, chap. 1). In his analysis, Koo makes the following assumptions: the U.S. steel industry behaves oligopolistically (i.e., it faces a declining marginal revenue curve and equates marginal revenue and rising marginal cost); steel imports are supplied competitively to the U.S. market; and the TPM minimum price is less than the U.S. price with tariffs imposed. He concludes that under the TPM not only will the U.S. price of steel be below that under tariff protection, but imports can be less and U.S. production (and profits) greater as well. These results derive essentially from the TPM's making the U.S. industry marginal revenue curve discontinuous with a horizontal portion where the minimum price becomes relevant. However, this analysis ignores the distributional implications among buyers of steel, producers, and taxpayers, since tariff revenues accrue to the government and the trigger price minimum does not.

The TPM benefited foreign firms relative to the imposition of a tariff since the higher revenues went to them. In fact, the average cost formula made the unit profits on Japanese sales to the American market high indeed; it also made total profits even on a smaller export volume substantially higher than would have occurred under free trade during this period. It is not clear whether the TPM benefited Japanese firms relative to a quota. Presumably their prices and revenues would have been even higher under a quota system, but, since the administration apparently never seriously considered quotas, this question is moot.

While the TPM does not set a minimum price for steel imports, selling below it triggers immediate government investigation. Because the TPM is based on the average production costs of the most efficient producer (the Japanese industry), any firm selling to the United States below that price must be selling below its average production costs, that is, dumping. Moreover, the implication is that significant quantities of imports entail injury.

Note, however, that non-Japanese foreign firms exporting to the United States at the trigger price are selling below their average production costs, since they are (by definition and in actuality, in most cases) less efficient producers. In effect they have a license to dump as defined in terms of average costs. The argument is that these sales do not constitute injury to the American industry, as they simply reflect competition between Japanese and non-Japanese foreign producers in the American market for a given total import share as determined by the interaction of U.S. demand and supply at the given trigger price, so long as efficient foreign producers have excess capacity (Solomon report 1977, p. 18). This argument is valid since Japan had a large excess capacity during the 1975-80 period. And yet, because Japanese firms are forced to sell at average costs while others can sell at marginal costs, conceptually the Japanese are at a competitive disadvantage vis-à-vis other foreign suppliers.

The position of the U.S. government has been that the TPM is an efficient way to administer the antidumping law, and is not in itself a protectionist instrument. The Solomon report (1977) suggests two major criticisms of the case-by-case antidumping procedure: the long time it took to process a dumping complaint by a U.S. producer; and the draconian impact on imports where dumping is found.[8]

In fact the TPM is an instrument of protection: it is a more comprehensive means of administering the average cost (constructed value) definition of dumping under U.S. law. The Gilmore case was the first application of the constructed value approach since the passage of the 1974 Trade Act. The TPM is an extension of this new, and protectionist, principle applied to

8. Once an antidumping suit was filed, it took the Treasury Department and ITC thirteen months on average to process the complaint; the six-month lapse between preliminary and final determination so increase the uncertainty and risk of duties to be paid that imports of affected products cease, as noted earlier.

all steel trade. Moreover, it is based on a particularly protectionist interpretation of the 1974 Trade Act. The act requires that sales be made "at prices which permit recovery of all costs within a reasonable period of time in the normal course of business." It can be argued that over a reasonable period in the business cycle boom-time profits offset losses or very low profits in recession, and hence marginal (or less than average) cost pricing is acceptable as long as profits are reasonably averaged over the cycle. However, the TPM requires continuous covering of costs. "The lack of a cyclical allowance [for profits] appears to be at variance with the intent of Congress" (Morkre and Tarr 1980, p. 171).

ADMINISTRATION OF THE TPM

The monitoring and enforcement of the TPM is done by U.S. Customs at the various ports; responsibility for its general guidance fell on the Treasury Department until early 1980, when the Commerce Department took over this function. A General Accounting Office study (U.S., GAO 1980) provides an evaluation of the monitoring of the TPM from its inception through early May 1979. It documents that the initial administration was rather loose: lags in customs reports to Washington; errors in calculating trigger price comparisons; inadequate evaluation of related-party transactions; inadequate case follow-up from Washington to determine whether dumping had actually occurred. The study also found that, once initial investigations had been done for clearance of specific Canadian mill products, all Canadian steel had been entering under automatic clearance at below trigger prices. The GAO estimated that about 6 percent (355,700 tons) of steel imports between October 1978 and March 1979 were in serious violation of the trigger price floors. Of this, cases involving only 61,800 tons had been investigated for antidumping. Only one case involved a Japanese company and it was not acted on.

The GAO study was critical of the Treasury Department's administration of the TPM. Certain of the GAO recommendations have been put into practice by the Commerce Department. However, the GAO criteria for evaluation are narrow. The Treasury Department argued that the main purpose of the TPM was to eliminate injury to the American steel industry. It suggested that serious violations (the estimated 6 percent of imports) were minimal, and caused no injury relative to over-all U.S. consumption. However, the relevant criterion is whether specific products are being imported at less than fair value. The results of the antidumping investigations to date suggest that injury has not been substantial. The Treasury Department further argued that the day-to-day administration, although in need of improvement, was cost-effective despite delays.

To some extent the GAO report was counterproductive because it implied the government was not seriously enforcing the TPM, so evasion seemed a relatively low-risk strategy. There is some suggestion that by late 1979 evasion was becoming a real problem, especially where foreign producers and American importers were related (as subsidiaries, for example). Their share of total imports had risen from 40 to 60 percent (GAO 1980, p. 21). Their activities were inadequately monitored. No transactions between these firms (or others) above trigger prices were ever audited—a major GAO criticism. The one case of possible fraud in misrepresenting import prices brought before a federal grand jury in early 1981 concerned allegations Mitsui and Co. USA had made false declarations to U.S. Customs on steel imports to West Coast markets in 1979 and had sold below the trigger price. This somewhat surprising situation, given the general policy of the Big Six to exercise self-restraint in exports, may be due to Kaiser Steel's— the main West Coast producer—institution of a vigorous program of pricing its products below the trigger prices.

THE ECONOMIC IMPACT OF THE TPM

It is difficult to determine with much accuracy the effect of the TPM on American and Japanese producers and consumers of steel because so many factors influence supply and demand and because it is not clear what the alternative American policy would have been. Nonetheless, some crude appraisals can be made. The volume of imports and the ratio of imports to domestic supply dropped sharply following the imposition of the TPM in May 1978 (table 8.3). A disproportionate share of the decrease was borne by Japan. This evidently was the result of decisions by Japan's Big Six to exercise self-restraint in the American market (see references to this in STC 1979 and Kawahito 1980a). This was not in the form of a (known) private voluntary agreement among the Japanese producers, which would have been illegal under U.S. antitrust laws, nor was it the result of Japanese government legislation or even MITI formal guidance. Rather, it seems to have been the consequence of a general consensus within the industry and a fear of antagonizing competitors, perhaps enhanced by the leadership of Nippon Steel and its chairman, Mr. Inayama. Japanese producers have continued to hold back in the American market even at the trigger prices. EC producers reduced their exports much less sharply, and Canada actually increased exports. A rule of thumb developed among Japanese industry leaders (not necessarily shared by smaller firms) that the United States would accept a 15 percent import penetration rate, and that it was reasonable for that to be shared among Japan, the EC, and others, with each of these getting roughly one-third. Given Japan's strong competitive position, this seems a remarkably conservative stance, though it may in fact have been profit-maximizing.

The decrease in imports came at a time when American demand for steel was rising. American industry benefited by substantially increased shipments in 1978 and the first three quarters of 1979. It is hard to specify how much the TPM contributed to the decrease in import volume. The decline is attributable not only to the initial rise in the import price of steel to TPM minimum levels, but also to the subsequent increases in the trigger prices, which made imports less competitive. In 1978 this was due almost entirely to the deprecation of the dollar relative to both the yen and the European currencies. In one sense this was a windfall to American producers since it was built into the TPM minimum price formula, and had not been anticipated by policymakers. But the U.S. steel industry had also been penalized in competing with imports by the overvalued dollar, so depreciation was no more than a macroeconomic adjustment toward an equilibrium rate. However, relative strength of the dollar between early 1979 and early 1981 offset part of this windfall. All of the increase in the trigger import price since early 1979 has been due to rising costs, common in degree if not absolute amount for all steel producers.

Table 8.4 provides comparative data on annual rates of price increases in the United States for general producer prices, steel mill products, steel import prices, and the trigger price. It is striking that domestic steel prices rose less rapidly following the imposition of the TPM than the general producer price index. Bradford (*Steel Quarterly*, February 1979, p. 4) points out that discounts from list prices (used for the index) were prevalent in 1977 so the 1978 increase was closer to 15 percent than the 10.7 percent recorded. There was also some discounting from list prices in late 1980.

The sharp increase in import prices in the first year of the TPM is also noteworthy. Part was probably due to the once-and-for-all upward adjustment to the TPM minimum price levels; most however is attributable to the appreciation of foreign currencies. This makes it all the more difficult to distinguish between the effects of dollar depreciation and the TPM on domestic steel prices and levels of imports. Crandall (1980a, p. 23) estimates that through 1979 the TPM raised steel import prices by about 10 percent, prices of U.S. mill products by about 1 percent, and steel prices in the United States by about 2.4 percent; the direct effect on the U.S. price level in 1978-79 was no more than 0.1 percentage points. The rise in prices due to the TPM cost American consumers about $1 billion annually. Since the major impact of the TPM was on import prices, roughly two-thirds of this transfer accrued to foreign exporters (in dollars, but less in terms of their own appreciated currencies) and one-third to American steel producers. Roger E. Alcaly, chief economist for the Council on Wage and Price Stability, in testimony at hearings on the TPM in December 1979, estimated that the TPM increased steel import prices by about 8 percent and domestic steel prices by about 1.5 percent; of the $1.1 billion increase in revenues, $600 million went to foreign firms, $500 million to American firms (GAO 1981, pp. 6-15). The price impact was too small to help the American industry much; it benefited more from a decrease in imports. The effect on steelworker employment was minimal—a maximum of twelve thousand jobs according to Crandall (1980a, p. 24). In steel as in other industries, protection is a very expensive way to create or maintain jobs.

The TPM has proven highly profitable for the Japanese steel industry. The formula 8 percent pretax profit rate on current costs translates into a

TABLE 8.4

AMERICAN STEEL PRICE INCREASES
(Annual rate, %)

	General Producer Price Index	Steel Mill Products (Producer price)	Carbon Steel Products Import Prices	Yen Appreciation (Trigger price)	Trigger Price Index[a]	Japan Average Export Price of Steel to U.S. Amount	% Increase
1975	11.5	16.0	1.9			$357.52	
1976	4.6	6.3	-17.5			315.96	-11.6
1977	6.2	9.6	3.4			352.12	11.4
1978	7.8	10.7	14.5		23.0	460.21	30.7
1979	12.6	10.2	21.3		1.6	506.51	10.1
1980	14.0	8.0[a]	13.6		13.1	575.18[c]	14.8[c]
May-Oct. 75	7.9	2.8					
Nov. 75-April 76	2.7	8.3					
May-Oct. 76	7.3	13.8	9.7				
Nov. 76-April 77	6.9	7.2	-0.3				
May-Oct. 77	6.0	11.7	-2.5				
Nov. 77-April 78	6.8	12.9	11.9				
May-Oct. 78	8.7	7.3	31.4	20.8	19.1	455.99	
Nov. 78-April 79	14.5	9.8	35.0	16.7	14.0	503.95	21.0
May-Oct. 79	13.2	9.8	-6.3	-20.3	-2.8	502.31	-0.1
Nov. 79-April 80	9.0	10.9	22.0	-18.4	6.2	520.37	7.2
May-Oct. 80	9.6	2.2	1.1	1.8[b]	24.2	596.72	29.3
Nov. 80-May 81				4.5[b]	10.6		

SOURCES: U.S. Department of Labor; AISI; Bradford 1980

[a]Second-fourth quarterly comparison at annual rate

[b]Comparison with first quarter 1980

[c]Through November (annual rate)

pretax return on equity for Japanese firms of 41 to 46 percent because of the high debt/equity ratios. (For 1975-77 current costs were 82 to 83 percent of sales and sales were 6.18 to 6.95 times the equity [*Tekkō tōkei yōran* 1979]). In 1976 and early 1977 the depressed Japanese steel industry had engaged in vigorous price competition in the U.S. market. Yet, American consumers were benefiting, not Japanese producers. It is not surprising that the Japanese industry was willing to negotiate any restriction on its exports that would result in substantial price increases. Thus, the TPM has been a particularly beneficial mechanism for Japanese producers. It meant high profits at TPM prices below which its foreign competitors could not readily compete (without invoking the threat of an antidumping investigation), and below which the American industry usually chose not to compete.

The alternatives for the Carter administration were the TPM, antidumping suits, or import quotas. Quotas seemed clearly inferior; antidumping has high political costs as well as direct and indirect (retaliatory) economic costs. Crandall (1980a, p. 23) argues that antidumping suits would have disrupted the flow of imports far more, and would have made possible greater price increases by American producers. Certainly antidumping suits increase sharply the risk and uncertainty of importing, as stressed earlier. Thus, the TPM appears to have been a reasonable political compromise under the circumstances, but it is nonetheless a substantial step in the protectionist direction.

FUTURE PROSPECTS

U.S.-Japan trade in steel has now developed its own mechanisms and behavioral patterns. In this section we briefly consider six broad areas: world steel supply and demand; the TPM; the Japanese steel industry; American steel industry modernization; U.S. government policy options vis-à-vis the American steel industry; and, briefly, some of the broader implications.

First, how long will the present world excess steel capacity persist? The key is the European steel industry, in terms both of trade policies and trade flows. As long as the European industry has substantial excess capacity it will expect to export to the United States at less than average costs of production. The lesson of the TPM experience is that it has the political clout to do so. American steel users benefit, and the wider economic and political costs to the United States of imposing antidumping duties on imports are too great. Two factors will reduce European excess capacity: a growth of world (especially European) demand for steel; and a restructuring of the steel industry by scrapping or modernizing obsolete steel production facilities.

Forecasts of world steel demand are hazardous, more so even than steel capacity. It seems unlikely that by the mid-eighties shortages will occur, despite some projections to that effect. Substantial excess capacity exists in Europe and Japan, and modest increases can be fairly readily achieved in existing facilities. The expansion of capacity in developing countries is likely to be commensurate only with the growth of demand in the next five years (Florkoski 1980, p. 11). Moreover, the world price of steel is low—below the level necessary to sustain existing capacity levels indefinitely. As the world supply-demand gap narrows, the relative as well as absolute price of steel can be expected to increase. But that appears to be some years away. In the interim the steel industries of Europe, the United States, and perhaps Japan are unlikely to achieve average levels of profitability of all manufacturing unless the rules of the trade game are substantially altered to provide very substantial insulation from import price competition. This seems unlikely, and certainly would be undesirable.

Second, what are the prospects for the TPM? There is always the possibility the Reagan administration will end it (we consider some alternatives below). Here the issue is whether the revised TPM will be a credible deterrent. Much lies in the effectiveness, real or perceived, of the administration of the TPM. There are many avenues for evasion by opportunists. The GAO (1981, pp. 7-24) is skeptical that it can be administered effectively. The Commerce Department staff is small. Much will depend on success in auditing transactions, and in generating highly publicized cases of fraud resulting in severe penalties, as well as antidumping investigations. The administrative difficulties in enforcing the TPM are in effect a built-in mechanism to ensure its temporariness. Apparently some of its inventors were aware of that from the start.

From the perspective of steel consumers, the optimal system under current law is one credible enough to ensure that the American steel industry does not bring it down with antidumping suits and yet porous enough in terms of low Japanese production costs, preclearance of even more efficient firms in other nations, and evasion, to maintain a high degree of import competition. This balance is difficult to achieve—as the 1980 US Steel suit demonstrated.

Third, what about the Japanese industry? It is secure in its current position as world low-cost producer, and confident that in the long run it can remain competitive through product specialization and innovations that raise productivity. Yet it is unlikely that Japan will build any new, major integrated plants in the foreseeable future. As a mature industry with sophisticated leaders, it is likely to continue its policy of caution and high unit profits in the American market in anticipation of potential political problems, and to continue to seek export diversification. The industry will generate substantial cash flow; while some will be used to reduce debt/equity ratios, investment in foreign iron ore and coal mines also appears likely.

The TPM has some inherent problems for the Japanese industry, though so far it has proven an immensely profitable device. While Japanese firms appear to be willing to play by the rules, they fear others will not—that Japan will be undercut by others evading the trigger price floors. Several Korean pipe producers have recently requested preclearance. Apparently they are purchasing steel from Japan at relatively low (marginal cost?) prices, and hence are able to fabricate pipes at costs below Japanese average costs. More-over, not only Canadian firms but very efficient European producers of certain steel products are currently requesting preclearance at prices below the TPM applicable to Japanese firms. If this should become widespread it could both reduce Japanese competitiveness and undermine the political assumptions of the TPM itself.

Fourth, what are the prospects for the American steel industry? It faces fundamental structural problems: it has lost comparative advantage, and has substantial obsolete capacity. Its wage rates are relatively high (now 75 percent above those for all American manufacturing), and almost double Japanese steelworker wages; union power has been strong, and it has decreased considerably the American ability to compete against imports. The industry's application of process technology lags—the still-low rate of continuous casting is an outstanding example. Its rate of research and development is low and declining (see OTA 1980, pp. 96-97). Investments to modernize steelmaking facilities rapidly have been inadequate. It has poor access to finance—perhaps its most serious problem. The ratio of total liabilities to equity by 1979 was 124 percent; profit rates are below the average for all manufacturing and dividend rates remain high. The industry argues it is difficult to increase private long-term borrowing or equity significantly, and hence funds must be obtained through higher profits and faster rates of capital-cost recovery through more rapid depreciation rates.

Industry strategy has involved a mix of investment for modernization of steel capacity, diversification into nonsteel activities, and the seeking of government assistance through import protection and a variety of domestic programs. In recent years about one-quarter of new investment has gone into diversification. This is not an unwise policy—so long as the American people are not asked to subsidize the industry. Investment rates are inadequate to bring about rapid restructuring of the industry; the incentives are apparently insufficient, judged by industry statements and performance.

Whether the industry can restructure itself to become more competitive is the key trade policy issue. Indications so far have not necessarily been bad. For the first time in recent years, US Steel reported a small profit in its steel division for 1980. This was made possible in part by permanently closing fifteen older plants employing 12,500 workers in 1979. The company seems determined to continue this consolidation. Many firms are adopting Japanese technology and production methods. Indeed, US Steel was seeking assistance from Sumitomo Metals and Nippon Steel for blast furnace technology even while preparing its antidumping cases. Nonetheless, it appears unlikely that the industry will succeed both in restructuring itself and in maintaining an 85 percent share of the American market without government support in one form or another.

This brings us to U.S. government policy options for the American steel industry. There are three broad choices, including the efficient core option, the renewal option, and the high investment option.

The efficient core option is to scrap obsolete plants and base the industry on the modern integrated and electric furnace mills. At its most pessimistic, the AISI estimates that up to 20 percent of capacity could be eliminated (AISI 1980, p. 39). This would still leave capacity in excess of 113 million tons, which as Crandall stresses, is far more than enough to cope with a national security crisis (1980a, p. 24). Crandall is one of the main proponents of the efficient core option. There also seems to be implicit support for it in the Japan-United States Economic Relations Group *Report* (January 1981, pp. 76-77). This option, like the others, would benefit from a general policy to increase incentives for investment, saving, and research and development for all industries; it would not require specific policies targeted for steel. It would make possible free trade in steel even with marginal cost pricing.

The renewal option is suggested by OTA (1980, especially chaps. 2,10). It would require an increase in industry investment for modernization from the past average of $2 billion to about $3 billion (1978 dollars). The main emphasis would be on new electric furnace mills, with some modernization of integrated mills; the electric furnace market share would almost double to 25 percent. Capacity would expand to meet demand growth; imports would be at about the 15 percent level (apparently assuming that the TPM would remain in place). This option would require a modest amount of direct government support to the steel industry.

The high investment option is propounded by the AISI, and was supported by the STC under the Carter administration. It would require annual investment rates for modernization of about $4.9 billion (1978 dollars). Most would go for modernization and capacity expansion of existing integrated mills. This option requires substantial government support—through greater restriction of imports, and/or capital subsidies and related measures. Crandall (1980a, p. 24) estimates that a 9 percent increase in relative prices would generate $4 billion in annual profits (at the expense of consumers), and would employ 36,000 new people at most. This annual subsidy for employment would be expensive—about $110,000 per new job created.

Implementation of these options implies alternative policy packages. The renewal and high investment options require some government support for the industry. The cost falls on American taxpayers and consumers, who on average are less well off than steelworkers, management, and stockholders. For import protection the government can choose among quotas (OMAs, VRAs), industry antidumping suits, or the TPM, at least for the period of restructuring. If the government intends to move toward the free trade position it would have to get rid of the TPM. But that would imply a more fundamental reform: revision of the 1974 Trade Act to return to the original, price criteria for dumping, and to relegate average cost of production and constructed value to a minor role.

Finally, one should be aware of the broader implications of U.S. steel trade policy for trade policy generally, American industrial structure, and U.S.-Japan relations. The extension of the average cost of production criterion for dumping to other industries would be a major protectionist step, as would attendant extension of the TPM to other products. Moreover, trade in steel must not be viewed in a partial equilibrium context. The price of steel in the United States has become substantially higher than in Japan, and indeed in a number of countries. This directly affects the competitive strength of industries using steel. The automobile industry is one obvious and extreme example, but the high cost of steel will hurt, to varying degrees, the competitiveness of many other steel-based American industries, too.

We will not attempt to predict what will occur in steel trade and trade policy. Our guess is that in five years, when the TPM is due to expire, these basic problems will still be with us. Neither the American nor European steel industries will have restructured sufficiently to restore adequate competitiveness. Excess world steel capacity will be diminished but not eliminated. A more liberal definition of dumping will be too politically difficult to legislate in the United States or in GATT. Problems in steel trade will not disappear; trade will be substantial but at higher prices and lower volumes, and will be less competitive than it would be under true free trade. The TPM, with all its problems, is likely to remain for some time since it embodies a political compromise among all the main actors.

The pattern of politicization of the U.S.-Japan steel trade issue has followed a pattern similar to that of other trade issues. First, growing Japanese imports cause a U.S. domestic industry to seek import relief from the government. Then, the U.S. government asks its Japanese counterpart to accept some type of export quantity restraint. The Japanese government refuses to comply due to domestic industry opposition, and the issue becomes increasingly politicized as long as it remains unresolved. This was clearly seen in the U.S.-Japan textile wrangle of 1969-71 (Destler, Fukui and Sato 1979). The steel issue, however, has not fully conformed to this pattern.

It is true that increasing Japanese steel imports did cause the U.S. industry to seek government action to reduce imports in 1977, but intergovernmental negotiations did not ensue. The United States never asked Japan, formally or informally, for export quantity restraints. Nor did the Japanese and U.S. industries maintain incompatible interests causing their governments to clash. On the contrary, the U.S. industry wanted Japan to implement voluntary quotas—exactly the kind of solution the Japanese industry was prepared to accept. The Japanese government, too, was willing to acquiesce to such a settlement. Nevertheless, the steel issue became a major source of friction between Japan and the United States, largely because of the unduly slow response of the U.S. government. U.S. officials at first ignored domestic industry pressures because they were preoccupied with broader issues (the curbing of inflation and expansion of U.S. trade through the MTN) and did not fully realize the potential seriousness of the issue from the standpoint of *domestic and alliance politics*. Government inaction induced the steel industry to escalate its anti-import, anti-Japanese campaign through media exposure and lobbying in Congress. Thus, disagreement between government and industry in one country intensified a bilateral issue even when the two industries and the two governments did not have mutually contradictory interests because the mechanism for protection became as important as the issue of protection itself.

The auto issue of 1980-81 falls somewhere between the different patterns represented by the textile wrangle and the steel issue (Destler and Sato 1981, pp. 12-14). While the Japanese government (particularly MITI) was prepared to make necessary adjustments, the U.S. government remained indecisive, thus contributing to the prolongation and escalation of the issue. On the other hand, the Japanese auto industry was not nearly as united and cooperative as the steel industry had been—though Japanese automakers in 1980-81 were not as intransigent as Japanese textile producers in 1969-71. Since MITI has become more internationally sensitive and cooperative in settling trade disputes—in contrast to the time of the textile issue—it may well be that in future trade disputes Japanese government willingness and industry reluctance, the pattern present in the auto issue, may be more typical. In this respect the steel industry is an exception.

For the United States the steel issue was far more than one of bilateral relations with Japan. The European factor played an important role in 1977 and again in 1980. Apart from macroeconomic (and legal) considerations, it would have been difficult for the U.S. government to accept the Japanese offer of export restraint short of a similar offer from the EC in 1977. As soon as massive antidumping suits were filed against the Europeans in the fall of 1977 the Carter administration sought the new TPM approach, which clearly favored the EC. And no sooner had US Steel threatened to file major antidumping complaints against the Europeans in late 1979 (thus challenging the TPM) than the U.S. government began talks with the EC Commission and US Steel to avert a political confrontation. All this suggests that in the eyes of American policymakers the U.S.-Japan relationship is more asymmetric than the U.S.-EC relationship, and that, ceteris paribus, the United States continues to tend to be more sensitive to European interests than to Japanese. The auto issue was seen more exclusively as a U.S.-Japan issue since Japan was by far the most dominant foreign supplier of automobiles to the U.S. market in 1980-81. West Germany was not made a target of anti-import attacks since Volkswagen had begun producing cars in the United States several years earlier. Nevertheless, individual European countries, notably Great Britain, France, and Italy, had already been limiting Japanese auto imports, a fact sometimes used by those Americans seeking protection. And as the possibility of a Japanese export quota to the United States increased in spring 1981, the Europeans exerted pressure on Japan to accept a similar arrangement with the EC. In 1976 the Europeans succeeded in getting Japanese steelmakers to restrain exports to the EC, and then the AISI filed the 301 complaint, charging that the Japanese were unfairly diverting steel exports from Europe to the United States. The trilateral relationships among the United States, Japan, and the EC are complex and difficult. Where any two agree on a bilateral restraint arrangement, almost inevitably the third seeks a similar accommodation. This is a major weakness in bilateral solutions when both partners are so large in the world economy.

CODA

In January 1982 seven American steel firms, led by US Steel, once again formally filed antidumping suits against European and other, but not Japanese, producers. The industry was under the twin pressures of domestic recession in steel demand and an overvalued dollar. The Commerce Department once again promptly suspended the TPM, and began antidumping investigations as required by law. At the same time negotiations were inaugurated once again with the European Community. As of late April 1982 the immediate issues had not been resolved, and the basic issues remain as intractable as earlier.

REFERENCES

Adams, Walter. 1977. "The Steel Industry." In *The Structure of American Industry*, ed. Walter Adams. New York, Macmillan.

—— and Joeb B. Dirlam. 1979. "Unfair Competition in International Trade." In *Tariffs, Quotas, and Trade: The Politics of Protectionism*, ed. Walter Adams et al. San Francisco, Institute for Contemporary Studies.

American Iron and Steel Institute (AISI). *Annual Statistical Report*, various issues.

——. *Selected Steel Industry Data*, monthly publication.

——. 1980. *Steel at the Crossroads: The American Steel Industry in the 1980s*. Washington, D.C., AISI.

Bradford, Charles A. 1977-1980. *Steel Industry Quarterly Review*. New York, Merrill Lynch, Pierce, Fenner & Smith, various issues.

Crandall, Robert W. 1978. "Competition and 'Dumping' in the U.S. Steel Market." *Challenge*, July-August.

——. 1980a. "Steel Imports—Dumping or Competition?" *Regulation*, July-August.

——. 1980b. "The Economics of the Current Steel Crisis in OECD Member Countries." In *Steel in the 80s*. Paris, OECD.

Destler, I. M., Haruhiro Fukui, and Hideo Sato. 1979. *The Textile Wrangle: Conflict in Japanese-American Relations, 1969-1971*. Ithaca, N.Y., Cornell University Press.

—— and Hideo Sato. 1981. "Political Conflict in U.S.-Japan Economic Relations: Where It Comes From; What to Do about It." In *Appendix to The Report of the Japan-United States Economic Relations Group*, ed. The Japan-U.S. Economics Relations Group, April.

Federal Trade Commission (FTC). 1977. *Staff Report on the United States Steel Industry and Its International Rivals: Trends and Factors Determining International Competitiveness*. Washington, D.C., FTC, Bureau of Economics.

Florkoski, Edward S. 1980. "Policy Responses to the Problems of the World Steel Industry." In *Steel in the 80s*. Paris, OECD.

Gordon, Michael R. 1980. "U.S. Steel's Dumping Complaints—The Start of a New Trade War?" *National Journal*, April 5.

Imai Ken-ichi. 1975. "Iron and Steel: Industrial Organization." *Japanese Economic Studies* 3 (Winter 1974-75):

Interagency Task Force on Steel (Solomon Task Force). 1977. *Report to the President: A Comprehensive Program for the Steel Industry*, Dec. 6. Washington, D.C. Department of the Treasury, mimeographed.

Japan Iron and Steel Exporters' Association (JISEA) 1977. *U.S.-Japan Steel Trade: Basic Views on Current Issues*. Tokyo, Overseas Public Relations Committee.

Japan Iron and Steel Federation (JISF). *Monthly Report of the Iron and Steel Statistics*, various issues.

———. *Tekkō tōkei yōran* [Steel statistics survey] , annual, various issues.

Japan Ministry of International Trade and Industry (MITI) *Tekkō tōkei geppō* [Steel statistics monthly] , various issues.

Japan-United States Economic Relations Group. 1981. *Report of the Japan-United States Economic Relations Group*. Washington, D.C. and Tokyo, Japan-United States Economic Relations Group. January.

Kawahito Kiyoshi. 1972. *The Japanese Steel Industry*. New York, Praeger.

———. 1978. Letter in *Challenge*, November-December.

———. 1979. *Sources of the Difference in Steel Making Yield Between Japan and the United States*. Monograph Series, no. 20. Murfreesboro, Tenn., Business and Economic Research Center, Middle Tennessee State University.

———. 1980a. *Anatomy of Conflicts in the U.S.-Japan Steel Trade*. Conference Papers Series, no. 60. Murfreesboro, Tenn., Business and Economic Research Center, Middle Tennessee State University.

———. 1980b. *Issues of World Steel Production and Trade in the 1980s*. Monograph Series, no. 26. Murfreesboro, Tenn., Business and Economic Research Center, Middle Tennessee State University.

——— and Hans G. Mueller. 1978. *A Close Look at Steel Dumping Allegations*. Conference Papers Series, no. 35. Murfreesboro, Tenn., Business and Economic Research Center, Middle Tennessee State University.

Koo, Anthony Y. C. 1979. "On the Equivalence of Reference Price with Tariffs and Quotas." *American Economic Review*, December.

Lynn, Leonard Harvey. 1980. "Institutions, Organizations, and Technological Innovations: Oxygen Steelmaking in the U.S. and Japan." Ph.D. dissertation, University of Michigan.

Morkre, Morris E. and David G. Tarr. 1980. *Staff Report on Effects of Restriction of United States Imports: Five Case Studies and Theory*. Washington, D.C., Federal Trade Commission, Bureau of Economics.

Mueller, Hans, and Kiyoshi Kawahito. 1978. *Steel Industry Economics: A Comparative Analysis of Structure, Conduct and Performance*. New York, Japan Steel Information Center.

———. 1979a. *The International Steel Market: Present Crisis and Outlook for the 1980s*. Conference Papers Series, no. 46. Murfreesboro, Tenn., Business and Economic Research Center, Middle Tennessee State University.

———. 1979b. "The Recent American-Japanese Discord over the Steel Dumping Issue: An Examination of the Causes of the American Misconception, with Some References to Japanese Business Culture." Unpublished paper, Middle Tennessee State University.

Organization for Economic Cooperation and Development (OECD). 1980a. *The Steel Market in 1979 and the Outlook for 1980*. Paris, OECD.

———. 1980b. *Steel in the 80s*. Paris OECD.

Putnam, Hayes, and Bartlett, Inc. 1977. *Economics of International Steel Trade: Policy Implications for the United States*. Report prepared for the AISI. Newton, Mass.

———. 1978. *The Economic Implications of Foreign Steel Pricing Practices in the U.S. Market*. Report prepared for the AISI. Newton, Mass.

Sato Hideo, and Michael W. Hoding. 1980. "The Politics of Trade: The U.S.-Japanese Steel Issue of 1977." In Appendix to the Report of the Japan-United States Economic Relations Group, Washington, D.C. and Tokyo, Japan-United States Economic Relations Group, April 1981.

Solomon Report. See Interagency Task Force on Steel.

Steel Tripartite Advisory Committee. 1979. *Steel Trigger Price Mechanism: A One-Year Review for the Steel Tripartite Committee.* Department of Labor, mimeographed.

——. 1980. *Report to the President on the United States Steel Industry.* Department of Labor, mimeographed.

——. n.d. "Initial Report to the Working Group on Modernization and Capital Formation on the American Iron and Steel Institute Paper." *Steel at the Crossroads: The American Steel Industry in the 1980s.* Department of Labor, mimeographed.

Takano Hiroshi. 1980. "A Response to Recent Allegations by American Steel Representatives." Tokyo, Overseas Public Relations Committee, Japan Iron & Steel Exporters' Association.

U.S., Council on Wage and Price Stability. 1977. *Report to the President on Prices and Costs in the United States Steel Industry.* Washington D.C., Government Printing Office.

U.S., Congress, Office of Technology Assessment (OTA). 1980. *Technology and Steel Industry Competitiveness.* Washington, D.C., Government Printing Office.

U.S., Department of Commerce. 1980. "Statement Concerning Reintroduction of the Trigger Price Mechanism." Washington, D.C., Department of Commerce.

——. *Survey of Current Business* (monthly).

——, International Trade Administration. *Steel Import Data* (monthly or quarterly).

——. *Trigger Price Mechanism Price Manual* (quarterly).

U.S., Department of Labor, Bureau of Labor Statistics. *Employment and Earnings* (monthly).

U.S., Department of Treasury. *Notice* and *News* (various issues).

U.S., Federal Trade Commission. 1977. *Staff Report on the United States Steel Industry and Its International Rivals: Trends and Factors Determining International Competitiveness.* Washington, D.C., Government Printing Office.

U.S., General Accounting Office (GAO). 1980. *Administration of the Trigger Price Mechanism.* Document no. ID-80-15. Washington, D.C., Government Printing Office.

——. 1981. *New Strategy Required for Aiding Distressed Steel Industry.* Document no. EMD-81-29. Washington, D.C., Government Printing Office.

U.S., House, Committee on Ways and Means, Subcommittee on Trade. 1980. *Problems in U.S. Steel Market.* Washington, D.C., Government Printing Office.

U.S., Senate, Committee on Finance. 1975. *Trade Agreements Act of 1974.* Public Law 93-618. Washington, D.C., Government Printing Office.

——. 1979. *Trade Agreements Act of 1979.* Washington, D.C., Government Printing Office.

Walter, Ingo. 1979. "Protection of Industries in Trouble—The Case of Iron and Steel." *The World Economy,* vol. 2, no. 2 (May).

Watanabe Tsunehiko, and Soshichi Kinoshita. 1970. "An Econometric Study of the Japanese Steel Industry." Discussion Paper, no. 155. Cambridge, Harvard Institute of Economic Research.

White House Press Release. 1980. "A Program for the American Steel Industry, Its Workers and Communities." Washington, D.C.

Woolcock, Stephen. 1980. "The Problems of Adjustment in the Iron and Steel Industry." Paper read before the Study Group on the Implications of Newly Industrializing Countries (NICS) for Trade and Adjustment Policies, January 24, 1980. Royal Institute of International Affairs, Chatham House, London.

Evolving Comparative Advantage
and Japan's Imports of Manufactures

GARY SAXONHOUSE

DOES JAPAN RESTRICT IMPORTS of manufactured products more than other industrial nations? This question is critical in the formulation of U.S. trade policy vis-à-vis Japan, and more generally the views the American (and European) public holds of Japanese trade policies and nontariff barriers. Most frequently cited as evidence of Japan's restrictive trade policy is the significantly smaller amount of manufactured products it imports (relative to total imports) in comparison to other Western industrial economies.

However, understanding just what accounts for the low share of manufactures in total Japanese imports is extremely difficult. In part this is because the few theories that relate to the commodity composition of trade are not easy to test empirically and because there have been structural and policy changes in Japan, with respect to the imports of manufactures, that have in all likelihood rendered earlier research obsolete.

Table 9.1 presents the relative import share of manufactures for Japan and other major Organization for Economic Cooperation and Development (OECD) countries since 1971. At first glance it appears that particularly since 1973 there has been a major constriction in the access of foreign manufactured products to the Japanese market. Of course, the change after 1973 is largely the result of major price increases in imported fuels, minerals, and agricultural products. Since 1973, imports have taken a much larger share of the Japanese gross national product. When current import quantities are valued at 1970 prices, conceptual difficulties aside, the relative share of

Some of the work in this paper was done as part of a joint project by Hugh Patrick and myself on Japanese trade structure in the 1980s. Patrick has graciously allowed me the use of joint material. I am grateful for useful comments on this paper to Yoichi Shinkai, Yukio Noguchi, and Kozo Yamamura. None of these scholars is responsible for failures resulting from my unwillingness to always follow their good advice.

TABLE 9.1

SHARE OF MANUFACTURES IN TOTAL IMPORTS

Year	Percent	Year	Percent	Year	Percent
		Japan			
1971	28.6	1974	23.6	1977	20.8
1972	29.6	1975	20.3	1978	24.6
1973	30.5	1976	21.5	1979	24.5
		United States			
1971	66.8	1974	55.7	1977	53.2
1972	67.9	1975	53.8	1978	59.0
1973	64.8	1976	54.3	1979	55.0
		United Kingdom			
1971	50.9	1974	51.5	1977	58.4
1972	54.7	1975	52.2	1978	63.9
1973	56.2	1976	54.3	1979	65.7
		West Germany			
1971	58.1	1974	52.9	1977	57.0
1972	59.9	1975	55.1	1978	59.4
1973	57.9	1976	55.4	1979	57.9
		France			
1971	66.3	1974	57.8	1977	58.0
1972	64.6	1975	57.3	1978	60.3
1973	64.8	1976	58.7	1979	60.2
		Italy			
1971	48.5	1974	43.5	1977	45.1
1972	49.2	1975	42.1	1978	46.6
1973	49.3	1976	44.5	1979	48.1

SOURCE: Organization for Economic Cooperation and Development (hereafter cited as OECD) 1980

manufactured products is far above what it was in the early seventies. As seen in table 9.2, in 1970 prices, 1979 imports of manufactured products comprised a full 50 percent larger share of total imports than in the early seventies.

This is not to say that current concern is entirely artificial. Far from it. While Japanese imports of manufactures measured in 1970 prices are a much more respectable share of total imports than before, this improvement is significant only by the standards of the early seventies. Excepting the

TABLE 9.2

SHARE OF MANUFACTURES IN 1970 PRICES OF TOTAL IMPORTS

Year	Percent	Year	Percent	Year	Percent
		Japan			
1971	29.8	1974	40.2	1977	35.8
1972	30.1	1975	35.0	1978	40.1
1973	35.1	1976	36.2	1979	44.2
		United States			
1971	69.3	1974	71.1	1977	68.3
1972	70.1	1975	67.8	1978	67.3
1973	66.9	1976	68.1	1979	73.5
		United Kingdom			
1971	52.9	1974	76.4	1977	82.1
1972	57.3	1975	74.1	1978	77.3
1973	58.4	1976	78.4	1979	82.4
		West Germany			
1971	59.4	1974	74.7	1977	77.2
1972	63.1	1975	77.3	1978	83.1
1973	62.6	1976	78.1	1979	84.3
		France			
1971	68.7	1974	78.4	1977	78.1
1972	65.2	1975	76.9	1978	83.7
1973	68.1	1976	79.2	1979	81.9
		Italy			
1971	50.2	1974	68.2	1977	69.8
1972	51.5	1975	66.5	1978	72.1
1973	54.3	1976	69.4	1979	74.7

SOURCE: UN 1970

United States, all OECD countries have responded to much higher energy prices by curtailing imports of oil (see tables 9.3 and 9.4).[1] Consequently, in real terms, though not with respect to current value, the share of manufactures in total imports has risen. Yet, by the standards of the import shares of other OECD countries, Japanese performance has not improved at all. It this is true (see table 9.5), then the question of whether, as the *United States Japan Trade Report* put it, "Japan today is generally an open trading nation" and/or whether foreigners have been slack in their efforts to pene-

1. As table 9.4 indicates, American energy conservation performance since 1973 is comparable with the Japanese record. Unhappily, even as the American household and industrial sectors have cut their demand for energy on the supply side, imported oil has been heavily substituted for domestic oil. Ever-increasing American demands on the world oil market after 1973 are at the heart of foreign criticism of American energy policies.

TABLE 9.3

NET IMPORTS OF IMPORTED OIL

(Barrrels per day, % W from last year)

Year	Bpd	%	Year	Bpd	%	Year	Bpd	%
Japan								
1973	5552	(—)	1976	5229	(+5.1)	1978	5331	(-2.1)
1974	5404	(-2.7)	1977	5446	(+4.1)	1979	5625	(+5.5)
1975	4976	(-7.9)						
United States								
1973	6025	(—)	1976	7072	(+21.0)	1978	8002	(-6.6)
1974	5868	(-2.6)	1977	8565	(+21.1)	1979	7790	(-2.6)
1975	5847	(-0.4)						
United Kingdom								
1973	2342	(—)	1976	1660	(-6.1)	1978	872	(-20.2)
1974	2264	(-3.3)	1977	1093	(-34.2)	1979	436	(-50.0)
1975	1767	(-22.0)						
France								
1973	2875	(—)	1976	2514	(+14.0)	1978	2494	(-0.8)
1974	2742	(-4.6)	1977	2514	(-3.2)	1979	2762	(+10.7)
1975	2278	(-16.9)						
Italy								
1973	2090	(—)	1976	1963	(+7.3)	1978	1908	(-1.4)
1974	2093	(+0.1)	1977	1936	(-1.4)	1979	—	(—)
1975	1830	(-12.6)						
West Germany								
1973	2869	(—)	1976	2675	(+12.4)	1978	2724	(+3.2)
1974	2597	(-9.5)	1977	2639	(-1.3)	1979	2837	(+4.1)
1975	2380	(-8.4)						

SOURCE: U.S., Central Intelligence Agency, 1980

trate the Japanese market deserves further scrutiny *(United States-Japan Trade Report 1980).*

HISTORICAL BACKGROUND

No student of Japanese-American economic relations would argue that the late sixties and early seventies was a golden age of Japanese imports of manufactured products. Yet then, too, there was at least as much criticism of the small role of foreign manufactured products in the Japanese economy. The major difference between the early seventies and now is that there is less emphasis today by foreign critics and foreign governments on Japan's formal restrictions on manufactured imports and direct foreign investment. The following is from a 1972 article:

While these [trade and investment] restrictions may well have once played a central role in calling forth a more socially optimal amount of modernizing activity on the part

TABLE 9.4

Oil Consumption/GNP Index
Energy Consumption/GNP Index
(1973 ≡ 100)

Year	Percent	Year	Percent	Year	Percent
Japan					
Oil consumption/GNP					
1973	100.0	1976	89.1	1978	85.3
1974	97.9	1977	88.5	1979	81.4
1975	90.6				
Energy consumption/GNP					
1973	100.0	1975	94.0	1977	89.7
1974	99.5	1976	93.0	1978	85.9
United States					
Oil consumption/GNP					
1973	100.0	1976	97.9	1978	96.1
1974	97.6	1977	98.2	1979	92.1
1975	96.8				
Energy consumption/GNP					
1973	100.0	1975	96.1	1977	93.3
1974	98.4	1976	96.7	1978	89.1
West Germany					
Oil consumption/GNP					
1973	100.0	1976	89.7	1978	87.0
1974	89.0	1977	86.5	1979	86.0
1975	87.3				
Energy consumption/GNP					
1973	100.0	1975	93.9	1977	92.4
1974	97.5	1976	97.0	1978	92.6
France					
Oil consumption/GNP					
1973	100.0	1976	86.0	1978	80.8
1974	91.5	1977	79.7	1979	—
1975	83.9				
Energy consumption/GNP					
1973	100.0	1975	86.2	1977	89.1
1974	94.9	1976	91.0	1978	86.4
Italy					
Oil consumption/GNP					
1973	100.0	1976	93.4	1978	92.3
1974	96.4	1977	89.9	1979	9.1
1975	96.5				
Energy consumption/GNP					
1973	100.0	1975	99.7	1977	96.5
1974	99.4	1976	97.8	1978	93.5

Source: U.S. Central Intelligence Agency 1980

TABLE 9.5

Manufactured Import Shares Relative to Average OECD Performance

Year	Percentage of Average	Year	Percentage of Average	Year	Percentage of Average	Year	Percentage of Average
			Japan				
1970	0.49	1972	0.46	1974	0.43	1976	0.38
1971	0.46	1973	0.49	1975	0.36	1977	0.37
			United States				
1970	1.07	1972	1.09	1974	1.02	1976	0.98
1971	1.10	1973	1.06	1975	0.99	1977	0.95
			West Germany				
1970	0.96	1972	0.96	1974	0.97	1976	1.00
1971	0.95	1973	0.95	1975	1.01	1977	1.02

Source: Bank of Japan 1980

of Japanese management, do they remain important today? It has been noted that elements of the Japanese trading pattern appear highly unusual by international standards. The very low ratio of manufacturing production, the lack of intra-industry specialization, and the high ratio of raw materials to total imports, cannot be explained simply by Japan's resource endowment, its physical distance from other countries, its cultural distinctiveness or special characteristics of its wage structure. Other developed countries with comparable resource bases do not exhibit this Japanese phenomenon. Similarly as distance and cultural distinctiveness present no problems for Japanese manufacturing exports and for raw material imports, why should manufactured imports present a special case? Japanese trade restrictions probably play an important role in explaining the unusual pattern. [Saxonhouse 1972]

In 1971 and 1972, virtually all the present rationalizations for the low share of manufactures in imports were already being made. At that time there was certainly a consensus on both sides of the Pacific, officially and privately, that Japanese commercial policy was a major cause. This view was expressed in Japan in the Economic White Papers of 1970 and 1971, in articles, public statements, and widely circulated research memoranda by some officials at Tsūsanshō (Tsūshō Sangyōshō, the Ministry of International Trade and Industry [MITI]). The same view appeared in popular articles by prominent academic economists in such journals as *Kikan gendai keizai, Ekonomisuto,* and *Chūō kōron* (see Yamada 1970, pp. 42-57; Shinkai 1972, pp. 8-23; Uzawa 1972, pp. 102-19).

There was also a good deal of basic research supporting this joint point of view. For example, in a series of articles, Keio University economists Iwao Ozaki and Yoko Sazanami (1973, pp. 612-43; see also Sazanami and Hamaguchi 1974) attempted a comprehensive comparison of the trade structure of West Germany and other OECD countries to Japan, using 1965 and 1970 input-output tables constructed for use with highly disaggregated international trade data. They found that, by comparison with Canada, the United

States, Belgium, the Netherlands, West Germany, France, Italy, and the United Kingdom, Japan's manufactured imports were not closely related to its manufactured exports. In 1965 and 1970, there was only limited intra-industry specialization so characteristic of trade among other advanced industrialized countries. Ozaki and Sazanami concluded that Japan's divergent pattern was the result of the government's policy of curbing imports of manufactured products.

Domestic and international pressure led to an acceleration of the liberalization of Japan's trade policies in the early seventies. Between September 1970 and April 1972, the number of items restricted under the General Agreement on Trade and Tariffs (GATT) fell from ninety to thirty-three. Hand in hand with this trade liberalization came changes in the two other factors widely held at this time as major barriers to foreign access to the Japanese market. As a result of the Nixon administration's new economic policy, the yen appreciated markedly after August 1971, and major liberalization in Japanese government policies toward foreign investment in Japan followed.

In Japan the belief was that these policy changes would mean a radical change in import structure. Consider table 9.6, a projection made by the

TABLE 9.6

THE STRUCTURE OF JAPAN'S IMPORTS, 1960-1980
(Shares)

Year	Total Imports	Food and Beverages (SITC 0, 1)	Raw Materials (SITC 2, 4)	Mineral Fuels (SITC 3)
1960	100.0	13.6	49.5	14.1
1965	100.0	19.3	36.5	19.0
1969	100.0	14.2	33.0	20.3
1980	100.0	9.0	19.2	18.8
		Chemicals (SITC 5)	Machinery (SITC 7)	Other (SITC 6, 8)
1960		6.4	9.0	7.3
1965		5.2	9.6	9.8
1969		5.5	10.6	15.3
1980		5.8	19.0	28.1

SOURCE: Japan Economic Research Center 1980

Japan Economic Research Center in 1972. Then it was expected that by 1980 almost 53 percent of Japanese imports would be manufactured products.[2] Both the United States and others were hopeful of a dramatic change. Quoting again from my 1972 article:

2. The great changes projected for 1980 were not entirely attributable to trade liberalization. The projection assumed a 10 percent average annual growth in GNP with

Historically the Japanese have given only lip service to the concept of free trade. As early as the 1870s the great Japanese statesman Okubo Toshimichi noted that England enacted heavily mercantilist laws in the seventeenth century when its industrial structure was underdeveloped, adopting free trade policies only in the nineteenth century when it had become the world's leading manufacturing power. In the last two years, there has been a remarkable change in outlook. Among Japanese policy-makers and businessmen, one has seen emerging a consensus in favor of liberal trade policies. There are signs that this change in outlook has its roots not simply in a reaction to American and world insistence on these matters, but also in the conviction that liberal trade is good for Japan and good for the world economy. [Saxonhouse 1972]

Nevertheless, there were those who doubted that it was really a matter of formal restrictions after all:

There seems to have been and there continues to be widespread belief in the United States that the removal of any or all formal controls by itself may mean very little in the short run and in the long run. So much has been written in the American press regarding the intimate connection between government and business in Japan that many believe that what was formerly handled by explicit measures now will be handled by the almost legendary (though perhaps non-existent) informal mechanisms of administrative guidance. Or perhaps it will be argued that the formal restrictions were never really important at all and the informal measures will go on as before. [Ibid.]

This concern—that informal government restriction and government protection of an archaic distribution system are limiting the access of foreign manufactures to the Japanese market, is one important focus, by no means the most newsworthy, of the present difficulties in U.S.-Japan commercial relations. This system, purportedly discriminating against foreign goods, thereby limiting foreign access to the Japanese market, bespeaks the present difficulties in U.S.-Japan commercial relations. By contrast, concern about formal barriers, excepting agricultural products, has become insignificant.

On the Japanese side, the optimism prevalent in the early seventies that Japanese imports of manufactured products would approach European levels in the near future vanished soon after the Arab oil embargo. Consider the post-oil embargo projections in the tables 9.8, 9.9, and 9.10 and compare them with the 1972 projection for 1980 in table 9.7.

None of these projections was anywhere near as optimistic for future Japanese imports of manufactures as the 1972 projections. Even the projection of import shares in 1970 prices, a projection that proved to be quite accurate, had Japanese shares still well below the levels for other advanced industrialized countries.

EXPLANATIONS OF CURRENT LOW SHARE

If the actual experiences of 1980, or more recent projections for 1985 seem unsatisfactory, it is appropriate to distinguish what might be a reasonable import structure for Japan, given its resource base and location. Does Japan now have surprisingly low aspirations?

---

all the structural transformation that such a high rate of growth for eleven years might bring.

TABLE 9.7

AVERAGE TARIFF LEVELS ON MINING AND MANUFACTURING
PRODUCTS BEFORE AND AFTER TOKYO ROUND

Countries	Before	After
Japan	9.9%	5.5%
U.S.	8.2	6.0
European community	9.7	7.0

Residual Imports Restrictions of Major Countries

Countries	Agricultural Products under Quota	Industrial Products under Quota	Total Items
Japan	22	5	27
U.S.	1	6	7
Norway	51	1	52
Sweden	5	2	7
Denmark	5	1	6
France	19	27	46
Germany	3	11	14
Italy	3	5	8
U.K.	1	2	3

SOURCES: Ministry of International Trade and Industry 1976 and Ministry of Foreign Affairs

TABLE 9.8

JAPAN ECONOMIC RESEARCH CENTER
IMPORT PROJECTIONS FOR 1980
(Share)

Food and beverages (SITC 0,1)	11.5%
Raw materials (SITC 2,4)	12.0
Mineral fuels (SITC 3)	43.2
Chemicals (SITC 5)	4.4
Other manufactured products (SITC 6,8)	21.9
Total imports	100.0

SOURCE: Japan Economic Research Center 1976

In a brief memorandum circulated in the spring of 1980, the Ministry of Finance (MOF) emphasized that Japan's dependence on raw materials imports is far greater than that of any other industrialized country. Second, it stated that the low level of manufacture imports exists because Japan is not surrounded by other industrialized nations. If intra-EC trade is excluded, the EC import share of manufactured goods falls from 55 percent to only 43 percent, and if trade with adjacent OECD countries is also excluded, manufactured products comprise only 35 percent of its imports. This ap-

TABLE 9.9

SANGYŌ KŌZŌ SHINGIKAI (INDUSTRIAL
STRUCTURE COUNCIL) VISION OF
IMPORT STRUCTURE FOR 1980
(In 1970 prices; share)

Food and beverages (SITC 0, 1)	12.0%
Raw materials (SITC 2, 4)	27.3
Mineral fuels (SITC 3)	19.5
Chemicals (SITC 5)	7.4
Other manufactured products (SITC 6, 8)	33.8
Total imports	100.0

SOURCE: Ministry of International Trade and Industry 1976

TABLE 9.10

KEIZAI KIKAKUCHŌ (ECONOMIC PLANNING AGENCY),
KEIZAI KENKYŪSHŌ (ECONOMIC RESEARCH
INSTITUTE) HYPOTHETICAL FORECAST FOR 1980
(Share)

Food and beverages	15.0%
Raw materials	25.3
Mineral fuels	30.2
Chemicals	2.6
Other manufactured products	25.5
Total imports	100.0

SOURCE: Economic Planning Agency 1976

proaches the 24 percent level Japan maintained in 1978 and is not far from the share of manufactured goods in Japanese imports in 1973 (MOF 1980).

Pointing to Japan's natural resource base and its distance from other advanced industrialized countries, the MOF confirms a continuance of its post-oil embargo attitudes and suggests that a European-style import structure for Japan is far away. In making its projections, the report assumes that the import of manufactured goods elasticity of total import demand will be 1.35. This figure is one of the great constants in the last twenty years of the Japanese economy's experience. Despite all the great differences in the periods from 1959 to 1973 and from 1973 to 1979, this elasticity, when imports are measured in real terms, is the same for both periods. With this elasticity, the MOF calculates that if imports grow 10 percent a year, it will take eighteen years for the share of manufactured goods in total imports to reach current EC shares—excluding intra-EC trade. Even if total Japanese imports increase 15 percent a year, it will be well after 1990 before the Japanese catch up with the Europeans.

The MOF analysis is certainly arguable. Is it really appropriate in making the comparison to net out trade with nearby OECD countries, some of whose distance from, say, West Germany is at least as far as that from Japan to South Korea, Taiwan, and perhaps some areas of Southeast Asia? Furthermore, is it anything more than a statistical coincidence that the manufactured imports' arc elasticity of import demand should be the same for 1959 to 1973 and 1973 to 1979—could it really be the same for the 1980s? That the arc elasticity is the same for the two periods, notwithstanding the sharp shifts in relative prices between 1973 and 1979, would seem to imply that the pace of Japanese commercial liberalization relative to the amount of real import growth slowed rather than quickened in the seventies.

Scholarly research on the commodity composition of trade should be helpful in deciding whether Japan's low import share of manufactured goods is prima facie evidence of informal restrictions. Yet, unfortunately, this has not been the case. As mentioned earlier, most careful empirical studies of Japan's commodity composition of trade concentrate on the period up to 1973, and like Sazanami's study, when they do find Japan's trade pattern unusual from an international perspective, they attribute this to formal restrictions—restrictions since abandoned.

Even where such studies are available for more recent periods, they are not entirely helpful given the character of the debates between Japan and its trading partners. Japan argues that its natural resource endowment is exceptionally poor and that it is uniquely far from its major trading partners. Given, however, the natural resource endowments of countries such as Italy, among other European countries, it is necessary that the characterization of the resource vector in empirical studies of commodity composition be handled with some subtlety. Typically, in general equilibrium, multicountry empirical models of international trade that focus on the relationship between factor endowments and trade structure, natural resources are proxied by population density or not represented at all.[3]

By contrast, more and more studies do relate distance to the commodity composition of trade. Leamer, in a study of the import/GNP ratio for two-digit commodity groups for Standard Industrial Trade Classification (SITC) groups five through eight, finds that distance along with GNP, population, and tariff variables are excellent predictors of trade dependence (Leamer

---

3. In Keesing and Sherk 1971, the population density variable is used as explicit, preferred proxy for natural resources per capita. Such well-known studies as Leamer 1974 and Hufbauer 1970 leave out the impact of natural resources entirely. Given that the interest of most of the early work on the commodity composition of trade was an attempt to validate a two-factor (capital and labor) version of the Hecksher-Ohlin-Samuelson model, this neglect is not surprising. At the same time, because of the newly enhanced importance of natural resources some more recent sources reflect that finally scholars are beginning to make more of an effort in this area. See Leamer, Stern, and Baum 1977, pp. 1-20. Unfortunately this study does not deal directly with the commodity composition of trade.

1974, pp. 350-74). Unfortunately, Leamer's cross-country sample includes only Atlantic area countries, so that the distances between Japan and its major markets are outside the sample range. Within the sample range, for most of the twenty-eight commodity groups, Leamer finds distance elasticities of import dependence close to unity. Given the distances between Japan and its major markets, were these elasticity coefficients applied—regardless of their validity—a strong possibility exists that a significant proportion of the difference in behavior between Japan and other advanced industrialized countries might be explained.[4]

A GENERAL EQUILIBRIUM MODEL OF TRADE STRUCTURE

UNDERPINNINGS OF THE THEORY OF COMPARATIVE ADVANTAGE

Too much of the discussion on the modern development of the Japanese economy stresses the unique characteristics of Japan as explanations of this development. In turn, the aggressive Japanese business expansion pattern, the unique style of decision making, unusual business groupings, the special ways of handling the labor force, the clinging to traditional consumption patterns, the strength of the family in the context of loyalty to national symbols, and the singular capacity to absorb from other cultures have all been touted separately and collectively as a means of understanding what has happened during the last 120 years and also particularly in the last 30 years. This tendency is not surprising. On the one hand many, though certainly not all, of these explanations have been developed by some of the same individuals who have helped establish Japanese studies as a separate field of inquiry in the United States. On the other hand many Japanese, in an effort to turn the discussion of commercial disputes away from low wages and unfair trade practices, have also openly promoted explanations emphasizing the superiority of distinctively Japanese behavior and practices.

It is hardly surprising or inappropriate that either group should emphasize the gains from cultural considerations. Understanding of the Japanese economy cannot be entirely divorced from an intimate knowledge of Japanese personality, society, and culture, but surely the situation at least in the policy context has already gone too far. In the U.S. congressional U.S.-Japan Trade Task Force report issued in September 1980 it was suggested, as previously noted, that "Japan is generally an open nation" but that "private [cultural?] barriers to trade are very serious and may account for billions of dollars in lost U.S. export opportunity" (*United States-Japan Trade Report 1980*). Indeed, when the areas of the economy are listed where such barriers are important they turn out to cover nearly three-fourths of total Japanese manufactured imports. Can this be true? Is Japanese behavior really so distinctive in its economic consequences?

4. Note in Leamer, Stern, and Baum 1977 the distance variable is not important. But Tanaka (1968), in a multivariate analysis, finds the distance elasticity of Japan's export demand to be greater than one. Among other studies on Japan stressing distance as a highly significant variable is Hirayama 1965.

Given this perspective, and given the desire to pose the analysis in the broadest possible context to ultimately facilitate long-term forecasting, the empirical work in the present study is undertaken within an analytical framework that is self-consciously comparative. This approach presumes that Japanese phenomena can be explained by theories that are general over time and space. It is hoped that Japanese phenomena can be understood in the context of general explanations relevant for all countries. The analytical framework of this work is an adaptation of the Hecksher-Ohlin-Samuelson Theory of Comparative Advantage (HOS).[5] This theory (a long-time favorite of instructors of international trade), emphasizes that in a freely competitive environment the structure and level of international trade can be explained by the distribution of inputs of the production process among the world's many economies. The original formulation of this model stressed a country's availability of capital, labor, skills, social organization, and natural resources.

Now, thirty years since it first gained wide acceptance, the HOS theory seems a bit shopworn. Since the famous Leontief Paradox results in 1953, numerous attempts have been made to verify the theory empirically. A review of this literature is curiously unsatisfying (Leontief 1956; see also Baldwin 1971). The algebra of HOS has been worked out in very great detail by a generation of theoretical economists. Strangely enough, however, tests of HOS make almost no direct use of this formal framework. Often the functional forms imposed in these tests cannot be derived from HOS mathematics.

It is occasionally suggested that the strong assumptions necessary to the development of the formal structure of HOS leave little doubt about the outcome of such a test. The theory is too unrealistic to explain real-world phenomena. Such an attitude seems in some respects unscientific. Theories are generally judged by their explanatory power, not by the nature of their assumptions. There is a rich body of theoretical literature delineating the conditions of and possible exceptions to the HOS theory of comparative advantage. It has been shown that what appears intuitively plausible rests on certain more or less restrictive assumptions, which may pose problems when this theory is used for empirical analysis and projection. These assumptions can be divided into three categories: those for which the exceptions are intellectually interesting but so unlikely in the real world as to be trivial; those for which exceptions may be potentially significant but for which it is virtually impossible to adjust directly by refining the theory so that some assessment of their importance is needed; and those for which exceptions are potentially significant and for which theoretical and empirical refinements are possible to overcome their restrictiveness, thereby making the theory more effective for analysis and projection.

The real-world exceptions to category one and two assumptions do not

5. For a thorough discussion of the logical underpinnings of this theory, see Bhagwati 1965. A good textbook treatment of the theory and some empirical tests of it appear in Carrs and Jones 1980, chaps. 8-11.

necessarily make the HOS theory of comparative advantage a weak or poor theory. After all, all theorizing represents an effort to simplify the complexities of the real world by focusing on the most important causal relationships that constitute the dominant explanation of any phenomenon. Are the exceptions empirically important? The proof of the pudding is always in the eating. Can this theory as it is empirically modeled actually predict trade levels and patterns? Its satisfactoriness as a theory depends on its performance, not on the literal accuracy of its assumptions. If accurate predictions result, the restrictive nature of the assumptions required to eliminate those exceptions need not be of great concern.

Category one assumptions. One exception of the first category has to do with the extreme difference in consumption preferences one nation might have in comparison to others. Suppose a country with many engineers has a strong demand for integrated circuits, but has little use for oil; it might then import some integrated circuits despite high levels of local production and export oil despite low levels of production. There is little if any empirical evidence to indicate that such extreme differences in consumer preferences, taking income levels into account, exist for any important commodities for Japan or any other nation. It is easy to see then why exceptions to category one assumptions can be readily dismissed.

Category two assumptions. The restrictiveness of category two assumptions are intellectually somewhat more troublesome, though fortunately the results of the empirical study imply that they do not constitute a serious obstacle to acceptance of this approach. Nonetheless, rather than simple dismissal, it may be worthwhile to discuss these basic assumptions.

Essentially, category two assumptions are all aspects of one basic assumption: domestic and international markets for commodities, capital, labor, and natural resources are perfectly competitive. A corollary is that there are no economies of scale in production (i.e., when all productive inputs are doubled, output is exactly doubled). Economists have long argued over the assumption of competition, which is used in almost all empirical analyses. The wide range of empirical evidence shows that, while monopolistic or oligopolistic markets and production economies of scale exist and are not insignificant, the assumptions about competition do not vitiate the theoretical framework of comparative advantage. Certainly Japan has oligopolist industries and enjoys certain economies of scale, yet they are common to all industrial market economies. Not only is the degree of over-all oligopoly the same in Japan as in major Western industrial nations, but more important, those industries characterized by oligopoly are the same, as is the degree of concentration (Pryor 1972).

Another corollary of the competitive assumption is that the size of any given industry in a specific country is sufficiently small relative to world production that a slight decrease in the foreign price of its product will result in all its output available for export being sold abroad. Certainly there are commodities for which this is not the case—Brazilian coffee, and probably Japanese oil tankers. In such instances, special attention must be paid to the market structure for the specific commodity by using information not contained in the model. Yet such cases are relatively few for Japan and for almost all countries, especially in the longer run, when producers throughout the world are able to adjust facilities and output in response to sustained changes in price. In general, the world demand for most Japanese exports is highly responsive to changes in their prices.

A related assumption inherent in the HOS theory of comparative advantage is that aggregate inputs of capital, labor, and natural resources at the national level—relative, of course, to amounts of these inputs elsewhere in the world—determine the level of production for each specific commodity. Thus, an increase in a country's supply of its relatively abundant factor of production, everything else unchanged, will increase the production of those specific commodities using that productive input the most. Using the earlier example, this assumes that a country with many engineers has a comparative advantage in producing integrated circuits and that an increase in the number of engineers, everything else unchanged, would result in increased integrated circuit production. But suppose in fact engineers in that country do not well understand the production technology for integrated circuits? Then the country might export its meager supply of oil and import integrated circuits. This may occur due either to the quality of the engineers or to the specificity of their knowledge. Thus, when Leontief found, paradoxically, that the presumably capital-rich, labor-scarce United States exported relatively labor-intensive goods and imported capital-intensive goods, contrary to the standard version of the theory of comparative advantage, subsequent research indicated that his original method of empirical estimation did not adequately take into account American abundance of natural resources, especially agricultural land, and more important, did not take into account the higher quality of American labor. In the next section the HOS theory of comparative advantage is extended to account for evolving differences in the quality of labor and other production factors.

Category three assumptions. The discussion of the preceding paragraphs points to two major, quite restrictive assumptions of the HOS theory of comparative advantage: production technology is the same for every country, and consumption preferences (consumer demands) are identical for all countries in the world. These are in the third category of assumptions—important ones, but about which something practical can be done. Both these assumptions violate reality, and each can have a serious effect on levels and structures of trade.

In particular, the assumption that the same technologies are available throughout the world, in the absence of economies of scale, implies in the extreme that wages and the returns on capital are the same for all countries. For example, theoretically as a result of trade, unskilled labor in India, Japan, and the United States would be paid the same. This is clearly not the case. The quality of even unskilled labor differs considerably among these three nations.

While the possibility of extreme differences in consumer tastes and preferences among nations, as a practical matter, has been dismissed, nonetheless the assumption that all nations have identical consumption preferences also seems an unwarranted simplification. It is desirable to accommodate the possibility of national differences in consumer preferences in an empirical formulation of the model, especially for forecasting purposes, where different assumptions might be significant. Therefore, national differences in both the quality of inputs and in consumer preferences have been incorporated into the model in the subsequent sections of this paper to resolve these difficulties.

First, however, the discussion can be summarized schematically, as shown in figure 9.1.

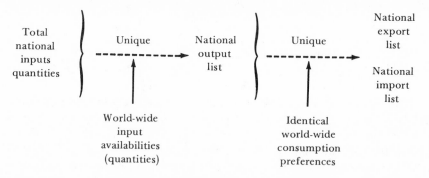

Fig. 9.1

In this schema a country's supplies of labor, capital, and natural resources relative to world quantities determine what that country produces; consumer preferences determine what is consumed. The difference between amounts produced and consumed is the amount traded—exports or imports. At this stage differing national qualities of factor inputs and consumption preferences have not been taken into account.

Phrases such as "factor inputs" or "capital, labor, and natural resources" may seem vague: seven factors are utilized to explain Japan's (and the world's) production and trade of goods. These include production capital stock, labor, education attainment, petroleum resources, iron ore resources, arable land, and distance. These seven aggregate inputs for each nation determine the production of and trade in each specific commodity and the total level of trade. Further detailed treatment of natural resources, labor, and educational attainment is desirable, as is clear from the earlier discussion, but even this minimal level of detail is a significant improvement over previous research on the commodity structure of trade.

DIFFERENCES IN INPUT QUALITIES

The assumption that factor productivities are identical for all nations is restrictive and contradictory (see, for example, Tinbergen et al. 1972, especially the essay by Abram Bergson). Productivities differ among nations substantially beyond what is explained by differences in amounts of capital, labor, and natural resources. Wages, even by degree of labor skill, are not identical in all countries; this is the most extreme gap. Returns on capital also differ by nation, though less than wages. One way to handle this difficulty is to assume that countries are simply at different technological levels in their utilization of inputs.

Conceptually, one might argue that what are termed differences in technology levels are no more than differences among disaggregated lists of specific productive inputs. If only complete data were available on all the productive inputs, and if one could correctly delineate their causal effects on output, then the production of any commodity could be fully explained without recourse to assumed differences in technological level. Such disaggregation might list all occupations by age and education, machines by type, buildings by age, natural resources by physical characteristics and access to transport, and the like—all in immense detail. But not nearly enough data are available to make this a feasible solution, and, even if all the data were available they would be so vast that their manipulation would be too expensive to be economically beneficial.

The approach here falls between the assumption of national differences in technology levels and the complete, disaggregated inclusion of all productive inputs. Basically, it is assumed that observed national differences in productivity levels (and differences in wages and payments for other production factors), beyond those due to educational levels and relative amounts of inputs themselves, are attributable to cross-country variation in the qualities of these inputs. So, in principle, the same production technology is available in all countries, as assumed in the theory, but some countries know how to use those technologies better than others. Part of this is due to differences in labor skills and this is already incorporated in the model through the education variable. However, all inputs—especially labor—exhibit further quality differences internationally. This approach then seems a plausible and reasonable way to close the gap between the theory and the facts of the real world, and to rescue the model for empirical use.

It may be useful to explain in somewhat more detail what is meant by quality differences. In large part, as the above discussion implies, a quality difference arises from the lack of disaggregated information in specifying a substantially larger number of inputs than the seven used in this study. If each of the seven were subdivided so that quantity differences among nations could be better specified, quality differences would be correspondingly reduced. This can be illustrated by considering some of the differences in labor, for example, that might result in measured differences in its quality among nations.

When, for example, it is assumed that labor of the same educational level in the United States or Japan is of higher productive quality than in India, it does not mean that there must be inherent differences. Rather there are a

host of socio-political-economic forces (broadly defined) that cause international differences in the quality of labor of the same educational level.
Even the quality of education for any given number of years varies substantially by nation. Values and attitudes regarding work assignments, incentives,
structures for economic performance, general competence and organizational-
entrepreneurial skills of management and the like all affect labor effectiveness. So too does government policy and institutional arrangements. Moreover, in some countries labor may be underemployed, the economy not reap-
ing full productive advantage of labor skill levels. In very low income countries, unskilled workers may be so poor that they cannot afford sufficient
nutrition and health care to be able to work as well as the unskilled worker
in a richer country. Thus the quality of labor measure is a summary or proxy
indicator for a large number of forces that affect worker productivity.

The statistical estimation of quality differences is rather complicated. It
is explained more rigorously and in more detail in the next section. In
essence, it is assumed that directly productive capital, labor, and educational
attainment for each country have a certain quality level that, though it
changes in time, is a constant ratio of their quantity at any given time. The
quality component of each input differs from country to country but is the
same within a country at a given point for all the various commodities being
produced. The introduction of quality variables for national inputs means, in
effect, that the measured sizes of the input quantities are adjusted by a
multiplicative quality factor, resulting in what is often termed in the technical literature as efficiency units of labor, capital, or natural resources.

As shown in figure 9.2, reading from left to right the schema reflects the
transformation of a country's productive inputs into output and into international trade. National production structure is also influenced by the possibilities of competitive production elsewhere in the world, by domestic consumption preferences, and by foreign demand (world-wide consumption
preferences). All inputs are adjusted for their international differences in
quality.

DISTANCE AND COUNTRY-SPECIFIC TERMS

Central to this approach is the basic hypothesis that every country's trade,
including Japan's, can be explained by essentially the same causal forces.
Differences in trade levels and structures are the consequence of different national endowments of labor, capital, and natural resources, all adjusted for quality. No country is presumed to be unique in the underlying
causes of its trade performance, though each has its own set of inputs and
preferences. Thus Japan is being compared explicitly with the rest of the
world, as measured by some nine important market economies. In a sense, a
world norm is defined based on the inputs, consumption preferences, and
commodity trade of a large number of countries that vary widely in economic size, level of income, natural resources, and other input factors. Japan
is then compared with this complicated average world norm. Any country

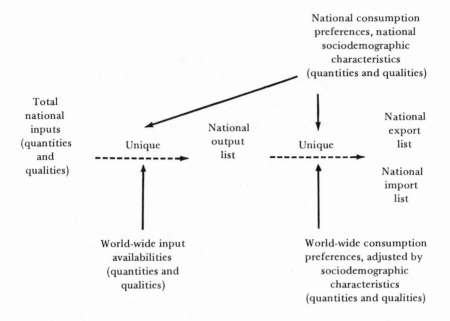

Fig. 9.2

with the same, quality-adjusted inputs and the same sociodemographic characteristics as Japan would be expected to have Japan's level and pattern of trade.

This is still a simplification in two respects. First, a country's distance from its major trading partners introduces an additional trade cost—the greater the distance the less trade, and the more trade is geared toward commodities whose values are high relative to transportation costs. Second, there may be unique elements influencing a country's trade; for instance, policies may be pursued for the protection and/or encouragement of particular industries, or indeed all industries—pursued to a greater or lesser extent than in other countries on average as measured by the world norm. The model is adjusted to incorporate both influences on the level of a country's trade, in total, and that structured by commodity.

In general, the farther a country is from other major national markets and sources of supply, the greater the costs of trade. The most obvious cost is simply the transportation of commodities. But there are other, related costs—delay in delivery, the interest cost of financing commodities being transported, and so forth. And there are less apparent costs; the farther one country is from another, the less each is likely to know about the other's markets, production, and prices. It may also be that distance is a proxy for degree of knowledge of each other's languages. Other research corroborates the assumption that distance is an important variable in explaining trade, especially for Japan (see, for example, Hirayama 1965; Nihon Keizai Shimbun 1972, p. 244).

A distance variable, measured as the average number of miles of each country from its major trading partners, weighted by the share of trade with each, is therefore explicitly introduced into the model. In practice this means that most European countries are very close to their major markets (other European countries), the United States is somewhat farther away on average from its major trading partners (though of course close to Canada), while Japan is one of the countries farthest away from its major trading partners. Australia is like Japan in that respect. Distance enters the model as a distinct variable for each country's trade equations; it is added as a separate source of explanation.

The general analytical framework of the model is based on the assumption that the major causes of the nature of Japan's trade practices are the same as for other countries. Yet, as noted earlier, it has been alleged that Japan is so different, or pursues such different policies, that it may be deemed unique. In particular, it has been alleged that the Japanese government has over the past two decades systematically engaged in import restriction and export promotion—much more so than other nations in comparable positions. This is an important issue, and deserves careful explicit analysis. The framework used in this study makes it possible to test this proposition for the over-all level of trade for broad commodity groups and also for particular commodities. This is accomplished by adding to each country's commodity equation a special variable designed to estimate that portion of trade attributable to special national features and policies affecting the import or export of that commodity in a way different from the world norm set of policies.

A GENERAL EQUILIBRIUM TREATMENT OF TRADE STRUCTURE IN MATHEMATICAL TERMS

This section is a technical treatment of the material covered in the previous section.

DEMAND

Suppose that national preferences may be summarized by a positive, continuous, nondecreasing, quasi-concave, utility function (for the conditions under which this is true, see Samuelson 1956; and Eisenberg 1961). Suppose further that the reciprocal, indirect utility function derived from this utility function can be approximated by the functional form.[6]

$$h(v) = \sum_{i=1}^{N} \sum_{j=1}^{N} b_{ij} v_i^{1/2} v_j^{1/2} + 2\sum_{j=1}^{N} b_{oj} v_j^{1/2} {}^6$$

$$+ b_{oo} \tag{1}$$

$$\text{where } b_{ij} = b_{ji}$$

where $b_{ij} = b_{ji}$

and where $h \equiv$ reciprocal indirect utility function (see Diewert 1974)

$v \equiv$ income normalized prices

If preferences are homothetic, that is, the direct utility function is homogeneous, the following system of consumer demand equations can be derived from (1):

$$X_i(P_1/Y, \ldots, P_N/Y) = \frac{\sum\limits_{j=1}^{N} b_{ij} P_i^{-1/2} P_j^{1/2} Y}{\sum\limits_{k=1}^{N} \sum\limits_{m=1}^{N} b_{km} P_k^{1/2} P_m^{1/2}} \tag{2}$$

where $X_i \equiv i^{th}$ good

$P \equiv$ price

$Y \equiv$ national income

Let income be equal to the weighted sum of factors, where the weights are unit factor rewards. Substituting this into (2) we get:

$$X_i = G_i \sum_{s=1}^{K} W_s a_s L_s$$

where $G_i = \dfrac{\sum\limits_{j=1}^{N} b_{ij} P_i^{1/2} P_j^{1/2}}{\sum\limits_{k=1}^{N} \sum\limits_{m=1}^{N} b_{km} P_k^{1/2} P_m^{1/2}}$ \qquad (3)

$L =$ factor of production

$W =$ factor reward

$a =$ quality of factor

SUPPLY

Suppose the technology of an economy may be summarized by a variable profit function,[7] and suppose that this profit function is approximated by:

6. h is the Generalized Leontief indirect utility function and was first presented by W. E. Diewert (1974).

7. The concept of a variable profit function was first suggested in Samuelson 1953.

$$\pi(P_i L) = \sum_{i=1}^{N} \sum_{j=1}^{N} \sum_{s=1}^{K} d_{is} (\tfrac{1}{2}P_i^2 + \tfrac{1}{2}P_j^2)^{1/2} a_s L_s$$

$$+ \sum_{i=1}^{N} \sum_{s=1}^{K} C_{is} P_i a_s L_s + \sum_{i=1}^{N} \sum_{s=1}^{N} \sum_{r=1}^{N} f_{sr}(a_s L_s)^{1/2}(a_r L_r)^{1/2} P_i \qquad (4)$$

where $d_{is} = d_{si}$, $f_{sr} = f_{rs}$; $d_{ii} = 0$ for $i = 1, 2, \ldots, N$

and where $f_{ss} = 0$ for $s = 1, 2, \ldots, K$

and where $\pi \equiv$ profit function

Using Hotelling's lemma, (4) may be differentiated with respect to each of the output prices to obtain a system of derived supply functions (Hotelling's lemma is discussed in Gorman 1968):

$$X_i(p_i L) = \sum_{j=1}^{N} \sum_{s=1}^{N} d_{ij} (\tfrac{1}{2}P_i^2 + \tfrac{1}{2}P_j^2)^{-1/2} P_i a_s L_s$$

$$+ \sum_{s=1}^{K} C_{is} a_s L_s + \sum_{s=1}^{K} \sum_{r=1}^{K} f_{sr}(a_s L_s)^{1/2}(a_r L_r)^{1/2}$$

$$i = 1, 2, \ldots, N$$

$$= \sum_{s=1}^{K} Q_i a_s L_s + \sum_{s=1}^{K} \sum_{r=1}^{K} f_{sr}(a_s L_s)^{1/2}(a_r L_r)^{1/2} \qquad (5)$$

$$= \sum_{s=1}^{K} Q_i a_s L_s + \sum_{s=1}^{K} \sum_{r=1}^{K} f_{sr}(a_s a_r)^{1/2} L_s^{1/2} L_r^{1/2}$$

$$i = 1, 2, \ldots, N$$

where $Q_i \equiv \sum_{j=1}^{N} d_{ij} (\tfrac{1}{2}p_i^2 + \tfrac{1}{2}p_j^2)^{-1/2} p_i + C_{is}$

Provided the much debated Law of One Price and the Factor Price Equalization Theorem hold, and the price of a particular good and reward of a particular factor are everywhere the same, G_i, and Q_i, and w_i may be treated as constants and (5) may be subtracted from (3). The resulting equation explains the net trade in goods, X_i, and is linear in parameters and has a nonarbitrary functional form derived explicitly from preferences and technology.[8]

$$X_i(L) = \sum_{s=1}^{K} U_i a_s L_s - \sum_{s=1}^{K} \sum_{r=1}^{K} f_{sr} (a_s a_r)^{1/2} L_s^{1/2} L_r^{1/2} \qquad (6)$$

$$i = 1, 2, \ldots, N$$

where $U_i = G_i - Q_i$[9]

ESTIMATION

(6) is to be estimated for N commodity groups from international cross-section data. Were it not for unknown variation in the quality of inputs across countries, estimation of (6) might proceed using ordinary least squares methods. Formally, the estimation of (6) with a_s unknown and differing across countries is a multivariate errors in variable problem.[10] Instrumental variable methods will allow consistent estimation of the U_i and f_{rs}. Also, it is possible to identify a_s for each economy up to an arbitrary normalization on one factor and one country.[11] These estimates of a_s can then be used to obtain new new Aitken efficient estimates of Q_i and f_{rs}.

DATA

(6) is estimated with data taken from nine countries for 109 internationally traded commodities for the years 1959, 1962, 1964, 1967, 1969, 1971, and

8. Unlike the Factor Price Equalization Theorem, the Law of One Price has been hotly debated in recent years. See in particular the discussions in Isard 1977; Kravis and Lipsey 1977; and Richardson 1978. The opposing view is summarized and extended in Frenkel 1978. How good an approximation of the Law of One Price is to reality is a most important issue for understanding the present-day workings of the international monetary mechanism. For the purposes of the econometric analysis here, how fast and in what manner domestic prices respond to exchange rate adjustment is not of critical importance. Deviations from constancy across countries of G_i and Q_i may be correlated with exchange rate changes, but such changes in turn may reasonably be assumed to be orthogonal to the independent variables in equation (6). Note that a number of different versions of the Generalized Leontief Production Function will rationalize the estimation motivated by equation (6).

9. Strictly speaking, equation (6) describes trade in finished goods. For intermediate goods, equation (5), which is formally identical up to a sign with (6) must be estimated.

10. In actual estimation an additive error term for equations will also be assumed.

11. For any given cross-section a_s will not be identified. In the particular specification adopted here, however, at any given time, there are i cross sections that contain the identical independent variables. This happy circumstance will permit consistent estimation of a_s.

1973. The nine countries are Canada, France, Germany, Italy, Japan, Korea, the Netherlands, the United Kingdom, and the United States. The seven factors treated as central to the explanation of trade flows are directly productive capital stock, labor, educational attainment, distance, petroleum resources, iron ore resources, and arable land.[12] The quality of only the first three of these seven factors is assumed to change over time.

In estimating (6) using a time series of cross-sections it is assumed that with the exception of input quality and disembodied technology time trends, the preferences and technology underlying (6) do not change. Even so, because prices and wages change over time, in (6) only f_{rs} will be time invariant. The a_s and U_i will change from cross-section to cross-section.

IS JAPAN DIFFERENT?

As noted earlier, each equation in (6) contains a set of country specific additive dummy variables that are also assumed to be time invariant. These variables are meant to allow for those characteristics not otherwise provided for in the analysis. Such variables might reflect national policies of protection and encouragement of particular industries. They might also reflect private, possibly ultimately more important pattern of protection. A positive, statistically significant country term for Japan for passenger cars (SITC 732.1) might well signify a distinctively successful policy of protection. Japan would be exporting more automobiles than expected considering the quantity and quality of its natural resources, labor force, capital, and consumption priorities. A statistically insignificant variable in any given equation does not mean that the development of an industry has necessarily conformed to liberal trade canons. If all countries with a comparative advantage in steel resorted to roughly comparable dumping practices, the variables would be, in all likelihood, statistically insignificant. While this investigation is interested only in examining whether Japan's low share of imported manufactures is really evidence for distinctive Japanese behavior and practices, this limitation in scope by no means undermines the interest of the results here. Japan's exporters and customs officials may engage in unsavory, even illegal activities, but within the limits of this type of evidence, a statistically insignificant variable would suggest that Japanese behavior is no different from other comparably structured countries. Of course, in the present study special pains have been taken to define comparably situated in a theoretically defensible fashion.

In actual estimation, relatively few of the terms for Japan are statistically significant. In 109 commodity equations, only fifteen variables were statistically significant. The relevant commodities include: maize (unmilled), SITC 044; other fruits and nuts, SITC 057.2; sugar, sugar preparations, honey,

---

12. The capital, labor, and educational attainment data are adapted from materials assembled by Christensen, Cummings, and Jorgensen for their study, "Economic Growth, 1947-1973: An International Comparison." The trade data and the natural resource variables are adapted from data reported to the United Nations, while the arable land data are collected from the Food and Agricultural Organization.

SITC 06; crude fertilizers, SITC 27; rubber manufactures, SITC 62; plywood veneer, SITC 631; pearls, precious, semiprecious stones, SITC 667; aluminum, SITC 684; silver and platinum, SITC 731; aircraft and parts, SITC 734; footwear, SITC 85; medical instruments, SITC 872; pianos and other musical instruments, SITC 891.4.

Although some of the products are closely associated in the public mind with Japan either as exports or imports, taken together they comprise no more than 4.3 percent of Japan's gross external trade. By contrast, twenty-one variables covering 10.4 percent of its trade were statistically significant for Italy. Not surprising, the impact of France's policies appears to have been greater still: fully thirty-one French variables are statistically significant. These thirty-one terms account for 15.9 percent of France's foreign trade. While this sort of information is never really conclusive, particularly in view of the absence from the list of commodities such as rice, it now appears that special undefined Japanese characteristics or particular foreign failures in the Japanese domestic market do not play a central role in explaining the postwar pattern of Japan's trade. The pattern of Japanese trade can be explained within a framework common to most other participants in the world economy.[13] Once again, it must be emphasized that this does not mean Japan has, in practice, liberal trade policies. Rather, when it has been illiberal, it has behaved as other similarly situated countries.

These results help rationalize some of the changing expectations regarding the share of manufactures outlined earlier in this study. In the early seventies, consistent with Sazanami's and other interpretations, it was expected that the removal of formal restrictions and changes in Japanese attitudes toward imports would drive at least manufactured imports as a share of total imports to European levels. When this failed and when the manufactured imports elasticity of import demand remained constant (rather than rising sharply), it was natural to assume that the grave uncertainties of a newly perceived energy-scarce world had caused a reevaluation of the Japanese commitment to liberal commercial attitudes. The results here suggest that the commercial policy changes and attitudinal changes of the seventies did not bring great alteration in the Japanese commodity structure of imports, not because of foreign cultural insensitivity to Japan, but because these policies involved only relatively small distortions. When the differing quantity and quality of Japanese labor, capital, natural resources, and distance are properly given their full allowance then, as the Ministry of Finance suggested, the Japanese share of manufactures in total imports is comparable to European and American experiences.

13. The results for Japan do not change when the investigation is carried out at a higher level of aggregation. Nor do they change when an attempt is made to assess statistical significance of the 109 country terms taken as a whole on the entire pattern of trade.

TABLE 9.11

Country Specific Constants by Commodities

Commodity	Japan	Italy	France	Canada	$\overline{R}^2$
Meat and preparations	—	—	*	—	.32
Dairy products and eggs	—	—	—	—	.28
Fish and preparations	—	—	*	—	.42
Wheat unmilled	—	*	*	—	.43
Rice	—	—	—	—	.17
Maize unmilled	*	—	*	—	.52
Other cereals	—	—	—	—	.31
Bananas and plantains	—	—	—	—	.19
Other fruits and nuts	*	—	—	—	.41
Tobacco and manufactures	—	*	—	—	.38
Hides, skins, and furskins	—	—	—	—	.42
Soya beans	—	—	—	—	.71
Oil seeds, excluding soya beans	—	*	*	—	.82
Crude and synthetic rubber	—	—	*	—	.51
Saw—veneer logs—conifer	—	—	—	*	.81
Saw—veneer logs—nonconifer	—	—	—	*	.85
Shaped wood	—	—	—	—	.58
Pulp and waste paper	—	*	—	—	.67
All other wood—lumber and cork	—	—	—	*	.71
Silk	—	—	*	—	.13
Wool and animal hair	—	*	*	—	.42
Cotton	—	—	—	—	.24
Synthetic regenerated fibers	—	—	*	—	.11
All other waste fibers	—	—	—	—	.23
Crude fertilizers	*	—	—	—	.41
All other fertilizers and crude materials	—	—	—	—	.44
Iron ore concentrates	—	—	—	*	.28
Iron and steel scrap	—	—	—	—	.36
Copper ores and concentrates	—	—	—	—	.31
Nickel ores and concentrates	—	*	*	—	.45
Zinc ores and concentrates	—	*	—	—	.49
Manganese ores and concentrates	—	*	*	—	.68
All other metalliferous ores and concentrates	—	—	—	—	.43
All other crude minerals	—	—	—	—	.52
Coal, coke, and briquette	—	—	—	—	.65
Crude petroleum	—	—	—	—	.85
Petroleum products	—	—	—	—	.89
Natural gas and manufactures	—	—	—	—	.91
All other minerals	—	—	—	—	.45
Organic chemicals	—	—	—	—	.69
Inorganic chemicals	—	—	—	—	.73
Manufactured fertilizers	—	—	—	—	.83
Plastic material	—	*	—	—	.78
All other chemicals	—	—	—	—	.61
Leather, pressed fur	—	—	*	*	.65
Rubber manufactures	*	—	*	—	.54
Cork manufactures	—	—	*	—	.23
Veneer plywood	*	—	—	—	.45
Paper, paperboard, and					

TABLE 9.11—*Continued*

Commodity	Japan	Italy	France	Canada	$\bar{R}^2$
manufactures	—	—	—	*	.73
Grey cotton yarn	—	—	—	—	.28
Yarn, synthetic fibers	—	—	—	—	.81
Cotton, fabric, woven	—	—	—	—	.68
Silk fabrics, woven	—	—	—	—	.73
Wool fabric, woven	—	—	—	—	.85
Cement	—	*	—	—	.89
Glass	—	—	—	*	.91
Glassware	—	*	*	—	.67
Pearls, precious, and semi-precious stones	*	—	—	—	.63
Pig iron	—	—	—	—	.85
Iron and steel, primary forms	—	—	—	—	.92
Iron and steel, bars and rods	—	—	—	—	.94
Iron and steel, universal plates and sheets	—	—	—	—	.94
Iron and steel wire, excluding wire rod	—	—	—	—	.79
Iron and steel, tubes and pipes	—	—	*	—	.83
All other iron and steel	—	*	*	—	.67
Silver and platinum	*	*	—	*	.52
Copper	—	—	—	—	.60
Nickel	—	*	*	*	.85
Aluminum	—	—	*	—	.65
Lead	—	*	*	—	.84
Zinc	—	—	*	*	.86
Tin	—	—	*	—	.79
All other basic manufactures	—	—	—	—	.58
Aircraft engines	—	—	—	—	.81
Piston engines	—	—	—	—	.68
Nuclear reactors	—	—	—	—	.48
All other engines	—	—	—	—	.67
Agricultural machinery	—	*	—	—	.91
Office machines	—	—	—	—	.97
Machine tools for metal	—	—	—	—	.92
Textile machinery	—	—	—	—	.95
Sewing machines	—	—	*	—	.95
Other clothing equipment	—	*	*	—	.75
Paper mill machinery	—	—	—	—	.84
Printing and binding machinery	—	—	*	—	.59
Construction and mining machinery	—	—	—	—	.84
Heating and cooling equipment	—	—	*	—	.78
Pumps and centrifuges	—	—	—	—	.85
Ball, rollers, etc., bearings	—	—	—	—	.78
Electric power machinery	—	—	—	—	.91
Switch gear	—	—	—	—	.93
Electric distribution machinery	—	—	—	—	.92
Radio	—	—	—	—	.85
Television	—	—	—	—	.90
Other sound equipment	—	—	—	—	.85
Domestic electrical equipment	—	—	—	—	.89
Transistors, valves	—	—	—	—	.91

TABLE 9.11—*Continued*

Commodity	Japan	Italy	France	Canada	$\overline{R}^2$
Railway vehicles	—	—	—	—	.88
Passenger motor vehicles	—	—	—	—	.88
Lorries, trucks	—	—	—	—	.86
Motor vehicle parts	—	—	—	—	.93
Motorcycles	—	*	*	—	.91
Aircraft and parts	*	—	—	—	.94
Ships and boats	—	—	—	—	.94
Clothing	—	—	—	—	.88
Footwear	*	—	—	—	.92
Optical equipment	—	*	*	—	.94
Photographic equipment	—	*	—	—	.92
Medical instruments	*	—	—	*	.80
Photo cinema supplies	—	*	—	—	.90
Pianos and other musical instruments	*	—	*	—	.92
Printed matter	*	—	—	—	.45
Fishing, hunting, and sports equipment	*	—	*	—	.67

*Statistically significant at 5 percent level

APPENDIX

TABLE 9.12

Explained Change in
Aggregate Trade Flows, 1959-1973
(In percentages)

	Japan	Italy	France	Canada
Proportion of export growth (1959-73) attributable to:	100.0	100.0	100.0	100.0
Δ in quantity of capital	22.8	13.2	18.0	19.5
Δ in quantity of labor and education	28.1	24.4	29.1	15.2
Δ in quality of capital	10.5	11.6	6.5	-3.7
Δ in quality of labor and education	15.2	17.1	9.2	5.9
Δ in U_i	22.1	22.0	21.5	26.2
Proportion of import growth (1959-73) attributable to:	100.0	100.0	100.0	100.0
Δ in quantity of capital	33.9	17.3	24.1	19.5
Δ in quantity of labor and education	15.7	15.9	16.3	20.4
Δ in quality of capital	3.1	-1.8	1.7	7.1
Δ in quality of labor and education	21.5	26.7	16.2	15.2
Δ in U_i	23.1	19.2	20.1	26.3

TABLE 9.12—Continued

	West Germany	Nether-lands	United Kingdom	United States
Proportion of export growth				
(1959-73) attributable to:	100.0	100.0	100.0	100.0
Δ in quantity of capital	29.1	16.4	34.3	26.2
Δ in quantity of labor and education	33.4	23.5	28.1	23.9
Δ in quality of capital	6.0	12.9	-4.3	0.5
Δ in quality of labor and education	7.5	8.1	7.2	11.2
Δ in U_i	27.7	32.4	28.5	20.1
Proportion of import growth				
(1959-73) attributable to:	100.0	100.0	100.0	100.0
Δ in quantity of capital	39.6	23.4	40.4	29.2
Δ in quantity of labor and education	20.3	16.9	21.9	18.2
Δ in quality of capital	6.7	7.2	0.8	5.7
Δ in quality of labor and education	13.1	14.2	10.1	14.9
Δ in U_i	24.7	30.9	24.1	28.5

REFERENCES

Baldwin, R. E. 1970. "Determinants of the Commodity Structure of U.S. Trade." *American Economic Review*, vol. 61 (March).

Bank of Japan. See Nihon Ginkō.

Bhagwati, J. 1965. "The Pure Theory of International Trade: A Survey." In *Surveys of Economic Theory: Growth and Development*, vol. 2, ed. N. Buchanan et al. New York, St. Martin's Press.

Caves, R. E., and Jones, R. W. *World Trade and Payments*, chaps. 8-11, 3rd ed. Boston, Little, Brown and Co.

Christensen, L., Cummings, D., and Jorgensen, D. 1977. "Economic Growth, 1947-1973: An International Comparison." *Harvard Institute of Economic Research Discussion Paper*, no. 193.

Diewert, W. E. 1974. "Application of Duality Theory." In *Frontiers of Quantitative Economics*, ed. M. D. Intriligator and D. A. Kendrick, vol. 2. New York, North Holland Publishing Co.

Economic Planning Agency. See Keizai Kikakuchō.

Eisenberg, E. 1961. "Aggregation of Utility Functions." *Management Science*, vol. 7 (July).

Frenkel, J. A. 1978. "Purchasing Power Parity: Doctrinal Perspective and Evidence from the 1920s." *Journal of International Economics*, vol. 9 (May).

Gorman, W. M. 1968. "Measuring the Quantities of Fixed Factors." In *Value Capital and Growth*, ed. J. N. Wolfe. Chicago, Aldine Publishing Co.

Hirayama, Y. 1965. "Nihon keizai ni okeru kokusai bungyō no rieki" [Japanese economic gains and international trade]. In *Kanshū kōza nihon keizai* [A course on the Japanese economy], ed. S. Inaba, S. Okita, and M. Sakisaka, vol. 5, *Kokusai keizai to bōeki* [The world economy and trade]. Tokyo, Nihon hyōronsha.

Hufbauer, G. 1970. "The Impact of National Characteristics and Technology on the Commodity Composition of Trade in Manufactured Goods." In *The Technology Factor in International Trade*, ed. R. Vernon. New York, Columbia University Press.

Isard, P. 1977. "The Law of One Price."*American Economic Review*, vol. 64 (December).

Japan Economic Research Center. See Keizai Kenkyū Sentā.

Keesing, D. B., and Sherk, D. R. 1971. "Population Density in Patterns of Trade and Development." *American Economic Review* 62 (December):956-61.

Keizai Kenkyū Sentā. 1976. *The Japanese Economy in 1985*. Tokyo.

———. 1980. *Sekai no naka no Nihon keizai–1980 nen* [The Japanese economy in the world–1980]. Tokyo.

Keizai Kikakuchō, Keizai Kenkyūsho. 1976. *1980 nen no sekai bōeki kōzō* [World trade structure in 1980]. Tokyo.

Kravis, L. B., and Lipsey, R. E. 1977. "Export Prices and the Transmission of Inflation." *American Economic Association Papers and Proceedings* (February).

Leamer, E. 1974. "The Commodity Composition of International Trade: An Empirical Analysis." *Oxford Economic Papers* 26 (November):350-74.

———, Stern, R., and Baum, C. 1977. "An Empirical Analysis of the Composition of Manufacturing, Employment in the Industrialized Countries." *European Economic Review* 9 (April):1-20.

Leontief, W. W. "Factor Proportions and Structure of American Trade: Further Theoretical and Empirical Analysis." *Review of Economics and Statistics*, vol. 38 (November).

Ministry of Finance. 1980. "Nihon bōeki kōzō" [Japanese trade structure]. Tokyo, MOF.

Ministry of Foreign Affairs. n.d.

Ministry of International Trade and Industry (MITI). 1976 *Sangyō kōzō no chōki bishon* [Long-term vision of industrial structure]. Tokyo.

Nihon Ginkō [Bank of Japan]. 1980. *Kokusai hikaku tōkei* [International comparative statistics]. Tokyo.

Nihon Keizai Shimbun. 1982. *Shiryō keizai hakusho nijūgonen* [A summary economic survey of Japan for twenty-five years]. Tokyo, Nihon keizai shimbunsha.

Organization for Economic Cooperation and Development (OECD). 1980. *Statistics of Foreign Trade*. Paris.

Ozaki, I., and Sagara, J. 1973. "Sangyō kōzō no henka" [Changes in industrial structure and trade structure]. *Mita gakkai zasshi* 66 (September):612-43.

Pryor, Frederic L. 1972. "An International Comparison of Concentration Ratios." *Review of Economics and Statistics*, vol. 54, no. 2 (May).

Richardson, J. D. 1978 "Some Empirical Evidence on Commodity Arbitrage and the Law of One Price." *Journal of International Economics*, vol. 8 (May).

Samuelson, Paul A. 1953. "Price of Factors and Goods in General Equilibrium." *Review of Economic Studies*, vol. 21 (June).

———. 1965. "Social Indifference Curves." *Quarterly Journal of Economics*, vol. 70.

Saxonhouse, Gary. 1972. "Review of U.S.-Japanese Economic Relations." *Asian Survey* (October).

Sazanami, Y., and Hamaguchi, N. "Process of Production and Intra-Industry Trade." Mimeographed, 1974.

Shinkai, Y. 1972. "Wagakuni tsūshō seisaku no kihon rinen" [Fundamental doctrine of Japanese commercial policy]. *Gendai keizai* 5 (June):8-23.

Tanaka, T. 1968. "Nihon no yūshutsu shiba kōzō no keiryōteki kenkyū" [Quantitative research on the structure of Japan's export markets]. *Kokusai keizai* 19 (March): 152-63.

Tinbergen, Jan et al. 1972. *Optimum Social Welfare and Productivity*. New York, New York University Press.

United Nations. 1970. *Yearbook of International Trade Statistics*. New York.

U.S. Central Intelligence Agency. 1980. *International Energy Statistical Review*.

U.S. Congress, House, Committee on Ways and Means, Subcommittee on Trade. 1980. *U. S.-Japan Trade Report.* Washington, D.C.

Uzawa, H. 1972. "Nihon keizai—no kokusaiteki koritsu—tsuka chōsei no shindankai o megutte" [Japan's isolation in the international system—over the new stage of currency change] . *Chūō kōron* (February), pp. 102-19.

Yamada, T. 1970. "Yunyū jiyūka to bukka no sōkan bunseki" [Import liberalization and the analysis of price change] . *Bōeki to kanzei* 18 (January):42-57.

Policy Interactions and the

United States–Japan Exchange Rate

KOICHI HAMADA

IN 1971, a basic change took place in the international monetary system. After strong resistance from Japanese monetary authorities against revaluing and floating the yen, President Nixon's new economic policy of August 1971, called the "Nixon shock" in Japan, drastically changed the course of events in the international monetary sphere. The rules of the game in the world economy changed from the dollar standard system, based on fixed exchange rates, to the system of floating exchange rates that allows some degree of government intervention in the exchange market. This meant a fundamental change in the international environment for Japan, which had managed to keep the exchange rate of ¥360 = US$1 that had originated during the occupation in 1949.

The Smithsonian system was in effect from December 1971 to February 1973, and provided a short interlude of fixed exchange rates with a wider band of permissible fluctuations. However, due to the decline in public confidence in the fixity of exchange rates, the exchange market during the Smithsonian system worked quite differently from that in the dollar standard system before Nixon's new economic policy.

One can easily compare the difference of these two regimes by looking at movements in prices and interest rates between the United States and Japan. During the 1960s, the WPI in the United States did not deviate from that in Japan by more than 2 percent. After 1971, the WPI in the United States deviated from Japan's plus 10 to minus 8 percent per year; accordingly, the differential in comparable three-month interest rates between the U.S. and Japan varied from minus 9 percent in 1975 to plus 7 percent in 1978 and 1980.[1]

The author thanks Masashi Ohshita for his research assistance. I am also indebted to Kazuo Sato for his helpful comments.

1. It is hard to find figures of comparable interest rates in Japan before 1971, partly because of regulations in the Japanese financial market.

The period after 1971 is interesting not only because of the change in international monetary regimes, but also because of the intensity of real disturbances that attacked both economies from outside. OPEC learning how to organize a monopolistic cartel had tremendous price and output effects on both the American and Japanese economies. The fear of quantity constraint created pessimistic expectation in the public. An extreme example was the panic situation in the first oil crisis that caused Japanese consumers, frightened by the prospect of rapid inflation, to run into supermarkets to buy up all the toilet paper. The terms of trade index fell after the first oil crisis from 100 in 1971 to 75 in 1974. It then recovered to 81, but after the second oil crisis, triggered by the revolution in Iran and the Iraq-Iran war, it came down to 56 in 1980 (cf. figure 10.8).

One can say that this period has been the *Sturm und Drang* period for the Japanese economy. It has experienced its most severe external shocks since World War II. In 1973 and 1974, the Japanese people suffered from double-digit inflation, and the real growth rate turned negative for the first time since the war. Inflationary pressure had already been fueled into the Japanese economy by government attempts to resist the revaluation of the yen, when the oil crisis hit Japan. On the other hand, monetary policy has reacted skillfully against the second oil crisis since 1979. It succeeded in preventing imported inflation from becoming "homemade" inflation without serious recessions. Unemployment figures varied around 2 to 2.4 percent in recent years, which is of course worse than the record of the sixties when unemployment was 1 to 1.5 percent. Nevertheless, unemployment has stayed within reasonable limits during recent years.

The economic thinking of both policy makers and economists changed substantially during the last decade. First of all, the obsession with which policy makers adhered to the fixed exchange regime, which was so strong in the early seventies, has disappeared. Now policy authorities, especially central bankers in Japan, recognize that flexible exchange rates are an effective means of isolating the Japanese economy from foreign inflationary pressure. Economists, who advocated the flexible exchange rate system as an ideal system for international adjustment, now recognize that the story is not so simple. There is still interdependence, in spite of flexible exchange rates, through capital movements and terms of trade. Also, we now realize that flexible exchange rates may equilibrate the over-all account in the balance of payments, but that they cannot necessarily balance the current account. The current account imbalances may, however, create various policy issues and trade disputes among countries. For example, the locomotive theory of business cycles is related to current accounts in the balance of payments.

At the same time, the efficacy of discretionary monetary and fiscal policies are thrown into doubt by many economists. Even though a majority of macroeconomists in Japan apparently still believe in some efficacy of Keynesian economic policies, the Bank of Japan seems to have a self-renewing mechanism to produce economic research based on the doctrines of monetarism, rational expectation, time series analysis, and so forth. Thus one can see that the trend of economic thinking also underwent a substantial change during this decade.

The purpose of this paper is to study the movement of exchange rates and the course of the balance of payments during this interesting period, and to relate it to macroeconomic performances and policies in the United States as well as in Japan. It is designed to give a general bird's-eye view of the issues involved in the U.S.-Japan monetary relationship. The concern, therefore, is not so much with presenting completely new ideas as with synthesizing existing views on monetary relations between the two countries. Emphasis will be on data and research from Japanese sources.

THE JAPANESE EXPERIENCE IN FLEXIBLE EXCHANGE RATES

Nixon's new economic policy opened a new era in the international monetary regime. This change was very important to Japan, which had adhered to the rigid par-value of $1 = ¥360 for a long period of its rapid economic growth. We shall study the Japanese experience in floating exchange rates by looking at movements of exchange rates, the degree of intervention by government, the intensity of exchange control, components of the balance of payments, and stances of economic policies.

EXCHANGE RATES

Figure 10.1 shows the course of the dollar-yen exchange rates. The vertical line shows the maximum and the minimum value of spot exchange rates during a quarter. From this we notice that the dollar-yen exchange rate has undergone rather volatile fluctuations since 1971. During the Smithsonian period, the dollar-yen rate remained at the lower bounds of the widened band of the Smithsonian system, that is, around $1 = ¥301. After the collapse of the system in February 1973, the value of the yen showed a rapid increase and reached around $1 = ¥265. Around these values the Japanese monetary authorities made attempts to support the dollar until the outbreak of the first oil crisis in the fall of 1973. The oil crisis reversed the course of exchange rates, and reversed the direction of intervention as well. In spite of heavy operations to sell the dollar, the value of the yen dropped to the trough value around $1 = ¥306 at the end of 1974. After the beginning of 1975, the yen recovered its value and kept appreciating, with minor oscillations, until it reached its peak in October 1978 at an exchange rate of almost $1 = ¥175. Thus the exchange rate of the yen in terms of the dollar more than doubled in seven years after the suspension of the fixed exchange rate.

On November 1, 1978, the United States announced a set of policy measures to keep the dollar exchange rate from depreciating further. In addition to adopting contractive monetary policies, the United States committed itself to intervention in the exchange market by using funds provided by the swap agreement (reciprocal currency arrangement). This change in attitude in the United States reversed the trend of exchange movements. The depre-

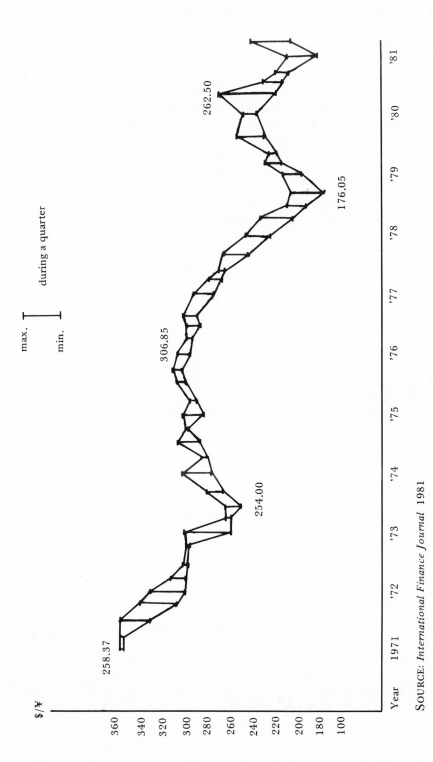

SOURCE: *International Finance Journal* 1981

Fig. 10.1. Interbank exchange rate (daily median)

ciation of the yen was then reinforced by the outbreak of the second oil crisis. The dollar continued to appreciate sharply in the spring of 1980. This
was caused partly by the high interest rate in the U.S. and the Eurodollar
market that reflected inflationary expectations in the United States. On
March 2, Japan announced, after consultation with the United States, West
Germany, and Switzerland, a series of countermeasures for preventing the
depreciation of the yen. The U.S. monetary authorities announced also that
they were ready to intervene in the New York exchange market and that
they were prepared to effectuate a swap agreement of up to five billion dollars between the Bank of Japan and the Federal Reserve Bank of New
York.

Japan also made a swap contract with the Swiss National Bank of up to
200 billion yen (less than one billion dollars). Still, the dollar did not stop
appreciating until it reached $1 = ¥264 on April 8. Then expectations for
lower interest rates prevailed. The yen recovered steadily. By the beginning
of 1981, the dollar exchange rate had crossed the bench mark of $1 = ¥200,
though the dollar has bounced up again since then.

It is an interesting coincidence, if it were coincidence at all, that, in both
of the first two major turning points, announcement of international cooperation in intervention changed the direction of exchange rates, immediately
in the first case, and quite soon in the latter.

In sum, the dollar-yen exchange rates fluctuated quite violently during
the ten years after the collapse of the Bretton Woods regime that relied on
fixed exchange rates.[2] These volatile movements are, as we shall see later,
influenced by the change in the trend in the current account of the Japanese
balance of payments. The changes are also affected seriously by incentives
for capital movements, which in turn depend on expectations of the future
course of the exchange rate.

GOVERNMENT INTERVENTION IN THE EXCHANGE MARKET

As we shall see later, intervention by the United States was not substantial,
so let us consider first the intervention by the Japanese monetary authorities.
During the last ten years, the degree of intervention by the Japanese monetary authorities was quite substantial. Thus, one may characterize the experience of the Japanese economy not as genuine float but as a managed or dirty
float. Japanese international reserves moved quite variably because of monetary authorities' intent to resist rapid appreciation of the yen in the earlier

2. Amano (1980) puts it as follows: "Since Japan joined the generalized float on
February 14, 1973, the yen/dollar rate has exhibited wide fluctuation, as have most other
major currencies: a 13 percent appreciation from December 1972 to July 1973; a 14 percent depreciation from July 1973 to December 1974; an 18 percent appreciation from
December 1976 to December 1977 after a relatively calm period of 1975-76; appreciation from January 1978 to December 1978." If we update his description, it would be
roughly 30 percent depreciation from December 1978 to April 1980, and 21 percent appreciation from April 1980 to January 1981.

years, and their intention to prevent its rapid depreciation after the oil crisis. Figure 10.2 indicates the variation of Japanese international reserves. Abso-

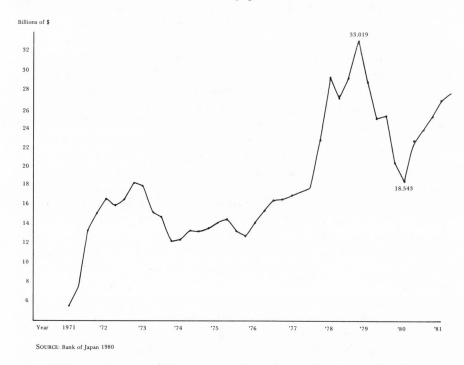

SOURCE: Bank of Japan 1980

Fig. 10.2. International reserves held by the Japanese monetary authorities

lute magnitude of variation was in fact much greater during this floating period than during the period with fixed exchange rates when monetary authorities intervened in the market to keep exchange rates constant. International reserves of Japan varied only from 1.5 to 5.5 billion dollars in the 1960s under the fixed exchange regime. One can see from figure 10.2 that the Japanese monetary authorities intervened not only to smooth daily fluctuations in exchange rates but also to affect some trends by substantial buying and selling operations. The level of international reserves had an upward trend in general, but they fell sharply during the two oil crises.

Here arises the question of whether or not the intervention of the Japanese monetary authorities was successful in stabilizing the movement in exchange rates. The transition to the float just after the breakdown of the Bretton Woods system in summer 1971 was accompanied by an unusually active buying operation of the dollar by the Japanese monetary authorities. This brought a huge capital loss to the Bank of Japan, an agent of the Japanese government, which in turn meant a loss to the Japanese public. Later, however, the Bank of Japan seems to have been making profit, on the average, when it intervened. If one follows Friedman's argument that profitable speculation tends to stabilize the course of exchange rates, then it is likely that intervention worked toward stabilizing the yen.

In this connection, however, Amano (1980, p. 43) maintains on the basis of his FLEX model that heavy and defensive intervention in the last quarter of 1977 and the first quarter of 1978 provided apparent profit opportunities for private short-term speculative capital. Whether this intervention was stabilizing or destabilizing, of course, is a different matter.

Let us consider here the role of intervention from the American side. Theoretical difficulty involved in the U.S. intervention is known as the (n-1) problem, and this will be discussed later. The Federal Reserve Bank of New York in fact engaged in intervention in European currencies for a long time. The United States first intervened in the yen market after the mutual cooperation announced in November 1978. In two months on the New York market, 274 million dollars were sold by the United States utilizing the swap arrangement with the Bank of Japan and financing from the International Monetary Fund (IMF). But the scale of intervention was much smaller than that made in the Tokyo market by the Bank of Japan (see Holmes and Pardee 1979, Pardee 1980, Bank of Tokyo 1979). The U.S. government has now decided to assume an almost complete laissez-faire policy in the exchange market.

DEGREE OF EXCHANGE CONTROL

The third factor that we should notice, in addition to exchange rate movements and the role of intervention, is exchange control by the Japanese government. Figure 10.3 indicates by vertical segments the maximum and minimum values of premium or discount, namely, the spread between the dollar forward rate and the dollar spot rate expressed in terms of the annual rate of increase. One can see that wide divergence between forward and spot rates existed until the middle of 1974. The interest parity theory teaches us that, in the absence of exchange control, this forward premium or discount should roughly correspond to the interest rate differential between domestic and foreign interest rates. The dotted line indicates the difference between the short-term (tegata) discount rate in Japan and the Eurodollar rate of three-month maturity. Therefore, the large divergence between the forward premium (discount) and the interest rate differential implies the existence of barriers to inflow (outflow) of short-term capital. For 1971 we notice a discount of 25 percent, which means that inflow of capital is blocked; in early 1974 the dollar had a premium of 39 percent, which meant that outflow of capital was blocked. After the third quarter of 1974, there was not such a wide variation in the forward premium (discount) of the dollar. This must imply that exchange control was substantially weakened. Since the middle of 1974, the exchange market seems to have been under less control. Premiums or discounts of the dollar on the Tokyo market remained within a more reasonable limit, even though there was a mild exchange control against inflow of capital from the last quarter of 1977 to the last quarter of 1979. Ironically, Japanese exchange control seems to have been eased when the oil crises worked toward depreciation of the yen.

Incidentally, the large discount after 1978 indicates the divergence of the

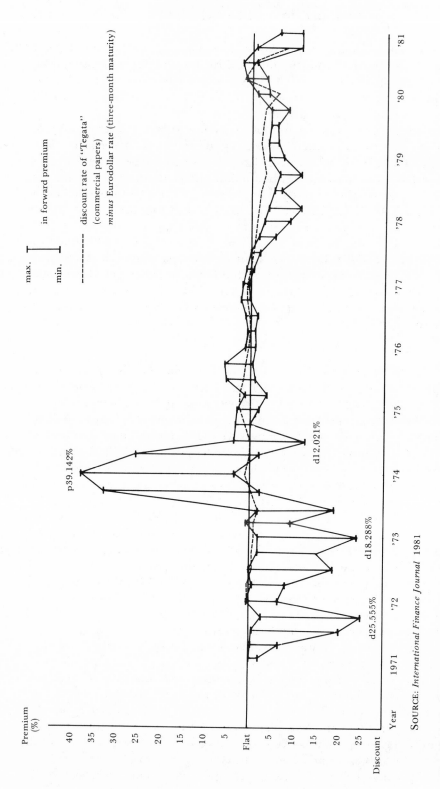

Premium (%)

40
35
30
25
20
15
10
5
Flat
5
10
15
20
25

Discount

Year 1971 '72 '73 '74 '75 '76 '77 '78 '79 '80 '81

max.
min.

in forward premium

discount rate of "Tegata"
(commercial papers)

minus Eurodollar rate (three-month maturity)

p39.142%

d12.021%
d18.288%
d25.555%

SOURCE: *International Finance Journal* 1981

Fig. 10.3. The three-month forward premium (discount) of the dollar in terms of annual rate and the differential between the Japanese and the Euro-dollar interest rate

Eurodollar's interest rate and Japanese short-term rate that arose from the divergence in the rate of inflation between the United States and Japan. From this statistical evidence we can divide the years of floating rates into two periods: from 1971 to 1974 with intensive exchange control, and following the last quarter of 1974 with less exchange control.

What were the institutional changes that caused the 1974 reduction of exchange control? There were not many drastic changes in regulations in that year. In July, the upper limit for the receipt of advance payments for export by Japanese exporters was raised to a half million dollars. In August 1974, the acquisition of government short-term securities was liberalized. Also the reserve requirement for free yen deposit was waived completely. These changes do not look conspicuous, but judging from the interest parity relationship, there must have been a substantial change of attitude by the monetary authority, particularly toward inflow of funds.

In 1980, the Foreign Exchange and Foreign Trade Control Law was amended to liberalize Japan's external transactions. With this amendment, the principle of freedom for external transactions was established. Article 1 of the new law states that regulatory measures should be limited to "necessary but minimum control or adjustment."

Composition of the Japanese Balance of Payments

Let us turn to the course of the balance of payments of Japan. Under the system of perfect floating without any government intervention in the exchange market, the over-all balance of payments would be in equilibrium. Therefore, the imbalance in the over-all account under floating exchange rates must imply that there is some intervention in the exchange market. A balance in the over-all account does not generally mean a balance in each component of the balance of payments, particularly, the balance in the trade or current account. Trade disputes and macroeconomic disputes are, however, very often concerned with the trade account or the current account. Thus it is important to trace the course of the components of the Japanese balance of payments.

Figure 10.4 indicates the composition of the Japanese balance of payments since 1971. The trade account and the current account showed a surplus until 1973 when the first oil crisis occurred. After the middle of 1974, the trade account regained its large surplus. Because the invisible or service account is always in deficit for Japan, the current account followed a pattern similar to the trade account, with less surplus. After the second oil crisis, both the trade and the current account ran into substantial deficit again; both accounts have been improving since then. Figure 10.5 shows the annual performance of the Japanese balance of payments vis-à-vis the United States.

In light of national accounting, the imbalance in the current account equals the net absorption of a domestic economy. Thus, as Komiya (1979) argues, the discrepancy between business cycles in the two countries can

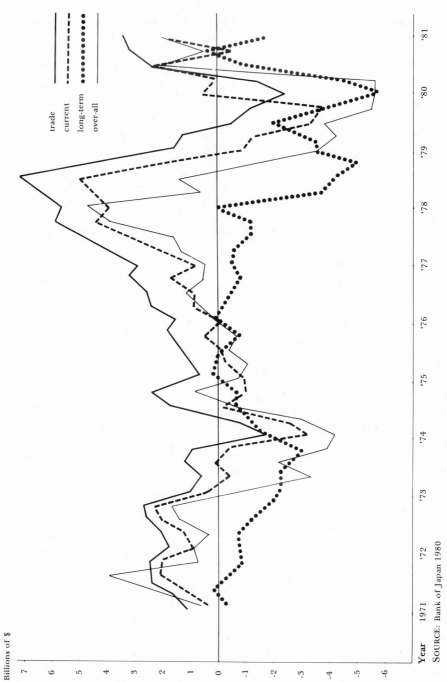

Billions of $

7
6
5
4
3
2
1
0
-1
-2
-3
-4
-5
-6

Year   1971   '72   '73   '74   '75   '76   '77   '78   '79   '80   '81

trade
current
long-term
over-all

SOURCE: Bank of Japan 1980

Fig. 10.4. Components of the Japanese balance of payments

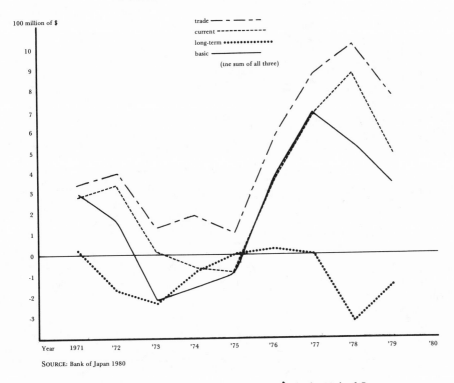

SOURCE: Bank of Japan 1980

Fig. 10.5. Japanese balance of payments vis-à-vis the United States

explain most of the imbalance in the current account. The course of GNP growth rates in both countries is depicted in figure 10.6. In this respect, the large deficit in the government sector in the recent Japanese economy may be one of the main reasons for the recent deficit in the Japanese current account.

ECONOMIC POLICIES IN JAPAN AND IN THE UNITED STATES

To close this section, let us look at the basic character of monetary policy in these two countries. Figure 10.6 indicates the money growth rate in the two countries. As stated at the beginning of this paper, the Japanese monetary authorities expanded money supply excessively even before the outbreak of the oil crisis. This was done because Japanese monetary policies tried to prevent revaluation of the yen at that time. Thus inflationary pressure already existed when the first oil crisis hit, and the period of severe monetary constraint followed. From this unhappy experience, the Japanese authorities learned a lesson. They controlled the money supply quite successfully, so that the adjustment of the Japanese economy during the second oil crisis was quite remarkable. In this second crisis, imported inflation did not turn into "homemade" inflation, according to the phrase in the economic report of the Economic Planning Agency.

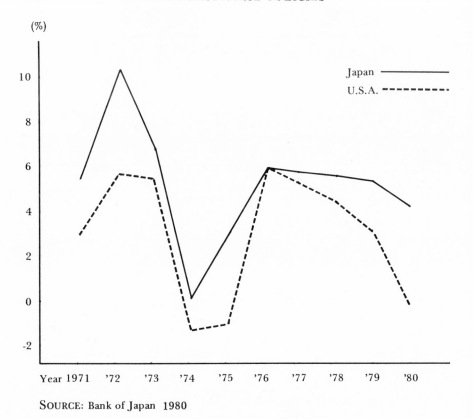

SOURCE: Bank of Japan 1980

Fig. 10.6. GNP growth rate (real)

In the United States, the constraint on monetary policy is also being exercised severely. But because of the unexpected variation in velocity due to institutional innovation in the banking sector, and because of the unexpected slow growth in productivity, monetary policy does not seem to have succeeded in stabilizing the price level. Recently, in Japan also, monetary velocity is becoming volatile, because, in addition to the process of financial innovation, the deposit in postal savings, not included in M_2, is replacing much of the savings deposit in the banking sector. M_2 growth rates are drawn in figure 10.7.

Finally let us turn to fiscal policy in the two countries. We know that the United States is suffering from government deficit. But the recent increase in the fiscal deficit of the public sector in Japan and the resulting accumulation of public debt is really remarkable. About 33 percent of the Japanese national budget for 1980 came from borrowing, and 26 percent in 1981. The accumulated public debt will reach 70 trillion yen (more than 30% of GNP) soon. The emergence of this large deficit is worth noting when we consider the effect of the macroeconomic policies on exchange rates and the balance of payments.

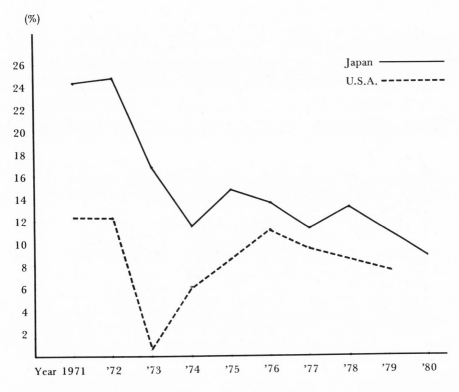

SOURCE: Bank of Japan 1980

Fig. 10.7. M_2 growth rate

Then what is the relationship between these characteristics of monetary or fiscal policy and the course of exchange rates and the balance of payments? What are the effects of real disturbances exemplified by sharp changes in terms of trade for Japan (cf. fig. 10.8)? To answer these questions, I will develop a theoretical framework for this task.

THEORETICAL FRAMEWORK FOR UNDERSTANDING
THE BEHAVIOR OF EXCHANGE RATES

Let us discuss briefly the framework suitable to the understanding of determinants for the U.S.-Japan exchange rates and the balance of payments. There are many studies in determinants of exchange rates. However, few of them present an integrated picture of exchange rate determination and the course of balance of payments in a world of nontraded goods, capital mobility, and sluggish adjustments in goods or the labor market. Very often the real picture is condensed into the familiar two-by-two cross diagram. Admittedly, simplification is the very essence of a good theory, but a good theory must also clarify the structure between the explicit variables under consideration and the implicit or suppressed variables behind the scenes.

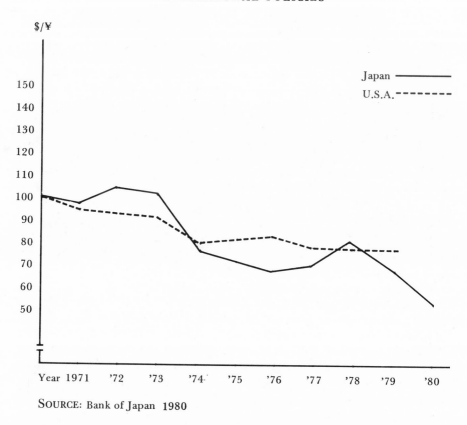

SOURCE: Bank of Japan 1980

Fig. 10.8. Terms of trade index (1970 = 100)

In this sense one cannot help wondering if economists are still like the blind groping an elephant in the classic Chinese story.

I do not dare present here another simplified theory, much less a really integrated story. However, my view on determinants of exchange rates and the balance of payments follows: The exchange rate is a relative price between financial assets denominated in one currency and financial assets denominated in another currency. Therefore, the relative price should be determined in the market of outstanding assets. The interest parity relationship is nothing but an expression of the equilibrium of this market of the outstanding stock of assets, under the assumption that interest bearing assets denominated in each currency are perfect substitutes except for the consideration of exchange rate fluctuation. The relationship states (cf. fig. 10.3): domestic interest rate = foreign interest rate + forward premium of the foreign currency, where forward premium is expressed as the annual rate equivalent of forward rate – spot rate/spot rate. If the future value of the exchange rate is given, then the expected value of the future spot rate will be reflected in the value of the forward exchange rate today. Interest parity says that an economic agent will earn the same gain regardless of where he invests.

Suppose that we regard forward rates as the average of expected future spot rates. Then, given the expectation of future spot rates, the spot exchange rate of today is determined so that people are satisfied to hold just outstanding assets denominated in dollar and in yen. Thus today's exchange rate is determined by the expectation of tomorrow's exchange rate, and the expectation of tomorrow's exchange rate is determined by the expectation of the next day's exchange rate. The determination of the exchange rate therefore has a recurring structure as in many other asset markets. Of course, one cannot go on into the future forever. Somewhere there is a horizon where one has to stop judging. The determination of asset prices is a difficult problem.

What businessmen call "fundamentals" in the exchange market are in fact determinants of these expectations in the future. In my view, exchange rate expectations are formed by individual agents according to the rule that one country cannot accumulate deficit or surplus forever, or beyond the limit thought to be reasonable for international resource allocation. For example, a fast-developing country may play the role of a debtor for a substantial period of time in the world economy. This is justified by the standpoint of international resource allocation over time (see, e.g., Hamada 1966). But if a country goes into deficit beyond the reasonable creditor-debtor range, the situation could be judged to be out of equilibrium. Therefore, the long-term exchange rate path is considered as the path that does not interfere with normal trade and investment patterns under the given expected stances of monetary policies. Although the exchange rate of today is determined as the relative price of assets denominated in dollars and those in yen, the value itself is influenced by the anticipation of the future exchange rate, which is in turn dependent on the long-run trade pattern between countries. Exchange rates are expected to follow a path that won't create a large accumulated asset for one country.

One can conceive a set of ideal conditions under which the purchasing power parity (PPP) theory and the asset market approach in the determination exchange rate can coexist without contradiction. Under these conditions the monetary approach can also be accommodated.

Consider a world that consists of only two countries. Let us assume the following: (1) both economies are in stationary equilibrium (population, technology, and capital stocks remain the same); (2) every commodity is tradable without transportation cost and there are no nontraded goods; (3) direct investments as well as financial capital movements are free; (4) in both economies, real wages are flexible enough to keep every market in equilibrium; (5) the velocity of money is constant in both economies; and (6) every agent has perfect foresight.

Under these conditions, there exists no contradiction between the PPP theory and the interest parity relationship. By assumption (2), PPP holds and, by assumption (3), the real rate of interest is equated between the two countries. In each country the nominal rate of interest is the sum of the real rate of interest and the expected rate of inflation. Under the assumption of perfect foresight, the expected rate of inflation equals its actual rate. Moreover, under the rule of the PPP and perfect foresight, the difference in the rate of inflation is reflected in the expected rate of depreciation (or appreciation) of exchange rates. Therefore interest parity coexists with the PPP. The system of asset prices conforms to the system of real prices without contradiction.

Similarly one can easily show that the monetary approach can be justified under these ideal conditions. Under an additional assumption of superneutrality of money that the rate of inflation does not influence the real rate of interest, monetary policies do not affect the real courses of events at all.

These properties will hold true, even if we relax assumption (1) and instead assume that each economy is on a path toward balanced growth, possibly with different rates of real growth. The monetary approach will hold true if we state it in such a way that the relative change in the exchange rate between two countries is determined by the difference in the rate of excess money supply, that is, the excess of the rate of monetary expansion over the real rate of growth. The existence of nontraded goods will, however, alter the nature of the determination of the exchange rate as many authors have pointed out. If there is a difference in the trend in relative price between nontraded goods and traded goods, then the course of the exchange rate will differ from what the simple PPP theory predicts. Moreover, if imperfection is introduced in market clearing and errors in expectations, the course of events that are expected under the ideal conditions will no longer hold.

Let us consider the short-term and medium-term effect of monetary and fiscal policies in more realistic cases, where "stickiness" in the goods or labor market and errors in expectation exist in both Japan and the United States. Let us start with the effect of monetary policy. Suppose a change in monetary policy takes the form of reduction in the discount rate in one country, say, in Japan. Then, provided that the expectation on the future course of the yen is given, incentives for arbitrage will create short-term capital outflow from Japan due to the accompanying decline in market interest rates. Since this deficit in the capital account must be balanced by the surplus in the current account, the yen should be devalued. Komiya and Suda (1980a) pointed out that these effects are by themselves quite small. An interest differential of 1 percent will cause less than a one-yen change in the dollar-yen exchange rate. If the reduction of the discount is regarded as a sign of loosening monetary control in the future, then it will create expectations toward the devaluation of the yen, which could cause the price of yen in the forward market to go down. This will tend to depreciate the spot rate of the yen as well. However, when the reduction of the discount rate was expected, or the actual amount of reduction is short of the expected reduction, then it will keep future expectation constant or even lead to the appreciation of the future yen rate. However, as Mundell (1967) argued, under a special assumption on the forward rate with unitary elasticity of expectations, we still consider that relatively tighter monetary policy with higher interest rates is most likely to result in (relative) capital account surplus and current account deficit, in accord with the depreciation of the home currency. Therefore, the maintenance of higher interest rates in Japan will attract more recycling funds from OPEC, which keeps Japan's current account in deficit. The maintenance of a lower interest rate policy will promote capital exports as well as commodity exports, and perhaps create more trade disputes because of the relatively lower value of the yen.

Now let us turn to the effect of fiscal policy. Mundell argued that under flexible exchange rates fiscal policy hardly affects domestic aggregate demand because the change in fiscal absorption is offset by the change in external absorption (=export--import) caused by the change in exchange rates. This implies, at the same time, that fiscal restraint is a very effective means for correcting a current account disequilibrium. Therefore, if the Japanese government were to succeed in reducing its huge budget deficit, such a reduction would work to improve the current account (or even worsen trade disputes), and have little effect toward depressing the domestic economy. (A different situation emerges if we believe in the superrationality of the public in response to government deficit. If the public reduces savings in response to the reduction of spending by the government, the total absorption will not change, and neither will the domestic aggregate demand.)

EMPIRICAL ANALYSES OF THE EXCHANGE RATE AND THE BALANCE OF PAYMENTS

As I mentioned, Komiya (1979) analyzes the relationship between current account and desynchronization of business cycles. Komiya and Suda (1980b) (1981) also present detailed critical views on the role of exchange rate policy taken by the Japanese government. Amano (1980) studies in his FLEX model the role of government intervention in exchange markets. He incorporates the reaction function of the monetary authorities and evaluates the function of the flexible exchange rate in insulating external disturbances, which was found effective. Because his results depend crucially on the particular structure of the FLEX model he developed, it is difficult to relate his analysis directly to the observed data that are discussed in this paper. However, we must notice his estimation of the relationship between the effective exchange rate of the yen and its dollar rate. This is an aspect I have neglected so far. His equation is (for 1973 I-1979 I quarterly) where EERI is the IMF

$$\ln \text{EERI} = \underset{(67.23)}{10.07} - \underset{(34.97)}{0.9369} \ln \text{FXS}$$

$$\bar{R}^2 = 0.981, \quad \text{S.E.} = 0.0197, \quad \text{D.W.} = 0.69$$

effective exchange rate index and FXS is the yen-dollar spot rate. Thus the effective exchange rate is explained well by the yen-dollar rate. Now I am quite certain that concentration on the yen-dollar rate is justified.

Three studies allow us to examine some of the components of my theoretical framework in light of the Japanese experience.

The simplest story of the determination of exchange rates is the PPP theory. Sato studied extensively in his M. Phil. thesis at Oxford (1979) how the Japanese yen followed or diverted from the PPP relationship. Seo (1981) also studied the relationship between price levels and exchange rates. Figure 10.9, essentially similar to Sato's, is taken from Ohashi (1980). Here Ohashi computed the hypothetical exchange rate that would have prevailed if it had followed the theoretical value implied by the PPP theory based on CPI, WPI, and WPI-manufacturing indexes respectively. As seen in the figure, the yen has actually been much stronger than the theoretical trend predicted by the CPI indexes. It became stronger than predicted by the WPI indexes and others during 1978.

Sato and Seo attribute the divergence of actual values from theoretical values based on the PPP theory to several factors, the following being the most important:

(a) The change in relative price between traded and nontraded goods. In Japan the export-goods sector enjoyed a higher rate of productivity growth than the industrial-goods sector in general, and much higher than the consumer-goods sector. This explains the yen's divergence toward the stronger side of the theoretical value based on the WPI, and the remarkable divergence from that based on the CPI.

(b) During these periods the United States kept its domestic price of petroleum products much lower than the international standard. If one may oversimplify Sato's argument a little, commodity prices lower than the international standard work as if subsidies were imposed on them. Subsidies would promote the depreciation of the dollar as compared with theoretical values predicted by the PPP theory.

(c) The causality may work in a different direction. As Sato analyzes, using time series techniques, the PPP relationship may result from, rather than cause, the change in exchange rates.

Shirakawa, on the other hand, directly applied the monetary approach to the exchange rate determination of the yen in his careful study (1978). He found that the monetary approach equation could explain well the actual performance of the yen exchange rate from March 1973 to January 1978. His equations are in terms of M_1 and M_2 (March 73-January 78):

$$\log S = 3.59 + 0.85 \log M_1 - 1.77 \log M_1^* - 0.74 \log y$$
$$\quad\quad (4.89) \quad\quad (5.09)\,(-5.92) \quad\quad\quad (-5.04)$$

$$\quad + 0.87 \log y^* + 0.06\,i - 0.01\,i^*$$
$$\quad\quad (3.99) \quad\quad\quad (6.37) \quad\quad (-3.27)$$

$$\bar{R}^2 = 0.813, \quad \text{S.E.} = 0.03, \quad \text{D.W.} = 1.28$$

$$\log S = \begin{matrix} -2.33 \\ (-1.22) \end{matrix} + \begin{matrix} 1.34 \\ (3.95) \end{matrix} \log M_2 - \begin{matrix} 1.77 \\ (-4.35) \end{matrix} M_2^* - \begin{matrix} 0.84 \\ (-5.15) \end{matrix} \log y$$

$$+ \begin{matrix} 0.88 \\ (3.59) \end{matrix} \log y^* + \begin{matrix} 0.88 \\ (8.47) \end{matrix} i - \begin{matrix} 0.01 \\ (-4.42) \end{matrix} i^*$$

$$\bar{R}^2 = 0.77$$
$$\text{S.E.} = 0.03$$
$$\text{D.W.} = 1.28,$$

where notations imply (starred variables referring to the United States):

S: end of month closing rate (the value of dollar in terms of yen)
M, M^*: average monthly balance in money supply with seasonal adjustment
y, y^*: mining-manufacturing production index with seasonal adjustment
i: interest rate on Free Yen time deposit (three-month maturity)
i^*: interest rate on Eurodollars (three-month maturity).

Shirakawa also drew an interesting scatter diagram relating the rate of money supply divided by both the real growth rate and the effective exchange rate of major advanced countries.

His equations above conform to the general view that monetary expansion in Japan eventually leads to the depreciation of the dollar (see also Dornbusch [1980] for similar estimates). According to the monetary approach, the balance of payments is the excess demand for money of a country as a whole; exchange rates are determined approximately by the difference between excess money creation by one country and that by another. Shirakawa's results (1978) support this view in general. However, this approach is usually developed on the assumption of the PPP relationship. Therefore one has to reconcile this finding with the direct inapplicability of the PPP theory. Shirakawa's approach can probably be refined, taking account of the difference in productivity growth.

Another interesting fact is provided by Ohashi in a journal published by the Ministry of Finance (1900). He shows, influenced by suggestions by Kanemitsu (1978), that there has been a strong coincidence between the accumulated value of current accounts and the exchange rate since 1973. Figure 10.10 is a scatter diagram drawn relating accumulated current account and the yen rate. The values before the first quarter of 1973, when Japan entered the floating system after the Smithsonian period of quasi-fixed rates, are depicted by a dotted line.

One can see very close positive correlation between accumulated current account (since 1971) and the dollar-yen since 1973 I to 1978 IV. The first oil shock does not seem to have had much effect on this relationship. The second oil crisis, indeed, had a negative impact on the dollar-yen rate as com-

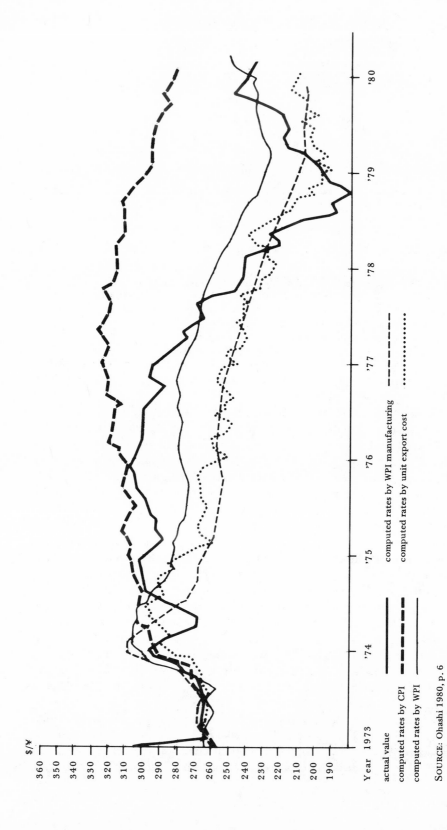

$/¥

360
350
340
330
320
310
300
290
280
270
260
250
240
230
220
210
200
190

Year 1973   '74   '75   '76   '77   '78   '79   '80

actual value ——————   computed rates by WPI manufacturing ——————
computed rates by CPI ——————   computed rates by unit export cost ··············
computed rates by WPI ——————

SOURCE: Ohashi 1980, p. 6

Fig. 10.9. The dollar-yen rate and hypothetical rates based on PPP theory

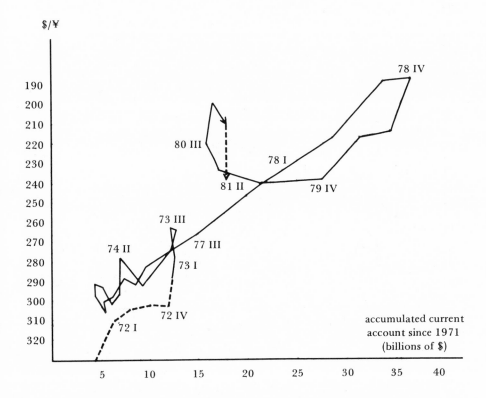

Fig. 10.10. Accumulated current account and the dollar-yen rate (Japan)

pared to computed values from this relationship. It is interesting to note that during 1980 the yen became much stronger than this simple relationship indicates. A similar diagram for the United States in figure 10.11 is provided for interested readers.

This quite remarkable correlation in the Japanese case can be interpreted in various ways. First, it may be interpreted just as the manifestation of the simple Walrasian process that the exchange rate moves responding to excess demand for foreign currencies. But this interpretation is too simple. Another explanation would be that the increase in accumulated current accounts generate expectations of the appreciation of the home currency in the future, which in turn appreciate the spot rate as well. Finally, it can be interpreted as evidence for the validity of the asset approach. The asset approach maintains that the accumulation of foreign assets tends to depress the price of foreign assets due to the portfolio selection process of the public. The oil crisis in 1979 created a large downturn in the yen exchange rate. This would imply that expectations for the future course of trade patterns are an important determinant of the spot exchange rate right now. This relationship is worth studying further by considering the stances of macroeconomic policies in the two countries.

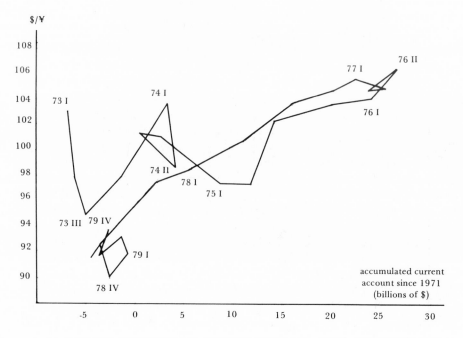

Fig. 10.11. Accumulated current account and the dollar-yen rate (U.S.)

THE SCOPE FOR POLICY COORDINATION

On the basis of the above analysis, let us now turn to one of the main themes of this paper, the question of policy coordination between the United States and Japan. What kind of coordination in exchange rate policies and, more generally, in economic policies, is possible or desirable?

First, we need to recognize the need for cooperation in exchange rate intervention. If one country engages in selling a currency when the other country engages in buying the same currency, the two operations will cancel each other out. A tug-of-war will emerge. This is one example of the well-known (n-1) problem in the determination of exchange rates: there are (n-1) relative prices of n-currencies so that one of the policy instruments, the intervention by the nth country, is redundant. To avoid this inconsistency in intervention, policy coordination is always necessary. Between the United States and Japan this type of coordination seems to have been successful. In fact, the sharpest changes in the value of the yen in recent years occurred just after the two governments agreed to intervene jointly in November 1978 and in March 1980. One form of coordination is of course the perfect passive attitude of one partner. The effect of the passive exchange rate policy of the Reagan administration remains to be seen.

Second, to keep exchange rates within a suitable range, we need the cooperation of monetary policies as well. The monetary approach or general equilibrium approach to balance of payments tells us that exchange rates are determined by interaction of monetary factors as well as real factors in the two countries, and that domestic credit expansion affects the course of exchange rates just as intervention in the exchange market does. Therefore it is impossible to keep the dollar-yen exchange rate within a target range for a substantial length of time unless there is some coordination in monetary policies between the two monetary authorities. This type of policy coordination does not seem to exist between the United States and Japan. There remains the question of whether or not we should work for stable exchange rates at the cost of independent monetary policy to be aimed at domestic objectives.

The third problem in economic coordination concerns the coordination in demand management. In an ideal world without friction, one such as that described in the last section, monetary or fiscal policies would hardly affect the course of real events. In the actual world, however, there are a great deal of friction and adjustment costs. In spite of the theoretical argument by the new classical macroeconomicists that predicted policies do not matter, governments are impelled to pursue countercyclical policies in case of severe recession. In the actual world, the transmission problem of the business cycle presents itself as a serious problem. Demand expansion in one country may be transmitted as an expansionary pressure in the other country. This is why the locomotive theory of international business fluctuations is popular among politicians. Every country wants the other country to follow an expansionary policy, hoping to enjoy the external demand pressure originated in the other country. As developed elsewhere (Hamada and Sakurai 1979), the terms of trade effect may create the chain of transmitting business cycles. However, the faster people adapt their expectations policies, the less effective the impact of macroeconomic policies. Moreover, the merit of a flexible exchange rate lies in absorption by fluctuation in exchange rates of most external monetary disturbances and the blocking of these disturbances. I therefore do not consider this element of interdependence extremely important. Of course, this aspect will be raised repeatedly in the future. It will be raised, however, not necessarily from a macroeconomic standpoint but from political pressures reflecting industrial adjustments in particular sectors to abrupt changes in trade patterns.

To conclude this paper, let me point out the prospect of the yen becoming an international currency. This implies a partial substitution of U.S. dollar by the Japanese yen in providing a medium of exchange in the world economy. This could also be regarded as a form of coordination. It is called for because it would make Japan share some of the burden of adjustment in the current account in the balance of payments needed for advanced countries in the face of the huge current account surplus by OPEC. If Japan succeeded in making the yen one of the vehicle currencies, it would imply that Japan would act as financial intermediary in the international financial market. Japan would be able to invest in long-run securities by issuing short-term liabilities. In fact, this is the role that the United States has played for a long time. In the large transfers of income to OPEC, and the need to recycle oil money to nonoil-producing developing countries that often lack abilities to finance by themselves, a partial transformation of the yen to an international currency should at least be welcomed. Further deregulation in the Japanese financial market as well as in the exchange market must be called for to attain this goal.

REFERENCES

Amano Akihiro. 1980. "Flexible Exchange Rates and Macroeconomic Management: A Study of the Japanese Experience, 1973-78." *Annuals of the School of Business Administration,* no. 24. Kobe University.

Bank of Japan. See Nihon Ginkō.

Bank of Tokyo. 1979. "Bei-tōkyoku ni yoru kawase shijō sōsa no kaiko" [Summary of exchange interventions by the U.S. monetary authorities]. *Tokyo Ginkō geppō* [Bank of Tokyo report], vol. 31, no. 5 (May).

Dornbusch, Rudiger. 1980. "Monetary Policy under Exchange-Rate Flexibility." *Managed Exchange-Rate Flexibility: The Recent Experience.* Conference Series no. 20 of the Federal Reserve Bank of Boston.

Economic Planning Agency. See Keizai Kikakuchō.

Gaikoku Kawase Bōeki Kenkyūkai. 1981. *Kokusai kinyū* [International finance journal]. Tokyo.

Hamada Koichi, 1966. "Economic Growth and Long-Term International Capital Movements." *Yale Economic Essays* 6, no. 1 (Spring):49-96.

——, and Sakurai Makoto. 1978. "International Transmission of Stagflation under Fixed and Flexible Exchange Rates." *Journal of Political Economy* 86, no. 5 (October): 877-95.

Holmes, Alan R., and Pardee, Scott E. 1979. "Treasury and Federal Reserve Foreign Exchange Operations." In *Quarterly Review* (Spring), issued by the Federal Reserve Bank of New York.

Kanemitsu Hideo. 1978. "En-daka no gen'in to kongo no ugoki" [Causes of appreciation of the yen and the yen's future]. *Nihon keizai shimbun* [Japan economy], August 21-22.

Keizai Kikakuchō. 1980. *Nenji keizai hōkoku* [Annual economic report]. Tokyo: Government Printing Office.

Komiya Ryutaro. 1979. "The American–Japanese Trade Conflict: An Economist's View from Japan." (Revised 1980). Mimeographed.

——, and Miyako Suda. 1980a. "Kanri furōto-ka no tanshi-idō" [The short-term capital movement under the managed float]. *Keizaigaku ronshū* [Journal of economics], vol. 46, no. 1.

——. 1980b. "Furōto-ikō zengo no kawase-seisaku" [Japan's foreign exchange policy in the beginning of the managed float]. *Keizaigaku ronshū,* vol. 46, no. 3.

——. 1981. "Sekiyu-kiki to kawase-seisaku" [The oil crisis and Japan's foreign exchange policy]. *Keizaigaku ronshū,* vol. 46, no. 4.

Mundell, Robert A. 1968. *International Economics.* New York, Macmillan Co.

Nihon Ginkō. 1980. *Keizai tōkei nempō* [Economic statistics annual].

——. 1981. *Keizai tōkei geppō* [Monthly report of economic statistics] (March).

Ohashi Muneo. 1980. "Furōto-sei ikō go kakkoku no kawase rēto no bunseki" [Studies in the exchange rate determination of major countries after floating]. In *Zaiseikinyū tōkei geppō* [Finance statistics report], no. 338 (June), issued by the Ministry of Finance.

Pardee, Scott E. 1980. "Treasury and Federal Reserve Foreign Exchange Operations." In

Quarterly Review (Spring), issued by the Federal Reserve Bank of New York.

Sato Setsuya. 1980. "The Purchasing Power Parity Theory of the Exchange Rate." Master of Philosophy thesis, Oxford University.

Shirakawa Masaaki. 1978. "The Monetary Approach to the Balance of Payments and the Exchange Rate: An Empirical Study of Japan's Case." In *Kinyū kenkyū shiryō* [Finance data], no. 3, issued by the Bank of Japan, Special Economics Studies Department (English translation 1980).

Seo Junichiro. 1981. "Kawase-rēto hendō to bukka hendō no kankei" [Exchange rate variations and price fluctuations]. In *Kinyū kenkyū shiryō*, no. 7, issued by the Bank of Japan, Special Economic Studies Department.

Determinants of the Yen-Dollar Exchange Rate:

The Course of the United States and Japanese Policies

JOHN MAKIN

THE LAST TEN YEARS have seen major developments in the theory of exchange rate determination. Two fundamental elements characterize these developments: exchange rates are determined by stock-equilibrium conditions in asset markets; exchange rates are determined by market participants' (rational) current expectations of all future values of relevant exogenous variables operating upon exchange rates.

These two developments, particularly the second, may seem somewhat rarefied to be taken seriously by policy makers. It is the aim of this essay to advance a convincing argument that the implications of modern exchange rate theory can and should be considered by policy makers in operating existing policies affecting asset markets where interest rates and exchange rates are determined. Further, a sophisticated theory of asset pricing, which is what these developments really provide, can supply valuable insights regarding implications of new policies that may be affected by the Reagan administration or by the Suzuki government.

It will come as no surprise to those familiar with "new" developments that in some sense there is nothing new in the stock equilibrium approach to exchange rate determination. It is really an updating and application to exchange rate behavior of the original formulation by Hume (1752) of the specie-flow mechanism for determination of equilibrium national gold stocks. The role of (rational) expectations is perhaps more novel, but undoubtedly any respectable historian of economic thought could find passages written hundreds of years ago by economists who understood the essential message that formation of expectations ought to be consistent with relevant economic theory and not just captured by some ad hoc (adaptive) formulation describing expectations.

In addition to major theoretical developments regarding exchange rate determination, those attempting to explain the behavior of exchange rates have had to deal with the fluid, hybrid exchange rate regime that evolved after the final collapse of pegging in March 1973. Central banks have tended to follow "leaning-against-the-wind" intervention policies with varying intensity. The intervention may or may not be allowed to affect the monetary base, and thereby the money supply, depending upon the ability and/or desire of central banks to insulate their economies ("to sterilize" inflows or outflows) from the effects of asset accumulation or decumulation when exchange rates are at disequilibrium levels.

The realities of intervention and sterilization must be incorporated into a modern theory of exchange rate determination. Obviously, the effect will be to modify somewhat the implications drawn from theory developed for the polar case of freely flexible rates. In particular, it will become clear that current expectations about future changes in intervention and sterilization policies will affect exchange rates today. Further, a theory of exchange rate behavior that ignores these phenomena and thereby implicitly sets them constant at zero will likely be contradicted when tested empirically against the actual behavior of exchange rates.

The primary aim of this essay is well served by beginning with a discussion of U.S. and Japanese policies, which carry important implications for the behavior of exchange rates and for the closely linked behavior of interest rates.

U.S. AND JAPANESE FINANCIAL MARKET POLICIES

REDIRECTION OF U.S. POLICY

The outcome of the 1980 U.S. presidential election indicated, among other things, that Americans were willing to risk dismissing an incumbent administration to lower inflation. It is not likely that the Reagan administration will forget that a president under whom inflation rises significantly for any reason short of an all-out war is not likely to be re-elected.

Knowing the seriousness of the political consequences of inflation, however, does not always insure a solution. Under the Carter administration, the Federal Reserve launched two major efforts to reduce inflation and calm financial markets. The November 1978 initiative was highly significant insofar as it was largely precipitated by a "crisis" (rapid dollar depreciation) in the foreign exchange markets. After an initial success, that initiative foundered as money growth reaccelerated during the summer and fall of 1979. The October 1979 initiative by the Federal Reserve seemed to suggest that operating procedures (targeting interest rates instead of the money supply) were responsible for the policy failure. The Federal Reserve reaffirmed its determination to lower and stabilize money growth and adopted a direct money-base targeting approach to increase confidence in the goal.

While debate persisted regarding whether the Federal Reserve had "really" abandoned interest rate targets, and while both interest rates and money growth became more volatile, the Carter administration did little to abate inflation after two years of trying, although it knew that inflation could prevent re-election. Therefore it is not surprising that interest and exchange rates did not, upon election of a new president, immediately reflect anticipation of inflation control merely on the strength of his obvious awareness that his re-election would require inflation control. In short, the election of a new president did not greatly affect the current expectations held by market participants about the future course of exogenous variables relevant for the determination of exchange rates and interest rates.

POSSIBLE IMPACT OF ALTERED U.S. POLICY

It is useful to speculate, in the light of relevant policies now in effect in Japan and the United States, about the implications for the yen-dollar rate of alternatives in future U.S. monetary policy.

The key to understanding the consequences of significant policy changes for exchange rates lies in understanding the crucial role played by what is termed here the momentum of expectations. At any point, the level of exchange and interest rates reflects asset prices determined by the efforts of international investors to obtain optimal portfolios contingent upon their expectations regarding rates of return on assets denominated in different currencies. In the simplest bilateral framework, those expected rates of return depend largely upon the current expectation of all future supplies of money relative to commodities.

Early in 1981, for example, the yen-dollar exchange rate reflected the best forecasts (guesses?) of market participants about the commodity value of the yen relative to the dollar over the lives of various assets. The expected commodity value of the dollar reflects both the political and operational difficulties the United States has had in recent years in trying to lower and stabilize money growth. The future commodity value of the yen reflects, on the one hand, Japan's perception of its vulnerability to changes in supplies of imported raw materials, particularly petroleum, but on the other hand its formidable display of adaptability to such problems, particularly coupled since 1979 with a demonstrated ability and determination to control the money supply.

Given this scenario, suppose as one possibility that the Reagan administration shows signs of achieving success in lowering government expenditures and effecting stimulative tax cuts while the Federal Reserve begins to achieve a sustained reduction and stabilization of money growth. Due to the momentum of expectations the initial response in exchange markets will likely be modest. Since exchange rates do represent asset pricing, which is in turn contingent on all currently anticipated future events, given the largely unsuccessful history of such policy initiatives, most market participants will see such success as temporary and may only wish to add to the share of short-term dollar assets in their portfolio. If U.S. interest rates fall by about the amount of an anticipated drop in inflation, exchange rates will be little affected. In short, the momentum of expectations can produce some initial results that may be somewhat discouraging to policy makers.

The most interesting results follow if a significant change in either direction does actually occur in the outlook for the commodity value of the dollar or the yen. Very little is known about the process whereby, say, initial signs of success in controlling U.S. inflation begin to be extrapolated well into the future as a fundamental change in the U.S. monetary environment. It is important to understand implications of stock equilibrium and expectations for the impact of such a change on financial markets in the United States and its major trading partners, like Japan.

Given a fundamental improvement in the relative and absolute outlook for the dollar in purchasing power over commodities, there naturally follows an increase in the demand for dollar assets. Given some intervention in foreign exchange markets, a transition period ensues during which large stocks of assets are bought and sold in the shortest possible time. Given, say, an unchanged outlook for the commodity value of the yen, a sharp improvement in the outlook for the commodity value of the dollar will cause a sharp but temporary outflow of capital from Japan if authorities "lean against the wind" to prevent full adjustment of the exchange rate. Alternatively, with no intervention in foreign exchange markets, the incentive created for a capital flow from Japan to the United States will result in appreciation of the dollar in the forward market by an amount that cuts the forward premium on the dollar to a level equal to the reduced nominal interest differential between the United States and Japan.

It is important to remember that just as a finite movement of the forward premium restores equilibrium with zero intervention, so a finite movement of capital restores equilibrium even when intervention in foreign exchange markets prevents full exchange rate adjustment *provided that the negative (positive) impacts of capital outflows (inflows) on the monetary base are permitted to materialize.* The effect of capital flows on the monetary base must not be sterilized. The temptation to do so will be reduced if it is remembered that a reallocation of assets in response to a change in expectations is temporary since portfolio managers are moving toward a new stock equilibrium. Once the process is completed, equilibrium interest rates in the United States will be lower in view of reduced inflationary expectations. Also, when the reallocation of portfolios has fully reflected the reduced inflationary expectations in the United States, and a new stable outlook for the relative commodity value of dollars and yen is established, the incentive for capital to move will be eliminated.

Another way to view this transition is to consider the security arbitrage equilibrium condition—interest parity. With no intervention, the drop in the U.S. interest rate attendant upon lower expected inflation will occur simultaneously with the equal drop in the forward dollar premium. With some intervention, portfolio realignments will occur since exchange rates won't fully adjust to new equilibrium levels. The intervention implies that during the realignment period the monetary base will rise in the United States and fall in Japan. Ceteris paribus, U.S. interest rates will rise part of the way back up to original levels while interest rates in Japan fall until the interest differential is in line with the reduction in the expected dollar appreciation occasioned by monetary flows resulting from intervention in support of the yen. If sterilization were to prevent the adjustment of the relative money base levels while intervention continued to support the yen, the outflow of funds from Japan would accelerate, given the perception of an overvalued yen. Eventually, intervention or sterilization would have to end. The former would allow full exchange rate adjustment while the latter would permit required adjustment of relative money supplies. In the case of intervention and no sterilization, once portfolios are realigned, unless there is another change in expected dollar appreciation, capital flows will end.

Obviously, an improved U.S. monetary environment is only one possibility and I do not mean to suggest it as a forecast. Any significant deterioration of the U.S. monetary environment would produce reverse results. In my view, the United States in 1981 is poised on a knife-edge from which inflation and the general monetary environment will either improve or deteriorate dramatically. The outcome will depend on the power of constituencies such as homebuilding and automobile manufacture, which tend to benefit from accelerating inflation (and suffer badly when it slows down) relative to the power of inflation-losers such as lenders and those whose wages or salaries tend to lag behind inflation.

IMPLICATIONS OF U.S. POLICY INITIATIVES FOR JAPAN

The impact of a sharp change in the U.S. monetary environment carries important implications for financial markets in Japan, just as actions affecting the monetary environment and financial markets in Japan affect U.S. markets. The Foreign Exchange and Foreign Trade Control Law that went into effect on December 1, 1980, underlines both the rapid emergence of Tokyo as an international financial center and the increasing need for coordination of financial policies in the light of closer U.S.-Japan financial interdependence. I shall now give careful consideration to special situations in Japanese financial markets that may be significantly affected by the course of U.S. policy.

Major changes in U.S. monetary policy are particularly relevant for the interrelated Japanese policies concerning the finance of government budgetary deficits, foreign exchange market intervention, and liberalization of international capital flows.

Government budgetary deficits in Japan rose very rapidly after 1974 when the outstanding government debt was only about 12 percent of the gross national product (GNP). By 1981 it reached well over 30 percent, close to the level in the United States. The deficit for the fiscal year ending March 31, 1981, is expected to be between $65 billion and $70 billion and for the fiscal year, about $58 billion. As a share of GNP, these deficits are about three times greater than comparable U.S. figures.

The sale of a volume of government securities sufficient to finance such deficits at interest rates desired by the Ministry of Finance has placed strains on capital markets in Japan. The mechanism designed to compensate city banks for absorbing government bonds at a loss during periods of high market interest rates has broken down under the strain of a very large volume of new issues. Some relief has come from sales of Japanese government bonds abroad, particularly to OPEC investors, but even these sales will absorb, at most, 10 percent of new issues during the 1980 fiscal year. The pressure of a constant, large flow of new issues produces something of a dilemma for policy makers concerned with interest rates in Japan. Any sharp changes in U.S. monetary policy will present more difficult choices, especially given the existing policy of "leaning against the wind" in foreign exchange markets and the increased freedom of movement of financial capital into and out of Japan.

As an example, suppose that a sharp tightening of U.S. monetary policy initially places a strong upward pressure on U.S. interest rates. Yen depreciation against the dollar ensues. This causes direct inflationary pressure in Japan as the yen price of imports denominated in dollars rises. Indirectly, more exports may increase inflationary pressure if the economy is operating at close to capacity. A desire to mitigate the exchange rate source of inflationary pressures will likely result in "leaning against the wind" by the Bank of Japan.[1] The less the adjustment allowed for the exchange rate, the more pressure will be for interest rates to rise in Japan as capital flows out, given the portfolio reallocation desired in light of the enhanced attractiveness of dollar assets.

This situation puts heavy stress on efforts to finance ongoing large deficits with government bonds priced to yield subequilibrium yields. Losses mount for the banks absorbing such bonds. Fears mount that a high interest policy will cause a slowdown of economic activity. The temptation grows to impose strict controls on capital outflows.

This combination of circumstances suggests that pressure on financial markets in Japan could be mitigated by allowing more movement of exchange rates, especially since such movement will tend to stabilize once reallocation of portfolios is effected. In the case just considered, more yen depreciation in spot markets would cut capital outflows and attendant positive pressure on interest rates inside Japan. Export sales would be increased, mitigating any possible negative effect of higher interest rates on over-all economic activity. Further, the perceived need to control capital flows would be lessened.

A true internationalization of Japan's financial markets such as is envisioned under the Foreign Exchange and Foreign Trade Control Law is con-

1. Evidence presented below suggests that BOJ offsetting intervention has become more pronounced since the end of 1975.

sistent both with its role as a major economy and with its changing internal needs. Given Japan's admirable record of monetary stability, particularly the remarkable adaptation to the oil price shocks in the late seventies, a broadening and deepening of markets for yen assets will come about if participants develop an assurance that free movement of financial capital to and from Japan will not be interrupted. A major international role for yen assets would ease the burden on Japan's capital markets of financing large government deficits that are likely to persist in the foreseeable future.

The foregoing discussion of the implications of policy in Japan and the United States is predicated on a theoretical framework for the analysis of exchange rate behavior. It is perhaps useful to reinforce points made earlier, to reveal the analytical biases that produce such views, and to briefly explore that framework.

EXCHANGE RATE THEORY

Asset Market Equilibrium and Expectations

The theory of exchange rate determination employed here to investigate the behavior of the yen-dollar exchange rate since the era of quasi-floating began in March 1973 may be termed the monetary equilibrium, rational expectations (MERE) approach. MERE essentially views the exchange rate as the relative price of money assets determined subject to satisfaction of: (1) stable money demand functions; (2) interest parity; (3) the lack of bias of the forward exchange rate as a predictor of the future spot exchange rate; and (4) purchasing power parity (PPP). The last condition is often violated by movements in "real" exchange rates and explicit account is taken of real exchange rate changes in the formulation of the empirical tests reported later in this article (and in the appendix that follows).

Empirical testing of MERE also requires its extension to include the sterilization and intervention behavior of monetary authorities that characterizes the post-Bretton Woods system of controlled and varying degrees of permissible flexibility of exchange rates.

Rationality

The MERE approach to exchange rate determination embodies rational expectations about which there exists considerable controversy among economists and others interested in analysis of market behavior. It is useful to characterize pure rational expectations formulations as representative of a polar assumption about information costs. Rational models effectively assume that market participants extract without cost all systematic information about the behavior of exogenous variables relevant to the determination of, say, exchange rates. At the other extreme are the traditional, adaptive models that assume that market participants learn more slowly. Much empirical investigation will be required to ascertain which models most faithfully represent actual behavior. Considerable discussion and empirical testing of traditional models has already been done. Empirical testing of rational exchange rate models has not been extensive, particularly for models that explicitly incorporate the features of a system of limited flexibility of exchange rates. This paper aims at an initial effort to fill this gap.

BASIC CONCLUSIONS FROM MERE

The extended MERE model yields a number of basic conclusions regarding determination of exchange rates that need to be well understood by policy makers and exchange market participants alike. The conclusions are presented and discussed without formal derivation. The appendix provides the interested reader with full derivations of each of the propositions advanced.

MERE yields a solution for an exchange rate in terms of current actual levels and all expected future levels of money relative to real output at home and abroad. Such determinants can be more compactly described as current actual and expected future values of *relative* (to "foreign") *excess* (relative to real commodity output) *money supplies* (RXM). This result is straightforward enough. A rational model of the price level would determine it in terms of the current expectation of all future excess money supplies (or the current expectation of all future money supplies with exogenously determined real output; see Fischer 1979). As a natural extension of this line of thought, it can be demonstrated that the exchange rate summarizes market participants' current perception of the outlook for the purchasing power over commodities of a domestic money relative to that of foreign money.

With "leaning against the wind" intervention in foreign exchange markets, current actual and expected future values of RXM remain the fundamental determinants of the exchange rate. However, intervention (so long as sterilization is absent) effectively substitutes some adjustment of relative money supplies for movement of an exchange rate (relative price of money) as a means of resolving foreign exchange market disequilibrium. In short, the exchange rate responds less sharply to a current or expected future change in RXM if market participants anticipate some given degree of leaning against the wind by monetary authorities that will in turn cause relative money supplies to adjust so as to remove some of the RXM.

A corollary proposition is that unpredictable intervention policy makes exchange rate prediction more difficult than it would be under a system of freely flexible rates wherein a zero level of intervention is assured. The usual stated purpose of intervention is to smooth out unnecessary (i.e., ultimately reversible) exchange rate movements. However, if this rationale results in volatile intervention, the actual effect is to increase uncertainty about exchange rates. Volatile intervention results in much uncertainty regarding the future mix of changes in exchange rates and relative money supplies that will equilibrate foreign exchange markets.

It is important to distinguish between the effects of the level of intervention and its volatility. As long as intervention is not sterilized, the actual level of intervention is not so crucial to the orderly functioning of foreign exchange markets as is its stability. A high and stable level of intervention imparts the expectation that changes in relative money supplies rather than exchange rate movements will absorb a large part of the shocks to exchange markets.

The danger lies in the likelihood that high levels of intervention are likely to be more volatile, thereby imparting considerable uncertainty about the future path of exchange rates and making a rational solution for the current exchange rate difficult. In effect, a volatile intervention policy raises the cost of ascertaining the path of future relative money supplies required for a rational determination of the exchange rate.

Compounding the difficulties inherent in the likelihood that extensive intervention will be more volatile is the likelihood that aggressive intervention, which results in sharply rising (falling) money supplies for surplus (deficit) countries, will increase the temptation to sterilize the impact of intervention on domestic money supplies. Sterilization of course cancels the adjustment of the relative money supplies required in the absence of the exchange rate adjustment, which intervention prevents. It becomes far more likely where the requirements of external balance conflict with those of internal balance (e.g., deficit-recession or surplus-inflation). And, like volatile intervention policy, volatile sterilization policy increases exchange rate uncertainty. Partial sterilization only delays the process of adjustment toward equilibrium exchange rates while full sterilization is highly unstable. For all but reserve currency countries, full sterilization almost always results in an exchange rate crisis where a large, discrete exchange rate change is required to restore equilibrium. The "speculators" who foresee such crises are really prudent men if one considers the inevitable result of persistently offering to sell foreign exchange at a subequilibrium price.

If only one country sterilizes, then all of the burden of adjusting relative excess money supplies is thrust onto its trading partners. If it is a particularly large country that sterilizes, such a burden is particularly onerous for the smaller countries, which are left with the choice of coordinating monetary policies with the large country or suffering considerable volatility in the exchange rate between their currency and that of the large country. The only other alternative is controls on capital flows, commodity trade, or access to foreign exchange.

PROBLEMS WITH EMPIRICAL IMPLEMENTATION OF MERE

It has been explained that under the MERE theory an exchange rate is determined by the course of current and expected future relative excess money supplies. Empirical testing requires specification of a model to represent the future behavior of relative money supplies and relative real output, the elements of RXM. The future behavior of relative money supplies also depends on the specification of given intervention and sterilization policies over the forecast horizon. The result is that empirical testing of MERE also involves jointly testing the validity of its elements along with the validity of an arbitrarily chosen representation of future RXM for given intervention and sterilization policies.

A simple formulation describing the behavior of RXM over time that has some empirical support specifies growth of relative money supplies and relative real output as a random walk. This representation essentially says that all systematic information about the future values of a variable is contained in current values. The random walk formulation for RXM is shown in the appendix to imply a cyclical response of the exchange rate to components of RXM.

Given that ability to predict future relative money supplies is conditional upon stable intervention and sterilization policies (or upon foreseeable changes in these policies), it is important to identify any sharp changes in these policies within the sample period under investigation. Since monetary authorities do not announce changes in intervention or sterilization policies in advance, it may be assumed that such changes were not foreseen and therefore would entail a violation of the assumption that a single model would adequately predict relative money supplies over the full sample period.

The net result of these considerations is to suggest that a full explanation of exchange rate behavior, particularly under a hybrid system of variable quasi-floating, will be difficult. Empirical tests of MERE for the yen-dollar exchange rate presented below aim at identifying what portion of the exchange rate movements can systematically be explained with particular attention paid to difficulties introduced by volatile intervention and sterilization policies. Once this is done it becomes easier to understand the need for well-defined intervention policies as a means to avoid some of the uncertainty about the future behavior of exchange rates and the importance of eliminating sterilization if exchange market crises are to be avoided.

TESTING THE EXTENDED MERE MODEL
FOR THE YEN-DOLLAR EXCHANGE RATE

IMPLICATIONS OF THEORY

The theory developed above and in the appendix anticipates some specific forms of observable behavior. The response of exchange rates to components of RXM may be cyclical. Separate components of RXM may produce different cyclical impacts upon exchange rates due to differences in the income elasticity of money demand (impact on response to real income variables) and to different projections of expected future behavior of the determinants of RXM from observable current and lagged values.[2] Over time, estimated parameters may vary due to changes in intervention and/or sterilization policy.

2. In terms of the model described in the appendix, the p values describing the (AR-1) growth path of exogenous variables may differ. Alternatively, a more complex ARMA model may imply alternative cyclical response patterns.

The sample period employed here runs from March 1973 through December 1979. During that time there has been steady "real" depreciation of the dollar against the yen. As noted earlier, the log of the real dollar-yen exchange rate follows a random walk during the 1973-79 sample period. Therefore the rate of change of the exchange rate (log-first-difference) obeys PPP (see appendix for fuller discussion). All variables discussed here are in log-first-difference form. Any possible remaining systematic, temporal behavior of the differenced dollar-yen exchange rate is captured by a noise model in the transfer function estimates reported below. Given this formulation, RXM components must explain some part of the random residuals of a prefiltered series on the rate of change of the exchange rate.

CONTROLLING FOR INTERVENTION POLICY

As already noted, it is necessary to consider the implications for exchange rates of foreign exchange market intervention by U.S. and Japanese authorities. A model of "leaning against the wind" intervention was estimated for both Japan and the United States. Transfer function estimation procedures following Box and Jenkins (1970) revealed that the systematic portion of Japanese intervention as measured by changes in foreign exchange reserves is explained by yen-dollar exchange rate movements and an "ARMA noise model."[3] Systematic U.S. intervention was explained by movements of DM-dollar and yen-dollar exchange rates and a moving average noise model. The latter result is interesting in view of the conventional wisdom view that U.S. intervention is largely keyed only to the DM-dollar rate.

The MERE theory of exchange rate behavior with intervention implies that the impact of exogenous money or real income shocks upon exchange rates is contingent upon a given intervention (and sterilization) regime. Therefore, large intervention outliers (unusually high levels of intervention) may disturb reduced-form estimates of exchange rate equations based on behavior of relative excess money supplies. An attempt to control for this problem was made by employing a dummy variable for months when a large outlier for U.S. or Japanese intervention behavior coincided with a large residual in initial estimates of the basic exchange rate equation. The result saw dummy variables at June 1978 and November 1978. The June 1978 dummy captures an abnormally high level of Japanese intervention in support of the yen. The November 1978 dummy captures abnormally high U.S. and Japanese intervention in support of the dollar, most likely as a part of the November 1978 U.S. policy in response to heavy dollar depreciation.

A third dummy variable for March 1979 captures the cumulative impact of three months of large unanticipated reductions in the U.S. money stock from December 1978 through February 1979.[4] It appears that by March,

---

3. An ARMA noise model explains behavior of the exchange rate in terms of its own history.

4. The unanticipated drop in d_{us} is evident from the univariate model estimated to prefilter d_{us} for use in the estimation of cross correlations with the yen-dollar rate.

projections of longer run U.S. money growth were being lowered enough to strengthen the dollar.

Inclusion of these intervention dummies along with an extraordinary money-surprise dummy removed large residuals from the basic estimated exchange rate equation. While the "explanatory power" of such dummy variables is only illusory, their inclusion is significant as a means to allow the estimation of parameters that are not biased by the larger outliers that appear when no effort is made to control for intervention.

In addition to searching for intervention outliers for a single intervention model estimated for the entire sample period, it is possible to entertain the hypothesis that the underlying intervention model may change within any single sample period. In effect, there may be a significant change in the degree of "leaning against the wind." Investigation of this possibility and its implications is, however, best left until after consideration of the results of attempting to estimate a single exchange rate model for the full sample period while controlling only for outliers from a single intervention model.

METHODOLOGY

Transfer function estimation procedures following Box and Jenkins (1970) were also employed to estimate exchange rate equations. This methodology enables parsimonious representation of lengthy, cyclical, distributed-lag effects running from exogenous variables to the endogenous variable along with simultaneous prefiltering of the endogenous variable to "white noise" by means of an AR, MA, or ARMA model. In addition, cross correlations between the endogenous variable and lagged and leading values of the exogenous variables (prefiltered to white noise) can be obtained. The cross correlations for lagged exogenous variables enable the investigator to see if any additional explanatory power remains once some relationship between exogenous and endogenous variables has been estimated. Cross correlations between the endogenous variable and leading values of the exogenous variables enable a check on the feedback running from the endogenous variable to later values of the exogenous variables. The latter cross correlations will be employed below in a discussion of possible sterilization behavior.

Initial estimation using eighty-two monthly observations running from March 1973 through December 1979 indicated that most of the impact of the exogenous variables upon the endogenous variables occurred (via numerator parameters) contemporaneously and with a lag of one month. A notable exception was the U.S. money variable, which affected the exchange rate only after a lag of eight months. For all RXM variables further explanatory power appeared to be distributed over a long lag. Therefore a parameter (second order denominator) was included to allow for a cyclical or monotonic distributed lag impact running from exogenous variables to the endogenous variable.

ESTIMATION RESULTS

Table 11.1 reports on the estimation of a transfer function model with nu-

TABLE 11.1

Transfer Function Estimation
of the Dollar Price of Yen
(t-statistics in parentheses)

$$R^2 \, (\bar{R}^2) = 0.48 \, (0.39) \qquad F(12,68) = 5.31$$

Exogenous variable	0-n. (8-n.)	1-n.	2-dn.	Total Gain
d_{us}[†][‡]	0.0845 (2.17)		0.950 (16.54)	1.688
y_{us} [§]	0.5682 (2.26)	-0.5405 (2.08)	-0.8546 (10.17)	0.0149
d_j		-0.0518 (1.95)	-0.5438 (1.62)	-0.0336
y_j	0.0172 (0.26)	-0.0892 (1.18)	0.979 (37.57)	-3.379
Dummies	-0.0842 (5.68)			-0.0842 (5.68)
Noise (MA-7)[∥]				-0.1770 (1.28)

[†] All variables are in log-first difference form.

[‡] d measures the log of the domestic portion of the monetary base. For the U.S., the domestic portion of the monetary base is measured by monetary authority reserve money (line 14) less monetary authority foreign assets (line 11) in IMF international financial statistics. For Japan, d_j is measured by line (14) less the foreign exchange portion of international liquidity (line 1dd). The change in measures of d is necessitated by a break in the series on Japanese monetary authority foreign assets. Correlation between line 1dd and line 14 for Japan prior to the August 1978 break in the series was 0.81.

[§] y is industrial production (line 66c of IFS).

[∥] The spot exchange rate, s, is taken from the Harris Bank Tape of international financial statistics. Data are as of the last available reporting day of the month.

merator parameters at lags zero and one (0-n. and 1-n.) and a second-order denominator parameter (2-dn.). "Total gain" in table 11.1 refers to the full distributed-lag impact of an exogenous variable over a period of damped, cyclical oscillations or monotonic decay toward zero.

Obviously many alternative formulations including first- and third-order denominator parameters and other numerator parameters could produce an oscillatory or other distributed-lag impact running from RXM variables to the exchange rate. Some were tried. Numerator parameters beyond lag-one-month were generally insignificant (with the exception of U.S. money, 8-n.). In most cases third-order denominator parameters resulted in explosive oscillatory distributed lags for one or more RXM variables. The formulation reported in table 11.1 has uniformity and relative simplicity to recommend it.

However, any significant change in intervention or sterilization policy can and will disturb the appropriate form of the model, as we shall see below.

Over-all, the results in table 11.1 are consistent with the MERE theory of exchange rate behavior, but the explanatory power of RXM variables is not high and for one variable—real output in Japan, y_j,—results are contradictory to MERE. The explanatory power of RXM variables is exaggerated by the R^2, adjusted R^2 ($\bar{R}^2$), and F-statistics, which reflect the impact of highly significant intervention dummies. Without the dummies, $\bar{R}^2$ drops to about 0.12 and the estimated equation just passes an F test at the 0.05 level of significance. On the other hand, it must be recalled that the transfer function formulation with a noise model places a heavy burden on the explanatory variables included along with the own past history of the endogenous variable. They must significantly improve on the explanatory power of a univariate ARMA (noise) model on the endogenous variable. If any correlation exists between RXM variables and past exchange rates then there is a bias against finding significant explanatory power for RXM variables in the transfer function formulation.

The monetary variables in table 11.1 produce anticipated effects on the dollar price of yen, although the indicated over-all impact of the U.S. monetary variable, d_{us}, occurs with a considerable lag and is much larger than the impact of the Japanese monetary variable, d_j. The full set of distributed lag weights can be seen in the appendix (figs. 11.1 and 11.2). An oscillatory response of the dollar price of yen follows from an expansion of the Japanese money supply while U.S. monetary growth causes a lagged dollar depreciation that declines monotonically over time. The indicated net yen depreciation with cycling that follows from monetary growth in Japan is quite consistent with MERE. While the dollar depreciation that follows from U.S. money expansion is also consistent in sign with MERE, it is difficult to account for such a lag. It may be due partly to a statistical artifact caused by strong feedback from the exchange rate to subsequent U.S. money, which suggests U.S. sterilization. As a result, past exchange rates may be correlated with contemporary U.S. money. Given the transfer function noise model, the explanatory power of past values of the endogenous exchange rate may make contemporary and recent lagged values of U.S. money appear redundant as determinants of the contemporary exchange rate. This possibility is considered further when sterilization is discussed.

The exchange rate impact of both U.S. and Japanese real income is a long, cyclical distributed lag (see figs. 11.3 and 11.4 in the appendix). While the "total gain" impact of U.S. growth is dollar depreciation (under MERE, output growth elevates money demand and causes appreciation), it is very close to zero. Further, from figure 11.3 it can be seen that over the first quarter the estimated appreciation coefficient is -0.46, consistent with MERE. By contrast the cyclical impact of Japanese growth is to produce strong yen depreciation, contrary to MERE. As is evident in figure 11.4, this result follows approximately from asymmetric cycling of the exchange

Distributed Lag Weights · · · · · · · · · · · · · Range 0 to 0.08450

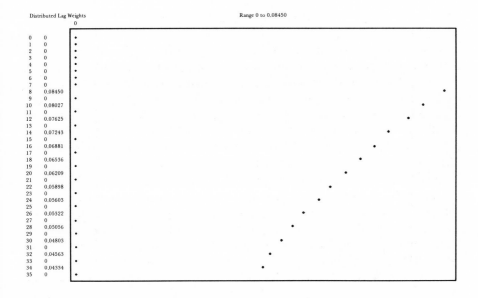

0	0
1	0
2	0
3	0
4	0
5	0
6	0
7	0
8	0.08450
9	0
10	0.08027
11	0
12	0.07625
13	0
14	0.07243
15	0
16	0.06881
17	0
18	0.06536
19	0
20	0.06209
21	0
22	0.05898
23	0
24	0.05603
25	0
26	0.05322
27	0
28	0.05056
29	0
30	0.04803
31	0
32	0.04563
33	0
34	0.04334
35	0

Fig. 11.1. Exogenous variable no. 1: domestic portion of base: U.S.

Distributed Lag Weights · · · · · · · · · · · · · Range -0.05181 to 0.02817

0	0
1	-0.05181
2	0
3	0.02817
4	0
5	-0.01532
6	0
7	0.008330
8	0
9	-0.004529
10	0
11	0.002463
12	0
13	-0.001339
14	0
15	0.0007283
16	0
17	-0.0003960
18	0
19	0.0002153
20	0
21	-0.0001171
22	0
23	0.00006368
24	0
25	-0.00003462
26	0
27	0.00001883
28	0
29	-0.00001024
30	0
31	0.000005567
32	0
33	-0.000003027
34	0
35	0.000001646

Fig. 11.2. Domestic portion of base: Japan

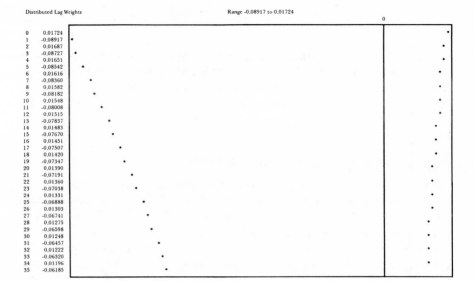

Fig. 11.3. Industrial production: United States

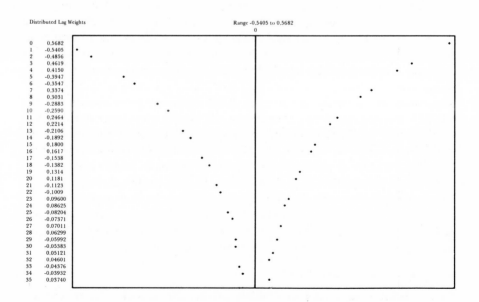

Fig. 11.4. Industrial production: Japan

rate in response to Japanese real income. Japanese growth does produce some periods of yen appreciation but alternating periods of depreciation as estimated here are dominant over a long period producing the large "total gain" with incorrect sign. This result and others in table 11.1 will be discussed further below in the light of significant changes in Japanese intervention policy.

FURTHER IMPLICATIONS OF ESTIMATION RESULTS

There is an additional important piece of information in the results shown in table 11.1, regarding the proper specification of models of exchange rate behavior. In view of the large difference in the estimated coefficients on U.S. and Japanese money variables and, also, income variables, it is clear that a serious misspecification is very likely to result from the common practice of regressing exchange rates on relative money supplies and relative real growth. That specification imposes the same coefficient (with sign reversed) on domestic and foreign money as well as on domestic and foreign real income. If different models are employed to project future values of money and income values, there will be a difference in the measured impact on the exchange rate of current, actual values of the domestic and foreign components of RXM like that reported in table 11.1. Cross-country differences in income elasticity of money demand will cause coefficients on domestic and foreign income variables to differ.

The general nature of the results reported in table 11.1 is not inconsistent with two basic notions about exchange rate behavior that imply difficulty in detecting systematic explanations for exchange rate behavior. First it is important to remember that exchange rates are prices, determined in asset markets where much of the information determining rates on a day-to-day basis is unforeseeable. Recall that MERE implies that current and all currently expected future components of RXM will determine an exchange rate. Regression of an exchange rate on RXM tests the joint hypothesis that MERE is an adequate theory of exchange rate behavior and that current and/or lagged values of RXM components are good measures of current expectations about future values of RXM. The fact is that RXM components are notoriously difficult to predict as are other unsystematic shocks with a significant impact on equilibrium exchange rates. In sum, empirical results reported here are consistent with the hypothesis that foreign exchange markets are best viewed as securities markets where behavior of asset prices is largely determined by a high volume of new information, most of which is impossible to predict or even to measure systematically ex post facto.

SHIFTS IN INTERVENTION POLICY

Even if RXM components were highly predictable, it is clear from extended MERE theory with intervention and sterilization that changes in either or both of these policies within a sample period being employed for estimation would disturb the relationship between exchange rates and RXM variables.

Beyond controlling for intervention outliers, an effort was made to test for a possible significant change in U.S. or Japanese "leaning against the wind" intervention policy after the December 1975 meetings at Rambouillet, where major countries attempted to formulate some revised exchange-rate-policy "rules of the game." Intervention equations of the form estimated for the full sample period were re-estimated for the subperiods from March 1973 to December 1975 and January 1976 to December 1979.

For the United States it was not possible to reject the null hypothesis that the intervention model was unchanged. The relevant F-statistic calculated was 1.03, well below the critical value of 1.93 required for rejection of the null hypothesis at the 5 percent level of significance. For Japan, the measured elasticity of intervention (reserve response to exchange rate movement) rose from an estimated 0.80 during the early period to 1.73 during the later period. This indicates more aggressive "leaning against the wind" by Japan after Rambouillet. Rejection of the null hypothesis of unchanged Japanese intervention was possible at about a 10 percent level of significance (calculated F=2.01). Some of the difficulty in estimating stable parameter values for RXM effects on exchange may be due to changes in intervention policy within the sample period. Efforts to re-estimate the table 11.1 equation for the sample subperiods before and after Rambouillet are, however, made difficult by the small number of degrees of freedom available, particularly during the early period.

FEEDBACK FROM EXCHANGE RATE TO MONETARY BASE: STERILIZATION

Chi-square tests of cross correlation between a prefiltered exchange rate and prefiltered series on all exogenous variables revealed positive feedback running from the exchange rate to the domestic portion of the U.S. monetary base. Dollar depreciation will, given "leaning against the wind" intervention, result in some reduction in the U.S. monetary base through sales of foreign exchange by the central bank. If simultaneously, or with a lag of two months as indicated by cross correlations, the central bank increases the domestic portion of the monetary base to offset (sterilize) some or all of the intervention reserve loss, the proximate result will be a positive correlation between the dollar price of foreign currency and the domestic portion of the monetary base (this can be seen from equations (5) and (6) in the appendix).

The result of such sterilization activity is to enhance the volatility of exchange rate movements in response to changes in the components of RXM. To see this, suppose that U.S. money growth accelerates. If the current expectation of market participants is for intervention with no sterilization, the result will be to dampen dollar depreciation because part of the adjustment to the U.S. excess money supply will be effected by the quantitative reduction in the U.S. monetary base (or increase in the foreign monetary base) implicit in "leaning against the wind." A sterilization offset to the negative pressure on the U.S. monetary base arising from intervention places the full burden of adjustment back upon the exchange rate (or upon the money supply of U.S. trading partners) and so implies more exchange rate volatility in response to a measured acceleration of U.S. money growth.

There is no evidence of significant feedback from the exchange rate to the domestic portion of the monetary base in Japan. This finding, along with "leaning against the wind" intervention by Japan, suggests an explanation for the smaller exchange rate response to the acceleration of money growth in Japan compared to that in the United States that is reported in table 11.1. Without sterilization, the indication is that some part of the adjustment to the excess money supply in Japan will be through a reduction of the monetary base resulting in turn from intervention.[5]

These results suggest that Japan, which has a more open economy than the United States, takes more seriously the rules of the game (no sterilization) required to effect external balance where intervention is present. The comparative emphasis on external balance in Japan relative to the United States is suggested in a study by Niho and Makin (1978) designed to reveal the tastes of policy makers. However, as the openness of U.S. economy increases it becomes more important to acknowledge before, rather than after a crisis like that in October-November 1978, some need to allow the behavior of the money supply to reflect the requirements of external balance. Consideration might well be given to articulation of U.S. exchange-rate policy that emphasizes the absence of conflict between domestic and international goals of U.S. monetary policy. Stability of the current and expected future purchasing power of the dollar is an appropriate, single goal for U.S. monetary policy that serves both domestic and foreign users and holders of dollars. Further, it satisfies a necessary condition for international monetary stability in a world where adoption of such a policy by all major central banks would satisfy necessary and sufficient conditions.

The U.S. policy of sterilization implies difficult choices for its trading partners. As noted earlier, sterilization by a large economy like the United States requires for equilibrium either more exchange rate adjustment, sharp changes in the money supplies for U.S. trading partners (especially smaller economies), or tying of monetary policy to U.S. policy. While this burden is relatively low for Japan as opposed to, say, Switzerland, it still is not incidental. Japan's money stock is roughly three quarters that of the United States so that a 1 percent change in the U.S. money stock equals about a 1.33 percent change in the money stock of Japan. Since Japan is not well advised to tie its monetary policy to that of the United States, sterilization by the

5. Professor Royama has suggested that institutional constraints upon the monetary authority may make some part of the domestic portion of the monetary base in Japan depend upon the exchange rate. Such endogeneity, which would be empirically the same as the result of sterilization, does not appear strongly in the data for the sample period under consideration here. Further investigation would be useful, particularly to see if an empirical test could be devised to distinguish the effects of possible sterilization from other sources of possible feedback running from the exchange rate to the domestic portion of the monetary base.

United States implies that a given degree of intervention by Japan will likely require more movement of the yen-dollar rate than would exist if such sterilization were ended and part of the adjustment burden borne by movements in the U.S. money supply. It is probably not, however, realistic for U.S. trading partners to expect an adjustment in U.S. sterilization policy. This implies that sustained high intervention levels will likely be accompanied by considerable volatility of local money supplies in view of the volatility in U.S. money markets. Alternatively, intervention levels may have to be reduced and more exchange rate volatility tolerated until conditions stabilize in U.S. money markets.

POLICY IMPLICATIONS OF EMPIRICAL FINDINGS
ON THE YEN-DOLLAR EXCHANGE RATE

LARGE UNSYSTEMATIC COMPONENT OF EXCHANGE RATE BEHAVIOR

It is clear that yen-dollar exchange rate behavior is not fully explained by the observable, actual behavior of relevant variables identified by theory. There are two basic reasons for this outcome. First, there is a large volume of unsystematic news (including real shocks like harvests, rainfall, oil price or availability, and election outcomes) that impinges on foreign exchange markets. Second, since exchange rates depend on the expected as well as the current behavior of the variables composing RXM, any empirical test necessarily involves a joint hypothesis regarding the validity of the basic theory and the ability of observable magnitudes to measure current expectations about the future behavior of exogenous variables.

Policy makers can do little about the large volume of unsystematic news affecting exchange rates. Likewise, the long-run path of real variables like growth rates is largely independent of policy measures. What can be affected by policy makers is the actual behavior of the money supply and the relationship between its current and its expected behavior. Crucial to the latter link is stability, and therefore predictability, of intervention and sterilization policies. Sterilization that accompanies intervention thrusts all of the burden of adjustment back on to exchange rates and recreates the exchange rate volatility that intervention seeks to avoid. It should therefore be avoided. Given this condition, intervention policies with a stable, systematic component and only a small unsystematic component should reduce the sensitivity of exchange rates to changes in relative excess money supply conditions.

IMPLICATIONS OF FINDINGS FOR U.S. AND JAPANESE POLICIES

In the light of this decision and the findings reported earlier on U.S. and Japanese policies, comments may be offered on each. The United States should end its policy of systematic sterilization, both intervention directed at the behavior of the yen-dollar rate and intervention directed at the DM-dollar rate (Makin 1981a). Further, while limited testing detected no significant change in U.S. intervention policy from the 1973-75 period to the

1976-79 period, care should be taken to avoid either sharp changes in underlying intervention strategy or large deviations from an existing strategy at some point. If a fundamental change in underlying strategy is deemed necessary, it should be clearly announced and subsequently adhered to.

The comments just offered would of course apply equally well to Japanese policies. The change in the underlying intervention policy detected for Japan may have served some perceived need but it also undoubtedly made the course of the yen-dollar rate somewhat harder to foresee, at least until the existence of the more aggressive intervention policy was detected by exchange rate analysts.

It is perhaps useful to close with an observation on Japanese sterilization policy. While cross correlations between the exchange rate and the domestic portion of the monetary base for the entire 1973-79 sample period revealed no tendency toward systematic sterilization activity by Japanese authorities, examination of cross correlations for the 1973-75 and 1976-79 subperiods indicates a possible change in policy. While no sterilization is evident during the earlier period, significant sterilization at a lag of two months is indicated during the 1976-79 period. Continuation of this pattern, coupled with U.S. sterilization and efforts in Japan to stabilize interest rates, could be expected to produce elevated volatility of the yen-dollar exchange rate.

CONCLUSION

Exchange rate behavior is difficult to explain in the sense of finding a few observable variables to account ex post facto for most exchange rate movements. This is essentially because exchange rates are affected by many unforeseeable events, while those variables that are accepted as relevant as a basis for a theory of exchange rate behavior are themselves difficult to measure.

In spite of these difficulties, a contemporary analytical framework is necessary to understand two very basic truths about exchange rate behavior. First, exchange rate movements are reflections of stock disequilibria and therefore are temporary in situations where policy makers do nothing. It is efforts to insulate domestic economic conditions from the requirements of external equilibrium through expedients such as sterilization or controls on movement of capital that perpetuate a disequilibrating shock and thereby produce chronic, one-way movements in exchange rates.

The significance of expectations about future events and policies and their crucial role in determining current exchange rates is the second basic truth about exchange rate behavior. It explains why dramatic announcements of policy changes may have little effect on exchange markets or other asset markets unless some record exists to establish credibility of announced goals. For central banks like the Federal Reserve System with a recent record of unfulfilled objectives, a significant period of actual achievement of objectives will be required to induce market participants to project, from a current stabilization of the monetary environment, a similar environment for the foreseeable future. This difficult truth does, however, have an encouraging corollary. Under any exchange rate regime that permits either continuous or periodic adjustment of exchange rates, policy makers can minimize the volatility of freely flexible rates or the uncertainty attached to partially or fully pegged rates by pursuing policies designed to stabilize the actual behavior of relative excess money supplies and to ease the prediction of future relative excess money supplies.

In light of the findings reported here, there are specific aspects of policy, in both Japan and the United States, that deserve attention to help assure orderly foreign exchange markets. The United States, and specifically the Federal Reserve, needs to continue with efforts to make operational the internationalization of monetary policy begun in November 1978. Particular care ought to be taken to avoid insulating the U.S. monetary base from the effects of external balance constraints transmitted through foreign exchange markets. The evidence suggests the existence of a policy that presumes sterilization of the effects of exchange market intervention upon the U.S. monetary base. Termination of this policy and maintenance of a stable and predictable intervention policy would mark an important step toward recognition of the reality that the United States has become a major international economy instead of the supranational economy it once was.

Japan too must recognize the need to adapt financial policies to major changes. The rapid increase in the annual sale of government bonds reflects the pressures for expanding social programs in Japan and the increasing international responsibilities (e.g., defense) of the world's second largest market economy. Efforts to peg interest rates at levels not consistent with world market conditions will bring increased exchange rate volatility and attendant volatility of inflation to Japan. Sharp changes in intervention policy or alteration of foreign exchange regulations that may be effected in the face of such pressures only serve to increase the uncertainty about future rates by making it more difficult to make predictions about the future monetary behavior required for the determination of equilibrium exchange rates and interest rates. In connection with this possibility it is perhaps worth noting that evidence is accumulating that suggests that inflation uncertainty can by itself depress real economic activity (see the suggestion by Friedman 1977 and evidence in Mullineaux 1980, Levi and Makin 1980 and Makin 1981a).

No country can effect policies directed at reducing exchange rate volatility and uncertainty by itself. Exchange rates depend upon projections of the behavior of relevant exogenous variables both at home and abroad. Still, in view of this fact and the somewhat disappointing record on past efforts at coordination of national economic policies, it is consoling to observe that countries acting completely in isolation to achieve a stable and predictable outlook for prices would simultaneously achieve a stable and predictable outlook for exchange rates. In view of this happy coincidence, if one considers the impressive record of monetary policy in Japan since 1975 and if one is willing to be optimistic about the ability of the Reagan administration to lower and stabilize U.S. inflation, then it may be possible to hope that determinants of a stable yen-dollar exchange rate may soon be in place. For now it is obvious, though still very suggestive, to observe how unfortunate it is that we cannot yet be sure of the outcome.

APPENDIX

A MONETARY EQUILIBRIUM RATIONAL MODEL
OF EXCHANGE RATE DETERMINATION

The simplest way to introduce the key stock equilibrium aspect of exchange rate determination is to specify a model of exchange rate determination based upon equilibrium money holding. A broader class of models including other assets is discussed in Dornbusch (1980). While many important questions regarding exchange rate behavior are usefully viewed employing models that admit a broad class of assets (wealth), the fundamental aspects of stock equilibrium exchange rate determination are adequately captured in a monetary formulation.

The approach followed here will be to extend Bilson's (1978, 1979) monetary-equilibrium, rational expectations approach to exchange rate determination to include sterilization and intervention behavior that characterizes the post-Bretton Woods system of controlled and varying degrees of permissible flexibility of exchange rates.

Specifying a Full-Equilibrium Rational Model

It is important to recognize that the MERE model avoids difficulties inherent in the simple monetary model of exchange rate determination described by Magee (1976) and criticized by Dornbusch (1980). The basic monetary approach to exchange rate determination begins with log linear money demand functions, takes money supplies to be entirely exogenous and imposes the PPP (equilibrium commodity arbitrage) condition to express the exchange rate in terms of relative money supplies, interest rates, and real outputs:[6]

$$s_t = (m - m^*)_t - b(r^* - r)_t - k(y - y^*)_t \tag{1}$$

where (all natural logarithms):

> s = logarithm of spot exchange rate (home currency price of foreign exchange) at time t
> m = logarithm of nominal money
> y = logarithm of real income
> r = logarithm of one plus nominal interest rate
> k = income elasticity of money demand
> b = interest elasticity of money demand with respect to r
> $*$ denotes foreign

Dornbusch (1980) reports that empirical tests of (1) fail to lend support to the monetary approach.

A major difficulty with equation (1) is the failure to recognize explicitly the link between actual and expected exchange rate levels and the interest rate differential. Arbitrage by international investors of comparable securities denominated in domestic and foreign currencies results in interest parity:

6. This result is fully derived in Makin 1980, 1981a as are all others presented in the discussion to follow.

$$f_t - s_t = r_t - r_t^*$$ (2)

where f_t is the natural log of the forward domestic currency price of foreign currency as of time t for time $t + 1$. More generally, equation (2) represents an equilibrium condition in the market for internationally traded assets.

In addition to capturing an important equilibrium condition, the interest parity condition opens the way to obtaining a rational solution for the exchange rate. Once the expected value of an endogenous variable appears in a model, it is possible to obtain a rational solution for that variable. A rational solution is one that is consistent with the model itself in the sense that the endogenous variable can be shown to depend, in a manner determined by the model, upon the currently expected values of the model's exogenous variables.

The first step to a full MERE solution is to invoke the simple efficient market hypothesis that states that under conditions of risk neutrality, zero transactions costs, rational use of information, and competitive markets:

$$f_t = E_t[S_{t+1}|\text{information}_t]$$ (3)

Equation (3) sets the forward rate at time t for time $t + 1$ equal to the mathematical expectation of the spot rate at time $t + 1$ conditional on the information set available at time t. Equations (1), (2), and (3) can be shown to imply a solution for the exchange rate (where for simplicity $k = 1$):

$$s_t = \frac{1}{1+b} \sum_{j=0}^{\infty} [\frac{b}{1+b}]^j {}_t[RXM']^e_{t+j}$$ (4)

where RXM' or relative excess money supply is defined as:

$$RXM'_t = [(m-y)_t - (m^* - y^*)_t]$$

Equation (4) expresses the actual spot exchange rate in terms of current actual and all currently expected future values of the determinants of the relative excess money supply.

Intervention and Sterilization

Equation (4) is an adequate expression for the exchange rate in a world of freely flexible exchange rates with no official intervention in foreign exchange markets and no efforts to sterilize the effects on the monetary base that follow from intervention. In a world of limited flexibility of exchange rates like that evolved in the wake of the Bretton Woods system, it is necessary to represent intervention and sterilization behavior. Basically, intervention links part of the monetary base, and therefore the money supply, to the behavior of the exchange rate by way of "leaning against the wind" efforts to stabilize exchange rates. Sterilization can, for a time a least, try to undo the link. The upshot is that in the absence of complete sterilization, which cannot persist for very long without precipitating some sort of an exchange market crisis, exogeneity of the money supply as specified in equation (4) no longer holds. Violation of that assumption will result in improper specification of tests of the theory represented in equation (4).

Correct modeling of exchange rate behavior under a system of limited flexibility of exchange rates requires careful presentation of money supply behavior as outlined in Makin (1980, 1981a). The money supply is determined, through a stable mutiplier, by the monetary base, which in turn depends on the domestic and foreign assets (foreign exchange reserves) of the central bank. Intervention links foreign exchange reserves of, say, country 1, x_1, to the currency 1 price of currency 2 or s:

$$x_1 = -\gamma_1 s$$ (5)

where γ_1 measures the elasticity of official reserves with respect to the exchange rate, s. The faster currency 1 depreciates (a rise in s) the faster reserves in country 1 are lost (and the faster "foreign" reserves rise).

Sterilization links the other determinant of the monetary base, domestic assets of the central bank, d, to the behavior of reserves and thereby, through intervention, to the exchange rate. For country 1, the domestic assets of the central bank are determined by an autonomous portion, de, not linked to reserves, and by reserves in a manner determined by the degree of sterilization. For country 1:

$$d_{1_t} = de_{1_t} - (1 - st_1) x_{1_t} \qquad (6)$$

where

de_{1_t} = log of autonomous portion of domestic assets of central bank in country 1

st_1 = sterilization coefficient in country 1 ($st_1 = 0$ implies full sterilization;

$st_1 = 1.0$ implies zero sterilization and $d_{1_t} = de_{1_t}$).

Applying analogous expression for country 2, the relative money supply for countries 1 and 2 can be written as:

$$\underline{m}_t = \underline{de}_t + \phi s_t \qquad (7)$$

where

$\underline{m}_t = (m - m^*)_t$

$\underline{de}_t = j_1 de_{1_t} - j_1^* de_{2_t}$

$\phi (\leq 0) \equiv [-\gamma_1(j_2 - j_1(1 - st_1)) - \gamma_2(j_2^* - j_1^*(1 - st_2))]$

If intervention dominates sterilization so that currency depreciation lowers x_1 and raises x_2 then ϕ is unambiguously negative. If sterilization eradicates intervention's effect on the monetary base then $\phi = 0$. In this case $\underline{m}_t = \underline{de}_t$ and there is no need to take account of either intervention or sterilization in modeling the money supply.

Employing (7) for the relative money supply term in equation (1) results in a modified, rational solution for the exchange rate:

$$s_t = \frac{1}{1+c} \sum_{j=0}^{\infty} [\frac{b}{1+c}]^j {}_t[RXM]_{t+j}^r \qquad (8)$$

where, now:

$$RXM = [(de_1 - de_2) - (y_1 - y_2)]$$

and

$$c = (b - \phi).$$

The exchange rate is determined by the current actual and expected future values of the relative excess money supply defined now in terms of the exogenous portion of the monetary base. The nature of this relationship is affected by the money demand (interest elasticity) parameter, b, as well as by the money supply parameter, ϕ, which reflects the state of intervention and sterilization policies.

A Rational Solution in Terms of Observable Variables

To derive from equation (8) propositions about the behavior of exchange rates in response to observable change in the relative excess money supply, it is necessary to model the way in which market participants form expectations, based on current RXM, about the path of all future RXM. A simple formulation with some empirical support specifies *growth* of exogenous variables as a random walk:

$$\Delta \underline{de}_t = \Delta \underline{de}_{t-1} + u_{d_t} \qquad (9.a)$$

$$\Delta \underline{y}_t = \Delta \underline{y}_{t-1} + u_{y_t} \qquad (9.b)$$

where

$$\underline{de}_t = (de_1 - de_2)_t$$

$$\underline{y}_t = (y_1 - y_2)_t$$

$$u_d, u_y = \text{error terms.}$$

Equations (9.a) and (9.b) make growth of the relative excess money supply a random walk. The resulting solution for the exchange rate in terms of observable levels of the excess money supply is given by:

$$(10)$$

$$s_t = [1/(1 - \phi)][(1 + b)[RXM]_t - b[RXM]_{t-1}]$$

where $RXM \equiv [\underline{de} - \underline{y}]$ or relative excess money supply.

Equation (10) implies a cyclical response of the exchange rate to RXM. If sterilization cancels the impact of intervention on the monetary base ($\phi = 0$), the elasticity of the exchange rate with respect to RXM is $(1 + b)$, implying an initial "overshoot" of amount b that is subsequently removed at $t - 1$. Sharpness of the cyclical response of the exchange rate to RXM is proportional to the interest elasticity of money demand. This result is most easily understood by first noting that interest parity, PPP, and lack of bias of the forward rate as a predictor of the expected spot rate together imply that Fischer equations describe nominal interest rates in each country.[7] These conditions are all implicit in (10). Given these conditions, a rise in RXM is exacerbated by a drop in the money demand at home relative to abroad, which in turn results from higher nominal interest rates at home relative to abroad. The latter results from a relative increase in expected inflation at home. The size of the additional negative effect on money demand depends on the size of b, the interest elasticity of money demand. In short a rise in RXM feeds on itself by causing anticipated inflation, which lowers steady-state money demand. Therefore the exchange rate must depreciate by more than a change in RXM to reduce domestic excess money supply. Once the initial overshoot reduces steady-state real money balances at home, the extra pressure on the exchange rate is removed and the overshoot portion of depreciation disappears.

These results are modified by intervention and/or sterilization. In the longer run ϕ cannot be zero, with intervention not allowed to affect the monetary base. If the base is not affected by the balance of payments disequilibria under nonzero intervention reserve, gains or losses will persist until some rapid adjustment of exchange rates to perceived equilibrium levels is permitted. This outcome implies that attempts to hold $\phi = 0$ will eventually cause γ (intervention) to fall until exchange rates reach perceived equilibrium levels. In any case, ϕ can be expected to vary over time.

If intervention is heavy and ϕ takes on a large negative value, the overshoot may seem to disappear, say over some sample period. The reason will be the market's per-

---

7. This condition holds given a constant ratio of domestic to foreign real interest rates.

ception of intervention to prevent exchange rate movement and not any failure of the monetary theory of exchange rate determination. A believable announcement or concrete evidence of a significant change in intervention policy will alter ϕ and thereby alter the measured impact of a given change in RXM upon the exchange rate during some finite sample period. The basic MERE theory that postulates a fixed impact would be contradicted by data drawn for that sample period. The reason would not be the invalidity of MERE but rather the failure to allow for a change in intervention (or sterilization) policy.

Allowing for Real Exchange Rate Change

In implementing empirical test of the MERE model of exchange rate behavior, it is necessary to deal with a problem related to PPP that it embodies. As Dornbusch (1980) and others have noted, the simple form of PPP embodied in equation (1),

$$s_t = (p_t - p_t^*) \tag{11}$$

where

$$p_t = \log \text{ of the price level}$$

is not consistent with actual data for many exchange rates. This is the cause for the yen-dollar rate during the 1970s. Deviations from PPP are often termed "real" exchange rate changes and represented as the residuals from PPP or

$$s_t = (p_t - p_t^*) + q_t \tag{12}$$

where q_t is the log of the real exchange rate. It is useful to examine the behavior of q for the yen-dollar exchange rate during the sample period employed to test the MERE theory of exchange rate behavior. Such an examination reveals that it is not possible to reject the hypothesis that q for the yen-dollar rate follows a random walk during the relevant sample period (Box-Pierce test for autocorrelations: $Q(12) = 11.7$; $Q(24) = 22.0$; $(36) = 26.4$). This implies

$$q_t = q_{t-1} + v_t \tag{13.a}$$

and

$$\Delta s_t = \Delta(p - p^*)_t + v_t \tag{13.b}$$

where $v_t = $ "white noise" residuals from an AR-1 model on $q_t (v \sim n, \sigma_t^2)$.

where $v_t = $ "white noise" residuals from an AR-1 model on q_t $(v \sim n, \sigma_t^2)$. Equation (13.b) indicates that PPP is satisfied by first differencing logs. All exchange-rate equations reported in the section on testing the extended MERE model are estimated in log first-difference form.

REFERENCES

Bilson, John F. O. 1978. "Rational Expectations and the Exchange Rate." In *The Economics of Exchange Rates: Selected Studies*, ed., Jacob A. Frenkel and Harry G. Johnson, chap. 5, pp. 75-96. Addison-Wesley, Reading, Mass.

———. 1979. "Recent Developments in Monetary Models of Exchange Rate Determination." *IMF Staff Papers* (June), pp. 201-23.

Box, G. E. P., and Jenkins, G. M. 1970. *Time Series Analysis, Forecasting and Control.* San Francisco, Holden-Day, Inc.

Dornbusch, R. 1980. "Exchange Rate Economics: Where Do We Stand?" *Brookings Papers on Economic Activity*, no. 1, pp. 143-86.

Fischer, Stanley. 1979. "Anticipations and the Nonneutrality of Money." *Journal of Political Economy* (April), pp. 225-52.

Friedman, M. 1977. "Inflation and Unemployment." Nobel lecture. *Journal of Political Economy* (June), pp. 451-72.

Gaikoku Kawase Bōeki Kenkyūkai. 1981.*Kokusai kinyū* [International finance journal]. Tokyo.

Levi, M. D., and Makin, J. H. 1980. "Inflation Uncertainty and the Phillips Curve: Some Empirical Evidence." *American Economic Review* (December), pp. 1022-27.

Magee, Stephen P. 1976. "The Empirical Evidence on the Monetary Approach to the Balance of Payments and Exchange Rates." *American Economic Review* (May), pp. 163-70.

Makin, J. H. 1980. "Techniques and Success in Forecasting Exchange Rates: Should It Be Done? Does It Matter? The Long and the Short of It." In conference volume on *Internationalization of Financial Markets and National Economic Policy,* forthcoming, New York University Press.

———. 1981a. "Exchange Rate Behavior Under Full Monetary Equilibrium: An Empirical Analysis." University of Washington, Department of Economics (January).

———. 1981b. " 'Anticipated' Money, Inflation Uncertainty and Real Economic Activity." *Review of Economics and Statistics* (forthcoming).

Mullineaux, D. J. 1980. "Unemployment, Industrial Production and Inflation Uncertainty in the United States." *Review of Economics and Statistics* (May), pp. 163-69.

Niho, Y., and Makin, J. H. 1978. "A Solution to the Inverse Problem of Optimal Control." *Journal of Money, Credit and Banking* (August), pp. 371-77.

Royama Sho'ichi. 1981. "The Japanese Financial System in Transition." Mimeographed. Paper prepared for presentation at the symposium on Japanese-United States economic relations, University of Washington, March.

Contributors

KOICHI HAMADA, Professor of Economics, University of Tokyo
KEN-ICHI IMAI, Professor of Economics, Hitotsubashi University
JOHN MAKIN, Professor of Economics, University of Washington
YASUSUKE MURAKAMI, Professor of Economics, University of Tokyo
YUKIO NOGUCHI, Professor of Economics, Hitotsubashi University
HUGH PATRICK, Professor of Economics, Yale University
HIDEO SATO, Associate Professor of Political Science, Yale University
KAZUO SATO, Professor of Economics, State University of New York at
    Buffalo
GARY SAXONHOUSE, Professor of Economics, University of Michigan
YOICHI SHINKAI, Professor of Economics, Osaka University
KOZO YAMAMURA, Professor of Economics, University of Washington

INDEX

Administrative guidance *(gyōsei shidō)*, 16-18, 86-87, 95, 102, 104, 246; investment coordination under, 13, 17-18, 85-86, 100; compliance with, 16-18, 38, 42-43, 49, 84; and competition, 18, 40, 82-83, 96-97, 107-8n, 117; future of, 42-44; definition of, 49n; form of, 83; decline of (1960s), 103, 107-8, 124-25. *See also* Bank of Japan; Cartels; "Excessive competition"; Ministry of International Trade and Industry

Agriculture, 18; households in, 29; subsidization of, 128-29; labor force participation rate in, 154-55

Alcaly, Roger E., 228

Amano, Akihiro, 275n, 277

Amaya, Naohiro, 119, 209

Antimonopoly Act (Japan, 1947), 103, 107-8n; amendment (1953), 4, 10-11, 81; proposed amendment (1958), 17; proposed amendment (1974), 89-90; amendment (1977), 90-91, 93, 96, 98-99

Armco Steel, 210

Australia: house ownership in, 34; steel industry in, 197-98

Balance of payments, 279-81, 292-93

Bank of Japan, 13, 17, 184, 191, 272-73, 276; interest rate policy of, 17, 42; exchange rate intervention of, 275, 277, 302n

Bethlehem Steel, 210

Bonds, 160

Bonuses: and savings rate, 32, 149; at retirement, 155

Bretton Woods Conference, 275, 276, 320

Bronfenbrenner, Martin, 96

Bruno, Michael, 118n

Budget (national), 125-29; industrial support from, 125, 128; and income redistribution, 126-29, 131

Canada: house ownership in, 34; steel industry in, 197-98; and steel exports to U.S., 214, 216, 217, 226, 227

Capital: flow of, 144, 166-67, 168-69; formation of, 156-58, 163-64

Cartels, 80-83, 95-96, 103, 117, 121; creation of, 9, 10-11, 17, 40, 43, 57-58, 81-86 passim, 92-96 passim, 104, 119; effect of, 9, 100, 103; number of, 81-82; laws concerning, 81-82; attitudes toward, 87-88, 89-91, 98-99, 101; MITI sponsorship of, 94-102. *See also* Administrative guidance; Ministry of International Trade and Industry

Carter administration, 201, 207-8, 209, 210, 230, 233, 235; inflation policy of, 298-99

Chandler, Alfred D., Jr., 61

Citizens' movements, 52, 58

Clean Air and Water Act (U.S.), 222

Consumer: goods, distribution of, 50, 56; movement, 52, 58, 87-88; price

PUBLICATIONS ON ASIA
OF THE SCHOOL OF INTERNATIONAL STUDIES
UNIVERSITY OF WASHINGTON

CHINA

BOYD COMPTON, trans, and ed. *Mao's China: Party Reform Documents, 1942-44.*
CHUNG-LI CHANG. *The Chinese Gentry: Studies on Their Role in Nineteenth-Century Chinese Society.*
PEDRO CARRASCO. *Land and Polity in Tibet.*
KUNG-CHUAN HSIAO. *Rural China: Imperial Control in the Nineteenth Century.*
NICHOLAS POPPE, LEON HURVITZ, and HIDEHIRO OKADA. *Catalogue of the Manchu-Mongol Section of the Toyo Bunko.*
FRANZ MICHAEL and CHUNG-LI CHANG. *The Taiping Rebellion: History and Documents.*
VINCENT Y. C. SHIH. *The Taiping Ideology: Its Sources, Interpretations, and Influences.*
TSI-AN HSIA. *The Gate of Darkness: Studies on the Leftist Literary Movement in China.*
JULIA C. LIN. *Modern Chinese Poetry: An Introduction.*
KUNG-CHUAN HSIAO. *A Modern China and a New World: K'ang Yu-wei, Reformer and Utopian, 1858-1927.*
HELLMUT WILHELM. *Heaven, Earth, and Man in the Book of Changes: Seven Eranos Lectures.*
JING-SHEN TAO. *The Jurchen in Twelfth-Century China: A Study of Sinicization.*
BYUNG-JOON AHN. *Chinese Politics and the Cultural Revolution: Dynamics of Policy Processes.*
MARGARET NOWAK and STEPHEN DURRANT. *The Tale of the Nišan Shamaness: A Manchu Folk Epic.*
JERRY NORMAN. *A Manchu-English Lexicon.*
HOK-LAM CHAN. *Theories of Legitimacy in Imperial China: Discussions on "Legitimate Succession" under the Jurchen–Chin Dynasty (1115-1234).* Forthcoming.
ALISON BLACK. *Nature, Artifice, and Expression in the Philosophical Thought of Wang Fu-Chih (1916-92).* Forthcoming.

JAPAN

MARLEIGH GRAYER RYAN. *The Development of Realism in the Fiction of Tsubouchi Shōyō.*
ROY ANDREW MILLER. *Origins of the Japanese Language.*
KOZO YAMAMURA, ed. *Policy and Trade Issues of the Japanese Economy: American and Japanese Perspectives.*

KOREA

DAE-SOOK SUH and CHAE-JIN LEE, eds. *Political Leadership in Korea.*
BRUCE CUMINGS, ed. *Child of Conflict: The Korean–American Relationship, 1945-1953.* Forthcoming.

SOUTH ASIA

EDWIN GEROW and MARGERY LANG, eds. *Studies in the Language and Culture of South Asia.*
BARRIE M. MORRISON. *Lalmai, A Cultural Center of Early Bengal.*
JAMES BROW. *Vedda Villages of Anuradhapura: The Historical Anthropology of a Community in Sri Lanka.*